D1453218

A Nation Fermented

A Nation Fermented

*Beer, Bavaria, and the Making of
Modern Germany*

ROBERT SHEA TERRELL

OXFORD
UNIVERSITY PRESS

Great Clarendon Street, Oxford, OX2 6DP,
United Kingdom

Oxford University Press is a department of the University of Oxford.
It furthers the University's objective of excellence in research, scholarship,
and education by publishing worldwide. Oxford is a registered trade mark of
Oxford University Press in the UK and in certain other countries

Published in the United States of America by Oxford University Press
198 Madison Avenue, New York, NY 10016, United States of America

British Library Cataloguing in Publication Data
Data available

Library of Congress Control Number: 2023938485

ISBN 978–0–19–888183–4

DOI: 10.1093/oso/9780198881834.001.0001

Printed and bound in the UK by
Clays Ltd, Elcograf S.p.A.

Links to third party websites are provided by Oxford in good faith and
for information only. Oxford disclaims any responsibility for the materials
contained in any third party website referenced in this work.

Contents

Acknowledgements

The journey that culminated in this book started in late 2008 as I was reconsidering my life choices. A couple years earlier, I had dragged myself over the graduation finish line at North Carolina State University and had since been following my love of food, working as a chef in Raleigh's up-and-coming restaurant scene. By the end of that summer, I was licking my wounds after opening a restaurant that might have bested a global recession if not for intense differences between the creatives and the capital. In that moment of reconsideration, I leapt from the proverbial frying pan of restaurant work into the fire of academia. The following year I moved to Philadelphia to begin a terminal Master's program at Villanova University, where I found the intellectual stimulation and passion that has, to date, fueled the next decade and a half of my professional life. Among the many debts I feel to that program, Paul Steege has been a consistent and generous mentor who always makes time to read work, grab a meal, or listen as unrefined ideas pour out of my mouth. From there, I crossed the country, beginning my PhD at the University of California San Diego, where Frank Biess offered precisely the mentorship I needed—expert guidance, humor, and a wonderful balance of rigor and flexibility. Frank and Paul have been generous advocates, and each in their way is a model for the type of scholar I hope to be. From Raleigh to Philadelphia to San Diego, Anthony La Vopa, Martha Lampland, Thomas Ort, Patrick Patterson, Jeremy Prestholdt, and Pamela Radcliff have each shaped the scholar and teacher that I am. They all have my thanks.

Formal mentors hold a special place in book acknowledgments—and in my heart—but many other colleagues and friends have shaped the evolution of this book, and of its author. John Gillespie and Julie Sneeringer each generously read the entirety of the manuscript, bringing their respective expertise and offering unique feedback. A lengthy list of other people has in one way or another influenced this book through conference comments and hallway conversations. Special thanks for their insights and support go to Greg Eghigian, Melissa Feinberg, Neil Gregor, Paul Hanebrink, Jeff Johnson, Rita Krueger, Jay Lockenour, Uwe Spiekermann, and Ulrike Weckel. Formative exchanges have also come at a bar, café, Biergarten, or Döner shop. In such settings, Julie Ault, Ian Beacock, Alissa Belotti, Jeremy Best, Adam Blackler, Mikkel Dack, Chris Fojtik, Patrick Hege, Andrew Kloiber, Melissa Kravetz, Jamie McSpadden, Alex Ruble, Lauren Stokes, and Teresa Walch have made life as a German historian a pleasure. Many people named in this paragraph have read or talked through sections of this book. But thanks are due especially to the members of the Philadelphia Area Modern

Germany Workshop for their thoughtful comments on an earlier version of Chapter 1. Similar thanks are also due to Alex Ruble for helping make Chapter 4 less of a thorn in my side. Other friends made along the way have proven a source of joy and fruitful distraction. Particularly appreciated for their joyful and distractive qualities over the years are Patrick Adamiak, Andrew and Lauren Aker, Matt Davidson, Katie Featherstone, DJ Guba, Bruce Hardy, Dave Henderson, Michael Keys, Annka Liepold, Joel Palhegyi, Jefferson Pooley, Norman Porticella, Urszula Pruchniewska, Dipankar Rai, Kelly Rembolt, Justin Rockwell, Scott Schabot, Alexa Schmitz, Katherine Sender, Nicholas Shapiro, Ben Smuin, Henrik Stephan, Meghnaa Tallapragada, Daniel and Dawn Taylor, Aaron Vaughn, and Tito Wright.

The research and writing of this book benefitted from numerous institutions and professional associates. The research for this project was funded by the J. William Fulbright Program, the German Historical Institute in Washington, DC, the German Academic Exchange Service (DAAD), and the Central European History Society. I owe these institutions many thanks for putting their faith (and money) into this project. The DAAD funded a stay at the Rachel Carson Center for Environment and Society, where Christof Mauch was far more welcoming and generous with his time and position than I could have ever hoped. In the archives, Laura Burgassi (HEAU), Katharina Köhn (ACSP), Eva Moser (BWA), and Susanne Millet and Johann Pörnbacher (BayHStA) were all particularly encouraging as I bounced around in German and European collections and worked to finish the manuscript. Thanks are also due to the Bayerischer Brauerbund and the Deutscher Brauer-Bund for their support. Content in Chapters 5 and 6, respectively, appeared in the journal *Contemporary European History* and the Routledge volume *Alcohol Flows Across Cultures*, edited by Waltraud Ernst. Thanks to Caroline Jennings, who lent her keen editing eye to several of the chapters. At Oxford University Press, Matthew Cotton, Imogene Haslam, and Stephanie Ireland were tremendously supportive and efficient in the production of this book. The anonymous reviewers Stephanie and Matthew organized have my deepest thanks for their thoughts and contributions. In Munich, Clay Mock was a lifesaver, hunting down printable versions of many of the images in the eleventh hour.

Since 2018, I have had the pleasure of working in a wonderful department and college at Syracuse University. My appreciation for the administrative wizardry of Christina Cleason and Faye Morse knows no bounds. Truly, little is likely to get done without them. Timur Hammond in the geography department has graciously read my work, organized crucial writing groups, and proven to be a supportive and positive voice in moments of self-doubt. The entire history department has my appreciation, but Susan Branson, Albrecht Diem, Samantha Herrick, Amy Kallander, Norman Kutcher, Tessa Murphy, and Junko Takeda have been particularly welcoming and supportive as I learned the institution, built a life in central New York, and worked toward completing this book.

Finally, I am tremendously grateful for the support of my family. My siblings, their spouses, and their children—Edward, Emily, George, Louisa, and Hugh Terrell, and Jane, Thad, Henry, and William Paul—have been a source energy and reprieve. My parents, Bob and Maria Terrell, have been unflinchingly supportive and have bravely endeavored to converse even when I was lost in the woods. My partner, Brooke Erin Duffy, and our daughter, Harlow Shea Terrell, have brought joy amidst the grinding moments of writing and finishing a book. Brooke has played every role imaginable, from critic and meal-maker to much-needed distractor. Her keen editing eye and "wordsmith-ery" helped punch up the language and make the text approachable to nonspecialists. Her silliness and humor provide welcome disruptions, and her love remains an anchor. Harlow has proven to be incredibly strong, generous, funny, and thoughtful. I cannot wait to continue watching her become who she is and wants to be. This book is dedicated to my parents, my partner, and our daughter.

Timeline

1516	Wittelsbach dynasty limits beer production to malted barley, hops, and water
1553	Wittelsbach dynasty restricts the production of beer in the summer (effectively banning the production of ales) in Bavaria
16th to 18th centuries	Persistence of numerous local cultures of production and consumption
	Wittelsbach wheat beer monopoly in Bavaria
	Early emergence of technical brewing literature in Bavaria
1842	Invention of Pilsner in Pilsen/Plzeň, Habsburg Empire
1871	German unification
	Bavaria, Baden, and Württemberg retain brewing standards and tax revenues through Reserve Rights (*Reservatrechte*)
1872	Founding of the North German Beer Tax Community (*norddeutsche Brausteuergemeinschaft*)
1894	Invention of Helles in Munich
1902	Saccharine ban prohibits the use of artificial sweeteners
1906	Yeast added to the list of permissible ingredients
	National law (effectively in northern Germany) adopts four-ingredient list (malted barley, hops, water, yeast) for bottom-fermented beer; top-fermented beer can still be brewed with malts from other grains and specified sugar sources
	Three southern states exercise Reserve Rights to unify around Bavarian production standards: four-ingredient list in all types of beer
1919	Southern states join the Beer Tax Community (*Biersteuergemeinschaft*) on the condition of retaining stricter production standards
	Beer tax integrated for equalization via the Reich Finance Ministry
1930	Bavarian People's Party (BVP) fragments, in large part over the beer tax
1931	German Brewers Association votes against national community advertising
1933	Adolf Hitler appointed Chancellor
1938	Reich Food Estate (*Reichsnährstand*) proposes brewing with the addition of sugar
1945–1948	Brewing bans (*Brauverbote*) variously in effect throughout occupied Germany
1949	West German Basic Law (*Grundgesetz*) Article 106 grants beer tax revenue to the federal states
1950–1952	Beer Tax Law (*Biersteuergesetz*) lowers tax rates (1950) and perpetuates 1906 standards of Lager/Ale production (1952)

1951	Founding of the Bavarian and West German community advertising organizations
1952–1956	Bavarian exporters hire patent lawyers for trademark disputes
1954	Beer production surpasses pre-war levels nationwide in West Germany
	Distribution Ban (*Vertriebsverbot*) against "sweet beer" (*Süßbier*) in Bavaria
1960	US Trademark on "Genuine Bavarian Beer" granted to the Bavarian Brewers Association
1962	Beer Transport Law (*Gesetz über den Verkehr mit Bier*) passes in Bavarian Landtag
1964	Bavarian beer exports see three-fold increase over 1954
1964–1965	New York World's Fair
1968	Beer becomes the single most consumed beverage in the Federal Republic
1969	Bavarian beer exports see five-fold increase over 1954
1970	European Economic Community (EEC) Directive to harmonize brewing standards
1974	Löwenbräu outsources production in the UK and US
1975	EEC Directive withdrawn
1987	European Court of Justice repeals the *Reinheitsgebot* as a non-tariff trade barrier
1989–1990	Fall of the Berlin Wall and national reunification
1991	Remaining East German breweries conform to the *Reinheitsgebot*
1995	European Commission recognizes "German Beer" as a traditional product
	Inaugural "Day of German Beer" celebration

List of Illustrations

Map Territorial changes and the German south in the 20th century.

Introduction

In a smoke-filled, working-class bar in Depression-era Berlin, a waiter delivers two glasses of beer to a table, adds the drinks to the coaster tallies, and moves on. One of the men at the table, Herr Völker, ponders his drink briefly before turning to his fellow communist, Herr Stoppel. "If I put a British beer here," he begins with an unmistakable Berlin accent, "and here a hearty Molle Helles, which one would you drink?" Stoppel answers as expected: he chuckles and declares he would prefer to drink the local Helles, "of course." Völker proceeds with a series of follow-ups centering on where the Helles is from: It is brewed in Berlin. But where is Berlin? On the Spree River. But where is the Spree? In Germany. "That's right," declares Völker. "In Germany. In our Germany. Think that over." Völker's line of questioning echoes an earlier conversation he had with the leader of his son's Hitler Youth group. In that instance, Völker was led through similar questions, again building toward the importance of the German nation as the foremost frame of reference. As he prods Stoppel along, Völker links local beer to his national awakening, questioning his communist convictions in favor of German nationalism and, presumably, National Socialism.

This scene comes from *Hitlerjunge Quex*, the first major Nazi propaganda film, which premiered about eight months after Adolf Hitler's appointment as Chancellor. The bar conversation and the film more broadly reflect the intense battle between the Nazis and their opponents on the left, most notably the communists. In this working-class bar, beer provides an opportunity for the characters and, presumably, the audience, to consider the national stakes of the mundane. The Helles creates cultural distance from Britain, and its origins in Berlin lead the characters to think of the city not as an industrial, workers' city on the Spree—a hub of international communism—but rather as part of a communal and national whole: "our Germany." From the perspective of the 21st century, it seems self-evident that beer from Berlin is German beer and that drinking it has something to do with *being* German. But if that were simply the case, Herr Stoppel should not need three chances and gentle prodding to make the realization. As a piece of National Socialist propaganda, the film unsurprisingly puts national belonging front and center, over and above socio-economic, local, or international loyalties and sentiments. In so doing, the scene illuminates how the German nation was

A Nation Fermented: Beer, Bavaria, and the Making of Modern Germany. Robert Shea Terrell, Oxford University Press.

and remains contested across multiple layers of connectivity and exchange, from the local pub to geopolitical conflict.[1]

Expanding our gaze beyond Berlin, the scene is yet more revealing in what it silences. Consider the seemingly obvious choice of the local Molle Helles. The Helles style was not a Berlin classic but rather a relatively new style, invented in 1894 at the Munich Spaten Brewery to compete with the ascendant hegemony of Pilsner beer. The two were among several lager-style beers—defined by their use of bottom-fermenting yeast—that took central Europe and the world by storm in the 19th and 20th centuries. Lager spread from Bavaria and Bohemia outward, at least in part thanks to imperial expansion, migration, and rapid economic development both in Europe and beyond.[2] In northern Germany, these brews were initially despised and discursively othered through the pejorative moniker "Bavarian beer." But with the explosion of urban and industrial development around the turn of the century, "Bavarian beer" increasingly became the standard, especially for the working classes. By the time *Hitlerjunge Quex* was produced, southern brewing standards and industrial cultures of production had solidified the association between lager and urban workers in Berlin and beyond.

This scene provides two of the main analytic threads that run throughout this book. The first is discursive. Just as Berlin and Germany are framed as nationalist rather than communist, beer provides a reference for articulations of place well beyond the 1930s. Throughout the period studied here—from the late 19th century to the end of the 20th—producers, regulators, lobbyists, advertisers, and consumer interest groups repeatedly laid claim to the political and cultural lives of the German people—that is, the very nature of "our Germany," as Völker put it in the film. But, moving beyond discourse, the second thread is structural. The beer in the scene can only be claimed as German because of an earlier process by which southern brewing practices and standards transformed production and consumption in the industrializing city. Just as "Bavarian beer" became a Berlin

---

[1] My thinking has been influenced by an insightful vignette from the geographer Doreen Massey, who compared a Kentucky Fried Chicken in Paris with a Parisian café. Our conviction that surely the latter must be the *real* Paris, she wrote, only holds water when we deny that what constitutes a Parisian café—coffee, croissants, bourgeois consumption habits—was at one time also foreign and new; not the real Paris. Articulations of place, like that made by Völker in *Hitlerjunge Quex*, pursue political aims by freezing temporality and the constant flow of goods and ideas. See Doreen Massey, 'A Global Sense of Place', *Marxism Today* (June, 1991): pp. 24–9; and Massey, 'Places and their Pasts', *History Workshop Journal* no. 39 (Spring, 1995): pp. 182–92.

[2] See for example, Jeffrey Alexander, *Brewed in Japan: The Evolution of the Japanese Brewing Industry* (Vancouver: University of British Columbia Press, 2013); Jeffrey M. Pilcher, 'National Beer in a Global Age: Technology, Taste, and Mobility, 1880–1914', *Quaderni Storici* 151, no. 1 (Apr. 2016): pp. 51–70; and Jeffrey M. Pilcher, 'Imperial Hops: Beer in the Age of Empire', *Global Food History*. Published online Jun. 21, 2023. DOI: 10.1080/20549547.2023.2226526. On empire, see Sabina Groeneveld, 'Far away at Home in Qingdao, 1897–1914', *German Studies Review* 39, no. 1 (2016): pp. 65–80; Malcolm F. Purinton, *Globalization in a Glass: The Rise of Pilsner Beer through Technology, Taste and Empire* (London: Bloomsbury Academic, 2023); and Tycho van der Hoog, *Breweries, Politics and Identity: The History Behind Namibia's Beer* (Basel: Basler Afrika Bibliographien, 2019).

staple, southern brewing standards and industrial values became increasingly national. The "hearty Molle Helles" thus not only functions as an object of Nazi claims to the nation, its unspoken history also testifies to how a southern style of beer transformed the landscape of production and consumption. Underpinning this particular Nazi contest over Berlin, it turns out, is a longer transformation of the city at the hands of southern practice.

A Bottom-Fermented History of Germany

Perhaps no commodity is as tightly entwined with the German nation as beer, but this is not a natural or timeless association. Indeed, the very idea of *German* beer is relatively new. For centuries, German-speaking Europe boasted a plurality of cultures and regulations around the production, sale, and consumption of beer. The emergence of something recognizable as "German Beer" and the imbrication of commodity and place are at the heart of this book. And, as the opening film analysis indicates, the pages that follow emphasize the role of southern—and, more pointedly, Bavarian—influence on the national whole. *A Nation Fermented* argues that Bavarian traditions and interests consistently shaped both beer and the German nation more broadly, from production standards and tax law to public health policy and consumer sensibilities.

Given the popularity of beer in Germany it is perhaps not surprising that a great deal has been written about the subject. By and large this scholarship takes one of several forms, from business histories of prominent breweries to localized studies of consumer practices and industrialization.[3] Much of this work parallels

---

[3] See, for example, Christian Schäder, *Münchner Brauindustrie, 1871–1945: Die wirtschaftsgeschichtliche Entwicklung eines Industriezweiges* (Marburg: Tectum Verlag, 1999); Wolfgang Behringer, *Die Spaten-Brauerei, 1397–1997: Die Geschichte eines Münchner Unternehmens vom Mittelalter bis zur Gegenwart* (Munich and Zurich: Piper Verlag GmbH, 1997); Wolfgang Behringer, *Löwenbräu: Von den Anfängen des Münchner Brauwesens bis zur Gegenwart* (Munich: Süddeutscher Verlag, 1991); Mikuláš Teich, *Bier, Wissenschaft und Wirtschaft in Deutschland, 1800–1914* (Vienna: Böhlau Verlag, 2000); Birgit Speckle, *Streit ums Bier in Bayern: Wertvorstellungen um Reinheit, Gemeinschaft und Tradition* (Münster: Waxmann Verlag, 2001); Eva Göbel, *Bayern in der modernen Konsumgesellschaft: Regionalisierung der Konsumkultur im 20. Jahrhundert* (Berlin: Weißensee Verlag, 2005), pp. 108–14; Nadine Mallmann, *Kölsch—mehr als ein Getränk: Eine Biersorte als Medium regionaler Identitätskonstruktionen* (Munich: GRIN Verlag, 2011); Jörg Spengler, 'Wer von Bier spricht, muss von Geschichte reden', *Jahrbuch der Gesellschaft für Geschichte des Brauwesens e.V.* (2007): pp. 221–48; Nancy Bodden, *Business as Usual? Die Dortmunder Brauindustrie, der Flaschenbierboom und die Nachfragemacht des Handels 1950 bis 1980* (Dortmund and Münster: Gesellschaft für Westfälische Wirtschaftsgeschichte e.V., 2019); and Franz Meussdoerffer, 'Beer and Beer Culture in Germany', in Wulf Schiefenhövel and Helen Macbeth eds., *Liquid Bread: Beer and Brewing in Cross-Cultural Perspective* (New York: Berghahn Books, 2011), pp. 63–70. Given the subject, there is also, of course, no shortage of more popular histories; see, for example, Horst Dornbusch, *Prost! The Story of German Beer* (Boulder: Brewers Publications, 1997). There remains an unfortunately small corpus of scholarship on German wine, but readers will find marked comparisons and overlaps there. See, for example, Kevin Douglas Goldberg, 'German Wine and the Fermentation of Modern Taste, 1850–1914' (PhD diss., University of California, Los Angeles, 2010).

other international histories of beer and brewing in a particular context: how technological or political shifts impacted brewing and commerce, or what sorts of consumer practices emerged among different social demographics.[4] Far too often, the inclination in histories of beer has been to add the drink and the industry to relatively well-known stories. This book, by contrast, analyzes rather than assumes the relationship between beer and Germany. In many ways, then, it is not a history of beer, and it certainly does not set out to analyze what beer meant to individual Germans throughout time and space. Instead, this is a history of Germany revealed through beer. It employs beer as a lens that reveals how the structures and practices of the German nation were transformed from the south up.

Germany has always been, and remains, a cultural and political patchwork, but this book grants the proposition—usually a dubious honor for Prussia alone— that one region can shape the nation. In their effort to repeal a Prussian-centered history culminating in Germany's grasps for world power, scholars have emphasized numerous regions and locales, highlighting plurality, and negotiations between larger and smaller scales of belonging.[5] But less attention has been given to precisely how those locales transformed the nation itself, particularly after the first half of the 20th century. In this book, provincialism not only directly shapes the national whole throughout the century, it is also part of Germany's shifting global presence. As we will see, Bavarian production practices and imagery inform not only the laws and consumer culture of beer in Germany, but also the international embrace of a set of beer-centric Oktoberfest stereotypes of Germany around the world. This book builds on recent assertions that there is no singular German nation or singular way to envision German history, and reveals a particular story of how provincial interests transformed different iterations of the nation-state throughout the 20th century.[6] It suggests another way that "the periphery became central" to the course of the nation and extends scholarship on provincialism not only beyond its conventional periodization in the decades before the First World War, but also into the global context.[7]

The central argument of this book can be broken down into three main components, each building on the last. First, brewers across Germany, but particularly

---

[4] For example, Alexander, *Brewed in Japan*; and Omar D. Foda, *Egypt's Beer: Stella, Identity, and the Modern State* (Austin: University of Texas Press, 2019).

[5] For an overview of how Prussia fits in histories of German federalism, see Abigail Green, 'The Federal Alternative? A New History of Modern German History', *The Historical Journal* 46 no. 1 (Mar. 2003): pp. 187–202; for two classic studies of provincial belonging, see Celia Applegate, *A Nation of Provincials: The German Idea of Heimat* (Berkeley: University of California Press, 1990); and Alon Confino, *The Nation as a Local Metaphor: Württemberg, Imperial Germany, and National Memory, 1871-1918* (Chapel Hill: University of North Carolina Press, 1997).

[6] Helmut Walser Smith, *Germany: A Nation in Its Time Before, During, and After Nationalism, 1500-2000* (London and New York: W.W. Norton, 2020); and H. Glenn Penny, *German History Unbound: From 1750 to the Present* (Cambridge: Cambridge University Press, 2022).

[7] I borrow the phrase from Astrid M. Eckert, *West Germany and the Iron Curtain: Environment, Economy, and Culture in the Borderlands* (Oxford: Oxford University Press, 2021), p. 6.

in Bavaria, were fiercely loyal to regional traditions, regularly prioritizing local values in their business calculations. They were no doubt profit-seekers, but they were also capitalists with a provincial face, and their actions must be understood in the context of such commitments. Second, the staunch regionalism of brewers and their legislative allies fundamentally shaped the production and regulation of beer across several iterations of the German nation-state. Whether in tax law or the fits and starts of European integration, Bavarians' ongoing intransigence and refusal to compromise regional tradition informed the economic, political, and social structures of Germany more broadly. Finally, regional identities and practices also pervaded the cultural discourses of Germany as a place. Bavarian brewers and legislators led the nation in its embrace of "beer purity" as a hallmark of German commercial sentiments and propped up an international stereotype of the beer-drinking, Oktoberfest German, in many cases stripped of its Bavarian origins. More than a history of modern Germany plus beer, *A Nation Fermented* uses beer to reframe how we think about modern Germany as a place under construction. From the late 19th century to the end of the 20th, the combined economic and regulatory power of intransigent Bavarian brewers, regulators, and others repeatedly transformed the production, consumption, and political economy of beer in Germany.

Provincialism and Capitalism

Understanding the actions of brewers, regulators, and marketers requires taking seriously that they repeatedly prioritized not just bottom-lines but also local traditions. In disputes over the taxation of beer—a hot button issue from the 1870s to the 1950s—or arguments about the inclusion of sugar—a topic which flared up in every decade of the twentieth century—Bavarian brewers and regulators invoked tradition, secured political allies, and wielded what levers of power were available to pursue regional interests. But profit and tradition were not always clearly separate. In some cases, Bavarian commitment to tradition appears as a sort of provincial curiosity, but in other cases, brewers, regulators, and marketers actively "invented" or "reinvented" traditions, infusing their practices with new meanings for the sake of political and economic utility.[8] Until the late 1940s, for example, Bavarian brewers held to their practices of— and legal protections for—brewing without the addition of sugar. But from the 1950s onward, they promoted the practice as a marker of regional and, later,

---

[8] Eric Hobsbawm and Terence Ranger, eds., *The Invention of Tradition* (Cambridge: Cambridge University Press, 1983); see also Roland Barthes, *Mythologies* Revised Edition (London: Vintage Books, 2009); and Jeremy DeWaal, 'The Reinvention of Tradition: Form, Meaning, and Local Identity in Modern Cologne Carnival', *Central European History* 46 no. 3 (Sept. 2013): pp. 495–532.

national culture, elevating the so-called *Reinheitsgebot,* or Beer Purity Law, as a national icon. While brewers of course desired profit, they also sought to retain their provincial identities. In the *Reinheitsgebot,* Bavarian brewers and their commercial and regulatory partners found a means to reconstruct both their industry and a bounded sense of cultural belonging in a series of integration moments—from the first years of the new West Germany to the early stages of European integration, and from the mounting influence of the United States to national reunification in 1989/90.

Rather than examining the particulars of Bavaria proper or even of beer itself, this book reimagines how a single region shaped the nation both from within and from without. It shows how an unsuspecting, regionally weighted industry informed both shifting iterations of the German nation and its symbolic presence on the global stage. Historians of the nineteenth century have been particularly insightful in their efforts to place the nation within a broad spectrum of connections. Classic studies of provincialism have shown, for instance, that local loyalties and identities existed side by side with national ones, and in fact that the former often supplied the lens for imagining the latter.[9] Outside the German case too, Kolleen Guy has demonstrated how, in the case of Champagne and France, regional commercial interests could be pivotal in the construction of national identities.[10] At the same time, but quite divorced analytically, other scholars have shown that the legal, discursive, and social practices that defined regions or the nation took shape in a transnational or global register of preconditions, connections, imaginaries, and transgressions.[11] The present book represents an effort to bridge these conversations, combining local histories with global and transnational ones in order to highlight the shifting constellations of forces that produce and shape the nation.[12] *A Nation Fermented* thus uses beer to show how Germany-as-global-nation is also Germany-as-provincial-nation;

---

[9] See, for example, Applegate, *A Nation of Provincials*; and Confino, *The Nation as a Local Metaphor.*

[10] Kolleen M. Guy, *When Champagne became French: Wine and the Making of a National Identity* (Baltimore: The Johns Hopkins University Press, 2003).

[11] See, for example, Andrew Zimmerman, *Anthropology and Antihumanism in Imperial Germany* (Chicago: University of Chicago Press, 2001); Sebastian Conrad, *Globalisation and the Nation in Imperial Germany,* trans. Sorcha O'Hagan (Cambridge: Cambridge University Press, 2010, orig. 2006); Dirk Bönker, *Militarism in a Global Age: Naval Ambitions in Germany and the United States before World War I* (Ithaca: Cornell University Press, 2012); Eva Göbel, *Bayern in der modernen Konsumgesellschaft: Regionalisierung der Konsumkultur im 20. Jahrhundert* (Berlin: Weißensee Verlag, 2005), p. 19; Manuel Schramm, *Konsum und regionale Identität in Sachsen, 1880–2000: Die Regionalisierung von Konsumgütern im Spannungsfeld von Nationalisierung und Globalisierung* (Stuttgart: Franz Steiner Verlag, 2002); and Hannes Siegrist and Manuel Schramm, eds., *Regionalisierung europäischer Konsumkulturen im 20. Jahrhundert* (Leipzig: Leipziger Universitätsverlag, 2003).

[12] In that respect the book is an exercise in "shifting between, and articulating, different scales of analysis." Sebastian Conrad, *What Is Global History?* (Princeton: Princeton University Press, 2016), p. 118.

Bavarian capital and regulatory interests operate across entanglements of scale from the local to the global.[13]

To be clear, the emphases on Bavaria and Munich should not suggest that regions or cities provide an analytic silver bullet that the nation-state does not. Beer and brewing, much like other goods and industries, depend on localized institutional power and cultural practice. They have particular centers and peripheries, and they are grown and sustained by their integrations and reconfigurations.[14] The usage of "Bavaria" here of course refers to an evolving territorial state. The political boundaries of Bavaria changed in the period studied here when the Palatinate—a Bavarian possession since the early 19th century—became part of a new federal state in West Germany. But beyond political boundaries, we will also see several scaled efforts to define and shape the structures and practices of something uniformly Bavarian. Indeed, Bavaria has long been a "region of localities," fragmented by intense divisions of religion, culture, and history.[15] But in the postwar moment, brewers and regulators sought to consolidate regional practice. Beginning in the 1950s, producers and their legislative allies in Munich and Upper Bavaria worked to influence and align production and consumption practices among Franconians that welcomed beer from other West German states into their homes and restaurants. In this case, Old Bavarian capital and regulatory interests fought to homogenize Bavarian commercial practices in a long-contested cultural and political battleground.[16] Bavaria has a marked "Janus face"—as *Der Spiegel* put it in 1964—characterized by "external struggles against every form of centralization; but from within, centralism at any price."[17] Viewing this subregional process of defining Bavarian practice in Franconia in the same frame as Bavarian influences on national laws or international stereotypes reveals a series of nested interactions: relationships such as those between Old Bavaria and Franconia, between southern Germany and Berlin, or between Munich and the Cold War West are each fluid and intersecting. Across them, brewers, regulators, and marketers with an interest in the success of Bavarian beer shaped the structures and discourses both of the market and broader cultural identities.

As this sketch of provincial interests suggests, this book focuses on places and processes that depart from the classic preserves of capitalism—whether material

[13] For a more in-depth consideration of this concept, see Robert Shea Terrell, "Entanglements of Scale: The Beer Purity Law from Bavarian Oddity to German Icon, 1906–1975," *Contemporary European History*. Published online Jan. 18, 2023. DOI: 10.1017/S096077732200087X.

[14] For a relevant American analogue, see Joshua Specht, *Red Meat Republic: A Hoof-to-Table History of How Beef Changed America* (Princeton and Oxford: Princeton University Press, 2019).

[15] Adam T. Rosenbaum, *Bavarian Tourism and the Modern World* (Cambridge: Cambridge University Press, 2016), pp. 4–8.

[16] On the longer roots of Franconian and Old Bavarian conflicts, see Ute Planert, 'From Collaboration to Resistance: Politics, Experience, and Memory of the Revolutionary and Napoleonic Wars in Southern Germany', *Central European History* 39 no. 4 (Dec. 2006), p. 689.

[17] 'Bundesländer—Bayern. Mir san mir', *Der Spiegel*, Jan. 8, 1964, pp. 30–42, here 34.

(i.e., coal, steel, or cotton), organizational (industrial labor and consolidated capital), or geographical (Britain, the Ruhr, and other industrial centers).[18] A more conventional history of capitalism centered on beer in Germany might revolve around Bremen, the Rhineland, or Dortmund in particular; these are common-sensical sites of inquiry, home to a consolidated handful of massive breweries.[19] But the history of capitalism, in both the German case and well beyond it, has increasingly broken with such conventional categories, fruitfully diversifying our understanding of capitalism and even the very concept of capital.[20] To borrow Kenneth Lipartito's words, Bavarian brewers, regulators, marketers, and other stakeholders repeatedly drew on "multiple motives and complicated subjectivities,"

---

[18] In this I have benefitted from the insights of non-western histories of capitalism that have recently emphasized that capitalism takes diverse forms beyond the ideal type of factory manufactur-ing and wage labor seen in Great Britain and other standard cases of industrial capitalism. See, for example, Andrew B. Liu, *Tea War: A History of Capitalism in China and India* (New Haven: Yale University Press, 2020); Kristen Alff, 'Levantine Joint-Stock Companies, Trans-Mediterranean Partnerships and Nineteenth-Century Capitalist Development', *Comparative Studies in Society and History* 60 no. 1 (Jan. 2018): pp. 150–77; and Omar Youssef Cheta, 'The Economy by Other Means: The Historiography of Capitalism in the Modern Middle East', *History Compass* 16 no. 4 (2018).

[19] While not framed as the history of capitalism, research on these regions includes Karl-Peter Ellerbrock, ed., *Zur Geschichte der westfälischen Brauwirtschaft im 19. und 20. Jahrhundert* (Dortmund: Gesellschaft für Westfälische Wirtschaftsgeschichte e.V., 2012); and Bodden, *Business as Usual?*

[20] The history of capitalism in Germany has long been shaped by two main interests. The first is a broader effort in the field to delineate temporally and spatially bounded "varieties of capitalism." Such work has sought to define so-called Rhenish capitalism: a combination of free-market and social interven-tionist impulses embodied in the West German social market economy. In the process, this work established a clear chronology gravitating around the "economic miracle" in the 1950s and 1960s. Historians working on either side of this period have subsequently debated the implications of this periodization, leading to a second major concern in the field—that of continuity and rupture. Perhaps one of the most vibrant debate in recent contemporary history has revolved around the extent to which the global recessions beginning in 1973 marked a fundamental rupture in the histories of the German economy and capitalism. There, as in work focusing on earlier periods including the Weimar Republic and Nazi Germany, scholars have cast doubt on singular cultures or mutually exclusive varieties of capitalism. This book thus speaks to the growing scholarly acceptance of overlap, multiplicity, and qualitatively different capitalisms by pointing to the ways that, throughout the century, before, during, and after the "economic miracle," provincial loyalties shaped commerce and the nation.
On "varieties of capitalism," see Peter A. Hall and David Soskice, eds., *Varieties of Capitalism: The Institutional Foundations of Comparative Advantage* (Oxford: Oxford University Press, 2001); Volker R. Berghahn and Sigurt Vitols, eds., *Gibt es einen deutschen Kapitalismus? Tradition und globale Perpektiven der sozialen Marktwirtschaft* (Frankfurt: Campus Verlag, 2006); and Hans Günter Hockerts and Günther Schulz, eds., *Der Rheinische Kapitalismus in der Ära Adenauer* (Paderborn: Schöningh, 2016). On the debate about continuity and rupture around the 1970s, see Lutz Raphael and Anselm Doering-Manteuffel, *Nach dem Boom: Perspektiven auf die Zeitgeschichte seit 1970*, 2nd ed. (Göttingen: Vandenhoeck & Ruprecht, 2010); Knud Andersen, Ursula Bitzegeio, and Jürgen Mittag, eds., '*Nach dem Structurbruch?' Kontinuität und Wandel von Arbeitbeziehungen und Arbeitswelt(en) sein den 1970er-Jahre* (Bonn: Dietz Verlag, 2011); and Sebastian Voigt, ed., *Since the Boom: Continuity and Change in the Western Industrial World after 1970* (Toronto: University of Toronto Press, 2021). On Weimar and Nazi Germany, see Moritz Föllmer and Pamela E. Swett, eds., *Reshaping Capitalism in Weimar and Nazi Germany* (Cambridge: Cambridge University Press, 2022). Finally, for more general commentary on the acceptance and importance of overlap and multiplicity, see Liu, *Tea War*, pp. 12–18; Kenneth Lipartito, 'Reassembling the Economic: New Departures in Historical Materialism', *The American Historical Review* 121 no. 1 (Feb. 2016): pp. 101–39; Jürgen Kocka, *Capitalism: A Short History*, trans. Jeremiah Riemer (Princeton: Princeton University Press, 2016), pp. 95–161; and Geoff Eley, 'Historicizing the Global, Politicizing Capital: Giving the Present a Name', *History Workshop Journal*, 63 no. 1 (Spring 2007): pp. 154–88, esp. 163–8.

bringing together "forms of knowledge, localized practices, and varied governance structures" to shape markets and commercial cultures.[21] Local and regional loyalties to tradition regularly cut across the placeless and valueless profit-making motivations we so often assume to characterize the modern business world. Beyond the aforementioned insistence on the *Reinheitsgebot*, Bavaria retained a notably decentralized industry structure, unique in comparison to most major beer-producing regions of the world until quite recently. While the number of breweries undoubtedly shrank in the period studied here, Bavarians insisted that industry decentralization was a crucial marker of their industry and culture and, as we will see in several chapters, this conviction, like the ubiquity of lager or the insistence on beer "purity," likewise took on national significance. This is capitalism with a provincial face, where brewers sought profit in markets ranging from the local to the global but also clung tightly to their local identities, rejecting centralization, open innovation, and any shred of faith in free markets.

These histories of provincialism and capitalism operate on a broad foundation of commodity history. As a whole, this field grants that "things" take on different meanings across time and place, thereby revealing the appropriations, translations, and power differentials between different cultures and regimes of policy and practice.[22] In recent years, commodity history has become so well established that new, seminal works rarely address such historiographical foundations, instead employing the lens to reframe other, often larger, stories. For example, historians have recently used commodities to reframe massive narratives including the global histories of capitalism, industrialization, empire, and mass consumerism.[23] Still, connections need not be grand to reveal the transformative power of commodity flows. While parts of this book follow beer beyond German borders, others drill down to interrogate the German case from within. Pulling commodity history into localized contexts and politics reveals how connections between

[21] Lipartito, 'Reassembling the Economic', pp. 121, 128.

[22] Arjun Appadurai, ed. *The Social Life of Things: Commodities in Cultural Perspective* (Cambridge: Cambridge University Press, 1986); Sidney Mintz, *Sweetness and Power: The Place of Sugar in Modern History* (New York: Viking, 1985); Marcy Norton, *Sacred Gifts, Profane Pleasures: A History of Tobacco and Chocolate in the Atlantic World* (Ithaca, NY: Cornell University Press, 2008); and Robert Batchelor, 'On the Movement of Porcelains: Rethinking the Birth of Consumer Society as Interactions of Exchange Networks, 1600–1750', in *Consuming Cultures, Global Perspectives: Historical Trajectories, Transnational Exchanges*, ed. John Brewer and Frant Trentmann (Oxford and New York: Berg, 2006), pp. 95–122; on the term itself, in addition to Appadurai, see Wim M.J. van Binsbergen and Peter L. Geschiere, eds., *Commodification: Things, Agency, and Identities (The Social Life of Things Revisited)* (Münster: LIT Verlag, 2005), especially the chapters by Roy Dilley and Peter Geschiere.

[23] Sven Beckert, *Empire of Cotton: A Global History* (New York: Vintage Books, 2014); Priya Satia, *Empire of Guns: The Violent Making of the Industrial Revolution* (New York: Penguin Press, 2018); Erika Rappaport, *A Thirst for Empire: How Tea Shaped the Modern World* (Princeton: Princeton University Press, 2017). The books by Beckert and Satia in particular capture some of the ways that commodity history has been bent by the gravitational pull of the new history of capitalism. The effect, for better or worse, has been a re-emphasis on structures of power, with less attention paid to the cultural contests and diversities of consumer valuation which were initially crucial to commodity studies.

different parts of the nation are just as in flux as those between opposite sides of the globe.[24] In the German case, studies of commodities have become increasingly common. Works focusing on individual German states—Imperial, Nazi, and East Germany, for example—have used material goods to recast major historical narratives, from the astounding economic importance of the German colonies to the role of East German consumerism in driving socialist globalization.[25] This book also sheds light on particular German states—the shifting political economy of the *Länder* in the Bonn Republic in Chapter 3, for example—but it also resonates with works that have used commodities—the Volkswagen or porcelain—to write across the broader siloing of political temporality that remains in German historiography.[26] *A Nation Fermented* offers a history of material culture grounded in the particulars of economic history that points to the ways that provincial differences in economy and industry manifest in larger cultural transformations across the twentieth century.[27]

German Beer? Integration, Industrialization, and the Rise of *Lagerbier*

While Germans have historically consumed a great deal of beer, the cultures of production and consumption have never been homogenous. Indeed, German-speaking Europe has long boasted a complex mosaic of cultures and regulations around the production, sale, and consumption of beer. Amid the diversity, however, one can discern a north–south split in both production standards and beer styles. It emerged over the course of hundreds of years and echoes throughout the 20th century.

Until the 19th century, a great deal of the production and consumption of beer in German-speaking Europe reflected the history of political fragmentation and decentralization, with states playing a crucial role. In the northern German lands,

---

[24] Commodity history in many ways emerged in lockstep with global history and initially centered on classic preserves such as the relationship between Britain and China, or the New World and the Old. This book has a global component but is more in line with commodity histories that center on national integrations and political economy. See, for example, Specht, *Red Meat Republic*; and Sarah Milov, *The Cigarette: A Political History* (Cambridge: Harvard University Press, 2019).

[25] Steven Press, *Blood and Diamonds: Germany's Imperial Ambitions in Africa* (Cambridge: Harvard University Press, 2021); Andrew Kloiber, *Brewing Socialism: Coffee, East Germans, and Twentieth-Century Globalization* (New York: Berghahn Books, 2023); and Nicole Petrick-Felber, *Kriegswichtiger Genuss: Tabak und Kaffee im 'Dritten Reich'* (Göttingen: Wallstein Verlag, 2015).

[26] For example, Bernhard Rieger, *The People's Car: A Global History of the Volkswagen Beetle* (Cambridge: Harvard University Press, 2013); and Suzanne Marchand, *Porcelain: A History from the Heart of Europe* (Princeton: Princeton University Press, 2020). Continuity and rupture have been the subject of an exceptionally large body of scholarship in German historiography. For a classic introduction, see Konrad H. Jarausch and Michael Geyer, *Shattered Past: Reconstructing German Histories* (Princeton: Princeton University Press, 2003).

[27] In this I take inspiration from Marchand, *Porcelain*, p. 5.

beer was most often produced by private individuals for private use or, at times, by larger landowners selling brews in their rural community for supplemental income. In smaller states and principalities, brewers developed a multitude of specialties underpinning a remarkable degree of market diversity. Just north of Leipzig, for example, brewers in the town of Zerbst were known for beer made with rosemary, and in other northern German locales beers contained everything from rye and herbs to spices and fruits.[28] This proliferation of styles in northern Germany reflected a relative absence of regulations that did not maintain in southern Germany, especially in Bavaria, which was quite early in developing "central sovereign legislation and administrative organization" that manifested in numerous regulations on production, consumption, and sales.[29] By far the most famous regulation—known since the 20th century as the *Reinheitsgebot*—was issued in Munich in 1487 and expanded to the Kingdom of Bavaria in 1516. According to the regulation—which initially aimed to limit competition for grain in the production of beer and bread—beer could only contain water, hops, and malted barley.[30] Innovation thus operated in a markedly narrower key as brewers developed techniques such as aggressively roasting malts. The Bavarian state also permitted a number of exceptions to the law; most famously, Bavarian Weißbier, or Hefeweizen, which is brewed with wheat, was brewed by royal decree, and royal monopoly, from 1520 to 1798.[31]

The Bavarian order of 1516 has become an icon of German beer—and, indeed, of Germany itself. This process is addressed in multiple chapters of what follows. But in the sixteenth century, it was soon joined by an equally important, if lesser-known, regulation on seasonality. Brewers had long been aware that beer fermented in at least two major ways: faster in the warmer summer months, and slower in the colder winter ones. More often than not, heat-tolerant, top-fermenting yeast strands fermented brews in the summer, producing ale, while more cold-tolerant, bottom-fermenting yeasts fermented beer in winter, producing lager (so named because the beer was fermented more slowly while stored in a cool storage cellar, or *Lagerkeller*). By 1553, the Wittelsbach dynasty all but banned the production of beer in the summer months, thereby effectively halting the production of ale. With the exception of some beers such as Weißbier, an ale

---

[28] J. G. T. Gräße, *Bierstudien: Ernst und Scherz. Geschichte des Bieres und seiner Verbreitung über den Erdball. Bierstatistik. Bieraberglauben. Bierfeste. Bierorden. Bierspiele. Bierlieder aller Zeiten und Völker. Biersprichwörter. Brauergeheimmnisse* (Dresden: R. v. Zahn Verlag, 1872), pp. 66–74; Hans Huntemann, 'Bierproduktion und Bierverbrauch in Deutschland vom 15. bis zum Beginn des 19. Jahrhunderts' (PhD Thesis, University of Göttingen, 1970).

[29] Karin Hackel-Stehr, 'Das Brauwesen in Bayern vom 14. bis 16. Jahrhundert, insbesondere die Entstehung und Entwicklung des Reinheitsgebotes (1516)' (PhD Thesis, Technische Universität Berlin, 1988): p. 364.

[30] On the beer and bread issue, see Schäder, *Münchner Brauindustrie*, p. 183; Hackel-Stehr, 'Das Brauwesen in Bayern', pp. 46–52.

[31] Karl Gattinger, *Bier und Landesherrschaft: Das Weißbiermonopol der Wittelsbacher unter Maximillian I. von Bayern* (Munich: Karl M. Lipp Verlag, 2007).

that could still be produced in the summer by royal decree, the vast majority of beers in Bavaria would henceforth be bottom-fermented lager by default.[32]

The effect of these two 16th-century Bavarian regulations was a balance of market homogenization and standardization that would thrive in the face of industrialization and increasing scientific control. As one of the fathers of organic chemistry noted in 1840, compared to British, French, and most German brews, Bavarian *Lagerbier* had solved the problem of long-term storage, leading "to the solution of one of the most beautiful problems of the theory of fermentation."[33] While most northern Germans continued to brew according to local practice and *Hausväterliteratur*, around the turn of the 19th century, Bavarian brewers embraced both specialized trade literature (*Fachliteratur*) and scientific innovations, including steam power, thermometers, and saccharometers. Alongside technological and scientific developments, private industry initiatives in quality control and Bavarian state investment and support for what would become the brewing technical school in Weihenstephan provided the foundation for industry standardization and rapid growth in the Bavarian brewing sector. By the middle of the century, Bavarian breweries employed an average of 3–4 workers; almost all mid- and large-sized breweries made use of steam power; and per capita beer consumption was four times higher than in the rest of the German lands. In Prussia, by comparison, most breweries had only one part-time assistant, while in the Rhineland and Westphalia there were almost no standalone breweries, each operating as a side business connected to a bakery, distillery, tavern, or agricultural farm.[34]

The industrialization of brewing gave rise to more productive and larger enterprises, but industry consolidation was less extreme than we might imagine. In Bavaria, total output increased from about 12 to 20 million hectoliters between 1880 and 1914. In the same period, the industry clearly consolidated, shrinking from more than 5,000 breweries to about 4,000.[35] This was a marked loss to be sure, but one that does not discount the fact that Bavaria remained home to perhaps the most decentralized industry in the world. Indeed, as late as 1950, Bavaria was home to twice as many breweries as the United States, four times as many as

---

[32] The Wittelsbach dynasty began regulating Winter- and Sommerbier differently as early as 1516 and issued a number of regulations related to them, such as levying different taxes for each in 1539. The 1553 regulation, however, allowed brewing in summer only by difficult-to-receive permits. Given that the distinction between ales and lagers was not entirely clear at this point, the resulting explosion of lager production should be seen as an effect of such regulations rather than a goal of them. See, further, Hackel-Stehr, 'Das Brauwesen in Bayern', pp. 57–59, 88, 281.

[33] Justus Liebig, *Organic Chemistry in its Applications to Agriculture and Physiology*, trans. Lyon Playfair (London: Taylor and Walton, 1840), pp. 294–5.

[34] Georg Wilhelm von Viebahn, *Statistik des zollvereinten und nördlichen Deutschlands*, vol. 3 (Berlin: Verlag Georg Reimer, 1868), pp. 793–5.

[35] Dirk Götschmann, *Wirtschaftsgeschichte Bayerns: 19. und 20. Jahrhundert* (Regensburg: Verlag Friedrich Pustet, 2010), pp. 224–9.

Great Britain, and more than the rest of West Germany combined.[36] Beyond Bavaria, the industrialization of the German brewing industry in the 19th century was shaped by Bavarian know-how, but it depended on the emergence and modernization of small- and mid-sized enterprises nationwide.[37] As we will see in later chapters, industry centralization undoubtedly accelerated from the turn of the 20th century onward, but in several key moments, usually around economic crises, it became a major force of industry anxiety, lobbying, and policy change. In the late 1940s, and especially in the 1970s and 1990s, Bavarian brewers led the charge to insist that small- and mid-sized production remained a hallmark of the national industry.

Beyond industry structure, southern-style lager began to rapidly conquer Germany by the mid-19th century.[38] "Bavarian beer" was increasingly available in central Europe and around the world thanks to expanding rail networks and industry innovation, with long-distance transport from railcars with evaporative cooling to ice-packed rooms on transatlantic steamers.[39] But such integration also forced small breweries throughout Germany to modernize production or lose their local market share. Indeed, already by 1868, more than 5,000 breweries in northern Germany reoriented their businesses around Bavarian-style bottom-fermented lager.[40] New breweries also cropped up across Germany to service the expanding centers of industrial and urban growth. In the coal and steel hub of Dortmund, the population exploded from about 50,000 at national unification to almost 400,000 by the First World War and, thanks to a boom of lager breweries in the 1860s and 1870s, became the third largest center of production behind Munich and Berlin.[41]

Lager quickly came to dominate German brewing, thanks in large part to the technological and scientific innovations of brewers in Munich and Bavaria more broadly. But many provincial differences remained. In fact, when the German Empire was unified in 1871 it not only perpetuated but codified the north–south split. As a condition of their entry into the German Empire, the three southern states—the Grand Duchy of Baden and the Kingdoms of Württemberg and Bavaria—maintained sovereign legislation on the production and taxation of beer. Such "Reserve Rights" (*Reservatrechte*) were federalist measures that aimed

---

[36] 'Anzahl der Brauereien auf der Welt', Bayerischer Brauerbund e.V. *Geschäftsbericht 1951/52 und 1952/53*, p. 124.

[37] Clemens Wischermann, 'Zur Industrialisierung des deutschen Braugewerbs im 19. Jahrhundert: Das Beispiel der Reichsgräflich zu Stolbergschen Brauerei Westheim in Westfalen, 1860–1913', *Zeitschrift für Unternehmensgeschichte/Journal of Business History* 30 no. 3 (1985): pp. 143–80.

[38] Hasso Spode, *Die Macht der Trunkenheit: Kultur- und Sozialgeschichte des Alkohols in Deutschland* (Opladen: Leske and Budrich, 1993), pp. 249–50.

[39] Schäder, *Münchner Brauindustrie*, pp. 165–6.

[40] Wischermann, 'Zur Industrialisierung', pp. 143–80, 149.

[41] Bodden, *Business as Usual?*, pp. 34–6.

to appease provincial concerns and decenter Prussian power. They ranged more broadly from the operation of free harbors in the Hanseatic states to the retention of semiautonomous militaries by the heads of Saxony, Württemberg, and Bavaria.[42] Not only did southern Germans retain their own standards, but in 1872 a new system of regulation and taxation came into effect in the rest of Germany, forming the North German Beer Tax Community (*Norddeutsche Biersteuergemeinschaft*), which set a common tax scheme and allowed brewers to include rice and various forms of sugar. The three southern states remained exempt, and, at the turn of the twentieth century, Baden and Württemberg exercised their Reserve Rights, formally adopting Bavarian production standards and thereby forming a large southern German bloc which both retained its own beer tax revenue and adhered to stricter standards of production. By the turn of the twentieth century, then, Bavarian and Bohemian *Lagerbier* had become increasingly ubiquitous even as the structures of the nation remained fragmented. From German unification to the eve of the First World War, the number of breweries in northern Germany producing anything other than bottom-fermented lager dropped from 10,170 to a mere 1,993.[43] Still, producers and consumers retained local pride, exceptions abounded, and regulations on production standards and taxation remained disjointed, making it difficult to pinpoint anything we might uniformly call *German* beer.

Outline of the Book

The structure of this book is roughly chronological. Chapter 1 begins at the turn of the 20th century when the enormously diverse German beer market faced a series of threats in regulation, taxation, and social reform that notably homogenized the market and galvanized myriad forms of industrial and political opposition. In the case of the Weimar-era beer tax, for example, Bavarian political intransigence destabilized Germany's first republic. Through the 1930s and 1940s, provincial politics and industrial convictions, particularly about production

---

[42] The Reserve Rights and their federalist implications remain an understudied area in the historiography of Imperial Germany. For a relevant overview of the federalist and constitutional histories of Imperial Germany, see Allan Mitchell, '"A Real Foreign Country": Bavarian Particularism in Imperial Germany, 1870–1918', *Francia* 7 (1979): pp. 587–96; more generally, George G. Windell, 'The Bismarckian Empire as a Federal State, 1866–1880: A Chronicle of Failure', *Central European History* 2, no. 4 (Dec. 1969): pp. 291–311; and Richard Dietrich, 'Foederalismus, Unitarismus oder Hegemonialstaat?' and Walter Peter Fuchs, 'Bundesstaaten und Reich: Der Bundesrat', in *Zur Problematik 'Preussen und das Reich'*, ed. Oswald Hauser (Böhlau, 1984); more recently, Dieter Grimm, 'Was the German Empire a Sovereign State?' in *Imperial Germany Revisited: Continuing Debates and New Perspectives*, ed. Sven Oliver Müller and Cornelius Torp, pp. 51–66 (New York: Berghahn Books, 2011).

[43] 'Reichstag Nichtamtliche Drucksache', no date, but included with other documents from 1912–1913, Bundesarchiv Berlin (henceforth BAB) R 2/1733.

standards, began to inform the structures of the nation. In the Nazi period, the subject of Chapter 2, state interventions moved southern brewers to present themselves and their product as a crucial part of everyday life—a lesson learned in combatting the temperance movement a decade earlier.[44] Southern brewers' refusal to accept sugar in beer set the foundation for decades of conflict over production standards. But, as Chapter 3 shows, Bavarian conceptions of beer also took on national significance beginning in the late 1940s as Bavarian agrarians in the new western German breadbasket used the production of beer to claim political and legislative power in the emerging postwar West. This emphasis on Bavarian influence explains in part the relative absence of East Germany until the final chapter of this book. While the production and consumption of beer remained crucial to everyday life and political rhetoric in East Germany, brewers there could not secure access to analogous levers of power and the influence of Bavaria—both politically, as in the case of curtailing adulteration with sugar, and culturally, with its increasing idolization of the *Reinheitsgebot* as a national commercial sensibility—was all but obliterated until after reunification.[45]

In the West, the remarkable growth of the economy in the 1950s and 1960s undergirded a number of processes by which Bavarian brewers, legislators, and marketers promoted beer not only as a popular drink, but as a fundamental characteristic of the (West) German nation. From the adoption of interwar advertising techniques that emphasized beer as a brandless good, the subject of Chapter 4, to market protectionism that saw the *Reinheitsgebot* become a staple of West German commercial values, the focus of Chapter 5, these were the decades in which beer took on increasing significance not just as a commercial good but as a national icon. The association also went global, as Chapter 6 shows, as Bavarian exports to booming markets shaped international cultures of consumption and the imagery of the nation abroad. Finally, as we see in Chapter 7, from the 1970s to the 1990s, the scaffolding of unprecedented economic growth and national division collapsed, but Bavarian influence remained in everything from global stereotypes to the insistence that German beer, even in the newly reunified nation, had to be "pure beer."

---

[44] See Chapter 1 of this book and Sina Fabian, 'Between Crisis and Innovation: Beer and Public Relations in the Weimar Republic', in Föllmer and Swett, *Reshaping Capitalism*, pp. 183–207.

[45] Brewers in the East who sought to export beer to West Germany were beholden to the import restrictions of West German brewing law and some, including Radeberger, Wernesgrüner, and Export Berliner Pilsner, did brew at least some beers according to the *Reinheitsgebot*, but this was a distinct minority and there was no official adoption of the regulation, first because the Soviet occupation authorities dismissed it in the late 1940s and second because few outside southern Germany had embraced the regulation before then. On the latter point, see Chapters 1 and 2. I am grateful to the insights and ongoing research of John Gillespie, whose dissertation "Beer Country: Beer, Identity, and the State in Postwar Central Europe" will prove to be a welcome addition to the entangled postwar histories of beer and brewing in the two German states and Czechoslovakia.

A Nation Fermented shows how brewers, regulators, lobbyists, and consumer interest groups consistently shaped the structures and practices of the nation in everything from production standards and tax law to public health policy, consumer sensibilities, and international stereotypes. Lessons learned in the Weimar era—about the incendiary qualities of the federal beer tax, for instance—directly shaped West German commerce. In that case, Bavarian intransigence from the 1920s to the early 1950s directly led to the beer tax emerging as the only consumption-based tax retained exclusively by the *Länder*, even to this day. But the same provincial values that animated southern brewers to reject state-driven efforts to change production standards during the Nazi period also led them to transform an obscure standard—the *Reinheitsgebot*—into an icon of national commercial sentiment beginning in the 1960s. To this day, Bavarian iconography, from the *Reinheitsgebot* to Oktoberfest and alpine idylls, continues to inform global conceptions of the German nation. Put differently, the beer-drinking German was not an accident of stereotyping but rather a product of enterprising brewers, importers, and marketers around the world who promoted the imagery to sell beer and, in the process, rebranded the (West) German nation.[46] We now turn to the beginning of the 20th century, well before *Hitlerjunge Quex* could assume the German character of lager in Berlin, to see how brewers, legislators, and social reformers contested the role of beer, Bavarian standards, and the centralizing state.

---

[46] Robert Shea Terrell, '"Lurvenbrow": Bavarian Beer Culture and Barstool Diplomacy in the Global Market, 1945–1964', in *Alcohol Flows Across Cultures: Drinking Cultures in Transnational and Comparative Perspective*, ed. Waltraud Ernst (London: Routledge, 2020), pp. 204–20; and Chapter 6 of the present book.

1

Integration and Its Discontents

Lager, Tax, and Temperance, *c.* 1900 to the 1930s

In 1901, the future Chancellor and Foreign Minister of the Weimar Republic, Gustav Stresemann, completed his doctoral dissertation on the bottled beer industry. As the son of a beer-bottler and distributor, Stresemann's thesis centered on a subject with which he was intimately familiar. His personal connection to the subject, and his love for his native Berlin, may be why Stresemann asserted a direct link between the rapid changes afoot across Germany and Berlin and throughout the world of beer. In particular, he bemoaned the loss of the "portly, thoughtful, and...philistine bourgeoisie of old Berlin." He waxed poetic over their penchant for sipping ales "at simple tables...reading newspapers, or speaking quietly and in modesty." In contrast, Stresemann blasted increasingly ubiquitous lager beer as both foreign to Berlin—he and others at the time called it "Bavarian beer"—and symptomatic of rapid proletarianization. "Bavarian beer" was not the beer of leisurely sipping, reading, and modesty, but rather of the

> eternal hustle and bustle, a coming and going of individuals...standing while eating one of the obligatory sandwiches or gulping down a half-pour (*Schnitt*)...and, with an eye on the clock, leaving after a few minutes to make room for others who, just like them, are "in a rush" to "enjoy" something.[1]

Lager beer embodied a two-sided assault on the city: from the provinces on the one hand, and from industrialization and proletarianization on the other. And while Stresemann and his contemporaries in northern Germany rightly understood *Lagerbier* as a southern German (and Bohemian) innovation, by this point most of the lager consumed in Berlin was in fact produced there, both to cater to the growing working class and because of southern-driven structural changes in production standards and regulation.

Stresemann was not alone in contesting changes in both beer itself and the social meanings it carried. From the turn of the century to the mid-1930s, three tensions of integration emerged that challenged the place of beer within the changing nation: the national regulation of production standards, a shifting tax

---

[1] Gustav Stresemann, 'Die Entwicklung des Berliner Flaschenbiergeschäfts' (PhD thesis, University of Leipzig, 1901), pp. 22–3.

A Nation Fermented: Beer, Bavaria, and the Making of Modern Germany. Robert Shea Terrell, Oxford University Press.
© Robert Shea Terrell 2024. DOI: 10.1093/oso/9780198881834.003.0002

structure, and the growing international temperance movement. In each, brewers, regulators, and social reformers contested how and what kind of beer fit in German society. And in each, opposition had a different geographical character. From the end of the 19th century to the first decades of the 20th, national legislative integration increased, with regulations on raw materials and permissible ingredients. These changes sparked opposition from brewers, most often in northern Germany, where regulations had been most lax and cultures of production were most diverse. Brewers and other commentators from the north repeatedly advocated for their industrial and social interests in response to federal interventions that ranged from the use of sugar to wartime measures designed to combat material scarcity. In the case of taxation, the stakes were highest in the three southern states which had long retained their own tax revenues on beer but faced a new federal fiscal structure in the Weimar Republic. The beer tax was a particular sticking point in Bavaria, such that by the Great Depression, alleged federal overreliance on Bavarian brewing undermined faith in the republic for many Bavarian parliamentarians. While these regulatory pressures prompted varying regional responses, brewers across Germany were largely united in the face of the temperance movement. Beer had long been such a staple of German life that many brewers had never realized the importance of public relations work. The coordinated and targeted assaults of temperance reformers changed that, and the national trade organization became a regular advocate, at exhibitions and in print, for beer as a public good.

Production standards, taxation, and public relations work, the three analytic themes of this chapter, are key elements of this book as a whole. The tensions of integration and the contestation of the social meanings of beer illuminate how industrial and political integration were never without their regional critics. Against the centuries-long backdrop of heterogeneous regional cultures of production and consumption, lager emerged as a distinct style in the 19th century and quickly conquered the national market thanks to its long shelf life, transportability, and lighter taste. By the turn of the 20th century, the dominant lager market was further buttressed by both product regulation and tax law, exacerbating the pressures on traditional beer styles and sparking broad industrial opposition, particularly in the north. In the realm of politics, however, the Weimar-era beer tax drew forceful opposition from southern brewers and parliamentarians, who adopted an increasingly uncompromising position on commercial and fiscal regulation. But while northerners like Stresemann railed against the ascendant hegemony of southern production standards, and southerners blasted federal overreliance on their regional industry, all proponents of beer—especially brewers themselves—could agree on their opposition to temperance and social reform. In all cases, brewers, parliamentarians, and social reformers used the production and consumption of beer to articulate claims to the popular interest. By the beginning of the 1930s, production standards had become so homogenous that the once pejorative "Bavarian beer" had been transformed into the standard German lager, even as brewers, regulators, and other advocates for beer remained divided on exactly how beer fit into the centralizing German state.

The Force of Regulation and Northern Industrial Backlash

Until the middle of the 19th century the production of beer in German-speaking central Europe was highly localized and fragmented, but in the course of industrialization, more and more brewers turned to the production of lighter *Lagerbier*. Not all brewers readily made the change, however, and for those who did, local differences remained regarding what, exactly, could be put in lager. In the last decades of the century, the federal state took on an increasingly important role in regulating and standardizing production. If urbanization and technical changes in refrigeration and logistics could affect industrial practices to reshape entire markets, the webs of regulation likewise hemmed in and shaped cultures and standards of production. These are but some of the structural issues at play in unraveling the relationship between political power, commerce, and consumer culture.[2] State interventions, from standards to resource management, significantly shaped what beers could be produced, dramatically furthering the homogenization of beer in Germany into something we might recognize as *German beer*. But such regulatory force triggered industrial backlash, most often from those areas of northern Germany where brewing practices had been most diverse.

The first wave of state intervention in production was the by-product of the industrializing food system and advances in food science. These processes sparked a wave of regulatory intervention, most notably for the brewing industry, regarding sugar and yeast. In most of northern Germany, brewing had come to depend on the use of a wide range of sugar alternatives, especially saccharin, the earliest synthetic sweetener, discovered in the United States in 1878 and first manufactured in Marburg in 1886. Cheaper and sweeter than natural sugar sources, saccharin production exploded, quickly drawing the ire of the established sugar industry, most notably the Association of the German Beet Sugar Industry (*Verein für die Rübenzuckerindustrie des Deutschen Reichs*), which was founded in 1850 and remained one of the oldest industrial organizations in Germany.[3] Under pressure from the beet sugar industry and its allies in associated business sectors, Imperial Germany passed a series of laws in 1898 and 1902

---

[2] See further, Arjun Appadurai, 'Introduction: Commodities and the Politics of Value', in *The Social Life of Things: Commodities in Cultural Perspective* (Cambridge: Cambridge University Press, 1986), pp. 29–41.
[3] Manfred Erdmann, *Die vefassungspolitische Funktion der Wirtschaftsverbände in Deutschland, 1815–1871* (Berlin: Duncker & Humblot, 1968), pp. 170–83.

which together banned the use of artificial sweeteners.[4] The regulations would prove catastrophic for top-fermenting (ale) brewers already struggling to keep pace with the production and consumption of lager beer.[5]

The effects of the 1902 saccharin ban were significantly compounded by a similar wave of regulations regarding yeast in 1906. Taken together, they precipitated a fundamental reorientation of the German brewing industry, reshaping regulation and taxation and forming the foundation of numerous conflicts over beer throughout the 20th century. Yeast had always been present in beer and, as we saw, strict Bavarian regulations in the 16th century underpinned a split in northern and southern brewing cultures, the latter eventually thriving in and driving the course of industrialization. In the same period, yeast had been the subject of prolific microbiological research and chemical isolation. In 1906, the relevant tax codes in both the north and south were amended to explicitly include both top- and bottom-fermenting yeast. In the south, Bavaria, Baden, and Württemberg simply added yeast, of both varieties, to their stricter three—or, rather, now four—ingredient list. The North German Beer Tax Community also tightened their regulations, but with an important distinction: while bottom-fermenting lager beers were limited to a four-ingredient list—water, hops, malted barley, and, now, yeast—as in the south, top-fermented ales could contain malts from other grains, technically pure cane, beet, invert, and starch sugar, as well as glucose and colorants derived from such sources.[6] By the turn of the 20th century, then, all beer regardless of type was required to adhere to the four-ingredient list in the south, while in the north, top-fermented ales could contain a series of additional ingredients. This regulatory split between north and south returns a number of times in subsequent decades, but at the turn of the century it was particularly consequential in the north because it both buttressed the 1902 saccharin ban and outlawed a significant number of historical additives, from citrus to herbs.

Some of the iconic ales that continue to exist to this day—Kölsch, Altbier, and Hefeweizen—do so because their relatively straightforward ingredient lists did not conflict with the new national law. The cases of Kölsch and Altbier, from Cologne and Düsseldorf respectively, demonstrate how local market diversity could exist within the narrow boundaries of integrating Germany, as each continued to be culturally and fiscally important in their home regions. The case of Bavarian Weißbier or Hefeweizen (literally yeast-wheat) is more curious. While this southern style conformed to the nationwide law, its inclusion of wheat was not in line with stricter southern regulations. But the style drew little critique. Within Bavaria, Weißbier had lost its royally decreed legal exemption and

---

[4] 'Süßstoffgesetz', *Deutsches Reichsgesetzblatt* (1902) Nr. 36, pp. 253–6; and, further, Anja Krumbe, 'Verboten, verbrannt, verschrien——Süße mit Geschichte', *VFED-Aktuell* Nr. 171 (2019), pp. 8–14.

[5] On the top- and bottom-fermenting taxonomy, see the Introduction to this book.

[6] 'Gesetz wegen Änderung des Brausteuergesetzes', *Reichsgesetzblatt* 98 (1906): pp. 622–31, esp. Section 1.

dynastic monopoly, but the culture of exception remained. No market protectionist campaigns emerged to push Weißbier to extinction, both because it met the nationwide regulation and, perhaps, because by 1906 it had dwindled to an almost negligible percentage of the Bavarian market.

While regional styles like Kölsch, Altbier, and Bavarian Weißbier survived, innumerable others were driven to near and sometimes total ruin. The production and consumption of beers that violated the 1906 legislation created tensions among provincial producers, the central government, and the national trade organization: the German Brewers Association (DBB), founded in 1871. Such conflicts were most prevalent in northern Germany, where the new legislation infringed on a far more diverse culture of production. There, brews commonly included alternative sugar sources like honey or molasses, fruit, roots, salt, herbs, and spices. Just a year after the ban, for example, the DBB worked with the Finance Ministry to prohibit the so-called Eckardt Method, a process by which north German brewers added winestone or tartaric acid during the production of top-fermented ale.[7] In other cases, such as that of Gose, entire styles nearly went extinct. For example, by the late 1930s only one brewery continued to make Gose, and in fact the style completely ceased to exist from 1966 until a revival in the 1980s.[8] The Eckardt Method, Gose, and any number of intensely localized beers and brewing practices faced the twin pressures of new legal restrictions and the industry turn to standardized lagers.

These relatively small cases of industry homogenization were indicative of a watershed in the national cultures of production. The combined effect of the 1902 saccharin ban and the explicit list of permissible sugars in the 1906 Beer Tax Law accelerated the threat already presented by industrial lager. In northern Germany, low-alcohol, top-fermented ales had long been king but had, in recent decades, been dramatically outpaced by lighter and stronger lager, at times shipped in but increasingly produced locally. From 1873 to 1911, while the total beer produced in the North German Beer Tax Community exploded from 19.6 million to 41.3 million hectoliters, the output of top-fermented beer was cut almost in half, from 8.4 million to 4.6 million hectoliters, or from 43 per cent to 11 per cent of total production. This figure is yet more striking in light of a population increase from about 41 million to 66 million in the same period.[9] Throughout the Kaiser Reich, then, the combined weight of industrial production and market regulation

[7] Melchior Busemann, *Der Deutsche Brauer-Bund 1871–1921* (Berlin: G. Asher, 1921), p. 110.
[8] Fal Allen, *Gose: Brewing a Classic German Beer for the Modern Era* (Boulder, CO: Brewers Publications, 2018), p. 23.
[9] Brewing figures taken from Busemann, *Der Deutsche Brauer-Bund 1871–1921*, p. 168; and 'Reichstag Nichtamtliche Drucksache' from the Vorstand des Vereins Berliner Weiß- und Braunbierbrauereien, no date, but included with other documents from 1912 to 1913, Bundesarchiv Berlin (henceforth BAB) R 2/1733; population statistics from Bernhard Weidenbach, 'Einwohnerzahl des Deutschen Kaiserreiches in den Jahren 1871 bis 1912', *Statista*, Jan. 20, 2021, https://de.statista.com/statistik/daten/studie/1091817/umfrage/einwohnerzahl-des-deutschen-kaiserreiches/.

sharply curtailed a once diverse and decentralized culture of production and consumption.

These shifts disproportionately disrupted small and mid-sized enterprises that had been the lifeblood of the industry and the root of broad pre-industrial market diversity, especially in the north. From 1873 to 1911, the sheer number of top-fermenting, ale-producing breweries fell from 10,170 to a mere 1,993.[10] Such a drastic shift led many to understand themselves to be in a common struggle against industry centralization, or what one contemporary called "the flag of capitalism."[11] The case of German beer thus complicates other histories of regulating foodstuffs in Europe and the United States. Throughout the industrialized world, concepts of "food purity" and "natural eating" emerged in the late nineteenth century as life reformers, food scientists, businessmen, and regulators eyed the potential harms of the modern food system, from meat-heavy diets to the increasingly adulterated and synthetic alternatives that occupied the growing space between food producers and consumers.[12] In the case of German beer, the drink remained outside the convictions of life reformers who tended toward temperance, localized production and consumption often remained the norm, and the pursuit of minimalism and later "purity" came from the modernizing industry itself. Small-scale producers, particularly in the north, ultimately rallied against this process. Around the turn of the 20th century, more than a hundred new local, regional, and national trade organizations formed throughout Germany, the vast majority in the North German Beer Tax Community.[13] Some represented local industries, from Chemnitz (1889) to Cologne (1902), or entire regions, from Bavaria (1890) to East Prussia (1893). But beyond specific place-based affiliations, many were explicitly organized around the interests of particular products and small enterprise. On the heels of the 1906 regulations on production standards, a slew of organizations representing top-fermenting breweries were founded in 1907, including the Association of Top-Fermenting Breweries in the Beer Tax

[10] "Reichstag Nichtamtliche Drucksache."

[11] Eugen Gütermann, 'Die Karlsruher Brauindustrie' (PhD Thesis, Ruprecht-Karls-Universität zu Heidelberg, 1908), p. 5. This sentiment may have been slightly inflated in reality. While the number of large joint-stock breweries increased from 263 to 514 from 1888 to 1911, and shareholder capital increased from 272 million to 615 million Marks in the same period, the average per brewery amounted to an increase of only about 160,000 Marks. Erich Borkenhagen, *100 Jahre Deutscher Brauer-Bund e.V., 1871–1971: Zur Geschichte des Bieres im 19. und 20. Jahrhundert* (Berlin: Westkreuz-Druckerei, 1971), pp. 65–6.

[12] On natural eating, see Corinna Treitel, *Eating Nature in Modern Germany: Food, Agriculture and Environment, c. 1870 to 2000* (Cambridge: Cambridge University Press, 2017); on purity and adulteration, see Uwe Spiekermann, 'Redefining Food: The Standardization of Products and Production in Europe and the United States, 1880–1914', *History and Technology* Vol. 27 No. 1 (Mar. 2011), pp. 11–36; and Benjamin R. Cohen, *Pure Adulteration: Cheating on Nature in the Age of Manufactured Food* (Chicago and London: Chicago University Press, 2019).

[13] This is only counting associations of breweries themselves, not those in malting, transport, or sales, which were also considerable. See Reichsamt des Innern, *Verzeichnis der im Deutschen Reiche bestehenden Vereine gewerblicher Unternehmer zur Wahrung ihrer wirtschaftlichen Interessen* (Berlin: Ernst Siedfried Mittler u. Sohn, 1903), pp. 409–23.

INTEGRATION AND ITS DISCONTENTS 23

Zone (*Verband obergäriger Brauereien im Brausteuergebiet*) and the Union of White and Brown Beer Breweries in Berlin and Environs (*Verein der Weiß- und Braunbierbrauereien Berlins und Umgebung*).[14]

By the eve of the First World War, the homogenizing pressures shaping the beer industry sparked organized opposition efforts from these trade organizations and industrial lobbies. Perhaps the most high-profile case originated around *Braunbier*, or brown beer, a sweet and sour sibling to Berliner Weisse. The color and flavor profile of the beer had initially derived from aggressively roasted barley malt, but by the late 19th century most producers had turned to saccharin to stay competitive in the booming lager market. The 1902 saccharin ban and the limitations on permissible sugars in brewing thus presented an existential threat.[15] By 1912, the Association of Top-Fermenting Breweries in the Beer Tax Zone advocated for lowering (if not abolishing) taxes on the sugars permitted in brewing. This request was echoed by the Union of Berlin White and Brown Beer Breweries, which petitioned the Reichstag not only to lower taxes on sweeteners but also to lift the saccharin ban for the production of *Braunbier*.[16] For the next two years, brewers appealed to the Reichstag, finding allies such as the senior civil servant Willy Pilger in the Imperial Treasury, who claimed the inclusion of saccharin would stabilize the *Braunbier* industry, and indeed the entire top-fermenting sector. Advocates repeatedly met intransigence, leading the ranks of petitioners to swell to more than 600 breweries, mainly small- and mid-sized enterprises claiming that the fate of their businesses and economic prospects hung in the balance.[17] If readers have never heard of *Braunbier* it is because the petitions failed to persuade the authorities to lift the ban. In the absence of cheap sugar alternatives, top-fermenting beer entered its death throes. In 1910, the number of top-fermenting breweries in Berlin had already been reduced to 112, and by 1925 only 40 remained.[18]

Advocates of top-fermenting ale and opponents of industry homogenization were given an opportunity by the material scarcities of the war years even as wartime regulations crystalized tensions between north and south. The war

---

[14] Ibid., and *Berliner Jahrbuch für Handel und Industrie*, annum 1907, vol. 1 (Berlin: Verlag von Georg Reimer, 1908), p. 89.

[15] In 1909, the north German *Brausteuergesetz* was amended to explicitly forbid the inclusion of artificial sweetners. See '*Brausteuergesetz* vom 15. Juli 1909', *Reichs-Gesetzblatt* Nr. 43 (1909), pp. 773–92; esp. p. 774.

[16] July 6, 1912, 'Denkschrift über die gegenwärtige Lage des obergärigen Brauereigewerbes sowie zur Begründung der Notwendigkeit, den lediglich zur Süßung und nach Abschluß des Brauverfahrens verwendeten Zucker von der Brausteuer zu befreien', BAB R 2/1733; and 'Reichstag Nichtamtliche Drucksache'.

[17] 'Ist dem Kleinbrauer nicht mehr zu helfen?' *Der klein- und mittelbrauer* Nr. 45, Nov. 8, 1913; 'Niederschrift über die Besprechung im Reichsschatzamt vom 20. Dezember 1913, betreffend die wirtschaftliche Lage der kleinen und mittleren Brauereien', BAB R 2/1733; 'Ein Antrag von über 600 deutschen Braumeistern an den Bund', *Der klein- und mittelbrauer* Nr. 1, Jan. 3. 1914.

[18] 'Die Biererzeugung', *Zeitschrift des Preuss. Statistischen Landesamts* (Berlin: Verlag des Preussischen Statistischen Landesamts, 1931), p. 205.

dramatically reduced the quantity and quality of beer in Germany and hurt bottom lines across the board.[19] At the same time, wartime conflicts over state regulations and permissible ingredients gave brewers an opportunity to roll back market homogenization and transformed the larger discourses of beer. Barley rationing had been introduced in 1915 and, in the second half of the war, the German state loosened the 1906 list of permissible ingredients to include additional sugar and malt sources, like rice and maize. Such regulations persisted after the war due to lingering scarcities and many northern brewers sought to make such changes permanent. In 1920, north German brewers denounced the 1906 regulation to the Finance Ministry and the Parliament. In hopes of continuing wartime exemptions which revived some of their pre-1906 practices, they critiqued the regulation as short-lived and "Bavarian," using the term, like Stresemann, to convey an internal otherness. To further distance themselves from the strict southern approach to beer, they aligned themselves with the rising power of the United States, reasoning that other grains, including rice, had worked particularly well for American brewers.[20] Their lobbying swayed the Reichstag to continue the exemption for rice and maize, and, into the 1920s, the federal government continued to allow exceptions on various sugar sources.[21]

In the south, meanwhile, brewers and their regulatory allies sought less to stop such exemptions than to ensure fair market competition in spite of them. Their most common strategy was to emphasize tradition and historical precedents, most often the 1871 Reserve Rights and their perpetuation in the 1906 Beer Tax Law. The deepest historicist claim of these years came in 1918 when, in a dispute over integrating the beer tax at the federal level, the Bavarian state parliamentarian Hans Rauch invoked Bavarian peculiarity with reference to the 1516 *Reinheitsgebot* or Beer Purity Law. Until this point, if the regulation was discussed at all it had usually been called, more prosaically, the *Surrogatverbot*, or surrogate prohibition.[22] While Bavarian insistence on the importance of the *Reinheitsgebot* would become crucial to the entire nation in subsequent decades—the subject of Chapter 5—this claim was part of a more limited effort in the early 20th century to secure the peculiarity of regional standards by federal exemptions. In fact, tighter production standards became a condition of the three southern states

[19] Sina Fabian, 'Between Criticism and Innovation: Beer and Public Relations in the Weimar Republic', in *Reshaping Capitalism in Weimar and Nazi Germany*, ed. Moritz Föllmer and Pamela Swett (Cambridge: Cambridge University Press, 2022), pp. 183–207, esp. pp. 186–7.

[20] Dec. 15, 1920, Schutzverband des Brauereien der ehemaligen Brausteuergemeinschaft to the Reichsfinanzministerium, BAB R 2/1736.

[21] *Akten der Reichskanzlei. Weimarer Republik. Die Kabinette Wirth I/II, Band 2, Doc. Nr. 294.5,* https://www.bundesarchiv.de/aktenreichskanzlei/1919–1933/0000/wir/wir2p/kap1_1/kap2_59/para3_5.html.

[22] Horst Dornbusch and Karl-Ullrich Heyse, 'Reinheitsgebot', in *The Oxford Companion to Beer*, ed. Garrett Oliver (Oxford: Oxford University Press, 2012), pp. 692–3. At the time, even the Bavarian Brewers Association only reluctantly referred to the law as the "so-called *Reinheitsgebot*." See Dec. 18, 1920, Bayerischer Brauerbund to Reichsfinanzministerium, BAB R 2/1736.

upon entering the federal fiscal system in 1919, and throughout the 1920s, southern producers and regulators contested northern exemptions on rice, maize, and other sugar sources.[23] They sought federal exemption in the name of market competition by seeking labeling measures and financial equalizations that would keep their products competitive in a market of cheaper, surrogate beers. By 1924, their pressure led the Reichstag to rule that exemptions on malts, sugars, and sugar-derived coloring agents did not apply in Bavaria, Baden, and Württemberg.[24] Such a decision perpetuated the north–south split in German production standards—enshrining 1871/1906 in the south, and undermining them in the north.

As the south clung to tradition, northern brewers continued to rally against national regulations throughout the 1920s, most frequently presenting their opposition as against the disproportionate influence of Bavaria. The brewers of Upper Silesia, for instance, echoed Stresemann, arguing explicitly and vehemently against Bavarian influence in industrial, legal, and consumer cultures. The Kretschmer brewers' guild in Breslau/Wrocław critiqued the "purism" (*Purismus*) of Bavaria, noting that the north German industry developed independently and "in full freedom." They maintained that even the distinction between top- and bottom-fermenting beer in 1906 was foreign to northern Germany. After 1906, much of northern Germany had continued to brew with the addition of sugar anyway, especially in those parts of Germany outside of major cities and in areas not dominated by lager. The Kretschmer guild lamented the decimation, and the resulting "fragile powerlessness" (*Ohnmacht schwache*), of the German ale industry and closed by suggesting that the German state should actively work to protect local production standards.[25] They were not alone in this sentiment. That same winter, more than 100 producers in Berlin rejected the nationwide departure from beer brewed with the addition of sugar, claiming that the national trend represented a fundamental threat to their businesses.[26]

Such petitions usually failed, and successes were often only temporary. By the 1920s, the standardization of production was increasingly total, as bottom-fermented *Lagerbier* came to dominate Germany. In Berlin, Stresemann's center of ale consumption, the production of lagers increased from less than 30 per cent in 1860 to a whopping 88 per cent by 1926. In subsequent decades, through to the 1970s, the national market share of top-fermented ale hovered between only

---

[23] 'Gesetz über den Eintritt der Freistaaten Bayern und Baden in die Biersteuergemeinschaft. Vom 24. Juni 1919', *Reichs-Gesetzblatt* 121 (1919), Section 2, Paragraph 2, p. 136; see, further, Helmut Klaus, *Der Dualismus Preußen versus Reich in der Weimarer Republik in Politik und Verwaltung* (Mönchengladbach: Forum Verlag Godesberg GmbH, 2006), pp. 196–8.

[24] See, for example, Nov. 27, 1922 memo from the Bayerischer Brauerbund e.V. in BayHStA MHIG 926.

[25] Dec. 30, 1925 Kretschmer Innung to the Reichsfinanzministerium, BAB R 2/1740.

[26] Jan. 2, 1926 Verein Gross-Berliner Jungbierverleger to the Reichsministerium der Finanzen, BAB R 2/1740.

4 per cent and 7 per cent of the national total.[27] Local variations continued to exist, from distinct styles like Kölsch or Altbier to locally produced lager. In the latter case, however, across Germany to this day, consumers will insist that their local Pilsner or Helles is fundamentally different from that of the neighboring town, but the differences often say less about the qualities of the thing itself and more about local efforts at differentiation within an increasingly homogenous form. They function as part of the unity in plurality that Celia Applegate dubbed a "nation of provincials."[28] But this celebration of minor differences is predicated on a larger process by which "Bavarian beer" simply became the standard German lager. To borrow and perhaps stretch the words of anthropologist Richard Wilk, this was a hegemony "not of content, but of form." Regulations and state interventions provided "structures of common difference...[which] celebrate particular kinds of diversity while submerging, deflating, or suppressing others."[29] In the case of beer, this process was never entirely complete, however. As we will see in several subsequent chapters, the 1906 schism between north and south over the use of sugar provided important fuel for future conflicts. In the early 20th century, however, production standards were not the only integrative force brewers and other advocates for beer had to worry about.

The Bavarian Politics of the Beer Tax

In northern Germany, brewers had balked at the tightening of production standards codified in the 1906 Beer Tax Law. In the south, the law appeared much in line with the region's stricter cultures of production and, as discussed, southerners even invoked their 1871 Reserve Rights to insist on maintaining yet narrower standards than the law imposed. Beyond production standards, however, the law did little to change the allocation of the beer tax, at least from a southern point of view. Since 1867, the three southern states of Bavaria, Württemberg, and Baden had retained their own tax revenues on beer and, by the eve of the First World War, the beer tax had become an important part of their budgets, respectively yielding 52.4, 13.9, and 11.9 million RM in 1913.[30] After the war, this changed dramatically as a new federal equalization program came into effect by which beer tax revenues would be collected by the federal Finance Ministry and redistributed to the *Länder* based on size. These fiscal considerations help explain why,

---

[27] Uwe Paulsen and Franz Meyer, *7. Statistischer Bericht des Deutschen Brauer-Bundes e.V.* (Bad Godesberg: Deutscher Brauer-Bund e.V., 1966), p. 67.

[28] Celia Applegate, *A Nation of Provincials: The German Idea of Heimat* (Berkeley: University of California Press, 1990).

[29] Richard Wilk, 'Learning to be Local in Belize: Global Systems of Common Difference', in *Worlds Apart: Modernity through the Prism of the Local*, ed. Daniel Miller (London and New York: Routledge, 1995), pp. 110–33, here p. 118.

[30] Busemann, *Der Deutsche Brauer-Bund 1871–1921*, p. 173.

while the beer tax would become a broadly contentious political issue, Bavarian regulators proved to be the most intransigent in the Weimar Republic. Bavarians across the political spectrum criticized increases of the beer tax and the alleged federal overreliance on the Bavarian brewing industry, but the position and stakes are particularly visible in the case of the only *Land*-specific party with a significant number of seats in the federal government—the *Bayerische Volkspartei* (Bavarian People's Party, or BVP). Bavarian intransigence on the politics of the beer tax, particularly that of the BVP, illuminates the enduring political influence of a single region in Germany's first republic. By 1930, the BVP and the Finance Ministry were so diametrically opposed over the beer tax that the party's willingness to work with the Weimar government had virtually dissolved. While many mainstream political parties struggled primarily to balance socio-economically, religiously, and regionally diverse electorates, the BVP was perhaps unique in that, as the only major *Land*-specific party, it stumbled on the issue of federalism itself.

The provincial politics of the beer tax bring into focus the tensions between *Land* and federal economic stability and the ways that regional political identities came to bear on national issues. The politics of the beer tax were not limited to Bavaria, but Bavarians undoubtedly contested Weimar-era legislation on the beer tax more consistently than other Germans. The single biggest reason for this was economic. By 1913, Bavaria produced 27 per cent of all the beer in Germany and, thanks to Reserve Rights negotiated in 1871, retained all taxes on beer, which amounted to more than a third of the entire budget of the *Land* government. From the start of the Weimar Republic the issue of taxation presented a challenge to the long-standing provincial politics of beer. Under the initial leadership of Matthias Erzberger, the Finance Ministry developed a redistribution mechanism for federal taxation and equalization among the *Länder*. As of 1919, Bavaria was allocated just 13.55 per cent of the federal tax revenue on beer in spite of its far greater share of beer production and sales. As a direct consequence, beer tax revenue in Bavaria dropped from about 40 million RM to less than 20 million RM in a matter of years.[31] At the federal level, the beer tax proved increasingly important for a balanced budget and a stable republic. In the course of inflation and hyperinflation, in the early 1920s, the beer tax rate quintupled while *Land* allocations decreased.[32] Such a state of affairs drew the ire of Bavarian politicians, who

---

[31] From 1910 to 1913, Bavaria raked in 47 million to 55 million RM a year; prior to that, however, it had consistently averaged around 35 million RM since the 1880s. Busemann, *Der Deutsche Brauer-Bund 1871–1921*, p. 173; Dirk Götschmann, *Wirtschaftsgeschichte Bayerns: 19. und 20. Jahrhundert* (Regensburg: Verlag Friedrich Pustet, 2010) pp. 248–52; Wolfgang Heindl, *Die Haushalte von Reich, Ländern und Gemeinden in Deutschland von 1925 bis 1933* (Frankfurt a.M.: Peter Lang, 1984), p. 289; Teich, *Bier, Wissenschaft und Wirtschaft*, p. 38; and *Akten der Reichskanzlei. Weimarer Republik*. Die Kabinette Luther I/II, Band 2, Doc. Nr. 336, https://www.bundesarchiv.de/aktenreichskanzlei/1919–1933/0000/lut/lut2p/kap1_1/para2_167.html.

[32] Heindl, *Die Haushalte von Reich, Ländern und Gemeinden*, pp. 289–91.

demanded that the original constitutional structure be revised. In January 1924, the Bavarian envoy Konrad von Preger delivered a memorandum "On the Revision of the Weimar Constitution" to Chancellor Wilhelm Marx. Among other things, the memorandum insisted on the restoration of the financial sovereignty of the *Länder*, most notably regarding the beer tax, which had been the "backbone of Bavarian finances."[33]

While equalization rates were improved in 1925 and 1927, there would be no reconsideration of fiscal integration until the late 1940s. If anything, the federal state became yet more dependent on tax revenue from beer and other key commodities as part of its political stabilization in the "golden years" of the Weimar Republic. According to the 1924 Dawes Plan, which had helped end hyperinflation and restructure war reparations, the German state had to pay successively increasing sums, building to 2.5 billion RM in 1928. Of this sum, fully half—or 1.25 billion—would be raised through income generated by taxes and tariffs on alcohol, tobacco, beer, and sugar.[34] Beyond reparations too, such taxation generated a massive amount of revenue for the Weimar state. From 1924 to 1931, annual tax revenues from these consumer goods alone climbed from 1.2 to 1.9 billion Marks. While the tax on sugar was the single most lucrative throughout, the tax on beer saw the greatest proportional increase, with beer tax revenues alone increasing from 196.5 million to 473.3 million RM. Such an escalation reflected the fact that the Finance Ministry had become increasingly convinced of the fiscal necessity of beer tax revenue.[35]

Across the political spectrum, Bavarians in the federal government used the issue of the beer tax to rail against the apparent overreliance on and exploitation of their regional industry. In February 1927, two Bavarians in the Reichstag traded verbal blows over a scheduled increase to the beer tax. According to Michael Horlacher (BVP), such an increase was not necessary for the 1927 budget and would amount to a price burden passed on to consumers. Such populist claims were denounced as political theater by Albert Buchmann (KPD), who argued that the beer tax should simply be abolished. Like all taxes, it "most heavily burdens the broad working masses," not only with price increases but with sinking wages and job losses among brewers and innkeepers. Gaining momentum, Buchmann knocked not only the machinations of the BVP but also the passivity of the Social Democratic Party (SPD) in tariff and tax debates—a passivity by which bourgeois parties aided German businesses and capital in their attacks

[33] *Akten der Reichskanzlei. Weimarer Republik.* Die Kabinette Marx I/II, Band 1, Doc. Nr. 63, https://www.bundesarchiv.de/aktenreichskanzlei/1919–1933/0000/ma1/ma11p/kap1_2/kap2_63/para3_1.html.

[34] Götschmann, *Wirtschaftsgeschichte Bayerns*, pp. 278–9.

[35] Gottlieb Schmucker, *Die wirtschaftliche Bedeutung des deutschen Braugewerbes* (Nuremberg: Verlag Hans Carl, 1951), p. 89; Theodor v. Pistorius, 'Die Entwicklung der Reichsfinanzen und das deutsche Wirtschafts- und Finanzelend', *FinanzArchiv/Public Finance Analysis* 48, no. 1 (1931): pp. 1–99; and, Klaus, *Der Dualismus Preußen*, pp. 196–8.

on the interests of the workers. The dispute came to an end when Dr Johannes Popitz, State Secretary in the Finance Ministry, inserted himself to note that such grandstanding was at best "wishful thinking" to reverse what had already passed into law—a reversal that would cost the federal budget 100 million Reichsmarks.[36] His deflation of the dispute not only motioned toward the apparent absurdity of such a proposition, it also revealed the importance of the beer tax in a functional federal budget. Already before the Depression, periodic increases to the beer tax provided political fodder for parties across the spectrum to claim that they—and not their opponents—were working most directly in the interests of the people.

While the beer tax could be adapted to different political agendas, it was Bavarians, and most visibly the BVP who illustrated how consequential the issue could be. Increases on the beer tax became a divisive political issue because the production and consumption of beer was disproportionately centered in Bavaria and because the BVP was a crucial if small component of a functioning coalition government. The claims by Horlacher and Buchmann were in fact more than

Figure 1.1 Emil Kneiß, "German Christmas (Stresemann with bandaged hand)" 12/23/1928, reproduced with the permission of Vanessa Wittmann, image thanks to Hermann Kurz and http://www.der-buzi-maler.de/

---

[36] *Verhandlungen des Deutschen Reichstags*, III. Wahlperiode 1924, Band 392, pp. 8943–4, http://www.reichstagsprotokolle.de/Blatt2_w3_bsb00000076_00046.html.

rhetorical, and Bavarian intransigence on the beer tax became increasingly insurmountable. In a 1928 cartoon by the Bavarian illustrator Emil Kneiß, Foreign Minister Stresemann tries to enjoy Christmas, nursing a hand he slammed on the table in vigorous protest at a Council of the League of Nations meeting earlier in the month. Coming home from the contentious world of foreign relations, he finds himself surrounded by the troubles of the Republic, from a "New Woman" rendering of Germania to Communist and Nazi ornaments on the tree. The naïve German Michel, pulling along a Bavarian lion, disturbs Stresemann's respite. Under the tree, the fairytales of peace and the Bavarian constitution sit below consumer taxes on alcohol, beer included. Of all the issues to disrupt Stresemann's peace, it is the immature Michel and his lion who features most prominently. And Kneiß was not the only illustrator to make the point. Several months later, the satirical *Simplicissimus* cast the beer tax as a distinctly Bavarian issue, which the intransigent southerners would happily ride into dictatorship. Indeed, the image implied a degree of sexual masochistic pleasure amongst the Bavarians by invoking the Austrian author Leopold von Sacher-Masoch, whose name had become the basis of masochism as a psychosexual condition.[37] In the caption, the Bavarian—who seems to be enjoying his subjugation—notes that the republic as a whole, beer tax included, would be tolerable if it came with political domination. Both of these images were Bavarian products—Kneiß was an illustrator for the *Bayerischer Zeitungsblock* and *Simplicissimus* was printed in Munich—suggesting that the allegedly pathological vehemence of Bavarian intransigence may not have been a uniformly held Bavarian sentiment. But, nonetheless, it was a staple of Bavarian politicians. In December 1928, the Bavarian Prime Minister Heinrich Held insisted that the issue of the beer tax had solidified provincial solidarity across the political spectrum. He argued that Bavarians in the Reichstag—regardless of party affiliation, SPD included—had agreed to oppose further increases on the beer tax.[38] The next month, in the ongoing coalition talks, parliamentary leader Johann Leicht (BVP) explained to Chancellor Hermann Müller that his party was willing to work with the other coalition parties but reserved the right to leave the government if it moved to increase the beer tax.[39]

In the eight months between Leicht's threat and the US stock market crash in October, the Finance Ministry relied on the beer tax as a federal cash cow, further aggravating Bavarian parliamentarians. In part, this was because the newly appointed Finance Minister, Rudolf Hilferding, was eager to establish the

---

[37] The use of his name was coined and defended by his contemporary in 1886: Richard von Krafft-Ebing, *Psychopathia Sexualis: The Classic Study of Deviant Sex*, trans. Franklin S. Klaf (New York: Arcade Publishing 2011), p. 87.

[38] *Akten der Reichskanzlei. Weimarer Republik. Das Kabinett Müller II*, Band 1, Doc. Nr. 98, https://www.bundesarchiv.de/aktenreichskanzlei/1919–1933/0000/mu2/mu21p/kap1_2/para2_98.html

[39] *Akten der Reichskanzlei. Weimarer Republik. Das Kabinett Müller II*, Band 1, Doc. Nr. 116, https://www.bundesarchiv.de/aktenreichskanzlei/1919–1933/0000/mu2/mu21p/kap1_2/para2_116.html.

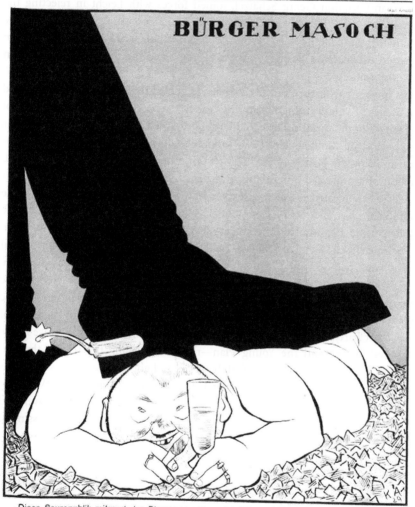

Figure 1.2 Karl Arnold, "Bürger Masoch" *Simplicissimus* Vol. 34, No. 2 (Apr. 8, 1929).

creditworthiness of the German state for the sake of the Young Plan, an emerging international restructuring of German reparations payments. In September, Hilferding introduced his new budget in the cabinet of ministers and revealed that it included a 50 per cent increase to the beer tax in order to add an additional

110 million RM to the federal budget. To appease Bavarian interests, he also revised the financial equalization structures so that Bavaria would receive a greater share of the federal revenue generated through the beer tax, which he calculated at an additional 18–20 million Marks. It was not a bad plan, but it crossed a line in the sand for the BVP. The lone BVP cabinet member, Minister of Post and Transportation Georg Schätzel, joined forces with Leicht in rejecting the increase on principle, going so far as to tie their opposition to the fate of the Young Plan in the Reichstag.[40] While many parliamentarians across the spectrum opposed the increase in private, the BVP remained the most publicly vocal in their opposition.[41]

As in so many histories of the Weimar Republic, the Great Depression fueled the flames of long-burning fires in the case of the beer tax. Feeling the weight of the emerging financial collapse, Hilferding resigned in December 1929, but his successor, Paul Moldenhauer (DVP), doubled down on his approach, and proposed raising the beer tax by 75 per cent in order to generate an estimated 240 million of a projected 305 million RM deficit. While 26.2 per cent of that was slated to be allocated to Bavaria, leaders in the *Land* government recoiled at the overall increase and warned of political consequences.[42] A few weeks before Müller's cabinet of ministers met in February, the Bavarian State Finance Minister, Dr Schmelzle, conveyed to Schätzel, Held, Leicht, and others his view that federal overreliance had disrupted regional interests and *Land* tax revenues, putting the very stability of the Bavarian state budget in jeopardy. The issue needed dramatic resolution "if the exit of the Bavarian People's Party from the coalition is to be avoided."[43] In the Reichstag, BVP leader Leicht was initially joined by members of the Center Party, the SPD, and the DDP against both the beer tax increase in the proposed budget and the Young Plan—rhetorically tying the fate of the two together. The bloc quickly crumbled, however, in light of other interests such as military and insurance spending.[44] Such tensions also plagued the BVP from within, cracking the party's seventeen-seat bloc, as the beer tax was weighed against the utility of a broad federal budget and debt restructuring. The passing of

---

[40] *Akten der Reichskanzlei. Weimarer Republik. Das Kabinett Müller II*, Band 2, Doc. Nr. 305.3, https://www.bundesarchiv.de/aktenreichskanzlei/1919–1933/0000/mu2/mu22p/kap1_1/kap2_49/para3_2.html.

[41] Diary entry, Dec. 25, 1929, ED 93/7, Papers of Hans Schäffer, Institut für Zeitgeschichte-Munich; and Feb. 1, 1930, letter from Rudolf Breitscheid to Hermann Müller, 1/HMAG00012, Nachlass Hermann Müller, Archiv der sozialen Demokratie der Friedrich-Ebert-Stiftung-Bonn; and *Akten der Reichskanzlei. Weimarer Republik. Das Kabinett Müller II*, Band 2, Doc. Nr. 383, https://www.bundesarchiv.de/aktenreichskanzlei/1919–1933/0000/mu2/mu22p/kap1_1/kap2_127/para3_1.html. My thanks to Jamie McSpadden for sharing his archival research into the Schäffer and Müller collections.

[42] *Akten der Reichskanzlei. Weimarer Republik. Das Kabinett Müller II*, Band 2, Doc. Nr. 454, https://www.bundesarchiv.de/aktenreichskanzlei/1919–1933/0000/mu2/mu22p/kap1_1/para2_198.html.

[43] Feb. 20, 1930, Schmelzle to Schätzel, BayHStA MA 103815.

[44] Christian Maga, 'Prälat Johann Leicht (1868–1940): Konservativer Demokrat in der Krise der Zwischenkriegszeit' (PhD thesis, Julius Maximilian University of Würzburg, 1990), p. 221.

the Young Plan in March 1930 came at the expense of isolating and fragmenting the BVP, which had played a not insignificant role in keeping the Weimar government functional. And so while the Young Plan passed, the new budget never did, and its failure fundamentally damaged the stability of the republic.

The beer tax was one of many issues that cracked the foundations of a functioning parliamentary system. The ultimate failure to pass a serviceable budget in March 1930 resulted in the fragmentation of the governing coalition and Müller's resignation, and conventionally marks the beginning of the republic's denouement. It kicked off the chancellorship of Heinrich Brüning, and brought about the September elections in which the Nazi Party surged from 12 parliamentary seats to 107. While the failure to agree on a budget hinged primarily on unemployment insurance rather than on the beer tax, the latter remained a sticking point in later efforts at fiscal stability. Brüning initially attempted to roll back the extreme increases proposed by the Finance Ministry under Müller, but he still met with heavy opposition, particularly from Schätzel, Leicht, and the BVP. Following a 1930 decree by Brüning and Reich President Hindenburg, a 50 per cent increase went into effect that exempted small-scale producers and allowed local communities and municipalities to levy a special community beer tax (*Gemeindebiersteuer*). Bavarian leaders increasingly sought to negotiate with the Chancellor directly and, in the spring of 1932, the federal government finally lowered the beer tax to between 25 and 32 per cent as part of a broad effort to align a range of state and federal policies.[45] The issue declined as a political dispute until the late 1940s, but not before the provincial politics of the beer tax in the Weimar Republic had undermined the stability of republican government and demonstrated just how enduring regional political issues could be for the trajectory of the nation.

The Common Good? Temperance, Public Health, and Brewers' Publicity Work

The third major force against which brewers and their allies struggled was the temperance movement. By the second half of the nineteenth century abstinence, prohibitionism, and other forms of temperance had emerged through an increasingly international network of religious organizations—the Order of Good Templars, the Women's Christian Temperance Union, and the Blue Cross—which did everything from attacking pubs to pushing for state-level prohibitions. According to historian Hasso Spode, the movements gathered steam thanks to two major structural shifts. First, the drinking habits of the broad working classes

---

[45] Oct. 27, 1931, letter from Leicht to Brüning, BAB R/431/2660; Heindl, *Die Haushalte von Reich, Ländern und Gemeinden*, pp. 289–91.

clashed with the new routines and expectations of an industrializing society; second, the expanding bourgeoisie developed an appetite for the accumulation of moral capital via self-restraint. In Germany, this took the form, for example, of the bourgeois German Association against the Abuse of Spirits (*Deutsche Verein gegen den Mißbrauch geistiger Getränke*, or DVMG), which was founded in 1883. Increasingly, temperance movements were internationalized through events such as the annual International Congress Against Alcoholism, which began in 1885 and promoted a shared vocabulary for social reform around alcohol. International sciencization in turn brought statistical firepower to moral discourses of temperance by linking drinking with illness, crime, moral decay, and (in the ascendant language of eugenics) collective degeneration (*Entartung*).[46] Temperance activism ranged from moral reformers touting moderation to hardline prohibitionists and racial hygienists. While full prohibition featured prominently in movements in the United States and Scandinavia, it had never been taken entirely seriously in Germany. Many members of the DVMG were teetotalers, but for practical reasons the organization never pursued full prohibition, focusing instead on excessive consumption and substance abuse.

Both critics and advocates of drinking laid claim to medical knowledge to support their positions, invoking nutrition and proper health—a curious state of affairs Michael Hau called the "dialectic of medical enlightenment."[47] Proponents of alcohol, including several brewers' organizations and a Defense League against the Outrages of the Abstinence Movement, publicized the work of public health researchers who claimed that drinking had healthful properties and benefits.[48] Such arguments squared with both popular convictions about beer as nutritious and a general scientific consensus that moderate alcohol consumption posed no major health threats. Still, conflicts over the nutritious properties of alcohol served to sow doubt and manufacture uncertainty.[49] In one example from the International Day of Good Templars in 1911, alcohol critic Max von Gruber took aim at the idea of alcohol as a nutriment, claiming that while it did indeed have notable caloric value, it also numbed the brain and disoriented the body, meaning whatever energy it provided was largely wasted. However, lobbyists in the German Brewers Union (*Deutsche Brauer-Union*, which would soon join forces with the

---

[46] Hasso Spode, 'Trinkkulturen in Europa', in Johannes and Christiane Weinand, eds., *Die kulturelle Integration Europas* (Wiesbaden: Springer VS, 2010), pp. 361–91, esp. 370–76; see, further, James S. Roberts, *Drink, Temperance and the Working Class in Nineteenth-Century Germany* (Boston: George Allen & Unwin, 1984), pp. 8–10, 110–12; and Heinrich Tappe, *Auf dem Weg zur modernen Alkoholkultur* (Stuttgart: Franz Steiner Verlag, 1994), pp. 281–355.

[47] Michael Hau, 'The Dialectic of Medical Enlightenment: War, Alcohol Consumption and Public Hygiene in Germany, 1910–1925', *History: The Journal of the Historical Association* 104 no. 359 (Jan. 2019), pp. 149–68.

[48] Hasso Spode, *Die Macht der Trunkenheit: Kultur- und Sozialgeschichte des Alkohols in Deutschland* (Opladen: Leske and Budrich, 1993), p. 230.

[49] See, further, Robert N. Proctor and Londa Schiebinger, eds., *Agnotology: The Making and Unmaking of Ignorance* (Palo Alto: Stanford University Press, 2008).

DBB), selectively edited the comments of this high-profile critic to suit their own public relations work, emphasizing his admission that alcohol had significant caloric value.[50] This type of reframing would become a common tactic in defense of beer as late as the 1940s (a subject taken up in the next chapter).

By the eve of the First World War, German temperance organizations boasted some 400,000 members. The war itself proved to be a boon to the claims of social reformers. Almost all belligerent countries in the Great War enacted some form of rationing or state intervention in alcohol markets, and social reformers often sought to extend such measures permanently. In Germany, temperance reformers petitioned the Reichstag in an effort to extend wartime measures. In Munich, opponents of beer and alcohol from twenty-seven different organizations joined forces to oppose an easing of wartime barley quotas. The petitioners embodied the tangled interests of social reformers, medical health experts, and racial party politics and included representatives of the Democratic Women's Group, the Central Institute for *Heimatdienst*, the Munich Psychiatric Clinic, and Hermann Esser, party member No. 2 of the Nazi Party (NSDAP) and cofounder of its predecessor the DAP. Advocating against the loosening of barley quotas, they demanded to know whether the "special interests of the brewing industry" were to outweigh the "*existential interests of the entire Volk.*"[51] The petition restated long-standing temperance discourses, noting that decreases in beer consumption correlated to less crime, fewer mental health conditions, and greater public security. But perhaps most pointedly in an era of war-related caloric scarcity and an uncertain postwar future, the petitioned criticized the use of barley for beer as a drain on the nutritional economy and even the future of Germany. The petitioners mocked the notion of beer as "liquid bread" and stressed that "everything must be done" to satisfy the "urgent need of the people" for abundant, high-quality bread.[52]

The 1920 petition came to naught, but it underscored tensions and divergences in the role of beer in national health and public policy. For some temperance reformers, drinking had been a question of public and indeed racial health since at least the turn of the twentieth century. As the Swiss physician Auguste Forel had put it, "a merciless war of eradication" had to be waged on alcohol, and drinkers themselves had to be hindered from reproduction and treated as "plague boils on the social body."[53] By the mid-1920s, racialized discourse of the national body took on increasing importance on the political right. These were the years in which the Nazi Party switched tactics. While never abandoning the revolutionary spirit of the Beer Hall Putsch, the late 1920s saw the party expand into

[50] Hau, 'The Dialectic of Medical Enlightenment', pp. 156–7.
[51] July 26, 1920, Petition to the Bavarian Landtag, BAB R 401/1529, emphasis in original.
[52] Ibid; and Hau, 'The Dialectic of Medical Enlightenment', pp. 165–7.
[53] Spode, 'Trinkkulturen in Europa', p. 375.

parliamentary politics seeking popular, nationalist support.[54] Far from the recognizable image of the *Sturmabteilung* (SA) beerhall brawler, many ideologues and party leaders framed beer (and alcohol more generally) as a threat to their vision of a new, healthy, and racially strong German nation. In March 1926, for example, the official paper of the Nazi Party, the *Völkischer Beobachter* (VB) lambasted alcohol consumption, arguing that rooting out both alcohol and alcoholism were part of "an unquestionable and undeniable moral national calling."[55] This rhetoric was deeply at odds with the routine alcohol-induced public violence of the Nazi SA, but it fit with broader claims to having popular and racial interests at heart.[56] The paradoxical place of alcohol in National Socialism receives fuller treatment in the next chapter, but here the early NSDAP operated in the ideological currents of temperance and public health, eyeing the popularity and ubiquity of drinking, and deploying it alongside myriad other claims to the national interest.[57]

The variegated pressures on the alcohol industry in general, and brewers in particular, galvanized increasingly organized opposition. The brewing industry remained regionally contentious; north German brewers no doubt continued to bemoan and contest the apparent market conquests of their Bavarian counterparts. Still, German brewers generally agreed that common challenges such as lingering wartime scarcities, the rising beer tax, and the abstinence movement translated into decreasing sales that presented holistic and collective threats. As Sina Fabian has recently shown, such challenges moved German brewers to significantly increase their public relations work via paid newspaper articles, tradeshow exhibitions, and film. In 1923, anti-alcohol reformers managed to land a piece of legislation in the Reichstag that would have institutionalized a local option (*Gemeindebestimmungsrecht*, GBR) allowing individual communities to vote on local prohibition. In response, the DBB paid freelance writers to tout the benefits of alcohol and, in 1926, launched a massive public relations event at the Exhibition for Healthcare, Social Welfare, and Physical Exercise in Düsseldorf.

---

[54] Peter Fritzsche, *Germans into Nazis* (Cambridge, MA: Harvard University Press, 1998), pp. 161–96.

[55] Qtd. in Jonathan Lewy, 'A Sober Reich? Alcohol and Tobacco Use in Nazi Germany', *Substance Use & Misuse* 41, no. 8 (2006), p. 1181.

[56] On alcohol and violence in the SA, see Daniel Siemens, *Stormtroopers: A New History of Hitler's Brownshirts* (New Haven: Yale University Press, 2017), pp. 3–31; and Edward B. Westermann, *Drunk on Genocide: Alcohol and Mass Murder in Nazi Germany* (Ithaca: Cornell University Press, 2021), pp. 24–39.

[57] The Nazi Party consistently worked toward the communitarian values of racialized Volk. In the case of economic thought, for instance, see Claus-Christian W. Szejnmann, 'Nazi Economic Thought and Rhetoric During the Weimar Republic: Capitalism and its Discontents', *Politics, Religion & Ideology* 14 no. 3 (2013): pp. 355–76. It is also worth noting that the NSDAP was not alone. Anti-alcohol rhetoric and policy gained traction across the political spectrum, often for diverse reasons beyond public health. For example, as early as 1909, the Social Democratic Party (SPD) promoted an unsuccessful alcohol boycott intended to gouge tax revenues for Schnaps-producing Junkers, the landed aristocrats of eastern Germany. See Roberts, *Drink, Temperance and the Working Class*, pp. 95–106.

The event was attended by some 7.5 million visitors, and the DBB exhibition space cost fully half a million Reichsmarks. The GBR was debated in the Reichstag in 1925 and 1926 and, while it never went into effect, it won support from almost every party across the political spectrum, with the most vehement opposition coming from the Bavarian People's Party (BVP) and the Wirtschaftspartei (WP).[58]

Throughout the Weimar Republic, German brewers repeatedly sought ways to secure the future of their product in the face of temperance reformers and hostile regulations, but one medium, market saturation advertising, remained elusive, at least on the national level. The Publicity Department (*Propaganda Abteilung*) of the DBB was responsible for industry-wide public relations, coordinating and orchestrating the sorts of episodic responses in media and exhibitions discussed above. The trade organization had considered a more far-reaching campaign of *Gemeinschaftswerbung*, or community advertising, to promote beer generally, regardless of brand. This embrace of extensive advertising at the national level met repeated obstacles until the 1950s. Regionally, however, the brewing trade organizations of Thuringia and Saxony had already begun to develop cooperative campaigns in 1931. Part of their approach relied on purchasing locally produced advertising material. At the height of the Great Depression, for example, brewers and innkeepers in Saxony could purchase paper coasters produced by the Holzfilz-Fabrik Kurprinz, a paper pulp works in Großschirma, near Freiberg. The coasters claimed that lowering the spiraling beer tax would mean higher consumption, which in turn would put many Germans to work in agriculture, brewing, transport, and service. More broadly, such consumerist activities would engender a more stable society where citizens could shop, enjoy material stability, and further feed economic growth. The coaster reflects how the highest level of government fiscal policy became the stuff of public relations and entered the intimate spaces of everyday consumption. Notably absent is any sense that drinking beer could be pleasurable—an end in its own right. As this coaster would have it, every glass of beer became a public service first and foremost.

Central German brewers also turned to professional advertisers, namely leading German ad man Hanns Brose. In the course of the Great Depression, Brose, like many advertisers in Germany and around the world, became increasingly convinced of the power of *Gemeinschaftswerbung*.[59] His initial campaign focused

---

[58] Sina Fabian, 'Between Criticism and Innovation: Beer and Public Relations in the Weimar Republic', in *Reshaping Capitalism in Weimar and Nazi Germany*, ed. Moritz Föllmer and Pamela Swett (Cambridge: Cambridge University Press, 2022), pp. 183–207; and Sina Fabian, 'Wet or Dry? Debates on a Local Option in Weimar Germany', unpublished conference paper from the 45th Annual Conference of the German Studies Association, Indianapolis, IN, Sept. 30–Oct. 3, 2021.

[59] Dirk Schindelbeck, '"Asbach Uralt" und "Soziale Marktwirtschaft": Zur Kulturgeschichte der Werbeagentur in Deutschland am Beispiel von Hanns W. Brose (1899–1971)', *Zeitschrift für Unternehmensgeschichte/Journal of Business History* 40, no. 4 (1995): pp. 235–52; for international comparison, see, for example, Robert Crawford, '"Drink Beer Regularly--It's Good for You [and Us]": Selling Tooth's Beer in a Depressed Market', *Social History of Alcohol & Drugs* 21 no. 2 (Mar. 2007), pp. 160–82;

Figure 1.3 "If the Beer Tax were lowered …" BayHStA Bayerischer Brauerbund 422. Reproduced courtesy of the Bavarian Brewers Association.

on "the value and meaning of beer for human nutrition and increased performance" with the slogan "beer has more value, it has nutritional value." The slogan featured in a poster campaign and a seventeen-part newspaper operation in more than a hundred dailies. In Erfurt, it ran in eight separate newspapers—national and party papers ranging from the Zentrum to the KPD—with an estimated circulation of some 200,000. Tens of thousands of posters went to restaurants, breweries, and bars, and more than 3,000 went up in urban spaces, with almost 800 in Leipzig alone. As Molly Loberg has shown in the case of Berlin, political and commercial values intermingled in urban spaces in a contest over the soul and trajectory of the nation.[60] The content of the ads showed Germans in their everyday live—at work, in their free time, and at small family celebrations—and positioned beer in each moment, highlighting its benefits of nutrition, strength, joy, and achievement.[61] At the height of the Great Depression, beer was thus aligned with meaningful work, economic productivity, a satiated stomach, and social and familial stability. Brose and his clients in Saxony and Thuringia were so pleased with the campaign, and so convinced of its efficacy, that within a matter of months the ad man had pitched expanding the campaign to the national level. Brose's messaging proved sufficiently broad and captivating for many German brewers,

and, more broadly in the German case, Dirk Schindelbeck, 'Werbung für Alle? Kleine Geschichte der Gemeinschaftswerbung von Weimarer Republik bis zur Bundesrepublik Deutschland', in Clemens Wischermann, Peter Borscheid, and Karl-Peter Ellerbrock, eds., *Unternehmenskommunikation im 19. und 20. Jahrhundert: neue Wege der Unternehmensgeschichte* (Dortmund: Ges. für Westfälische Wirtschaftsgeschichte, 2000), pp. 63–97.

[60] Molly Loberg, *The Struggle for the Streets of Berlin: Politics, Consumption, and Urban Space, 1914–1945* (Cambridge: Cambridge University Press, 2018).

[61] Pamphlet 'Gemeinschaftswerbung für Bier' (Berlin: Otto v. Holten, 1931), pp. 6–7, in BayHStA Bayer. Brauerbund 424.

regardless of regional and local differences. They were designed to combat the major obstacles to consumption faced by brewers in 1931, which Brose pegged as sizeable tax increases, strategic opposition from the temperance movement, and decreasing purchasing power in the Depression. According to Brose, brewers had been lazy and had taken for granted their place in the world of goods. They had wrongly believed "that beer had grown to be so fixed and indivisible from the German character—the German worldview and way of life—that an appeal to the goodwill of the consumer seemed superfluous." Brose proposed to change the very "consciousness of the broad masses," by developing ads which would solidify beer in "a category of indispensable foodstuffs."[62] Had the Great Depression not gutted the budget of the Publicity Department—down 33.33 per cent from 1930 to 1931—it is likely that regional differences would have given way and Brose's ads would have gone national. In the report of their vote against the campaign, however, the DBB cited budget reductions and cost as the decisive factors.[63]

While a comprehensive campaign of nationwide advertising did not become a reality until the 1950s, the national trade organization continued to work in the realm of public relations. Throughout the Depression years, the Publicity Department continued its promotional activities, secured celebrity endorsements, lobbied regulators, produced brochures and pamphlets, and participated in public exhibitions. The latter was perhaps the single greatest focus for industry-wide PR work and included sizeable events like the International Hygiene Exhibition in Dresden in 1929 and 1930 as well as smaller events in more than a dozen cities and towns. In 1930–1931, such exhibitions saw the distribution of almost a quarter of a million brochures emphasizing the good place of beer in health, nutrition, and exercise.[64] While the Depression strained the public relations budget, in March 1933 the DBB returned to exhibition work at a sizeable event called *Die Frau in Familie, Haus und Beruf* (The Woman in the Family, at Home, and at Work), held at the exhibition hall in the new Berlin Radio Tower. Their exhibit touted beer as "the German family drink," underscoring tranquil domestic life and idealizing masculine public sociability, nutritious home cooking, and beer's medical benefits as part of a heathy diet. Many of the long-standing strategies of combatting temperance had been rolled into the sort of holistic appeal advocated by Brose. Indeed, beyond the family unit, visitors could learn how beer benefitted the entirety of the German nation. One poster boasted that beer buoyed the entire economy with an estimated 2.22 billion RM, including some 300–500 million RM as wages for farm laborers, producers, transporters, and salaried employees, and a sizeable 664 million RM in government revenue.[65]

---

[62] Ibid, p. 4.
[63] 'Tätigkeitsbericht der Propaganda-Abteilung für das Geschäftsjahr 1930/1931', BayHStA Bayer. Brauerbund 422.
[64] Ibid.   [65] 'Bier, das deutsche Familiengetränk!' BayHStA Bayer. Brauerbund 422.

Like the Thuringian and Saxon community advertisements, the presentation of beer at *Die Frau* not only framed beer as a salve for the trials of the Great Depression, but more broadly aligned it with the common interest of the people. But in the context of the early 1930s, such claims were as ubiquitous as they were contentious. The exhibition opened in March 1933, just months after Adolf Hitler's appointment as Chancellor and only days before the infamous Enabling Law that cleaved the business of government from parliamentary accountability. The opening address of the exhibition was given by none other than Joseph Goebbels, and was his first public address as newly appointed Reich Minister of Propaganda and Public Enlightenment. In it, he laid claim to the importance of women in the Nazi worldview, where they provided the cornerstone for the reproduction of the race.[66] In subsequent years, many in the public health and propaganda apparatus understood alcohol as antithetical to the reproduction and purification of the nation. The claims made by Goebbels and the German brewers in the exact same space in March 1933 thus foreshadow a conflict at the heart of the next chapter. As one public health official reflected in 1941, "the National Socialist revolution was simultaneously a biological revolution."[67] Nazism represented not just a political mission but an effort to redefine Germany down to its biology. The eugenic obsession at the heart of National Socialism took many forms, one being extreme health consciousness and the pursuit of a healthy and "pure" lifestyle. The regime would increasingly weave racial and communitarian ideology into the practices and norms of consumption. As Jonathan Wiesen has written, consumer activity in Nazi Germany was meant to "serve a higher purpose, namely the enrichment of the Volk during its struggle for global and racial dominance. In this respect, goods and services had a national, even moral, rationale."[68] As we turn to the Nazi period, longer conflicts over the place of beer in the public interest undergird political–industrial tensions which would be exacerbated not just by racial thought but by wartime mobilization and state intervention in industry practices.

Conclusion

In the first decades of the twentieth century, industry standardization, fiscal policy, and conflicts over the place of beer in German society reflected both the transformative power of regional influence and the countercurrents of German

---

[66] Madeline James, 'Domesticating the German East: Nazi Propaganda and Women's Roles in the "Germanization" of the Warthegau during World War II' (MA thesis, University of North Carolina—Chapel Hill, 2020), pp. 14–16.

[67] Qtd. in Lewy, 'A Sober Reich?', p. 1179.

[68] S. Jonathan Wiesen, *Creating the Nazi Marketplace: Commerce and Consumption in the Third Reich* (Cambridge: Cambridge University Press, 2010), p. 36.

integration. As we have seen, industrial, regulatory, and social transformations undergirded the conquest of German production and consumption by bottom-fermented, southern-style lager. This trend would remain constant for decades to come, with the market share of top-fermented ales dropping from over 70 per cent in in the middle of the nineteenth century to less than 20 per cent by the 1920s. It was not until the 1970s that top-fermented ale crept above 10 per cent of national beer production.[69] While it became the norm, this homogenization in form initially drew sharp critique, as in the case of organized advocacy for *Braunbier*. This process of homogenization and integration was strikingly total. What was true of industry and regulations on production, however, was not true of state centralization and consolidation of beer tax revenues. Bavarian intransigence and opposition to the alleged federal overreliance on the regional brewing industry contributed to the gradual fraying of Weimar parliamentarism. The issue would not be given sustained attention in a functioning representative political system until after the Second World War. When it was, as discussed in Chapter 3, the legacies of the collapse of the Weimar Republic were powerful and would help enshrine the beer tax as the only consumption-based tax retained entirely by the *Länder* in the Federal Republic.

In the 1920s, numerous groups responded to the production, consumption, and regulation of beer, investing both process and product with deeper meaning. For some, including brewers, their arguments took on greater urgency but remained largely economic in nature. They pointed either to the damage done by restrictive legislation or to the threat of increasing tax rates. But for many others, including teetotalers and other social reformers, political upstarts, and established parliamentarians, the consumption and taxation of beer provided a discursive launching pad for divergent claims to the popular interest. Going into the Nazi dictatorship, German brewers had, in part, managed to put aside their regional differences in the face of common challenges. And while some of this solidarity continued throughout the Nazi period, state interventions in production standards once again triggered regional divisions. The provincialism of the Weimar Republic most certainly continued into the Nazi era, manifesting primarily in opposition by southern German brewers who understood the new regime as posing a significant threat to their economic livelihoods and cultures of production. In the course of the dictatorship, beer increasingly became a battleground for the regime and brewers—particularly in the German south—to make contradictory claims to the popular good.

---

[69] Deutscher Brauer-Bund e.V., *12. Statistischer Bericht des Deutschen Brauer-Bundes e.V.* (Bonn-Bad Godesberg: Leopold, 1975), p. 78.

2

The People's Drink in the Racial State

Debating the Interests of the Volk

In September 1935, Adolf Hitler addressed the Hitler Youth at the seventh party congress in Nuremberg. From year to year, he reflected, the organization had grown in quantity and quality, becoming, like all of Germany, "more disciplined, more strapping and tauter." Not long ago, and "almost incomprehensibly," he contemplated, the ideal youth was a "beer-drinking, hard-living fellow," which the Party was happy to see displaced. "Today," he explained, "it is not about how many glasses of beer he can drink, but how many blows he can take, not about how many nights he can stroll through, but how many kilometers he can march. Today we no longer see the ideal of the German people in the beer-drinking-bourgeoisie (*Bierspießer*) of yesteryear, but in men and girls who are taut and fit as a fiddle."[1] The ideal of the healthy, strapping, and abstinent German, which was touted by so many in the Party leadership, was often at odds with the cultural practices of drunken violence so central to Nazi expansionism and race war.[2] Beyond the cutting edge of violent conquest, however, the propaganda and public health apparatus of the Third Reich continually worked to define alcohol and other stimulants and intoxicants as antithetical to German racial purity.[3] Hitler's juxtaposition of beer-drinking individualism and the healthy future of the racial community reflects some of the ways that beer became a point of tension between public health officials and propagandists on the one hand, and brewers, food scientists, and regional political leaders on the other. Getting Germans to drink less beer would prove a big ask, and, indeed, in the pre-war years consumption rates steadily increased as the economy recovered, leaving most brewers with little to complain about. But as the Nazi dictatorship consolidated, mobilized for, and waged war, its increasingly heavy-handed interventions in the beer market triggered a critical response, particularly from brewers and their political allies in the south.

---

[1] 'Bei der Kundgebung der HJ', *Die Reden Hitlers am Parteitag der Freiheit 1935* (Munich: Zentralverlag der NSDAP, 1935), p. 57.

[2] Edward B. Westermann, *Drunk on Genocide: Alcohol and Mass Murder in Nazi Germany* (Ithaca: Cornell University Press, 2021).

[3] Robert N. Proctor, *The Nazi War on Cancer* (Princeton: Princeton University Press, 2000), pp. 134–54; Jonathan Lewy, 'A Sober Reich? Alcohol and Tobacco Use in Nazi Germany', *Substance Use & Misuse* 41, no. 8 (2006): pp. 1179–95; Nicole Petrick-Felber, *Kriegswichtiger Genuss: Tabak und Kaffee im 'Dritten Reich'* (Göttingen: Wallstein Verlag, 2015), pp. 47–82.

A Nation Fermented: Beer, Bavaria, and the Making of Modern Germany. Robert Shea Terrell, Oxford University Press.
© Robert Shea Terrell 2024. DOI: 10.1093/oso/9780198881834.003.0003

Like the other mass ideologies of the twentieth century—from communism to liberal capitalism—Nazism worked to align politics and material life. Each movement "promised their supporters a better life and developed strategies to harness consumption to their particular ends."[4] In Germany, Nazi economists and ideologues consistently worked "to align commercial morality and *völkisch* morality... by legislating a market sensibility that spoke to both older norms of public decency and to the new demands of the racial state."[5] In the case of beer, public health officials, propagandists, and other ideologues exerted manifold pressures on the industry and market, ranging from restrictions on advertising and anti-alcohol propaganda to changes in production standards in the name of centralized resource management. In the 1920s, brewers had turned to public relations and claims to beer in the public good as a way to cope with challenges ranging from material scarcity to social and temperance reform. By the 1930s, the pressures increased dramatically as many of the arguments that brewers deployed in the 1920s about the benefits of beer came under direct scrutiny from the commercial and propaganda apparatuses of the Nazi regime. If indeed Nazism drew support for its promise "to resolve the tensions of German capitalism," the response of the brewing industry shows some of the ways it failed to do that.[6] As the regime sought to bring commerce in line with ideology, brewers not only worked within the spaces that remained to them, but also invoked the communitarian ideals that underpinned the Nazi conception of the Volk.

In their effort to excise unhealthy consumer practices, the Nazi regime elevated many voices in the temperance and medical communities that had long been critical of beer and alcohol consumption. State critiques emanated primarily from the Ad Council (*Werberat*), the Propaganda Ministry, the Ministry of Food and Agriculture, and the Reich Food Estate (*Reichsnährstand*), which combined to undermine the place of beer and alcohol in German life. Advocating for their product and their livelihoods, brewers occasionally pushed back. In some cases, the ensuing conflicts were primarily cultural, for example in arguments over folk knowledge about beer as a foodstuff. Efforts to buttress beer as a cultural staple were most profound in Bavaria, where the trade organization continued to celebrate local and regional histories. In other cases, conflicts over beer sat more firmly in the formal sphere of politics and, indeed, racial war. In mobilizing for and waging war, the Nazi dictatorship worked to centralize resource management in order to insulate the regime from scarcity and a repeat of the so-called "stab in

---

[4] Frank Trentmann, *Empire of Things: How We Became a World of Consumers, from the Fifteenth Century to the Twenty-First* (New York: Harper Collins, 2016), p. 274.
[5] S. Jonathan Wiesen, *Creating the Nazi Marketplace: Commerce and Consumption in the Third Reich* (Cambridge: Cambridge University Press, 2011), p. 61.
[6] Moritz Föllmer and Pamela E. Swett, 'Introduction: Historicizing Capitalism in Germany, 1918-1945', in Föllmer and Swett, eds., *Reshaping Capitalism in Weimar and Nazi Germany* (Cambridge: Cambridge University Press, 2022), pp. 1–30, here p. 27.

the back"—the mythology of home front betrayal in the First World War.[7] By the late 1930s, food management collided with the production of beer, which depended on the use of bread grains, most notably barley. Food planners repeatedly attempted to alter production standards to optimize the grain economy, and each time their efforts met opposition, again from southern (and especially Bavarian) brewers who insisted on historical regional differences, claiming that altering production standards would spark consumer unrest—an argument to which the regime was particularly sensitive. Conflicts over production standards were merely the latest episode in longer struggles stretching back to the Reserve Rights of 1871 and the beer tax legislation of 1906 and 1919. But they took on a new urgency in the context of war as brewers found allies in provincial political institutions, including state chancelleries and ministries, that likewise argued that, rather than being detrimental, beer was firmly aligned with the interests and well-being of the Volk.

Many of those who opposed the valuation of beer emanating from public health officials, anti-alcohol ideologues, and food planners in the wartime economy were functionaries in the normative state: state ministers, members of government and economic organizations, and Nazi Party members. When they advocated for beer in the interest of the Volk, most of the actors here were not challenging Nazism writ large. Instead, their insistence on beer as part of German life might best be understood as an effort to include beer among the welfare concerns of the Nazi regime. Brewers primarily worked to ensure their own economic interests, but alongside their political allies they seem to have taken seriously that National Socialism was out for the best interests of the Volk. Beer, they contended, ought to be a part of that project. The unprecedented pressures of Nazi centralization galvanized a southern German bloc of brewers and politicians willing to actively engage in national political and cultural life. While Bavarians in many ways led the way, industrial and political allies in Baden and Württemberg quickly joined the chorus of southern Germans presenting a unified vision of beer as the national drink of the German people. More than a history of *Handlungsspielraum*—or the room for maneuver retained by private enterprise in Nazi Germany—conflicts over the people's drink in the racial state were also political conflicts over who the German people were and what their social, economic, and cultural life looked like.[8]

[7] Alice Weinreb, *Modern Hungers: Food and Power in Twentieth-Century Germany* (Oxford: Oxford University Press, 2017), pp. 43–4.

[8] On debates over *Handlungsspielraum*, see, for example, Peter Hayes, 'Corporate Freedom of Action in Nazi Germany', *Bulletin of the German Historical Institute* 45 (Fall 2009): pp. 29–42; Jochen Streb, 'Das Nationalsozialistische Wirtschaftssystem: Indirekter Sozialismus, gelenkte Marktwirtschaft oder vergezogene Kriegswirtschaft?'. in *Der Staat und die Ordnung der Wirtschaft: Vom Kaiserreich bis zur Berliner Republik*, ed. Werner Plumpe and Joachim Scholtyseck (Stuttgart: Franz Steiner Verlag, 2012), pp. 61–84; and Matt Bera, *Lobbying Hitler: Industrial Associations between Democracy and Dictatorship* (New York: Berghahn Books, 2016).

Brewers and the Biological Revolution

Nazism presented not just a political mission but an effort to redefine Germany down to its biology. Most infamously, of course, this manifested in the persecution and mass murder of millions of Jews and other so-called "undesirables." But the eugenic obsession at the heart of National Socialism also took the form of extreme health consciousness and the pursuit of a healthy and "pure" lifestyle for those included in the Nazi racial community. For many ideologues and party leaders, beer and alcohol more generally represented a threat to their vision of a new, healthy, and racially strong Germany.[9] But the Nazi "biological revolution"— to borrow a phrase from Hans Reiter in the Ministry of Health—was profoundly incomplete in the case of alcohol and drinking.[10] Historians have acknowledged that efforts to curb drinking were not only marginal in their success but also often at odds with the practices of everyday life ranging from college drinking cultures to the intoxicated hypermasculine community of the *Sturmabteilung* (SA), the *Schutzstaffel* (SS), and the military.[11] Looking from the perspective of the brewing industry, however, it becomes clear that there is more to this history than the tensions between eugenic prescriptions and consumer habits. As we have long known, the Third Reich was a sort of "systemless system," a morass of competing agendas and fluctuating commitments to social change. Off the bat, there was no clear administrative or structural consensus about the extent to which beer fit in the biological revolution. Indeed, brewers repeatedly worked to align themselves with the agendas of the regime by articulating their industrial interests in the language of national rejuvenation and the good of the Volk. So, as the propaganda and public health apparatuses of the dictatorship worked to sideline the central place of beer and alcohol generally in German society—especially in the spheres of advertising, gender norms, and the cult of youth—brewers sought to harness their economic fates to the discourses of the regime.

Emerging out of the Depression years, many German brewers found themselves exhausted by political turmoil and thirsty for economic stability. In this spirit, brewers across the country welcomed the new Chancellor and his government in January 1933. Beyond promises of economic growth, the National Socialist leader had famously burst onto the national political scene in the Beer Hall Putsch and had since built his movement in bars and beerhalls nationwide. Hitler, it seemed, was set to make a great ally for a brewing industry plagued by economic crisis and decades of assault by temperance reformers and high taxes. In August 1933, the German Brewers Association (DBB) even requested the

---

[9] Proctor, *Nazi War on Cancer*, pp. 141–53.   [10] Qtd. in Lewy, 'A Sober Reich?', p. 1179.
[11] Geoffrey Giles, 'Student Drinking in the Third Reich: Academic Tradition and the Nazi Revolution', in Susanna Barrows and Robin Room, eds., *Drinking: Behavior and Belief in Modern History* (Berkeley: University of California Press, 1991), pp. 132–43; and Westermann, *Drunk on Genocide*.

"publication of an official press release on the position of the Reich's Chancellor Adolf Hitler regarding the enjoyment of alcoholic beverages." At the core of this request was the hope that a public statement on Hitler's attitude would bring "absolute clarity" to those temperance reformers that had misunderstood his support for the production and consumption of alcohol.[12] To be sure, while brewers may have seen promise in the economic rhetoric and beerhall culture of Nazism, long-standing teetotalers and social reformers saw instead hardcore public health ideology. Such a statement was never released, and while propagandists and public health officials increasingly sought to crack down on alcohol and beer consumption, brewers worked to capture the momentum of other facets of the new regime—namely, discourses of health, strength, and the popular interest.

By the early 1930s, German brewers had taken to heart the importance of public relations and promoting the popular importance of beer. We have already seen how they worked to do this in the Depression years, and such practices continued into the consolidating Nazi dictatorship, in part because there was no uniform policy around beer, and brewers, like almost everyone else, worked to accommodate and navigate the new regime. In 1934, for example, the national trade organization participated in Green Week: an event dating to the mid-1920s that combined the annual meeting of German agrarians with public outreach and tourism. That year the event was organized by the Reich Food Estate, a new government institution intended to coordinate control of all aspects of the agricultural and food systems. Almost immediately upon its founding, the Reich Food Estate focused on food self-sufficiency and touted the imbrication of "blood and soil." At Green Week 1934, the DBB leaned into both central drives, organizing their exhibit around three main themes which highlighted the role of beer in the production and preservation of food, work, and race. The first—"From Farmer to Brewer"—located the brewery at the center of a food chain linking barley and hop farmers to German consumers. For these latter, the exhibition claimed, beer delivered 1.5 billion calories a year, and brewery by-products increased milk yields in dairy cows by some 450 million liters of milk. A similar holistic message characterized the second main theme, "German Volk—German Work," which covered more than 14 meters of exhibition space and conveyed all the labor and financial benefits of brewing and its many extensions into German life and stability. The third and final component embraced the regime's veneration of the German soil and peasantry. While the Reich Food Estate had yet to directly involve itself in the production of beer, brewers jumped at the opportunity to align themselves with what they recognized as a kindred interest in rurality. In their third display, the DBB captured the flow of material between industrial

---

[12] Aug. 9, 1933, letter from the Propaganda Division of the German Brewers' Union to the German Agricultural Council, and Aug. 7, 1933, to the Ministry of Public Enlightenment and Propaganda, both in Bundesarchiv Berlin-Lichterfelde (henceforth BAB) R8073/19.

and agrarian producers with the slogan "In German Beer—the Power of the German Earth." In no unclear terms, brewers emphasized that beer was of the land, resonating with broader efforts at aligning racial and agricultural sensibilities.[13]

While the relationship would become more complicated, in the early months and even years, brewers embraced the manifest values of the new regime. Indeed, it was not entirely clear that brewers and the Nazi Party had any internal tensions. The leadership had issued no clear statements, after all, and this ambiguity even trickled down to major Party publications. In May 1933, for example, the Nazi Party paper in Berlin, *Der Angriff*, ran an ad that framed beer as part of a timeless Germanic culture and tradition. Featuring a stereotypical ancient tribesman— wild hair and beard, well-muscled, and complete with an operatic fur pelt and drinking horn—the ad announced that "beer has been the national drink of the Germans since primitive Germanic times!" This connection between beer, race, and place similarly featured in printed materials included at Green Week 1934. In one such image, produced in poster and flier form, a tempting glass of beer is flanked by idyllic barley and hops and boasting the simple slogan, "In German Beer—the Power of the German Earth."

The persistent idea of beer as a popular and crucial part of German life in both industrial public relations and Nazi Party publications would come under increasingly close scrutiny by the joint efforts of the Ad Council (*Werberat*), the Ministry of Health, and the Reich Office for Alcohol Abuse (*Reichsstelle gegen den Alkoholmißbrauch*, henceforth RgA). In the sphere of advertising, the Ad Council gradually targeted everything from endorsements to claims about the healthful or popular cultural properties of beer. As recently as 1931, German ad man Hanns Brose insisted that brewers needed to emphasize "the value and meaning of beer for human nutrition and increased performance."[14] But increasingly, the Ad Council cracked down on such claims. In 1936, they restricted the use of medical endorsements, and in 1938 they forbade the comparison of beer and other foodstuffs, particularly the use of direct caloric comparisons. As a result, industrial practices of promoting beer with the visage of a doctor or a side-by-side comparison of beer, bread, or other foods largely ceased to exist.[15] Other campaigns in cultural tightening depended on cooperation with the Ministry of Health and the RgA.

---

[13] 'Sonderdruck aus der Sonderbeilage "Grüne Woche 1934" der "Deutschen Zeitung"', Bayerisches Hauptstaatsarchiv (henceforth BayHStA) Bayer. Brauerbund 422; On the *Reichsnährstand*, rurality, and blood and soil, see Weinreb, *Modern Hungers*, pp. 60–2.

[14] Pamphlet, 'Gemeinschaftswerbung für Bier' (Berlin: Otto v. Holten, 1931), pp. 6–7, in BayHStA Bayer. Brauerbund 424.

[15] Hinweise betr. Wirtschaftswerbung, attached to a Rundschreiben Nr. A 70, October 18, 1938; letter from Hunke to the Wirtschaftsgruppe Brauerei und Mälzerei, October 15, 1940, both in: BayHStA Bayer. Brauerbund 428. On the Werberat, more broadly, see Pamela E. Swett, *Selling Under the Swastika: Advertising and Commercial Culture in Nazi Germany* (Palo Alto: Stanford University Press, 2014).

Figure 2.1 "Beer has been the national drink of the Germans since primitive Germanic times!" *Der Angriff* Mar. 4, 1933. Thanks to Teresa Walch for sharing this image.

The overarching goal of the latter, which it saw as nothing less than the "will of the Führer," was to promote "popular consciousness for the entire nation concerning the dangers of alcohol...for the Volk and the race." Where the Ad Council focused on commercial advertising, the RgA engaged in business and finance, for example by promoting the construction and operation of alcohol-free restaurants as paragons of "healthy national nourishment," and overseeing the transfer of no less than one-third of tax revenue from alcohol and tobacco sales into housing developments for "genetically healthy, child-rich families."[16]

As such actions suggest, the RgA played a central role in advancing the interests and traditions of the temperance movement within the racialized and communitarian worldview of National Socialism. The organization took over publication of *Auf der Wacht*, a prohibitionist newspaper dating to the late 19th century, and worked in conjunction with the Ministry of the Interior, the Health Ministry, and the Reich's Health Press to produce fliers, pamphlets, posters, and books for popular circulation. One of the most common themes in such publications was generating broad social consciousness about the dangers of alcohol consumption for public health, social life, nutrition, and work safety.[17] In all such work, the individual—that bastion of classical liberalism—was made subservient to the primacy of the Volk. In a well-reviewed 1934 abstinence book, for instance, Erich Rätsch dedicated some thirty pages to the question "Why do people drink?" Omitting personal preference and cultural practice, Rätsch explained that drinking was little more than a symptom of psychological or social degeneracy.[18] In this view, the physical act of consuming alcohol was hardly a consumer *choice* at all but rather a symptom of socio-biological weakness—a lapse in communal responsibility at best, and a sign of biological degeneracy at worst. In these sorts of publications, individual choices and cultural preferences were often omitted in favor of moral, physical, and social degeneracy. This reframing of consumption as an affront to the well-being of the communal whole reflected a broader emphasis in Nazi Germany on public accountability as an avenue for encouraging broad participation in communal projects.[19] In ubiquitous fliers and oversized posters, potential drunk drivers were reminded that their actions hurt their friends, family, and, above all, their Volk.[20]

In the spheres of public health, the regime increasingly worked to curb alcohol consumption as a hyper-individualistic affront to the national community. Medical discourse provided one of the key rationales for such arguments, bringing state authority to old logics of medicalized temperance. Professional medical journals were quick to focus on alcohol poisoning and the inhibition of both motor skills and morality. According to one report, alcohol caused more than

---

[16] May 7, 1938, speech by Gauamtsleiter Dr Med. Erich Bruns, 'Die Arbeit gegen den Alkoholmissbrauch. Grundsätze und Organisation', delivered at the Hauptamt für Volksgesundheit der NSDAP, BAB R 36/1358.

[17] On the latter, see, for example, Ferdinand Goebel, *Schulungsheft der Reichsbahn-Zentralstelle gegen den Alkoholmißbrauch* (Berlin: Reichsgesundheitsverlag, 1940).

[18] Erich Rätsch, *Gefährliche Freiheit? Der Rausch als Regulierendes Prinzip* (Berlin: Kurt Elsner Verlag, 1934), BayHStA Bayer. Brauerbund 415. For reception see, review in *Forschungen zur Alkoholfrage: Alcohol studies. Études sur la question de l'alcool* 43 (1935): p. 81.

[19] Peter Fritzsche, *Life and Death in the Third Reich* (Cambridge: Harvard University Press, 2008), pp. 54, 81.

[20] 'Alkohol-Merkblatt für Kraftfahrzeugführer', 1934 bulletin by *Auf der Wacht*, BAB R 1501/116423.

60 per cent of all automobile accidents, and according to another it encouraged illegitimate sexual contact that threatened the core of Nazi bio-ethics, the nuclear family. The numerous social dangers of alcohol offered a justification for the "moral obligation" of state interventions in civic life in the name of public health.[21] In one of its most extreme forms, such a conviction placed alcoholism among the hereditary diseases of the ever-opaque "antisocial" population—a biological defect with social manifestations. Alongside the mentally and physically disabled, the epileptic, the blind, and many others, alcoholics were subject to forced sterilization according to the July 1933 "Law for the Prevention of Hereditarily Diseased Offspring." Some 350,000 individuals were forcibly sterilized in the 12 years of the Third Reich, 95 per cent of them before 1939. Alcoholism was an issue of "social hygiene" very early on, and was the fourth most common ground for sterilization. In some communities it was particularly common. In Hamburg, for example, of 1,364 "biologically defective" persons sterilized by 1935, 561 of them (or 41 per cent) were listed as severe alcoholics.[22]

Far beyond alcohol abuse and chronic alcoholism, however, Nazi ideologues increasingly worked to reframe the cultures and norms of consumption that influenced individual choice and behavior by locating them in larger medicalized and racialized conceptions of the Volk. Such efforts targeted key social groups, one of which was women. As Pamela Swett has shown more broadly, German companies and advertisers in the Third Reich actively targeted the consuming power of women, acknowledging the importance of managing the information that consuming women brought to their buying and homemaking.[23] The anti-alcohol propaganda directed at women emphasized communitarian values over liberal individualism, but also highlighted the stringent conservatism of Nazi gender norms. Women were portrayed not as individual and autonomous consumers but as social auxiliaries—as managers of the home, as wives and mothers, and as the guardians of the future of the Volk. In this view, a woman having a drink should be understood not as an individual in action but as a faltering piece of the nation and its future. As the head of the Hannover division of the Main Office for National Health (*Hauptamt für Volksgesundheit*) put it,

> When women drink, one can almost always determine it the result of defects in constitution...It is an old and deeply rooted view among the Volk that a woman drinking is "especially dangerous" and "reprehensible"...In all circles today, it is equally unfeminine and contrary to all good practices when a woman gets drunk and even begins to drink. A "tipsy" woman is no comrade (*Kamerad*) and

---

[21] The same was true far beyond alcohol. See, for example, Claudia Koonz, *The Nazi Conscience* (Cambridge: Harvard University Press, 2003).
[22] Lewy, 'A Sober Reich?', p. 1186.   [23] Swett, *Selling under the Swastika*, pp. 136–84.

no partner for a health-minded man. This view, anchored in popular sentiment, is now invested with full legitimacy by the genetic knowledge of our times.[24]

For many in public health, a woman's relationship to alcohol was one of reprehensibility and shortcomings in moral constitution. This position was no doubt anchored in the Party critique of the politically, socially, sexually liberated "New Woman" of the Weimar Republic. This reactionary approach to women's consumption habits captured the broader Nazi effort to "tame the excesses of consumer capitalism by legislating a market sensibility that spoke both to older norms of public decency and to the new demands of the racial state."[25] Indeed, far beyond notions of alcohol abuse or overindulgence, here even a tipsy (*beschwipste*) woman is rendered unworthy of a reproductive partnership with the modern German man. Rooting Nazi gender norms in traditional "popular sentiment" and modern "genetic knowledge" captures the extent to which attitudes about alcohol consumption were a microcosm of a much larger effort by the regime to justify and legitimate its approach to German culture and values.

While prohibitionists and temperance reformers had for decades given special attention to women and children, the Third Reich brought the weight of modern media and communication to align the discourse of alcohol in a mass consumer society with the foundations of racial ideology. For many in the Nazi state, women were potential wives and mothers and the stakes of women's alcohol consumption in the Third Reich were nothing less than the fate of the race. Circulating this message and encouraging women's awareness and vigilance took many forms in both coordinated social organizations and media production. For example, a 1935 book published by the National Socialist Women's League stressed the special alertness and concerns that women should have about the dangers of alcohol. The book, *Volksgift und Frauenpflicht* (*The People's Poison and Women's Duty*), was addressed to wives and mothers as well as working women who "feel themselves bound and committed to their Volk in spiritual motherhood."[26] It detailed the long-term effects of alcohol on genetic strength, fertility, pregnancy, and child growth. Employing scientific discourses, it explained that laboratory testing had recently shown that children of parents who drank were smaller, weaker, and performed worse in school. Similar claims came from social policy publications such as the journal *Soziale Praxis*, which claimed that alcohol damaged genetic material, and increased the frequency of abortions seven-fold and the likelihood of death in the first year of life by as much as 40 per cent.[27]

[24] Bruns, 'Die Arbeit gegen den Alkoholmissbrauch'.

[25] Wiesen, *Creating the Nazi Marketplace*, p. 61.

[26] Gertrud Kaetzel, *Volksgift und Frauenpflicht*. Hrsg. v.d. Obersten Leitung der Parteiorganisation, N.S.-Frauenschaft, (Berlin, 1935), p. 3. BAB NS 5/VI 4868.

[27] Helene Wessel, 'Warum Kampf gegen Alkoholmißbrauch?' *Soziale Praxis. Zentralblatt für Sozialpolitik und Wohlfahrtspflege*, Oct. 3, 1935, pp. 1146–56. BAB NS 5/VI 4868.

Alongside women, the youth also became a key demographic in the struggle to shape a new set of German values by aligning racial and commercial morality. The words of Adolf Hitler, which opened this chapter, were reproduced as gospel for many years, including by him. In succeeding years, he explained to the Hitler Youth that beer consumption was part of an outdated system of cultural values incompatible with the new Germany. Speaking in Nuremberg in 1936, he explained that "a new ideal of beauty is developing. No longer the corpulent beer-drinking-philistine (*Bierphilister*), but rather the fit and slender youth is the ideal of our time; standing on the earth with steady legs—healthy in his body and in his soul."[28] In the Third Reich, the vibrant and healthy youth were the symbol for—and, in fact, the literal future of—the new Germany. It was they who were meant to strengthen the genetic makeup of the Volk, and it was they who were to fight the war, win it, and consolidate the thousand-year Reich. Two years later, Hitler explained again that he expected the party leadership to "speak the word of temperance, condemn all abuses in the strongest terms, and especially that they admonish our youth again and again that the future of our people does not need a generation of drinkers but a generation of fighters."[29] The metaphor of generational conflict lent itself well to combining military and public health propaganda, especially in the context of war. For instance, the image "Two Men—Two Worldviews" first appeared in *Der SA-Mann* in 1938 and was reproduced in a number of publications, including the anti-tobacco publication *Reine Luft* in 1939. In it, an unhealthy and older beer drinker (perhaps a "corpulent beer-drinking-Philistine") stares left, or to the West, and wallows in its decadence, while the young healthy man heads purposefully to the right—the East—set to change the world in the Nazi image. The image stresses not only the infatuation with health, youth, strength, and action, but also that the regime in fact acknowledged there was a second "worldview" here too; there were people who, while not chronic alcoholics or "degenerates," were nonetheless resistant to the "biological revolution" and unwilling to revolutionize their lives and habits.

Like public health and women's organizations, the Hitler Youth pursued both tangible measures against alcohol and subtler cultural propaganda regarding consumer choice. In the spirit of youth abstinence, the Hitler Youth launched a 1939 campaign targeting alcohol and tobacco consumption. The initiative collected public abstinence endorsements from world-class athletes such as Gerhard Stöck, the 1936 Olympic gold medalist in the javelin throw, and encouraged denunciations for intoxication and underage drinking to the Security Service (SD) of the SS. The SD found that this campaign was moderately successful, most notably in the northeast, in Pomerania and East Prussia, with some minor increases in

---

[28] Speech from the 'Parteitag der Ehre' in Nuremberg, Sept. 12, 1936. Quoted in *Die junge Gefolgschaft. Monatsschrift der Fränkischen Hitlerjugend*, no. 9 (Sept. 1936).

[29] Qtd. in Bruns, 'Die Arbeit gegen den Alkoholmissbrauch'.

Zwei Männer — zwei Weltanschauungen

Figure 2.2 "Two Men – Two Worldviews" *Der SA-Mann* May 14, 1938.

arrests for drunkenness.[30] In addition, popular publications for the Hitler Youth stressed abstinence and encouraged children to make smart choices as consumers. They should drink other beverages, such as the alcohol-free Sinalco and especially milk. The latter was, as one promotion put it in 1936, "the only foodstuff that contains all the nutrients in the correct amounts and ratios necessary for the constitution, conservation, and performance of the youthful organism."[31]

Broad sections of the media and public health organizations as well as a number of key ideologues, Hitler included, worked to reshape racial and communitarian consumer values characteristic of a new Germany. While economic growth and increased consumption afforded the Nazi dictatorship a good deal of political legitimacy in a Germany climbing out of the Great Depression, these ideologues and bureaucrats nonetheless worked against longer traditions of consumption, injected medical and racial ideology into consumer values, and promoted communal strength over the hyper-individualism they associated with the Weimar Republic.[32] Conceptions of individual choice were subjected to moralizing

---

[30] Heinz Boberach, ed., *Meldungen aus dem Reich: Die geheimen Lageberichte des Sicherheitsdienstes der SS, 1938–1945*, vol. 1 (Herrsching: Pawlak Verlag, 1984), pp. 112, 272.

[31] Sinalco ads appear consistently in publications for the Hitler Youth, especially during the war years. This milk promotion comes from the back inside cover of *Die junge Gefolgschaft. Monatsschrift der Fränkischen Hitlerjugend* 8 (August 1936).

[32] On economic recovery and increased consumption as part of political legitimacy, see Gesine Gerhard, *Nazi Hunger Politics: A History of Food in the Third Reich* (Lanham: Rowman & Littlefield, 2015), pp. 19–46; Weinreb, *Modern Hungers*, pp. 49–66; and, more generally, Adam Tooze, *The Wages of Destruction: The Making and Breaking of the Nazi Economy* (New York: Penguin Books, 2006), pp. 135–65.

narratives of communal well-being and the strength of the Volk—values applied with particular vigor to key demographics, including women and the youth. But, more broadly, in the words of Heinrich Himmler, Germany needed the strength of every single German "for the preservation of its racial and economic freedom. No German, therefore, has the right to weaken their body and spirit through alcohol abuse. They damage not only themselves but also their family and above all their Volk."[33] Such high-flying rhetoric captured the way in which individual choices about consumption increasingly stood at odds with communitarian and racialized thought. But they also rang somewhat empty. Himmler's SS—the alleged racial and ideological avant garde—depended on a culture of hypermasculine drunken debauchery rooted in Weimar-era beerhall brawls that permeated all aspects of racial violence and mass murder in Eastern Europe.[34] Still, Himmler's words point to a Nazi future that would never be while the actions of the SS point to the most violent means of getting there. The regime sought to align individual consumer choice with increasingly radical ideologies, far beyond alcohol abuse and overconsumption, promoting traditional gender roles, the nuclear family, the exaltation of youth, and racial protectionism. Beer and alcohol generally were thus woven into a "regime of value"—a network of institutions, convictions, and value-makers that shaped the social meanings of material things.[35] Still, the Nazi dictatorship was never entirely total, and we ought not expect that a *völkisch* commercial morality was either. In a state that had embraced mass consumption as part of its legitimization, discourses and practices of production and consumption that pre-dated 1933 remained potent for companies and consumers alike.

Contesting the Value of the Thing: The Economic and Cultural Stakes of Racial Health

Getting Germans to drink less beer proved to be a difficult sell. Instead of revolutionizing their worldviews, Germans on average drank more beer each year as the country climbed out of the Great Depression and purchasing power increased.[36] While this trend reflected Germany's broader economic recovery, purchasing power is only part of the equation. Brewers also worked to stabilize the industrial and cultural scaffolding of the beer market. While brewers accommodated

---

[33] 'Der Feind der Volksgesundheit', *Nationalsozialistische Parteikorrespondenz* Jan. 13, 1938, Bundesarchiv Berlin-Lichterfelde (henceforth BAB) NS 5/VI 4875.

[34] Westermann, *Drunk on Genocide*.

[35] Arjun Appadurai, 'Introduction: Commodities and the Politics of Value', in *The Social Life of Things: Commodities in Cultural Perspective*, ed. Appadurai (Cambridge: Cambridge University Press, 1986), pp. 3–63, esp. pp. 15, 57.

[36] From 1933 to 1938, rates of consumption increased from 52 to just shy of 64 liters per person. Dec. 12, 1938, press release of the RgA, BAB R 36/1358.

campaigns targeting women and the youth, and made no objection to the criminalization and forced sterilization of alcoholics, they contested other, potentially existential efforts to undermine broadly held social convictions that beer was a nutrient-rich foodstuff and a people's drink embedded in the historical-cultural landscape.[37] The brewing industry, particularly in Bavaria, which was home to the greatest number of breweries, the highest rates of consumption, and the most expansive cultures of everyday beer drinking, actively worked to protect their markets. The ensuing conflicts over the meaning of beer recall the sorts of contestations and "tournaments of value" theorized by anthropologist and pioneer of commodity studies Arjun Appadurai. In his seminal work *The Social Life of Things*, Appadurai wrote that "demand" is neither the pure product of social manipulation, nor simply the manifestation of some basic human desire for stuff, but, rather, amounts to "the economic expression of the political logic of consumption."[38] The biological revolutionaries had targeted precisely the "political logic of consumption": the moral implications, market conditions, cultural values, and norms that informed the place of beer in German life. Throughout the 1930s and into the 1940s, Bavarian brewers turned both inward and outward, reinforcing their own narratives of tradition and culture in the trade press while also engaging with the regime over the place of beer as a popular and nutritious good.

Propaganda and public health efforts to render beer beyond the racial, nutritional, and cultural interests of the Volk triggered a response nationwide, but especially in Bavaria where the economic stakes were particularly high. Readers will recall that Bavarian cultures of production and consumption were markedly different than in much of the rest of the country. By quantitative measure alone, the peculiarities of the regional industry go a long way toward explaining why much of the opposition to state campaigns against beer emerged from Bavaria. Not only did Bavaria produce and consume more beer than the rest of Germany, it did so in decentralized and rural ways. In 1933 it was home to more than twice as many taxable breweries (those producing more than 20 hl a year) than second-place Prussia, and more than half of the national total.[39] The breweries were also significantly smaller. By 1937, Bavaria had almost three times as many full-scale breweries as all of northern Germany, and the smaller the scale, the more staggering the imbalance. So-called home brewers producing less than 20 hl a year were

[37] Many Germans maintained that beer was an important part of their daily lives, nutrition, and identity, and continued to drink beer because of its long-standing reputation as healthy, nutritional, and culturally popular. See, for example, Eduard Maria Schranka, *Ein Buch vom Bier. Cerevisiologische Studien und Skizzen*, 2 vols. (Frankfurt a.d. Oder: B. Waldmann Verlag, 1886); Carl Michel, *Geschichte des Bieres von der ältesten Zeit bis zum Jahre 1900* (Augsburg: Verlagsbuchhandlung von Gebrüder Reichel, 1901).

[38] Appadurai, 'Introduction', *The Social Life of Things*, p. 31; on tournaments of value, p. 21.

[39] 'Standort der deutschen Brauereien nach der gewerblichen Betriebszählung 1933', *Das Bier in Zahlen*, pp. 18–19.

tax exempt and numbered more than 35,000 in Bavaria, compared to just over 4,000 in all the rest of Germany combined.[40] The decentralization of the industry helps explain how rural Bavarians also managed to consume so much more beer at a time when the majority of the drink was still not bottled and sold in centrally located grocery stores. The average annual per capita consumption of beer in Bavaria in 1935/36 was 157.8 liters, compared to 98.5 liters in second-place Württemberg and only 50–60 liters in other regions including Hessen, Baden, Rhineland, and Westphalia.[41] Curbing beer consumption would not just impact consumers, it would also potentially decimate the economic livelihoods of Bavaria's only nationally relevant industry.[42] Brewers in Bavaria had a great deal to lose financially should the biological revolutionaries carry the day.

One of the first industry responses in the south was to turn inward, circling the wagons around the traditions and cultures of Bavarian beer in the trade press. In some ways this was an approach centered on emphasizing how beer mattered in German and Bavarian society—an approach developed in response to years of pressure by temperance reformers and spiraling taxes. Feature stories in *Der Bayerische Bierbrauer* regularly spanned ten to fifteen pages covering the history of specific breweries, the buildings and the brewers, the accommodations made for technological advancement, and the social role the breweries played from employment to sociability. The Hofbräuhaus was the subject of an entire edition which fused the beer to the richness of the place: "Munich and its Hofbräuhaus have, over the course of time, become a singular concept (*Begriff*)."[43] This was no small claim in the city that National Socialist propaganda and Hitler himself had long called "the capital of the movement." Other articles emphasized the geography of southern beer tradition and culture. The globally dominant hop-producing region of the Hallertau received lengthy treatment, as did the Upper Palatinate (*Oberpfalz*).[44] By mobilizing their trade publications in the praise of Bavaria, Munich, and countless other smaller locales and personalities, the Bavarian brewing industry promoted a distinct value system around beer that undermined ideological efforts to excise beer from German and Bavarian culture. Beer, in this view, was a crucial component of, rather than a blight on, daily life.

[40] 'Verteilung der Brauereien auf Süd- und Norddeutschland im Rechnungsjahr 1936/37', *Mitteilung der Wirtschaftsgruppe Brauerei und Mälzerei* 6 (1939): p. 143.

[41] 'Bierverbrauch im Rechnungsjahr 1935/36', *Mitteilung der Wirtschaftsgruppe Brauerei* 4. (1937): pp. 98–9.

[42] Dirk Götschmann, *Wirtschaftsgeschichte Bayerns: 19. und 20. Jahrhundert* (Regensburg: Verlag Friedrich Pustet, 2010), pp. 249–50.

[43] Hannes Schmid, 'Das k. Hofbräuhaus München', *Der Bayerische Bierbrauer* 45, Nov. 10, 1933; similar brewery-centric stories appear in M. Teichmann, 'Das Weiße Bräuhaus, München. G. Schneider & Sohn', *Der Bayerische Bierbrauer* 51, Dec. 22, 1933; and Franz X., 'Wiedereröffnung der Pschorrbräu-Bierhallen in München', *Der Bayerische Bierbrauer* 22, May 29, 1936.

[44] Fr. X. Ragl, 'Mainburg, das Herz der Hallertau, seine Brauereien und sein Hopfenbau', *Der Bayerische Bierbrauer* 40, Oct. 6, 1933; Fr. X. Ragl, 'Braugeschichtliches aus Kempten', *Der Bayerische Bierbrauer* 47, Nov. 20, 1942.

And it was a decidedly provincial effort. In one article, readers in the heavily Catholic German south could read about how, in the 17th century, the friar Barnabas Still of the order of Saint Francis of Paola brewed Paulaner Salvator, the first *Starkbier*, or double bock beer. Boasting an unusually high alcohol and caloric content, *Starkbier* was designed to be drunk in lieu of eating solid food during lent; a literal "liquid bread."[45] The core of these articles—tradition, culture, provincialism, economic stability, and nutrition—provided the fault lines of many conflicts throughout the 1930s. While trade journals remained largely internal to the brewing industry, the discourses developed there increasingly filtered into open conflicts over the social value of beer.

Unlike with the campaigns targeting women and the youth, brewers had reason to respond to efforts by public health officials that targeted the broadly held social conviction that beer was a nutrient-rich foodstuff and a people's drink. One of the most outspoken advocates for beer was Dr Ernst Röhm (no relation to his name-fellow, the Chief of Staff of the SA who was murdered in the summer of 1934). Röhm was the president of the national trade organization, the DBB, as well as the chairman of a brewery in Bad Reichenhall in the far southeast corner of Bavaria. On June 29, 1934, one day before the Night of the Long Knives, this lesser-known Röhm gave the closing address at the annual meeting of the DBB in Munich—the last before its official coordination into the Nazi economy. The address revealed both his optimism about the regime and his insistence that beer belonged in it. The core of it focused on economic recovery, which he explained in some depth by emphasizing industrial decentralization in Bavaria. The small- and mid-sized scale of the regional industry served local communities and fostered sociability. But perhaps most importantly in a moment of both widespread unemployment and apparent threats from the Left, the brewing industry created jobs in the small trades that helped to "de-proletarianize" Germany. In closing, he announced his aim to make beer affordable and available to all Germans. Throughout, Röhm balanced national and regional references, using the increasingly racialized category *Volksgenossen*, but signing off with the traditional Bavarian toast, "Hopfen und Malz, Gott erhalt's": roughly translated, "hops and malt, God save them."[46]

The speech delivered by Röhm was that of both a Bavarian businessman and an industry leader and was emblematic of the tensions between business interests and state interventions in commerce. For the next decade and more, Röhm walked a fine line between advocate for beer and moderate critic of the regime. To be sure, he was never fully the latter; he remained the head of the trade

[45] Fr. X. Ragl, 'Bayerische Braumeister-Pioniere', *Der Bayerische Bierbrauer* 49, Dec. 4, 1942, pp. 1–7.
[46] *Schlußwort zum Deutschen Brauertag 1934. von. Dr Ernst Röhm* (Berlin: Buchdruckerei Gebrüder Unger, 1934), BAB R 3101/13957.

organization even after it was "coordinated" as the Business Group for Breweries and Malthouses (*Wirtschaftsgruppe Brauerei und Mälzerei*, henceforth Business Group) in early 1935. Structurally, the Business Group remained largely the same organization as the DBB, focusing on relevant issues of industry and economy. Questions of agriculture and nutrition, however, increasingly became the purview of a completely new organization, the Central Association of the German Brewing Industry (*Hauptvereinigung der Deutschen Brauwirtschaft*, henceforth Central Association). A subsidiary of the Reich Food Estate, the Central Association became a near constant rival to the positions of the Business Group. That the two were in conflict until the end of the Reich undermines the American wartime assessment, re-presented in recent historical work, that "there was not a single agricultural product that was not rigidly controlled by some section of the Reich Food Estate."[47] The hopes of Röhm and the brewing industry more broadly that the regime "would usher in a new blooming for [their] local industry" faced pressures not only from propagandists, but also from institutions ranging from the Central Association to the medical complex.[48]

The initial optimism that many brewers felt toward the new government was confronted almost immediately by the increasingly entangled realms of nutrition, economic policy, and racial science. Already in late 1933, Dr Paul Schmidt of the Hygienic Institute at the University of Halle published an article suggesting how racial science, nutrition, and economic policy could be woven together. Schmidt's article, "On the Question of the Salubriousness of Beer," appeared in *German Medical Weekly* and was subsequently picked up for popular dissemination by the RgA rag, *Auf der Wacht*. In the realm of nutrition, Schmidt argued that the caloric value of an 80 Pfennig liter of beer could be met with a 10 Pfennig loaf of bread. Exemplifying the vanishing line between medical science and state policy, Schmidt went on to advocate raising taxes on beers above 4 per cent alcohol by volume (ABV) because they were an "unjustifiable waste of national wealth and simultaneously damaging to health."[49] Such an argument embodied the guiding ethos of Nazi nutritional science, which held, as Robert Proctor has shown, that good nutrition should not only be wholesome and unprocessed but should also be economical.[50] Medical and public health discourse beyond Schmidt's piece maintained that whatever nutritional value beer had, it did not make economical

---

[47] Qtd. in Weinreb, *Modern Hungers*, p. 50; see also Tooze, *The Wages of Destruction*, pp. 186–97.

[48] Bayerischer Brauerbund e.V. *Tätigkeitsbericht* April 1932–June 1933. (München: Bidel Söhne, 1933), p. 1; on the Central Association, see Dorothea Schmidt, *'Die Kraft der deutschen Erde': Das Bier im Nationalsozialismus und die Hauptvereinigung der Deutschen Brauwirtschaft in Berlin-Schöneberg* (Baden-Baden: Nomos, 2019).

[49] Paul Schmidt 'Zur Alkoholfrage der Bekömmlichkeit von Bier', *Deutsche Medizinischen Wochenschrift* 46 (1933), qtd. in 'Vom "flüssigen Brot" und vom täglichen "mäßigen" Trinken' *Auf der Wacht* 1/2 (Jan.–Feb. 1934): p. 7.

[50] Proctor, *The Nazi War on Cancer*, pp. 125–6.

or racial (*völkisch*) sense, rendering it neither nutritionally nor socio-economically worthy of being a drink of the people.

The article by Schmidt was part of an assault not only on alcoholism in the name of racial health but also on the more broadly rooted place of beer in German society. By the mid-1930s, as historical sociologist Herman Fahrenkrug has noted, an obsession with public health beyond chronic alcoholism took center stage in state discourse and policy regarding alcohol both as part of the broader remaking of German society and as part of war readiness.[51] Public health officials had rejected popular conventions that beer could be a medical aid (*Heilmittel* or *Medicament*) or a foodstuff (*Nahrungsmittel, flüßiges Brot*), and instead viewed it as a luxury, a poison of indulgence, or a national poison (*Genussmittel, Genussgift,* or *Volksgift*). Few issues better capture the conflicts between the interests of the regime and those of the industry than the idea of beer as a foodstuff. One example from a 1936 dispute over beer as "liquid bread" proves notable for both its content and its ultimate result. In May of that year, Dr Franz Wirz, a physician and member of the Expert's Forum for Public Health, argued in the *Berliner Tageblatt* that, among other changes required of national nutrition such as a high-protein diet, preferably of a "purified" nature such as vegetarianism, the German people also needed to abandon beer and the notion that it was a foodstuff.[52] Within a week this claim had garnered attention in Bavaria that bubbled up from the regional to the national offices of the Business Group. At stake, wrote the chairman of the Munich-based Spaten-Franziskaner-Leistbräu AG, was the fact that beer "used to be and remains to this day a foodstuff for large segments of the population; in Bavaria more than anywhere else."[53] But the extent to which beer was a foodstuff was an issue not just of consumer habits, but of the state management of nutrition.

The response from Wirz took over a month and demonstrates the extent to which disputes over beer revolved around nutrition, public health, and cultural peculiarity, as we have seen, but also increasingly were understood by the state as an issue of scarcity and caloric management. In his response, Wirz towed the line of the Reich public health initiatives by skirting the issue of cultural peculiarities and consumer preference and stressing that Bavarians drank more beer—and ate more radishes, he added—not because of a peculiar regional culture but because they otherwise lacked access to healthy goods. Fixing this and other regional scarcities, he claimed, was the very goal of Nazi diet reform and agricultural centralization. Leaning on much the same logic as Schmidt three years earlier, Wirz stressed that alcohol itself was unhealthy and that whatever nutritional value beer

---

[51] Hermann Fahrenkrug, 'Alcohol and the State in Nazi Germany, 1933–1945', in *Drinking: Behavior and Belief in Modern History*, ed. Susanna Barrows and Robin Room (Berkeley: University of California Press, 1991), pp. 315–34, here p. 328.

[52] Franz Wirz, 'Was sollen wir essen?' *Berliner Tageblatt* 238, May 20, 1936.

[53] May 25, 1936, letter from Gabriel u. Jos. Sedlmayr Spaten-Franziskaner-Leistbräu A.G. to the Bayer. Brauerbund, BayHStA Bayer. Brauerbund 416.

had, it could be made up elsewhere. The regime sought to increase consumption of whole-grain bread, for example, and, as this happened, "a decline in beer consumption will inevitably take place." If the brewing industry really wanted what was best for the Volk, Wirz suggested, it might be best served by allowing all grain to go toward bread and to turn to the "production of non-alcoholic beverages, especially good, natural, and cheap fruit juices."[54] This was the consolidating Nazi valuation of beer in miniature: beer lacked economic and *völkisch* practicality; it wasted bread grains, thus undermining more appropriate forms of consumption; and, through top-down reforms of the agricultural system, progress could be made toward completing the biological revolution and attaining self-sufficiency.[55]

This 1936 conflict fizzled out, but it constitutes part of the larger tension over beer as a foodstuff which continued well into the war years and was fought by industrial and provincial interests, especially in southern Germany. If Bavarian brewers failed to carry the day it is because they ran up against the bureaucratic morass of the Nazi dictatorship. This path was foreseeable and foreseen: When the Business Group initially forwarded along the critique, they warned that, while Bavarian traditions may run deep, "to take up the issue of beer as a popular food-stuff for all of Germany is unfortunately hopeless because according to the Ministry of the Interior, the highest authority responsible for these issues, beer can be considered a nutritious luxury but cannot be considered a food."[56] The logic was circular and resistant to critique. And, upon forwarding Wirz's response, they noted caustically that "his remarks are hardly likely to find our unqualified applause."[57] Facing such inflexibility, the only line of recourse was to appeal to the Central Association, an organization created to align brewing raw materials with agricultural centralization—that is, to do exactly what Wirz advocated. The course of this interaction is indicative of the shrinking space brewers had to lobby for beer in the popular interest, but such efforts remained. In 1940, for instance, four different breweries in and around Stuttgart drew the ire of the Ad Council for publishing local newspaper ads touting the nutritional qualities of beer and claiming that "beer is and will remain the German People's Drink."[58] In the preceding years, the RgA and the Ad Council had worked to prohibit advertising that

---

[54] June 26, 1936, letter from Franz Wirz to the Wirtschaftsgruppe Brauerei in Berlin, BayHStA Bayer. Brauerbund 416.

[55] On the ideological significance of bread, see, Uwe Spiekermann, 'Vollkorn für die Führer: zur Geschichte der Vollkornbrotpolitik im "Dritten Reich"', *Zeitschrift für Sozialgeschichte des 20. und 21. Jahrhunderts* 16 (2001): pp. 91–128; and, more generally, Weinreb, *Modern Hungers*, pp. 60, 67.

[56] June 2, 1936, Propaganda division of the Wirtschaftsgruppe Brauerei to the Bavarian Regional Group, BayHStA Bayer. Brauerbund 416.

[57] July 3, 1936, Propaganda division of the Wirtschaftsgruppe Brauerei to the Bavarian Regional Group, BayHStA Bayer. Brauerbund 416.

[58] Nov. 4, 1940, letter from Bezirksgruppe Württemberg-Hohenzollern to Röhm, BayHStA Bayer. Brauerbund 428.

promoted claims to the healthful and popular cultural aspects of alcohol. In this instance, Röhm came to the defense of the Stuttgart brewers, trading barbs with Dr Carole von Braunmühl of the Ad Council. The two agreed to disagree about the nutritional claims and completely stalled out over the nebulous term *Volksgetränk*, or people's drink. Von Braunmühl conceded that "beer is certainly a typical drink of the German people," but denied that "beer is the German *Volksgetränk*." Since 1933, he noted, certain words and concepts—like *Führer* or *Vaterland*—had taken on a "higher meaning" than they previously held. The word *Volk* (as in *Volksgetränk*) likewise had taken on greater meaning and, since 1935, was limited in commercial usage to only broadly beneficial consumer goods.[59] From bureaucratic to linguistic intransigence, advocates for beer could often only get so far.

While Röhm and the trade organization did much to contest the valuation of beer emerging from the public health and propaganda apparatus, so too did food and brewing scientists in Munich and Berlin. In-house brewing scientists of major breweries and teams of researchers at the Experimental and Teaching Institute for Breweries (VLB) and the research institute at Weihenstephan, in Berlin and Freising respectively, worked well into the war years to undermine scientific knowledge critical of alcohol. In many cases, the disputes came down to framing, a classic approach in contestations over the science of alcohol.[60] In 1940, for instance, Dr Ferdinand Goebel entered the debate over beer as a foodstuff in a book published by the Reich Health Press, in which he claimed that the fermentation process decreased the caloric value of the carbohydrates in barley. "Fermentation is a process of decomposition," he wrote, "and its products must be seen, purely calorimetrically... as being of lesser value. The myth of alcohol as a full-fledged food is thereby definitively refuted."[61] The logic seemed simple enough. And, indeed, when Dr Nowak, the brewing scientist for the Paulanerbräu-Salvatorbrauerei und Thomasbräu in Munich, complained to the Business Group, he agreed that fermentation decreased the carbohydrate value of the barley. He critiqued, however, that Goebel had not considered the value of the products of fermentation, most notably alcohol. Offering the counterpoint of ersatz coffee—which was made from malted barley and heavily supported by the Nazi state in wartime—a similar ingredient list produced a far less nutritious good precisely because of the lack of fermentation.[62] In truth, he argued, by gram, the caloric

---

[59] Nov. 18, 1940, v. Braunmühl to Röhm, BayHStA Bayer. Brauerbund 428.
[60] Michael Hau, 'The Dialectic of Medical Enlightenment: War, Alcohol Consumption and Public Hygiene in Germany, 1910–1925', *History: The Journal of the Historical Association* 104 no. 359 (Jan. 2019), pp. 149–68.
[61] Ferdinand Goebel, *30 Experimente zur Alkohol- und Tabakfrage* (Berlin-Dahlem: Reichsgesundheitsverlag, 1940), p. 3.
[62] Beer and ersatz coffee have many of the same ingredients and the two commodities frequently came into direct conflict. The malt coffee industry metaphorically threw brewers under the bus on a number of occasions, taking advantage of the anti-alcohol culture of the Third Reich in order to secure more raw resources and ensure market expansion. See, for example, Apr. 8, 1938, Rundschreiben Nr.

value of alcohol was more nutritious than protein or carbohydrate, coming in just behind fat. Alcohol—that is, the product of decreasing the caloric value of barley—is in fact "from a calorimetric standpoint the most valuable part of the beer. Therefore, the myth of alcohol as a full-fledged food is hardy definitively refuted, rather it is confirmed to be just the opposite."[63] Upon Röhm's request, the critique was considered by experts at both the VEB and Weihenstephan, all of whom wholeheartedly agreed with Nowak. One expert in Berlin went so far as to denounce the quality of Goebel's scientific work and its political purpose as nothing more than a "tale of the bogeyman!" (*Kinderschreck*)[64]

As the war intensified and the promises of a booming economy crumbled, the Nazi dictatorship both increased its interventionist approach and decreased its rigid opposition to pleasurable modes of consumption. As Nicole Petrick-Felber has shown in the case of tobacco and coffee, commodities that were initially of great concern to public health officials ultimately became essential to continuing the war effort. Such commodities were subjected to rationing for soldiers and civilians alike, and featured prominently in the political calculus of maintaining the loyalty of the home front.[65] In the case of beer too, as the Nazi regime prepared for and waged war, the moralizing, scientific, and public health discourses were joined, and ultimately displaced by, potential and then real concerns of wartime scarcity. Bavarian brewers continued to insist on the provincial peculiarities of production and consumption, to be sure, but they ran up against an increasingly heavy-handed wartime regime obsessively focused on food self-sufficiency. In this context, Bavarian brewers pushed back harder, finding industrial partners beyond Bavaria, new political allies within the regime, and an Achilles Heel in the threat of consumer unrest.

In the Name of the Volk: Southern Production Standards and the Language of Unrest

The pressures exerted on the production and consumption of beer by the Nazi dictatorship shifted significantly in preparation for, and in the ultimate waging of, war. As an agricultural product, beer fell into the larger structures of nutritional planning. Thanks in large part to the legacy of scarcity during the British blockade in the First World War and the mythology of the "stab in the back," the

21/38 der Fachgruppe Kaffee-Ersatz-Industrie der Wirtschaftsgruppe Lebensmittelindustrie, BayHStA Bayer. Brauerbund 415; 'Entwicklung und Steuerung des Bierverbrauchs in Deutschland', *Auf der Wacht* 1, 1938, pp. 10–16.

[63] Jan. 1, 1941, letter from Novak to Wirtschaftsgruppe Brauerei und Mälzerei, BayHStA. Bayer. Brauerbund 415.

[64] H. Haehn to the Wirtschaftsgruppe Brauerei und Mälzerei, qtd. in Jan. 1, 1941, letter from Nowak to the same office, BayHStA. Bayer. Brauerbund 415.

[65] Petrick-Felber, *Kriegswichtiger Genuss*.

Nazi Party and regime remained fixated on ensuring self-sufficiency and satisfying the material needs of the German people. In this spirit, the food planning division of the Four-Year Plan—designed to mobilize and coordinate the German economy for wartime autarky—worked to bring the production of beer into their larger designs of food management. It was in this context that provincial interests found their most powerful lever in the threat of consumer unrest. Efforts to centralize and standardize beer as an agricultural product ran up against intransigence among brewers in southern Germany who insisted that their regional production standards—that is, the *Reinheitsgebot*, though they rarely used the word—had conditioned provincial consumer expectations. Should the regime alter the standards of production, they argued, consumers might revolt. Finding allies among regional political leaders, an increasingly effective southern German bloc managed to avoid centralization, albeit in relatively small ways. These were not resisters in any meaningful sense of the word. Many of the opponents of centralization were officials in the Nazi regime: heads of provincial governments and functionaries in the coordinated economy via the Business Group. Their opposition nonetheless demonstrates the persistence of provincial politics and culture and the extent to which such blocs could manipulate concerns of popular opinion and unrest in the service of regional economic and cultural interest.

While the Nazi economy had been gearing up for war and self-sufficiency since at least the Four-Year Plan in 1936, pressures only directly reached brewers two years later. They initially came in the form of agricultural centralization by state secretary and later Food Minister Herbert Backe, who would go on to design the intentional starvation of Eastern European civilians in the so-called Hunger Plan.[66] That winter, one of Backe's tasks was to centralize domestic agricultural resources in the name of war-readiness. Limiting barley allocations to the brewing industry aimed to ramp up bread production, but it posed a problem for brewers. As the barley content of beer decreases, so too does the quality of the product, and the alcoholic and caloric content. Backe's initial limitation on barley allocations to 1 million metric tons per year was not a particularly Spartan amount; production in previous years had required just over that quantity. Hoping to keep brewers and beer drinkers happy, Backe and the Central Association—the new organization whose raison d'être was to manage the agricultural raw materials of the brewing sector—proposed the inclusion of raw sugar as a way of making up for lost barley. In the sugar sector, Germany faced far fewer scarcities. Thanks to a massive sugar beet industry, Germany was among the largest sugar-producing countries in the world; prior to the First World War, it had

---

edged out Cuba to become the single largest.[67] At the level of fermentation, the addition of raw sugar could effectively replace the sugars normally extracted from barley. The proposal reignited both regional and industrial tensions that had been simmering since at least the 1906 Beer Tax Law, which, as discussed earlier, split northern and southern production standards. Brewers in southern Germany who had long opposed the inclusion of sugar in beer vehemently rejected this relatively simple effort at food management, turning it into a battle in the cultural sphere. The Business Group, led by Röhm, provided the institutional mouthpiece for their opposition and came into direct conflict with the Central Association, which increasingly aligned with perspectives from brewers in northern Germany who had long been more flexible in their brewing practices.

In February 1938, the chairman of the Central Association, J. Immendorf of Cologne, held a confidential meeting in Berlin to discuss the implications of the sugar proposal. At this meeting, the north–south divide emerged almost immediately thanks to Röhm, who was the first voice of opposition. While his credentials as head of the Business Group had got him into the room, he clarified that he was speaking as a brewery chairman rather than an industry leader—that is, as a Bavarian rather than a German. This explicit signaling of regional and industrial identity was extended by his insistence on the "strictest form" of the *Reinheitsgebot* in southern Germany. He was the only speaker to refer to the *Reinheitsgebot* by name that day, signaling a sort of shorthand for decades of regional conflict over production standards. Throughout the meeting, brewers from northern Germany tended to side with the Central Association in favor of the sugar proposal, while southern Germans sided with Röhm and the Business Group. Berliners, Dortmunders, and Kölners argued that there would be no taste difference, but representatives from Karlsruhe in Baden, and from Stuttgart and Blaubeuren in Württemberg, sided with the Bavarians. For southern brewers, the sugar proposal not only challenged their traditions, it also threatened to backfire on the goal of minimizing the potential unrest caused by food scarcity. At the core of their opposition, they argued that the populace would begin deriding "sugar water" and may well become unruly. The suggestion sparked a fissure in the industry with northern brewers, long open to the inclusion of sugars, in favor, and southerners in opposition, insisting on their stricter production standards. While the fault lines of the debate were decades old, the language of popular opinion emerged as a key dynamic in the context of the mobilizing dictatorship. According to Herr Hollweck, a brewer from Ingolstadt, the issue threatened unparalleled social discontent. The inclusion of sugar in beer would "undoubtedly" lead to "great unrest…at least in the southern German population, as they would defend

---

[67] John Perkins, 'Sugar Production, Consumption and Propaganda in Germany, 1850–1914', *German History* 15 no. 1 (1997): pp. 22–33; here p. 23.

themselves...by any means." It was, therefore, "necessary for political reasons, to satisfy consumer desire and thereby avoid unrest in the consuming public."[68]

All the attendees understood the importance of mobilization and the role of agricultural autarky for ensuring a stable home front. What the southern Germans wanted to stress, however, was precisely how relevant their opposition to the proposal was for larger concerns about public opinion and domestic stability. While the ensuing dispute was rooted in provincial peculiarities of law, industry, and culture, it operated on the level of popular support for the regime. The language of consumer unrest resonated with a prevailing memory culture that pinned defeat in the First World War on the disgruntled and revolutionary home front. Southern brewers were likely motivated at least as much by industry practices and potential profit losses as by altruistic interest in public opinion. While it may be true that southern consumers had particular expectations of taste, almost none of them were aware of the existence of the *Reinheitsgebot*, and there is virtually no evidence of impending consumer unrest over beer. In many cases, it seems clear that southern brewers were primarily concerned with sinking profits; as two separate brewers from Württemberg pointed out that day, the inclusion of sugar was likely to push southern consumers toward wine and juice.[69] This was an old fight in a new context and consumer unrest provided a powerful lever for elevating business interests and provincial standards.

The language of unrest, whether driven by altruistic cultural preservationism or mere financial interest, took on a more robust political life in the weeks following Immendorf's heated meeting. In Bavaria, Röhm secured a political alliance with Ludwig Siebert, a loyal servant of the Party and the Reich. Siebert had been in Bavarian politics since 1908 and joined the Nazi Party in 1931 while serving as the mayor of Lindau, thus becoming the first NSDAP mayor in Bavaria. He went on to become one of the most prominent of Bavarian politicians, serving as State Minister of Economics and State Chancellor in the Third Reich. But Siebert also became a quick and close ally of the Bavarian brewers. At their request, he repeatedly appealed to Immendorf, to the Reich Ministry of Food, and to Backe himself. He explained at length his commitment to war readiness and stressed that his primary concern was about regional industry and consumer culture. He expressed uncertainty about "what effects a shaking of the *Reinheitsgebot* may have" if the addition of sugar became policy. Bavarians, he explained, had unique expectations and consumer desires that prioritized quality over quantity. They would be more amenable to "quantitative restrictions on beer consumption than to such a fundamental change in the production method."[70] This is likely untrue; Bavarian

---

[68] 'Niederschrift über Besprechung vom 10.2.1938 in den Diensträumen der Hauptvereinigung, Berlin', BayHStA Bayer. Brauerbund 586.
[69] Ibid.   [70] Feb. 23, 1938, Siebert to the Hauptvereinigung, BAB. R 3101/13958.

beer consumption was significantly higher than in other parts of Germany and the *Reinheitsgebot* remained broadly unknown among the general public. In any event, this and other formulations are taken almost verbatim from Röhm's statements weeks earlier. Siebert's parroting here indicates how tightly industrial and political interests were entwined in questions of provincial politics, economics, and culture. Bringing in reports from other regional industrial and political leaders from Baden and Württemberg, Siebert went beyond Bavaria to lend political voice to the idea of a distinct southern German bloc extant within the Reich. And the consequences, he claimed, going off Röhm's script to great effect, could be devastating. With the Great Depression barely in the rear-view mirror, he argued that consumers would not drink the new sugar-beer, destabilizing the brewing industry overnight and resulting in a recession that would hit Bavarian urban and brewing centers in Munich, Nuremberg, Würzburg, and Kulmbach especially hard.[71]

Siebert's claims to economic recession and consumer unrest, though likely hyperbolic, were nonetheless successful and point up the rhetorical power of unrest as a tool of political and economic provincialism in the Nazi dictatorship. The decision to allow southern German brewers to retain their regional production standards came down the pipeline in the beginning of March, about a week before the German annexation of Austria that marked the beginning of the Nazi conquest of Europe. The Reich Ministry of Food supported the adherence to southern German legal and cultural traditions precisely because they wanted to ensure there would be no unrest amongst the populace, the brewing industry, and the agricultural sector, especially in Bavaria.[72] As a result, the 1938 sugar proposal went into effect only in northern Germany, thereby preserving decades of north–south division over production standards. The threat of popular unrest in the south had proven sufficient to give pause. As the war began, raged, and turned sour, the barley supply predictably decreased, but southern brewers nonetheless held to their production standards. Equally predictably, less barley made for weaker brews, but as southern beers got thinner, brewers maintained their regional standards thanks to political and industrial manipulation of the regime's fears of unrest. In this, the centralizing and totalizing goals of the Nazi state and the dreams of a singular *völkisch* morality ran up against the intransigence of cultural, economic, and political provincialism.

The successful refutation of the sugar proposal in 1938 would go on to inform conflicts over production standards for decades, as we will see. As soon as 1941, however, the subject emerged once again. That year, Nazi Germany opened its two-front war which pushed the issue of resource management and concerns over popular unrest back into the spotlight. As the wartime food system began to

---

[71] Feb. 15, 1938, Siebert to the Hauptvereinigung. BAB. R 3101/13958.
[72] Mar. 3, 1938, letter from Siebert to Röhm, BayHStA Bayer. Brauerbund 587.

strain in the autumn of 1941, the regime again turned its attention to the grains being allocated toward beer. The upper leadership knew that less grain meant weaker beer, but the path forward remained unclear. Hitler himself rejected the idea that consumers would be able to tell the difference but, as Goebbels noted in his diary, the abstinent Führer was perhaps not the best judge of consumer expectations on the issue.[73] That winter, grain allocations were cut further and the Central Association issued a decree encouraging the practice of adding sugar to beer to make up for the shortfall. In response to the decree, the administrative board of the Bavarian Business Group immediately contacted all regional breweries to clarify that while sugar was allowed and now encouraged, it could not be mandated without changing legal codes and thus brewers could continue with business as usual.[74] As regulators in Berlin pushed to change brewing practices, southern Germans dug in their heels. For instance, in January, the Reich Finance Minister asked his regional counterparts in Bavaria, Baden, and Württemberg for their support in shifting brewing practices. The Bavarian Minister responded that he could not support the measure in good conscience. He further noted that any effort to change brewing practices for the sake of grain shortages would nonetheless have to honor the agreement of 1919 that had guaranteed Bavaria the retention of its stricter production standards.[75] The persistence of Weimar-era federalism is itself remarkable, providing a foundation of tradition and legal peculiarity on which regulators invoked the danger of public backlash. And the concern seems to have been taken seriously. The next month, an official in the Propaganda Ministry noted to the Food Ministry that since consumers "will undoubtedly recognize the decrease in quality," the introduction should be made "without any fuss" and with reasonable price cuts that would allay consumer objections.[76]

There is little evidence of consumer riots over beer quality, but the rhetoric remained remarkably powerful even as the realities of war became undeniable. As the war became increasingly total and economic controls tightened, supply and demand collapsed, and the consumerist utopia was postponed until an indefinite postwar period.[77] The anti-sugar campaign in southern Germany held strong through to the end of the war, but materials became so scarce, and taxes so high, that production and consumption largely collapsed in 1944 and 1945. Still, brewers effectively clung to the language of supplying beer to a volatile populace.

---

[73] *Die Tagebücher von Joseph Goebbels*, ed. Elke Fröhlich. Teil 2, Diktate 1941–1945, Band 2, Oktober–Dezember 1941 (Munich: K.G. Saur, 2001), 374. Thanks to Paul Steege for this reference in the 11th hour.

[74] Dec. 27, 1941, letter from the managing directors of the Bavarian Regional Group to the membership, BAB R 2/24316.

[75] Jan. 16, 1942, letter from Bavarian Finance Minister to Reich Finance Minister, BAB. R 2/24316.

[76] Jan. 15, 1942, letter from Alfred-Ingemar Berndt to the Reich Ministry of Food and Agriculture, BAB R 2/24316.

[77] Wiesen, *Creating the Nazi Marketplace*, p. 227.

As the bombs fell, many breweries were converted for the purposes of civil defense. Large urban breweries such as the Munich Spaten Brewery were home to large fire protection systems, often with independent water and power sources.[78] By the spring of 1943, Luftwaffe civil defense exerted pressure to convert as many breweries as possible. Such demands were hard to make mandatory, and brewers again argued that while they supported the war effort, such conversions should be taken case-by-case and avoided if possible, "especially due to the already palpable consequences of the increased air attacks for breweries and the beer supply."[79] This rhetoric intimated that popular support for the Reich and the appearance of consumer freedom were at stake in state efforts to control and restrict the Bavarian brewing industry. Beer, they seemed to suggest, held greater sway over popular morale than bombs.

Such a claim motions toward the increasingly ridiculous nature of industrial reluctance. The end of the Second World War brought catastrophic destruction to Germany, and while most Bavarian and southern German brewers held to their convictions to the end, for some the physical devastation of Germany undermined their insistence on regional differences in production and consumption. Provincialism and tradition could understandably take a backseat to the basic necessities of life in the rubble. For instance, one disgruntled brewer in Memmingen wrote to Röhm in February 1945 critiquing the trade organization and even rejecting the strict Bavarian aversion to brewing with the inclusion of sugar:

The workers in factories, meadows, fields, and forest want to have something, anything, to quench their thirst...What mistakes have we made in Bavaria in this war with the ban on sugar use?...And why? Because a couple uptight conservatives reject any innovation. I'm an old brewer and even I cannot understand that...In other conditions things might be different; but for the present time the order of the day is for German brewers to make enough thirst-quenching beverages available for the people.[80]

Ultimately, the devastation of bombing and Allied invasion undermined bickering over who best understood the needs and wants of "the people." If brewers truly imagined themselves patriotic Germans, they might have better given up their peculiar vision of the people's drink in favor of simply giving the people something to drink.

---

[78] July 3, 1942, letter from Luftschutzleiter and Polizeipräsidenten München to Luftgaukommando VII, BayHStA Bayer. Brauerbund 645.

[79] Mar. 22, 1943, letter from Proebst to the Berlin office of the Wirtschaftsgruppe Brauerei und Mälzerei, BayHStA Bayer. Brauerbund 645.

[80] Feb. 8, 1945, letter from Hugo Bilgram to Röhm, BayHStA Bayer. Brauerbund 582.

Conclusion

Seen from the south, the story of beer in Nazi Germany is a story of conflict between two different visions of beer and its relationship to "the people." The first understanding of beer—that of incompatibility—was constructed on the foundations of abstinence programs and eugenic thought by an array of ideologues, institutions, and interest groups. The second—that of essential necessity—rested on cultural provincialism and long-standing tensions over regional production standards, and was formed and advocated for by a reactionary southern brewing industry. From 1933 to 1945, beer became a site of conflict between two different conceptions not just of beer, but rather of the German people and their economic and cultural life. Germany was not, as many in the Nazi regime imagined it, a homogenous community of racial comrades. It was instead, as it had always been, a provincial patchwork of cultures and bounded political discourses, industrial practices, habits, and belief systems.[81] Contests over the value of beer in Nazi Germany capture some of the complexities and consequences of the Nazi dream of revolutionizing social norms in a country that remained home to deep provincial divisions in industry, politics, and culture. Dreams of totalization galvanized a southern bloc of diverse political, economic, and cultural discourses and values about the German people and their cultural life which would reverberate for decades to come. Beer had long been a drink common to Germany, but the reaction of southern brewers and their allies to the pressures of the dictatorship energized industrial and political conceptualizations of beer as the *Volksgetränk*—not just a habit of consumption, but a marker of collective identity. If we see in these conflicts a tension between different versions of Germany and German values, then we can also see in them part of the foundation for a new Germany. As we will see, the Bavarian and southern convictions about beer articulated in the Nazi period shape national policy and practice for decades after 1945. First, however, on the other side of their unconditional surrender, Germans were faced with extreme scarcity, shifting regimes of nutritional management, and an ascendant politics of beer and Bavaria in questions of national self-sufficiency.

---

[81] See, further, Claus-Christian W. Szejnmann and Maiken Umbach, eds., *Heimat, Region, and Empire: Spatial Identities under National Socialism* (New York: Palgrave Macmillan, 2012).

3

Liquid Bread

The New Politics of Bavaria from the postwar Occupation to the Federal Republic

On December 9, 1949, Max Solleder of the Christian Social Union (CSU), the exclusively Bavarian sister party to the West German Christian Democratic Union (CDU), was one of several parliamentarians to speak in a plenary session of the new West German Bundestag. That afternoon, the chamber spent a great deal of time discussing an issue that had long been a sticking point between the federal and *Land* governments: the beer tax. Until 1919, the *Länder* had retained their own tax revenues on beer and, as we have seen, efforts at fiscal centralization in the Weimar Republic sparked animosity from Bavaria, ultimately contributing to the collapse of a functioning parliamentary government in 1930. Now, the beer tax again loomed large and, advocating for a decentralized fiscal structure, Solleder urged the Bundestag to approve a motion to reallocate beer tax revenues to the *Länder*. In the course of the discussion, however, it became clear that the issue was not simply one of fiscal policy but of how Bavaria fit in the West German nation. Solleder was one of a chorus of Bavarians from four different political parties that spoke that day. Addressing the "ladies and gentlemen from the northern districts," he explained that while "you only see us Bavarians drinking beer at large folk festivals...that is the extraordinary exception, not the rule. For us, beer is really a daily liquid bread...It is part of our way of life!" Just as the chamber handled questions regarding Heligoland or Berlin "with seriousness and empathy," it had an "obligation" to do the same for Bavaria. Solleder entreated his colleagues "not to regard these things as a Bavarian matter, but as a German matter which, even if it takes place on Bavarian soil, nonetheless remains just as German."[1]

The arguments made by Solleder and others revolved around the conviction that federalist governance required sensitivity to the peculiarities of the *Länder*. Ultimately, the Bavarians swayed the chamber and the beer tax became—and remains to this day—the only consumption-based tax to be retained by the *Länder*. The decision was a culmination of historical tensions over the centralized state: decentralization as of 1871 was reversed in 1919 and the issue had

[1] *Plenarprotokoll*, Deutscher Bundestag 22. Sitzung, Dec. 9, 1949, p. 707.

A Nation Fermented: Beer, Bavaria, and the Making of Modern Germany. Robert Shea Terrell, Oxford University Press.
© Robert Shea Terrell 2024. DOI: 10.1093/oso/9780198881834.003.0004

smoldered ever since. But two further components undergird this moment in 1949. The first, as Solleder noted, was the role of beer in Bavarian life: "liquid bread" was a crucial component in the nutritional and agricultural systems of Bavaria. Beer energized farmhands, provided a much-needed sterile beverage in rural areas, and generated by-products that enriched livestock feed. But this long-standing role of beer in Bavaria took on new importance in the immediate postwar period. Second, therefore, it proves crucial to locate Bavaria in the shifting political economy of the German lands. Managing food scarcity was the order of the day in occupied Germany, and because the most food-rich regions of the former Reich fell under the authority of the Soviet Union, Bavaria quickly became the go-to breadbasket of the western zones.[2] The Bavarian "way of life" became an issue of federal policy because the conditions of defeat and division fundamentally shifted the relative importance of Bavaria in western Germany.

Histories of the seismic political transitions of the postwar years have, understandably, tended to focus on the political division of Germany into two Cold War states. This chapter similarly focuses on the early years of division, but emphasizes less the issue of division itself than the ways that it precipitated a reconfiguration of domestic political structures, from the food system to tax policy. As of 1945, the occupation authorities enacted a series of prohibitions on brewing beer that were designed to optimize bread production. Opposition emerged immediately, and most profoundly, from Bavaria, where beer played an important role in a stable food system. Over the next few years, ongoing food scarcity and worsening East–West relations resulted in increased agricultural reliance on Bavaria and created a fulcrum on which agriculturalists and local and regional politicians sought to move Allied and western German policy. Change was slow thanks to the reluctance of the US Congress, but came nonetheless as the Western Allies embraced German recovery and empowered German policymakers. As Bavarian political leaders and agrarians reframed beer as a nutritional, agricultural, and economic necessity, such arguments informed legislative structures, marking a reconfiguration of the relative power of the *Länder* in divided, post-Prussian Germany.

The late 1940s, as many have noted, were a period marked by both continuities and ruptures. In the present case, as elsewhere, many of the issues that plagued postwar Germany were inherited: excessively high taxes from a wartime regime and, crucially, an overstretched food system reliant on eastern Germany and colonial extraction in Eastern Europe. But such issues were also exacerbated by the conditions of defeat: the destruction of a regime with a manifest

---

[2] On food in the occupation, see, for example, Paul Erker, *Ernährungskrise und Nachkriegsgesellschaft: Bauern und Arbeiterschaft in Bayern, 1943–1953* (Stuttgart: Klett-Cotta Verlag, 1990); Paul Steege, *Black Market, Cold War: Everyday Life in Berlin, 1946–1949* (Cambridge: Cambridge University Press, 2007); and Alice Weinreb, *Modern Hungers: Food and Power in Twentieth-Century Germany* (New York: Oxford University Press, 2017).

interest—however partial—in consumer desires, astronomical tax increases designed to enforce partial prohibition, and a deteriorating geopolitical balance. Where the previous chapter demonstrated how the Nazi dictatorship galvanized southern opposition, here the Allied occupation and division of Germany opened space for Bavarian legislators and regulators to take an increasingly central role in emerging national politics. Allied policy—from the prohibition of beer to the increasing reliance on Bavarian agriculture—drew significant opposition on the ground. Beer and brewing played an important role in a functioning food system, especially in Bavaria, and as the occupation went on, such a conviction made its way into numerous petitions to the Military Government. Still, years of Bavarian critiques failed to sway Allied policies. As relations between the Soviet Union and the Western Allies deteriorated, however, the shift toward western reconstruction created new opportunities for Bavarian advocates for beer to leverage their role in agricultural and economic recovery into meaningful policy change. Some changes were relatively minor, such as tweaking the ration system, while others were more pivotal—namely, the 1949 resolution of a decades-long conflict over tax policy. Throughout the late 1940s, conditions in Bavaria and the conviction that beer held the key to stability and recovery radiated outward. Bavarian agrarians and legislators appealed to the Military Government and to German-led governing bodies in Frankfurt and later Bonn. In each case, they insisted that the peculiar importance of beer in Bavaria—laughable though it seemed to their interlocutors—ought to be of the utmost collective importance well beyond the rural southeast.

Beer as Food, Food as Beer: The *Brauverbot* and Caloric Scarcity

In the last months of the Second World War, the Allies enacted a series of prohibitions on the production of beer for civilian consumption. The initial goal of these *Brauverbote* was to funnel all available grain into bread production—a measure designed to manage the collapse of the German food system. In effect, however, limitations on both the production and consumption of beer had unintended and unforeseen repercussions, especially in rural Bavaria. Lacking alternatives such as juice or other soft drinks and even, in some cases, clean drinking water, beer had long been a crucial and calorically rich mainstay. In the absence of beer, farmers across Bavaria began consuming the milk they produced rather than delivering it to market, thereby straining the already weak dairy economy. But beyond beer consumption, beer production also played a role in a healthy agricultural food system. Brewing by-products such as spent grain traditionally went into animal feed and fertilizer and thus occupation regulations damaged agricultural productivity at a much deeper level. In effect, the *Brauverbot* worsened rather than alleviated food scarcity in occupied Germany, especially in the American Zone, where the brewing industry was most conservative in its production standards and where beer played a particularly important role in rural and agricultural life. The brewing bans were thus top-down managerial interventions—akin to the rationing system or UN relief programs—which, in their shortcomings, shaped German practices, political convictions, and discursive continuities in subsequent years and decades.[3] In particular, disputes over the *Brauverbote* illuminate the changes in agrarian politics and the role of Bavaria in the German nation.

The German food system had long been oriented toward the east. Prior to 1945, the parts of Germany that came to be administered by the Soviet Union and the newly formed Polish state had supplied almost half of Germany's national annual grain needs.[4] But beyond the borders of the former Reich too, the wartime food system depended on the conquest and plunder of food-rich Eastern Europe.[5] As the war ended, feeding the Germans was among the foremost concerns of the Allies and, in this spirit, Soviet premier Joseph Stalin had agreed at the Potsdam Conference to transfer eastern German foodstuffs and other essentials to the western zones. Conditions were exacerbated by the fact that in spite of the heavy casualties of the war, the expulsion of ethnic Germans from Eastern Europe amounted to a population *increase* of 16 per cent from 1939 to 1950. In Bavaria, on the southeastern border, the figures were yet more extreme, with a population increase of almost 30 per cent.[6] The reordering of space and the swelling population of the former Reich presented twin pressures that drastically increased demands on the shattered food system. The collapse of the Reich and the unraveling of Stalin's promise of food deliveries—already in early 1946—signaled the immediate need for a new breadbasket for the western zones. Bavaria, more so than any other German region, felt the pressure to provide foodstuffs for western Germany.[7] Comprised of highly localized smallholder farming and marked by

[3] Steege, *Black Market, Cold War*; and Alice Weinreb, 'For the Hungry Have No Past nor Do They Belong to a Political Party': Debates over German Hunger after World War II', *Central European History* 45, no. 1 (March, 2012): pp. 50–78; and Malte Zierenberg, *Berlin's Black Market: 1939–1950* (New York: Palgrave Macmillan, 2015).

[4] 'Rede des bayer. Staatsministers für Ernährung, Landwirtschaft und Forsten Dr Joseph Baumgartner anläßlich des 2. Gründungstages des Bayer. Bauernverbandes in Passau am 7. September 1947', (Manz A.-G. 1947), BayHStA NL Ehard 1310; see also Ulrich Kluge, *Vierzig Jahre Agrarpolitik in der Bundesrepublik Deutschland*, vol. 1 (Hamburg and Berlin: Verlag Paul Parey, 1989), pp. 41–4.

[5] Gesine Gerhard, *Nazi Hunger Politics: A History of Food in the Third Reich* (Lanham: Rowman & Littlefield, 2015), pp. 85–102; Alice Weinreb, *Modern Hungers: Food and Power in Twentieth-Century Germany* (New York: Oxford University Press, 2017), pp. 49–87; more generally, Timothy Snyder, *Bloodlands: Europe between Hitler and Stalin* (New York: Basic Books, 2010); and Snyder, *Black Earth: The Holocaust as History and Warning* (New York: Tim Duggan Books, 2015).

[6] Franz Bauer, 'Aufnahme und Eingliederung der Flüchtlinge und Vertriebenen: Das Beispiel Bayern, 1945–1950', in *Die Vertreibung der Deutschen aus dem Osten*, ed. Wolfgang Benz (Frankfurt am Main: Fischer Verlag, 1995), p. 201; and Wacław Długoborski, *Zweiter Weltkrieg und sozialer Wandel. Achsenmächte und besetzte Länder* (Göttingen: Vandenhoeck & Ruprecht, 1981), p. 119.

[7] Raphael Gerhardt, *Agrarmodernisierung und europäische Integration: das bayerische Landwirtschaftsministerium als politischer Akteur, 1945–1975* (Munich: Verlag C.H. Beck, 2019), p. 105.

decades of poor mechanization, Bavaria was woefully unprepared to deliver.[8] Still, the demand placed on Bavarian agriculture over the course of the occupation years became an increasingly potent condition on which advocates for beer would stake their claims to the popular interest.

The politics of beer production and consumption in the late 1940s depended on material and regulatory continuities from Nazism, the conditions of postwar food scarcity, and the managerial approach of the Allies. From the late Nazi period through to the early Federal Republic, beer and brewing were subjected to a remarkable array of restrictive legislation. As we saw, the Nazi regime began altering brewing standards as early as 1938, leading to the production of lower-quality beers. In both the south, where brewers clung to their stricter production standards, and in the north, where their counterparts turned to sugar and other surrogates, the calorie and alcohol content of beer dropped precipitously by the last years of the war. Permissible strength was constrained through restrictions on raw materials and heavy-handed tax laws. Since 1943, German beers averaged between 3.1 and 1.7 per cent original wort strength (*Stammwürze*), a quantity that had virtually no caloric or alcoholic value. After 1945, the raw materials shortages and the tax system of the Nazi dictatorship remained but were compounded by the *Brauverbote*. At their core, these measures, which initially applied to all four zones of occupation, had a similar goal as Nazi wartime regulations: to manage scarcity by betting the farm on bread production. But the caloric balance, it turned out, depended on the presence of full-strength beer. Occupation *Dünnbier*—or thin beer—that was typical of the American Zone, was limited to an original wort strength of 1.7 per cent. Such beer yielded a final alcohol by volume (ABV) of less than 0.5 per cent, and contained only 70 calories per liter. By contrast, a liter of beer with a 12 per cent *Stammwürze*, typical of peacetime brewing in Bavaria and equivalent to about 5.5 per cent ABV, contained almost 500 calories.[9]

Opposition to the Allied *Brauverbot* emerged across occupied Germany, but Bavarians made the most frequent, vocal, organized, and ultimately successful critiques. The brewing industry produced more, Bavarians consumed more, and, due to a lack of industrial centralization, there were significantly more breweries. As a result, restrictions on production and consumption were felt most acutely in Bavaria. But perhaps more importantly, beer fit into Bavarian culture in important ways. It was a staple foodstuff in the Catholic south, long thought of as liquid bread. Since the early 17th century, Catholic monks had been allowed by Vatican

---

[8] Alois Schlögl, *Bayerische Agrargeschichte: die Entwicklung der Land- und Forstwirtschaft seit Beginn des 19. Jahrhunderts* (Munich: Bayerischer Landwirtschaftsverlag, 1954); Erker, *Ernährungskriese und Nachkriegsgesellschaft*, pp. 155–9.

[9] July 23, 1945, Ernst Rattenhuber, 'Zur Frage der bayerischen Bierversorgung', NARA RG 260 390/47/34/1 Box 7; and Aug. 10, 1945, 'Memorandum on the Brewing Industry in Germany', NARA, RG 260 390/51/17/2-3. Box 716.

decree to drink beer during times of fasting. This was the impetus behind the creation of Paulaner Salvator, a double bock beer with high alcohol and caloric content. Some of the strongest and most nutritionally substantive of all German beers, Salvator and other "-ator" double bocks appear throughout southern Germany during strong beer season (*Starkbierzeit*), which directly corresponds to Lent each year. But beyond this cultural and religious association, Bavarian voices were most vocal about the importance of beer because of its role as a foodstuff. It was local political leaders, from mayors to agrarian politicians, tasked with feeding the German people that first relayed the importance of beer and the brewing industry for reconstructing the food system. In July 1945, the Mayor of Munich, Karl Scharnagel, may have been the first to complain to the Military Government, writing that "beer is for us in Munich, as in the entire Bavarian region, more than a refreshment. Beer has always been part of nutrition [and]…especially in the scarcity, beer is practically a necessity for our population."[10] While it would be easy to dismiss his rhetoric as either hyperbolic or mundane, Scharnagel's insistence on the role of beer in the Bavarian food system would become increasingly visible in the coming months and years.

Urban leaders such as Scharnagel repeatedly advocated for beer, but the most consistent critiques came from those with an eye on the caloric balance of the countryside. Ernst Rattenhuber, for instance, was the initial director, as of May 9, 1945, of what was then called the Office for Nutrition and Agriculture and later became the State Ministry of Food, Agriculture, and Forestry. In late July, he wrote to the Military Government explaining that beer was a crucial foodstuff, "in Bavaria…more so than in any other German state."[11] Postwar *Dünnbier*, Rattenhuber pointed out, was no longer liquid bread at all, but rather, "little more than a thirst quencher." Without beer as a nutritious option, he went on, "the farmer and his employees drink more and more milk" and, as a result, "the delivery of milk to the dairy farms, and accordingly the production of butter, have a strong retrograde tendency."[12] And logically so. In contrast to the 70 calories to be had from a liter of *Dünnbier*, milk with a typical fat content of 3.4 per cent delivered more than 600 calories.[13] As a result, Rattenhuber predicted that milk deliveries across Bavaria would drop by at least 30 per cent. Already that month the delivery of raw milk to a dairy farm in the town of Moosburg, outside Munich, had dropped dramatically from 32,000 liters a day to only 18,000.[14] Beyond Munich and its environs, the interim mayor of the Middle Franconian administrative seat of Ansbach, Hans Schregle, also noted that beer in Bavaria was a basic nutriment, that it was a part of agricultural wages, and that in the absence of the

---

[10] July 16, 1945, letter from Scharnagel to OMGB, BayHStA Bayer. Brauerbund 695.
[11] Rattenhuber, 'Zur Frage der bayerischen Bierversorgung'.   [12] Ibid.
[13] June 23, 1948, letter from Schlögl to Ehard, BayHStA, NL Ehard 1347.
[14] Rattenhuber, 'Zur Frage der bayerischen Bierversorgung'.

fuel required to boil water free of typhoid, "the people of Bavaria must have *something* to drink." He warned that farmers were being led into a regrettable decision between consuming the milk bound for distribution or the calorically weak *Dünnbier*.[15]

The production of beer became a part of agrarian politics because of its relationship to milk in rural Bavaria, a connection that tied the rural countryside and the Bavarian center. At an institutional level, the newly formed Bavarian Farmer's Association (BBV) took up the relationship between milk and beer at their very first meeting in the spring of 1946. Founded in the autumn of 1945, the BBV was one of the earliest professional organizations in postwar Germany and it grew into "undoubtedly the most important non-state actor in Bavarian agrarian politics," connecting rural sentiment and agrarian labor to the emerging state ministry system.[16] That spring, a special session of the Nutrition Policy Committee debated "Beer or Milk," stressing the severity of the need for beer in rural areas. As the Committee explained on the small scale,

> Assuming that instead of beer, the farmer drinks milk, he would drink 5 liters of milk a day during the harvest time. If one assumes a work force of 120 farmers per community (*Gemeinde*), this would mean that each day 600 liters of milk will be needed. In a circle of forty communities, this would amount to 24,000 liters of milk that would be extracted from the delivery per day.[17]

Expanding this out to encompass the almost two and a half million Bavarians working in rural agriculture was left implicit at this meeting—likely because some had better access to alternatives than others. But even expanding the estimate to half the farming population (1.2 million), the calculation would amount to more than 5 million liters of milk lost *per day* in Bavaria alone as a direct result of the brewing ban.

However dire the situation seemed, the link between beer and milk was only part of the problem. If beer was a crucial beverage and a calorically rich foodstuff, the production of other foodstuffs also depended on beer: beer was food, and food was beer. As milk entered the equation of rural consumption and production habits, simultaneous concerns erupted from local political leaders and agrarians that emphasized the crucial role of brewing by-products as fertilizers and ingredients in feed for livestock. From the beginning of the occupation, Rattenhuber had explained that, "in brewing beer, valuable waste products are

---

[15] Aug. 22, 1945, letter from Hans Schregle to the Office of MG, Ansbach, NARA RG 260 390/47/34/1 Box 7; see also, 'Halbmonatsbericht über die Landwirtschaftlichen Verhältnisse im Landkreis Aichach, June 21 to July 6, 1945', Staatsarchiv München (henceforth StAM), LwA 719.

[16] Gerhardt, *Agrarmodernisierung und europäische Integration*, p. 49.

[17] July 15, 1946, 'Aktennotiz. Betr. Sitzung des ernährungspolitischen Ausschusses des Bayerischen Bauernverbandes', BayHStA Bayer. Brauerbund 695.

obtained, namely malt residue and spent brewers' grain. These waste products increase milk production to a remarkable extent. For instance, 1 kilogram of dry malt residue yields about 2 liters of milk-value (*Milchwert*)."[18] Such small numbers may have minimized the force of this observation and exacerbated Allied innumeracy. But for the next few years a great many commentators made the same point: When grain is used for baking bread, it can only be used once, but when used for brewing beer, it has an afterlife. As one petition in the winter of 1947 put it, agriculturalists and food scientists agreed that "the byproducts of brewing are of the same fodder-value for cows as the original barley," and if farmers get "no malt husks, they will fodder barley."[19] Studies conducted at the Technical University in Munich and at Weihenstephan, the famed brewing and agricultural school, developed increasingly convincing reports on how to best optimize the caloric value of barley. Because this was a problem the Allies had inherited rather than created, many of these reports were based on research initially conducted during the Third Reich.[20] Still, the conclusion was simple: brewing, rather than baking, made the best use of barley because of the secondary value of the by-products.

German advocates for beer found support among the Allies, even including General Lucius D. Clay, the military governor of the American Zone. Yet, as consistent as critics were in their arguments for beer, they ran up against much larger political uncertainties, from the persistent intransigence of the US Congress to the rapidly deteriorating political balance between East and West.

Policy Appeals and the Obstinacy of Geopolitical Uncertainty

That the brewing ban exacerbated agricultural productivity was amplified by two main political uncertainties: Opposition to brewing beer in the US Congress, and the entangled fates of Germany, the Western Allies, and the Soviet Union. In the first instance, as Germans in the American Zone made their case to the Military Government, what advocates they won could only take policy change so far as

[18] Rattenhuber, 'Zur Frage der bayerischen Bierversorgung'.

[19] Dec. 10, 1947, letter to Van Wagoner signed by various associations, BayHStA Bayer. Brauerbund 695; See also Apr. 3, 1947, letter from Landesgewerkschaft Nahrung-Genuss-Gaststätten to OMGB and Dec. 5, 1946, Memorandum of the Brauwirtschaftsverband. NARA RG 260/390/46/24/3, Box 294.

[20] See, for example, the two 1947 reports by J. Paproth, 'Ernährungswirtschaftliche Ausnützung der vollkörnigen Sommergerste über Brauerei, Gerstenmüllerei, Schweinemast und Kaffeeersatzbereitung. Ein ernährungswirtschaftlicher Vergleich', and Paproth, 'Die Verwertung der vollkörnigen Sommergersten für die Volksernährung', reproduced in BayHStA Bayer. Brauerbund 404. These were based on research conducted in the 1930s and early 1940s that Paproth himself had been involved with. See, for example, the 1937 manuscript by H. Fink, K. Göpp, Fischer, H. Lüers, E. Röhm, and J. Paproth, 'Ernährungswirtschaftliche Ausnützung der Gerste bei der Bierbereitung', and E. Röhm's 1941, 'Politische und ernährungswirtschaftliche Wertung des Bieres und der bei der Verbrauung der Gerste anfallenden Nebenerzeugnisse', both in BayHStA Bayer. Brauerbund 585.

they ran up against opposition in the US Congress. Not only had Congress attempted to resuscitate American Prohibition as recently as the early 1940s, but wartime scarcities had led American brewers and distillers to face many of the same issues as their German counterparts. While American brewers mostly succeeded in navigating these pressures, the wartime premium on bread grains led to a decline in the production of spirits.[21] Put simply, Congress worried about allowing the defeated Germans to brew beer while Americans faced limitations on their own alcohol. And while there was some parallel reluctance in the British Parliament, the American–Bavarian case is somewhat unique. The Americans not only had the strongest culture of prohibition, but had also come to take on a leading role in managing food security and scarcity around the world.[22] The Bavarians, for their part, continued to insist on the need for barley, a stipulation of the *Reinheitsgebot* that remained less important elsewhere in occupied Germany. Indeed, the British, French, and Soviet Zones had lifted full prohibition already in the summer of 1945 and the Germans in those areas made do with beer containing surrogates such as whey, fruit, and other grains.[23]

Many in the American Military Government sympathized with the demands for beer in their zone but ultimately ran into organizational intransigence. In the summer of 1945, for example, American military assessments in the administrative districts of Hessen-Nassau and Bavaria relayed the importance of beer as a daily foodstuff and caloric alternative to milk. As a result, the Military Government advocated for restarting the brewing industry, and by November moved to loosen the initial full prohibition in favor of allowing weaker beer effective February 1946.[24] The measure was to be short lived. Not only did the planned rollback of the prohibition generate concern about German food self-sufficiency in Washington, it also stoked concerns about restrictions on alcohol production at home. As Lt. Col. James M. Gwin relayed it to the Deputy Director for Food and Agriculture of the US Zone, Stanley Andrews, American "public opinion in this regard is rather sensitive...Every German abuse might provoke a discussion on that matter in Congress."[25] For his part, the military governor of the US Zone, General Lucius D. Clay, sided with the advocates for beer. He understood the concerns back home but noted that beer was, "the native drink,

---

[21] On beer, see Lisa Jacobson, 'Beer goes to War: The Politics of Beer Promotion and Production in the Second World War', *Food, Culture & Society* 12, no. 3 (2009): pp. 275–312.

[22] See, for example, Nick Cullather, 'The Foreign Policy of the Calorie', *The American Historical Review* 112, no. 2 (Apr., 2007): pp. 337–64; and Alice Weinreb, ' "For the Hungry Have No Past nor Do They Belong to a Political Party" '.

[23] Sept. 13, 1945, 'Production of beer for Consumption by German Civilians', NARA, RG 260 390/51/17/2-3. Box 716.

[24] July 31, 1945, 'Beer—general discourse on'; Aug. 10, 1945, 'The Brewing Industry in Germany'; Sept. 13, 1945, 'Production of beer for Consumption by German Civilians'; Dec. 27, 1945, 'Beer for German Civilians'. NARA, RG 260 390/51/17/2-3. Box 716.

[25] Memorandum attached to Jan. 24, 1946, letter from Gwin to Andrews. NARA, RG 260 390/51/17/2-3. Box 716.

particularly in Bavaria," and that "even a small amount of beer will increase output of farmers and workers during [the] heavy working season."[26] Reluctance in Washington remained strong, however, and the next month the War Department pushed back by recalling a quarter of the barley released for beer production in the American Zone. For the rest of the year, the House of Representatives and the Senate debated a number of resolutions that cracked down on both the domestic use of grain in alcohol production and the cessation of grain exports to "nations which are manufacturing alcoholic beverages from agricultural products while their people are starving."[27]

The great irony of the tensions over beer is that both sides believed they were working in the interest of food production. Beyond food production too, all parties also concerned themselves with the financial and economic impacts, the creation of lawless black markets, and the political resentments fueled by the prohibition. Still, by the end of 1946 it was becoming difficult to understand why opposition remained, and Bavarian critics of the prohibition began to call into question the competence of the American Military Government. In December 1946 the complete argument for beer was laid out in a pro-brewing memorandum sent by the *Brauwirtschaftsverband Bayern* to Chief Food and Agriculture Officer for the administration of Bavaria, Colonel George R. Quarles. The memorandum detailed the case for beer from raw materials to employment and tax revenue, and from the absence of alternatives to the agricultural value of beer and brewing by-products. The fact that all of these arguments had "already been submitted on a large scale" could only lead the petitioners to conclude that "no office, competent for decision, took pains to take into consideration the real coherence."[28] Quarles was largely won over and forwarded the memorandum, confessing that "this office views the complete suspension of beer production with grave misgivings" and noting the "reduction in the amount of milk delivered to market and...an already precarious fat supply."[29] But such lamentations did not succeed in changing policy. Indeed, his letter came just three days after a different sort of policy change: as relations between the Western Allies and the Soviet Union deteriorated, the British and American authorities had made a decision that would come to further exacerbate agricultural tensions, especially in Bavaria.

The worsening relationship between East and West directly led to an increasing overreliance on Bavarian agriculture. As food scarcity persisted and deliveries of food from the Soviet Zone failed to materialize, the British and American

---

[26] 'Reopening German Breweries', Feb. 16, 1946, letter from Clay to Hilldring, in *The Papers of General Lucius D. Clay: Germany, 1945–1949*, vol. 1, ed. Jean Edward Smith (Bloomington: Indiana University Press, 1974), p. 161.

[27] Here, H. R. 5893, but see also S.J. Res. 149, H.J. Res. 334 and 337, and H.R. 665. 'History of Bills and Resolutions', *Congressional Record* Bound Edition, vol. 92 (1946).

[28] Memo by the *Brauwirtschaftsverband Bayern*, attached to Dec. 5, 1946, letter from Quarles to OMGUS Economics Division, Food and Agriculture Branch, NARA RG 260/390/46/24/3, Box 294.

[29] Ibid.

occupation authorities consolidated their zones into a joint administrative district called the "Bizone" at the end of 1946. American and British authorities claimed that the Bizonal Fusion Agreement was an effort to honor economic unity as agreed in Potsdam, and that the French and Soviet Zones were welcome at any time. In effect, however, it was a further step toward the ultimate division of East and West. The Bizone developed a system by which the British and American authorities would work with representatives of the *Länder* in an effort to ease resource management and food production and circulation.[30] In Bavaria, however, the Bizonal administration galvanized political resentments by levying high food quotas that Bavaria could scarcely meet.[31] As Bavarian Minister of Food, Agriculture, and Forestry Joseph Baumgartner put it in September 1947, "since the merger with the British zone, [the Bavarian] food situation has grown worse from month to month and if this is to be continued we are actually facing catastrophe" in a number of key food sectors. Noting the broader political shift, he emphasized that "the super abundance of the German eastern districts is no longer at our disposal." His own political solution was isolation. In later years Baumgartner would lead the arguably state separatist Bavaria Party, so it may be unsurprising that he demanded "that all food produced in Bavaria, remain in Bavaria."[32] But if his isolationism was a minority opinion, he was certainly not alone in his conviction that the abundance of Bavarian land was not being reaped by Bavarians.[33] The cities and environs of Ansbach and Furth, for example, became sites of unrest as the food supply dwindled, the refugee population swelled, and anti-American resentment peaked.[34]

Tensions around beer followed tensions around food more generally. Each time the Military Government or the Bizonal administration put more demands on Bavarian productivity and cut Bavarian rations, opposition grew. For example, in May of 1947, scarcities exacerbated by the formation of the Bizone led the US Military Government to once again enact a full prohibition restricting even the production of *Dünnbier*. The announcement sent shockwaves reverberating across the Bizone. There were more than forty popular demonstrations in Bavaria

[30] See 'Bizonal Fusion Agreement' and the various amendments to it, in United States Department of State, *Germany 1947–1949: The Story in Documents* (Department of State, 1950), pp. 450–81, esp., p. 450 and pp. 466–7; and 'Speech held by President Hoover in Stuttgart on Feb. 11, 1947', NARA RG 260 390/47/34/1 Box 9.

[31] See, for example, the case of potato export statistics, in 'Bayerns Lieferungen in die britische Zone', NARA RG 260 390/47/34/1 Box 9; the Bizonal office in Frankfurt ultimately admitted that it had placed impossibly high quotas on Bavaria; see Rede des Herrn Staatministers Dr Alois Schlögl am 12.5.1948 im Bayerischen Landtag', BayHStA NL Ehard 1311.

[32] 'Report about an extraordinary Session of the Senior-Council of the Bavarian Landtag', Sept. 5, 1947. NARA RG 260 390/47/34/1 Box 9.

[33] For another such argument, see May 30, 1947, Bavarian Trade Union Federation to Manpower Division of OMGB, NARA, RG 260 390/51/17/2-3, Box 716.

[34] Hans Woller, *Gesellschaft und Politik in der amerikanischen Besatzungszone. Die Region Ansbach und Fürth* (Munich: R. Oldenbourg Verlag, 1986), pp. 256–64.

alone, all producing petitions against the prohibition and the occupation administration itself. According to a widow in Straubing, near Regensburg, the prohibition spoke to her "deepest horrors," and drew the outrage of peasants and workers who were "utterly battered and disgusted and embittered."[35] Brewers in rural areas such as Tann, near the Austrian border, estimated that 80 per cent of their customers were agricultural workers, and that without beer it was unreasonable to expect them to bring in the harvest at all.[36] But the agrarian effects were not limited to Bavaria. Speaking well beyond it, and even beyond the Bizone, the increasingly important BBV issued a decree for the entirety of occupied Germany that was reproduced in publications throughout the Bizone: "without beer—no milk!"[37] And while the full prohibition did not last long, the issue of agrarian mismanagement via the Bizone remained a source of political tension. A broader series of ration cuts led more than a million laborers to go on strike across central Bavaria, from Regensburg and Ansbach all the way to Coburg. At their core, these strikes were about food scarcities that, in many cases, resulted from Bizonal and Allied overreliance on Bavaria.[38] Indeed, in his prescription for quelling the unrest, the president of the Bavarian State Police advised Minister President Hans Ehard to stress to the Bizonal and Allied administration that "Bavaria cannot be treated as only a supply-state."[39]

If many Bavarians imagined themselves the unheard subjects of an extractive and disinterested Allied or Bizonal regime, the reality was somewhat more complex. The twin political uncertainties of Congressional intransigence and deteriorating East–West relations hemmed in the possibility of brewing beer and exerted increased pressure on Bavarian agriculture. In most cases, the American and even Bizonal authorities listened quite closely but simply lacked the political or institutional power to enact lasting change. The Bizone, for example, did give some political power to Germans, but it simply had no mechanism for handling disputes between the *Länder* or between a given *Land* and the Bizonal Executive Council.[40] And while the Bizone undoubtedly exacerbated tensions around food and agriculture, it also ultimately opened the pathway for Bavarian agrarians to

---

[35] June 3, 1947, letter from Lina von Gaehler to Hans Ehard, BaySHtA StK 14541.

[36] June 18, 1947, letter from brewmaster of Gutsbrauerei Greiner Tann to Dr Fritz Höchtel, BayHStA Bayer. Brauerbund 695.

[37] See, for example, 'Brauverbot und Milchverbrauch', *Die Brauwelt*, June 19, 1947; 'Bier her oder—kein Milch!' *Rhein-Ruhr-Zeitung*, Feb. 17, 1948; 'Heil!—Bayerisch Milch', *Neue Ruhr-Zeitung*, Feb. 18, 1948.

[38] 'Bayerns Arbeiter streiken—über eine Million Werktätige folgen dem Ruf ihrer Gewerkschaften', *Frankenpost* Nr. 7, Jan. 24, 1948, p. 1; see also, Woller, *Gesellschaft und Politik in der amerikanischen Besatzungszone*, pp. 292–5.

[39] Jan. 23, 1948 Michael von Godin to Hans Ehard, Willi Ankermüller, and Captain Williams, BayHStA NL Ehard 1311.

[40] March 1948 report prepared by the Civil Administration Division, 'The Evolution of Bizonal Organization', pp. 6–7, University of Wisconsin Digital Collections, http://digital.library.wisc.edu/1711.dl/History.Bizonal.

wield disproportionate influence in the emerging political structures of the west. The Americans, for their part, remained reluctant to change their thinking on beer production. While they released some barley allocations in 1947, US Congress continued to opposed the idea of using grain for the production of beer through to the summer of 1948.

The *Brauverbot* was intended to alleviate caloric scarcity, but in effect exacerbated it due to the role of beer in Bavaria and the overreliance on Bavaria in Bizonal Germany. But as the food system continued to collapse, the Western Allies, and particularly the United States, began to imagine a political shift yet more radical than the formation of the Bizone. In the early summer of 1947, the American Joint Chiefs of Staff (JCS) changed tack from the strategy that had dominated the occupation since 1945. The earlier approach—embodied in the infamous JCS directive 1067, and true to the Potsdam Agreement—was to make no efforts to rehabilitate or maintain the German economy. But in July 1947, a new directive, JCS 1779, came into effect, in part due to pressure from US Secretary of State George Marshall, who believed that national security depended on the economic recovery of Europe. The transition toward economic recovery marked by JCS 1779 also created fertile ground for German-led agricultural recovery. Agrarian politicians, local political leaders, farmers, and brewers already largely agreed on the need for beer. And as German and Bavarian voices took on greater importance—from defeated subjects to fledgling allies—they found their way into offices "competent for decision" and used the production and consumption of beer to enact policy change and transform managerial competence into political authority.

The Politics of Beer and Bavaria Between Provincialism and Federalism

Tensions over food mismanagement and reliance on the Bavarian breadbasket highlighted the relationship between resource management, provincial politics, and broader western German and international administrative structures. Even as the Western Allies began to encourage and revive the western German economy, the US Congress remained skeptical about the utility and politics of rolling back restrictions on beer. Making real policy change to free beer from the unintended repercussions of the *Brauverbot* and excessive wartime taxation required the elevation of Bavarian voices. In several key cases—managing the rationing system, repealing the Allied prohibition, and reworking the tax system—Bavarian voices drove extra-Bavarian policy change. In the first case, in the spring and summer of 1948, a Bavarian-led coalition succeeded in reforming resource management structures in the Bizone by creating a new, flexible ration card which would allow Bizonal Germans to receive either bread or beer. Shortly afterward, as rationing and market restrictions were loosened, Bavarian insistence on the role of beer in a stable food economy moved the Military Government to lift the *Brauverbot*. Finally, after the founding of the West German Federal Republic in 1949, Bavarian politicians succeeded in retaining provincial legal peculiarities that supported rural Bavarian farmers and the tax revenues of the *Länder*. When the new federal parliament rolled back heavy tax legislation in 1950, it was driven by agrarian concerns rooted in Bavaria, and the new tax law ultimately reflected a conception of Bavaria as provincially peculiar but also legislatively instructive for the operation of a functioning federal state. From 1948 to the early 1950s, Bavarian arguments from the preceding years that beer was a boon to agriculture and a crucial part of a functioning food supply chain came to inform the discourse and legislative reforms of the emerging West German state.

While the Allied policy shift represented in JCS 1779 focused on German economic recovery and the political threat of communism, such economic and political arguments about beer failed to spark policy change in the Military Government. In spite of the broad turn toward rehabilitating western Germany in the summer of 1947, the *Brauverbot* remained in effect for more than a year. Beer seems to have stood outside the political imagination of early western anticommunism. In December 1947, one brewery proprietor complained to Hans Ehard that the *Brauverbot* was galvanizing opposition to the American occupation forces, who were "achieving the opposite of what they say and want by strengthening communism."[41] A similar argument appeared in perhaps the single most thorough and comprehensive petition, authored by a dozen trade associations in farming, malting, brewing, transportation, and retailing. Addressed to the Military Governor of Bavaria, Murray Van Wagoner, it played into the deteriorating political situation, noting repeated instances of American intransigence that may well "result in an increase of the radical mind of our population toward the occupation power and serve as propaganda for antidemocratic ideas." It also presented familiar arguments about milk consumption and brewing by-products while speaking to the newfound American interest in German economic recovery. Indeed, it noted that brewing was "a key trade" in Bavaria and beyond, accounting for some 250 million Marks in tax revenue and a quarter of a million jobs in brewing and associated industries.[42] The petition, and these arguments, once again had no effect. Van Wagoner advocated for repealing the *Brauverbot* to Lucius Clay just two days later.[43] But, as we have seen, Clay was already on board with reopening breweries as early as February 1946. When push came to shove,

---

[41] Dec. 2, 1947, letter from Lina von Gaehler to Hans Ehard, BayHStA StK 14541.
[42] Dec. 10, 1947, letter to Van Wagoner, BayHStA Bayer. Brauerbund 695.
[43] Dec 12, 1947, letter from Van Wagoner to Clay, NARA RG 260/390/46/24/3, Box 294.

the issue seems to have come down to a question of resource management and the prohibitionist convictions of US Congress.

In early March 1948, the new Bavarian Minister of Nutrition, Agriculture, and Forestry, Alois Schlögl, explicitly recast the familiar agrarian arguments within the context of recovery. The *Brauverbot*, he claimed, represented an outdated approach to managing Germany, a hangover from the destructive Morgenthau Plan and JCS 1067. Agricultural recovery and food self-sufficiency, he claimed, could only "be resolved when the *cause* [of the scarcities] is removed"—namely, the *Brauverbot*. Drawing attention to the massive caloric value of brewing by-products, he emphasized that beer would not only relieve the loss of milk through farm consumption, but fodder enriched with brewing by-products would both increase milk production per cow and help get animals to slaughter weight quicker.[44] Lucius Clay responded the next day, intimating the ongoing reluctance in Washington. Despite the strength of Schlögl's arguments, and "despite my personal views," the ongoing caloric hardship and grain scarcity rendered it "extremely difficult to explain the brewing of beer from barley in the Bizonal area."[45] For Bavarian agriculturalists, politicians, and brewers, the need for brewing beer was anything *but* extremely difficult to explain: as far as they were concerned, they had been explaining it for years. In the United States, however, brewers and distillers had similarly faced limitations to their grain supply, and Congress faced both industrial and popular pressure to free the domestic drink market.[46] From the perspective of Congress, allowing Germans—who continued to depend on a degree of American food exports—to produce beer while Americans faced their own limitations on using grain for alcohol production was a non-starter.

Efforts to repeal the *Brauverbot* through direct petitions to American power repeatedly proved fruitless, but advocates for beer also worked within their limited legislative options. The combination of Congressional opposition to brewing and regional adherence to stricter production standards meant that the *Brauverbot* was both longest lasting and most profoundly felt in Bavaria. In the British Zone, Germans had been permitted to brew medium-strength beer (above 4 per cent original wort) for several years, and did so through the use of grain malt alternatives such as fruit and whey. Still, Bavarian advocates for beer worked to find allies in the Bizone. In early 1948, advocates for beer in Bavaria and in British-controlled Hamburg joined forces to develop a flexible Bizonal ration card that could be exchanged either for beer or bread. It fell to the Bavarians

---

[44] Mar. 2, 1948, letter from Schlögl to Van Wagoner, BayHStA Bayer. Brauerbund 696. Emphasis added.

[45] Mar. 3, 1948, letter from Lucius Clay to Van Wagoner, NARA RG 260 390/47/34/2-3 Box 15.

[46] See, for example, 'Distillers Won't Reduce Grain Quotas', *The Washington Post* Dec. 18, 1947, p. 1; and 'Time for Common Sense: An Open Letter to the Congress of the United States', *Daily News* (New York), Jan. 19, 1948, p. 29.

to convince other western German leaders to endorse the program. In April, the Mayor of Munich, Karl Scharnagel, wrote to Hans Schlange-Schöningen, the Director for Nutrition, Agriculture, and Forestry in the Administrative Council of the Bizonal Administration in Frankfurt. Scharnagel addressed the many ways that Munich and Bavaria faced unique challenges in the Bizonal structure. He understood that the concerns of Bavarians were not shared everywhere and prefaced his pitch of the beer–bread ration card accordingly: "I know that the importance of this matter [the availability of beer] has not the found necessary understanding beyond Bavaria and is most often ridiculed and laughed at." This defense of provincial peculiarity had appeared in numerous critiques but became a common refrain among Bavarian legislators in subsequent years. Despite the apparent laughability, he went on: "when beer possesses a certain quality, it is actually a foodstuff, most notably for our laboring people."[47] Schlange-Schöningen may have been one of the first Bizonal administrators who sympathized with the Bavarian position and advocated for a federated policy that reflected provincial peculiarity, but other leaders in the Bizonal administration also came to understand that beer filled a vital niche in rural consumption and promoted the ration card.

The key to making the program politically viable was that it was not only pitched as a way to get more beer, but also as a way of improving the food situation in Bavaria and western Germany more generally that did not upset Allied emphasis on bread production. In May 1948, pamphlets were produced in Munich and Hamburg that spread the word around the Bizone that beer played a crucial role in the food economy. The small booklet offered a simple explanation and equation, and pointed out that by sacrificing only a small "sugar-cube sized" portion of bread (another source claims it was 6 grams) per week, consumers could also reap more calories from dairy and meat sources. On the back cover, it concluded that the relationship was win–win–win:

> Agriculture regains its largest and crisis-proof customers for barley and hops and in turn receives valuable feed enrichment from breweries [resulting in] an intensification of the dairy industry, an increase in the bread supply, and extensive pig fattening with a corresponding gain in protein and fat. Beer is a boon to the food- and national economy.[48]

In July, the flexible ration program became a reality, introducing new ration cards with coupons that could be redeemed either for 50 grams of bread or 1.5 liters of

---

[47] Apr. 8, 1948, letter from Karl Scharnagel to Hans Schlange-Schöningen, Bundesarchiv Koblenz (henceforth BAK), Z 6/I 123; thanks to Chris Fojtik for sharing this wonderful letter.

[48] Flier 'Bier lindert die Getränke-Not..', attached to May 11, 1948 correspondence between the Brewers Association of the British Zone in Hamburg and the Bavarian Brewers Association, BayHStA Bayer. Brauerbund 423.

Figure 3.1 "Beer mitigates the drink emergency," BayHStA Bayer. Brauerbund 423. Reproduced courtesy of the Bavarian Brewers Association.

beer.[49] While the ration cards specified that recipients were limited to *Dünnbier*, the thinking was that, over time, beer strength would rise as the meat and dairy economies rebounded.

The ration card program was emblematic of an important transition toward the promise of consumer preference, but it cannot be said to have fixed the problems it addressed. Combined with Congressional intransigence and the currency reform, it even exacerbated them. The currency reform and the rollback of production and price restrictions by Ludwig Erhard, Director of Economics in the Bizone, are often noted as the crucial turning point in the economic recovery of western Germany. The triumphalism of such a conviction does not maintain in the case of beer, where these transitions only made matters worse. Facing Congressional opposition, Erhard did not lift the brewing ban or the heavy wartime tax policies placed on beer and, as a result, beer-related agrarian crises

---

[49] July 15, 1948, 'Ministerial Resolution A/II 1-329/48', sent by Schlögl to Food Offices A and B. BayHStA Bayer. Brauerbund 696.

worsened even as the rest of the economy began to grow.[50] The currency reform compounded the entanglements of the agricultural system and forced the issue of tax reform. As Minister Schlögl explained to Bavarian President Ehard only three days after the currency reform, "an increase in beer consumption seems necessary" both for the caloric importance of beer and for its valuable by-products, and such an increase "can only be achieved by lowering excessive tax." From 1945 to 1947, he offered, the average milk price had not increased while, in the same period, the beer price had close to doubled due to heavy taxation designed to enforce the brewing ban. Fully 80 per cent of beer demand came from rural farmers and,

> with the price of beer at 72 Pfg per liter and a milk price of 24 Pfg per liter, it is obvious that the farmer, in the face of this huge price gap will choose milk instead of beer, which means milk consumption in agricultural areas will increase tremendously in the future.[51]

This was a familiar agrarian argument, but one made all the more urgent by fledgling economic recovery. The introduction of the Deutsche Mark undermined the surplus money and buying power generated by inflationary means of war finance and, as a result, the consumer had to pinch Pfennigs.[52] As they became more conservative in their purchasing decisions, demand for affordable, high-quality beer rose and occupation-strength ersatz beer was rendered unsalable. In the period between the currency reform and the return of full-strength beer, for example, Bavarian sales dropped between 90 and 95 per cent.[53] After the currency reform, as one Bavarian official put it, "the impossible prices will nearly prevent beer sales" and, once again, "much beer will be replaced with milk."[54] The peculiarities of Bavarian consumption thus became an explicitly economic—and not just agricultural—concern due to the prohibition and lingering tax burdens.

It was within this shift from managing scarcity to managing growth that the *Brauverbot* was finally repealed. The Marshall Plan goal of increasing consumption and economic growth required making beer more attractive to western Germans with their new Deutsche Marks. In August 1948 an economic advisory

---

[50] On the lingering importance of American prohibitionism in Congress, see, 'Biersteuer und Prohibition', *Münchner Merkur* Sept. 22, 1948, cited in Birgit Speckle, *Streit ums Bier in Bayern: Wertvorstellungen um Reinheit, Gemeinschaft und Tradition* (Münster: Waxmann Verlag, 2001), p. 57.

[51] June 23, 1948, letter from Schlögl to Ehard, BayHStA NL Ehard 1347; see also July 2, 1948, letter from Schlögl to Verwaltung für Ernährung, Landwirtschaft und Forsten des Vereinigten Wirtschaftsgebietes in Frankfurt, BayHStA MELF 1334.

[52] Michael L. Hughes, *Shouldering the Burdens of Defeat: West Germany and the Reconstruction of Social Justice* (Chapel Hill: University of North Carolina Press, 1999), p. 29; and Dirk Götschmann, *Wirtschaftsgeschichte Bayerns. 19. und 20. Jahrhundert* (Regensburg: Verlag Friedrich Pustet, 2010), pp. 408–13.

[53] Bayerischer Brauerbund e.V., *Geschäftsbericht 1948*, p. 10.

[54] Memorandum marked only 'received July 21, 1948', NARA RG 260 390/47/34/2-3 Box 15.

committee on brewing in the Bizone concluded that beer with such a high price would never be bought while the alcohol content and nutritional value were so low.[55] Bavarian voices were again the loudest. The Bavarian Brewers Association and the Bavarian Farmers' Association were joined by the Administration of Food, Agriculture, and Forestry in the United Economic Area in advocating repeal. On September 15, 1948, they succeeded, and Military Government Regulation 12-303.4 approved their petition, thereby lifting the *Brauverbot*.[56] As long as resources existed, stronger beer could be produced; whether it would be bought was a different issue. It was the currency reform and the hopes of economic growth that finally lifted the brewing ban, but these two alone would not be enough to fix the rural consumption problem—there needed to be tax reform. There, as in the ration card program and in the repeal of the *Brauverbot*, the logic of policy change was rooted in a strongly Bavarian argument about the relationship between beer and agricultural life. Such convictions would come to shape both parliamentary discourse and tax legislation in the young Federal Republic.

Just as the *Brauverbot* was lifted, Bavarian leaders brought the question of beer to other broader western German legislative questions—namely, the issue of taxation and the plans for a federal fiscal structure. Already at the Constitutional Convention in Herrenchiemsee in August 1948, the Bavarian Finance Minister Johann-Georg "Hans" Kraus (CSU) advocated that the beer tax should remain the preserve of individual German states. Kraus was a member of the Weimar-era BVP and a financial policy adviser to then Bavarian president Heinrich Held (1924–1933), thus bringing direct experience of the Weimar-era debates. His position became a CSU staple in the deliberations of the Committee on Questions of Finance (*Ausschuß für Finanzfragen*), which helped author the West German constitution or Basic Law (*Grundgesetz*). Most members of the committee viewed the beer tax as akin to any other consumption-based tax, but for the Bavarians, the legacies of alleged federal overreliance on a regionally strong industry in the 1920s and early 1930s remained palpable. The CSU proposal was initially rejected in the Finance Committee in October 1948, but by February 1949, under renewed pressure from the Allies and the president of the Parliamentary Council, Konrad Adenauer, the Finance Committee ultimately conceded the point on the beer tax.[57]

The fight was far from over, however. Early formulations granted the *Länder* autonomous retention of the beer tax in order to simply keep the larger constitutional conversation moving. The relevant sections of the draft of the Basic Law

---

[55] Aug. 2, 1948, signed Hans Podeyn, Director of the VELF, BayHStA Bayer. Brauerbund 696.

[56] See, for example, Sept. 22, 1948, 'Niederschrift über die 8. Sitzung des Beirats des Bayerischen Brauerbundes', BayHStA Bayer Brauerbund 696.

[57] On the pressure from Adenauer and the Allies, see, 'Einleitung', in *Der Parlamentarische Rat, 1948–1949: Akten und Protokolle*, vol. 12 Ausschuß für Finanzfragen, ed. Michael F. Feldkamp and Inez Müller (Munich: Harald Boldt Verlag, 1999), p. IL; on the initial rejection, see 'Sechzehnte Sitzung des Ausschusses für Finanzfragen—13. Oktober 1948', in ibid., pp. 475–82.

noted that a financial equalization system should be developed at a later date. The committee's working drafts of the Basic Law made explicit that the proviso was designed to "take into account the special interests of the state of Bavaria."[58] And, to be sure, the "special interests" of Bavaria went far beyond the beer tax; the so-called Free State of Bavaria did not even ratify the Basic Law, agreeing only to go along with it as long two-thirds of the other *Länder* ratified it. As the Basic Law came into effect, it kept the door open to debate about federal equalization. It established a written precedent for the Federal Republic that was the product of a long and contentious history of German integration—rooted in the Reserve Rights of 1871 and deeply influenced by the fiscal equalization structures of the Weimar Republic.[59]

The question of the beer tax landed on the national legislative stage quite quickly when it was the subject of several hours of parliamentary debate from December 1949 to July 1950. The first federal elections, in August 1949, had put the CDU/CSU at the head of the government coalition, but only by a razor thin margin, making the Christian Social Union (CSU) a crucial factor in the emerging political system. The Bavaria Party (BP) also did quite well and, between the two, Bavaria-specific parties accounted for more than 10 per cent of the parliament. The first wave of debate centered on tax retention by the *Länder*, the second on repealing the excessively high tax rates of the Nazi and Allied governments. Toward the end of 1949, both the BP and the CSU submitted petitions under which the *Länder* would retain beer tax revenues in perpetuity. As the statements from Solleder that opened this chapter suggest, the ensuing debate over the measure was not a conventional dispute over tax policy. Very little attention was paid to the fiscal issues at stake, projected budgets, or the like. Instead, the peculiarities of Bavarian culture were front and center. Parliamentarians from the BP and the CSU were joined by other Bavarians from national parties ranging from the liberal Free Democratic Party (FDP) to the more illiberal populist Economic Reconstruction Union (WAV). Reading the debates, it can be difficult to tease out how this was an issue of fiscal policy at all. At the core of it was the sense that the role of beer in Bavaria—which comprised the actual content of the debates—depended on a decentralized regional brewing industry that would be decimated by centralized taxation. And, indeed, in the years before the war, Bavaria had almost 2,800 breweries producing more than 20 hectoliters of beer per year—a number that nearly doubled the 1,506 found in the rest Germany combined.[60]

---

[58] 'Vorschlag des Fünfer-Ausschusses für die dritte Lesung des Grundgesetzes im Hauptausschuß— Stand vom 5. Febr. 1949', in *Der Parlamentarische Rat, 1948–1949: Akten und Protokolle*, vol. 7 Entwürfe zum Grundgesetz, ed. Michael Hollmann (Boppard am Rhein: Harald Boldt Verlag, 1995), pp. 339–95, esp. 386, Art. 138 c-4.

[59] See Chapter 1, and Article 106 of the *Grundgesetz*.

[60] 'Verteilung der Brauereien auf Süd- und Norddeutschland im Rechnungsjahr 1936/37', *Mitteilung der Wirtschaftsgruppe Brauerei und Mälzerei* 6 (1939): p. 143.

The finer points of industrial decentralization and, for that matter, tax revenue, however, were all but displaced by the insistence that Bavarian cultures, lifeways, and labor structures depended on beer. Advocates exchanged barbs with hecklers from industrial regions and the political left who critiqued claims of Bavarian difference as laughable at best, and separatist at worst. Proponents of Bavarian interests repeatedly insisted that the differences were real. Joseph Baumgartner, for example, now a representative of the BP, made the familiar point that beer was a necessity for laborers, especially Bavarian farmers, who now numbered about 9 million, in part because, unlike in other parts of West Germany, there were scant alternatives.[61] Further stressing the issue of laborers, Solleder (CSU) emphasized how farm hands would happily embrace their work if "at 8 o'clock in the morning" they have "a liter of beer, a *Leberkas*, and a couple of *Laiberl!*" Having used the Bavarian dialect in reference to common southern foods *Leberkäse* (a kind of baked forcemeat) and seeded rolls, he went on, as quoted earlier, to justify the quotidian importance of beer to the "ladies and gentlemen from the northern districts," insisting that "it is part of our way of life!"[62] Beyond Bavarian-specific parties, the conviction that Bavarian culture needed translation to other parts of West Germany transgressed party- and place-based identities. Hans Wellhausen, for instance, was an FDP parliamentarian hailing from the culturally contested Franconian region of northern Bavaria. He testified that drinking milk at mealtimes, as so many Bavarian farm workers had been forced to do, is not appropriate for the Bavarian spirit (*Gemüt*): "It does not matter whether you understand that or not. It is a fact."[63] Wellhausen's statements are interesting because, as a Franconian, he was both insider and outsider to Bavarian culture. Indeed, speaking on the subject again seven months later, Wellhausen had to stop to correct an SPD heckler who accused him of being Bavarian—a telling accusation—by noting that in fact he was from "the nine-hundred-year-old city of Nuremberg."[64]

As that exchange suggests, the discursive and legislative stakes of these parliamentary sessions centered on tensions of centralization and provincialism. At their most grandiose, the debates swung between accusations of separatism and deployments of the Nazi past. As the debate wore on, tensions rose. An SPD representative claimed there was no legal justification for the decentralized fiscal structure, while others blasted the Bavarians for borderline separatist antifederalism. Responding to the charges, Anton Besold of the BP shot back "I admit that it is simpler to build a centralized state eliminating the jurisdiction of the *Länder*; and it may be faster too because one can ignore the interests of minorities. But do not forget what we have just behind us." Flipping the charge of

---

[61] *Plenarprotokoll*, Deutscher Bundestag 22. Sitzung, Dec. 9, 1949, pp. 705–6; for farm labour statistics, see, Götschmann, *Wirtschaftsgeschichte Bayerns*, p. 488.
[62] *Plenarprotokoll*, Deutscher Bundestag 22, pp. 706–7.
[63] *Plenarprotokoll*, Deutscher Bundestag 22, p. 708.
[64] *Plenarprotokoll*, Deutscher Bundestag 77. Sitzung, July 19, 1950, p. 2766.

radicalism, he went on that in a centralized state, "a majority decision that suppresses minority rights may suffice, but in a federal state structure, higher statesmanship would have to prevail."[65] Claims for "higher statesmanship" from a former Bavarian separatist and monarchist (a member of the *Bayerische Heimat- und Königspartei* until 1947), should be taken with a boulder of salt. Still, the Bavarians maintained that they were not asking for more than fair treatment. It was in this context that Solleder eloquently insisted on the responsibility that the parliament had to consider issues specific to Bavaria just as thoroughly and fairly as those specific to Berlin or Heligoland. Even if the issue takes place on "Bavarian soil, [it] nonetheless remains just as German."[66]

After much debate, the measure passed, making the beer tax the only consumption-based tax to be retained by the states. But if the issue of tax revenues was settled, much work was still to be done to lower excessively high tax rates on beer. Both issues had long-term continuities and short-term causes. The question of fiscal federalism was one that had unfolded over the course of decades, rooted in 1871, but had been triggered most directly by the promises of the Constitutional Convention to account for Bavarian interests. The question of the tax rate was rooted in the historically decentralized nature of the Bavarian brewing industry, but took on immediate importance in the context of economic recovery. Across the political spectrum, all parties agreed that the beer tax was too high to encourage consumer spending. As Schlögl had pointed out as early as 1948, beer had been rendered practically unsalable thanks to high tax rates first levied by the Nazi regime and later increased in the occupation period. In overturning the tax rates, as in all questions of beer, Bavarian idiosyncrasies again loomed large. In particular, the issue centered on small-scale production and how to tax appropriately according to brewery size. In 1950, for example, Bavaria produced almost 6.4 million hl of beer, compared to 10.3 million in the rest of West Germany. But, as had been the case for at least the last century, it did so differently. In the early 1950s, the average Bavarian brewery produced about 3,700 hl, compared to roughly 8,300 hl in an average non-Bavarian brewery.[67] To compound matters further, Bavaria was also home to a remarkable number of small-scale brewers producing less than 20 hl a year. These *Hausbrauer*, or home brewers, were an almost uniquely Bavarian phenomenon. In the years before the war, Bavaria was home to 35,650 *Hausbrauer*, compared to only 4,271 in the rest of Germany.[68] At the core of parliamentary debate was a conviction that smaller breweries should not be taxed as much as large-scale producers.

---

[65] *Plenarprotokoll*, Dec. 9, 1949, pp. 710–11.   [66] Ibid., p. 707.

[67] Calculated from Bayerischer Brauerbund e.V., *Geschäftsbericht 1951/52 und 1952/53*, pp. 118 and 124.

[68] 'Verteilung der Brauereien auf Süd- und Norddeutschland im Rechnungsjahr 1936/37', p. 143.

In May, June, and July of 1950, the Bundestag debated numerous proposals that sought, in different ways, to grant the *Länder* the power to set and adjust their own tax rates. The thinking was that the peculiarities of the brewing industry in different *Länder* would require *Land*-specific tax rates. Ultimately, such proposals were rejected, and the 1950 Beer Tax Law, or *Biersteuergesetz*, which finally dramatically lowered the tax rate in August of that year, set national standards for tax rates. Internalizing the core of the debates, the rates were tiered, with higher taxes for both production quantity and strength of beer produced, and, in short, the reform roughly halved the tax rate on beer. The biggest sticking point, as the debates ensued, was the massive number of *Hausbrauer* in Bavaria. According to the new Federal Finance Minister (and founding member of the CSU), Fritz Schäffer, the issue was, "a local, decidedly Bavarian matter." Now reversing the rhetoric of Solleder that Bavarian affairs are national affairs, Schäffer claimed that the *Hausbrauer* question remained beyond the scope of the federal state, which had no reason "to intervene in the affairs of a *Land*...and do away with old rights and customs."[69] This about-face logic underwrote a practical tax exemption for *Hausbrauer*, who produced quantities of beer below the lowest tier of the new Beer Tax Law. Ultimately, parliamentarians from different parties yielded on the paradox of Bavarian logic, agreed, as they were, that the foremost issue was passing the law so that the market sector could recover. If Bavaria preferred to receive no tax revenue from its smallest producers, so be it.

Once approved by the Allied High Commission, the law went into effect in August 1950, and took its final shape in 1952.[70] In the estimation of the Bavarian Brewers Association, it was a windfall that "created a sound basis for the comeback of the [West] German brewing industry."[71] The 1950 tax disputes, like the flexible ration card and the repeal of the *Brauverbot*, reflect the extent to which Bavarian agrarian, political, and cultural interests could shape West German policy. What emerged out of the occupation was a West German state that relied on and privileged Bavarian agriculture and internalized the Bavarian conviction that the production and consumption of beer played an important role in a stable and productive agrarian and economic system. The point here is not to suggest that advocating for beer was somehow *the* central goal of Bavarian politics or of the (Bavarian-dominated) agrarian system. Instead, beer was integrated into agrarian and political discourse in Bavaria as a result of the scarcity of the immediate postwar period and the competing Allied and German claims to managerial competence. Even in the semi-sovereign Federal Republic of 1950, the importance of

---

[69] *Plenarprotokoll*, July 19, 1950, p. 2763.
[70] *Biersteuergesetz in der Fassung vom 14. März 1952 mit Durchführungsbestimmungen zum Biersteuergesetz (BierStDB) in der Fassung vom 14. März 1952* (Nuremberg: Brauwelt Verlag Hans Carl, 1952).
[71] Bayerischer Brauerbund e.V. *Geschäftsbericht 1950*, p. 16.

beer to agricultural workers and the peculiarities of the decentralized brewing industry shaped national policy decisions.

Conclusion

In the immediate postwar years, many regional and local political leaders, agriculturalists, farmers, and brewers located beer at the heart of agricultural and economic stability. This conviction emerged in several parts of occupied Germany, but nowhere as fully as in Bavaria. And, as the western zones came to lean on the new Bavarian breadbasket, the convictions of Bavarian agriculturalists carried greater political weight. Local and regional leaders, professional organizations, and agrarians found themselves managing daily subsistence and scarcity within shifting political constellations from the early heavy-handed military government, to the Bizonal Administration in Frankfurt, and, ultimately, the legislature of the Federal Republic. Operating within myriad political uncertainties, Bavarian convictions about the importance of beer for food self-sufficiency and economic recovery shaped emerging governmental structures, from rationing systems to new taxation policies. Political administrators, rural leaders, and heads of professional and labor organizations learned that beer was a particularly well-suited medium through which to assert their political viability vis-à-vis the occupation authorities and the new federal government.

Beer was not the be-all and end-all of postwar politics, but it does highlight a fundamental shift in the political economy of the German states. It took on increased political significance in the immediate aftermath of the war because of the conditions of scarcity and division. Long-standing practices and conceptions of beer—as a foodstuff, as liquid bread, as a part of stable rural life—that may have never taken on more significance than their provincial realities, became part of Allied deliberations and parliamentary debates precisely because of these postwar conditions. The balance of provincial power in Germany, long dominated by the Prussian north, shifted dramatically as the far east was shorn off and what remained was aligned with the Soviet Union. The long-standing German food system, which had depended on Prussian land and, since the late 1930s, on a racial war of conquest and agrarian extraction, collapsed in the late 1940s. The emergence of Bavaria as the new breadbasket of western and, ultimately, West Germany, meant that Bavarian agrarian interests took on new importance. The case of beer highlights but one example in which Bavarian convictions and practices came to inform the emerging agricultural, economic, and political structures of the Federal Republic.[72] By the early 1950s, then, the market was

---

[72] For a thorough analysis of the entanglements of Bavarian agriculture in both the Federal Republic and integrating Europe, see Gerhardt, *Agrarmodernisierung und europäische Integration.*

open, agriculture was on the rebound, tax rates were favorable, and, importantly, taxation receded as a political flashpoint between the *Länder*. That all being the case, we turn now to the so-called "miracle years" in which West Germany entered an unprecedented boom of about two decades and in which beer, and particularly Bavarian conceptions of beer, shaped everything from consumer culture to global stereotypes.

4

Brewing up a New Old Germany

Production, Consumption, and Social Order in the Miracle Years

In September 1963, Bitburg brewer and advertising expert Dr Theobald Simon addressed an international beer advertising conference in Munich. In his remarks, he applauded the successes of industry-wide public relations, or community advertising (*Gemeinschaftswerbung*), in making beer the West German people's drink. Beyond branding, *Gemeinschaftswerbung* had transformed beer into a "drink of conviviality and sociability...for young and old, for man and woman, and for everyone."[1] By the next year, West Germans had quadrupled their per capita beer consumption since 1950, and by the end of the decade, beer became the single most consumed beverage nationwide.[2] Such a transformation was far from certain. The Allied prohibitions, soaring tax rates, and lingering material scarcities combined to keep both the quality and quantity of beer production well below pre-war levels into the mid-1950s. Becoming West Germany's favorite drink a decade and a half later was no small feat. And while pent-up demand can explain part of the explosive growth, it would be a mistake to assume that beer consumption would simply bounce back out of some German consumer essentialism. Indeed, many brewers worried that decades of temperance moralizing and, most importantly, an overwhelming marketplace of choices would lead Germans to simply stop drinking beer. The turn to community advertising in the 1950s and 1960s was part of an industrial effort to solidify beer in the West German consciousness. But Simon was only partially correct in his triumphalism; consumption patterns continued to break along conventional lines such as social class, regionalism, and gender.

For all its shared qualities and community-building potential, beer was part of a conservative restoration by which political stability went hand-in-hand with the heavy labor of reconstruction and the hardening of conventional gender norms. In the first two decades of the Federal Republic, the drink emerged as a symptom

---

[1] 'Zehn Jahre Deutsche Bier-Gemeinschaftswerbung', speech by Theobald Simon delivered at the Internationaler Bierwerbe-Kongress held in Munich, 4–6 September, 1963, Bayerisches Hauptstaatsarchiv (henceforth BayHStA) Bayer. Brauerbund 443.

[2] 'Bier: Sieg der Flasche', *Der Spiegel* 43 (October 21, 1964), 54; 'Der Deutschen liebster Saft', *Der Spiegel* no. 33, (1968), p. 34.

A Nation Fermented: Beer, Bavaria, and the Making of Modern Germany. Robert Shea Terrell, Oxford University Press.
© Robert Shea Terrell 2024. DOI: 10.1093/oso/9780198881834.003.0005

and a symbol of uneven reconstruction; it refreshed laborers and lubricated sociability in the wake of dictatorship while also reinforcing social hierarchies and enabling Germans to define a new national culture. Beer followed a similar trajectory to that of other intoxicants that had been subjected to moralizing, critique, and prohibition throughout Europe and the United States. In the second half of the century, substances from tobacco to whiskey became "emissaries of freedom and prosperity...[and] symbols of good living and worldliness."[3] But, crucially, the economic boom and the rapid expansion in the production and consumption of beer was also undergirded by less self-congratulatory processes, including the silencing of the Nazi past and a restoration of normative gender inequalities. The rapid growth of beer in West Germany was thus part of a much larger process of political and economic stabilization predicated on the construction of a male producer-citizen and a female consumer-citizen.[4] At the intersection of advertising and consumption, beer informed an emerging pleasure-oriented mode of consumption that buttressed the central role of economic growth in West German political stability. Historian Julia Sneeringer has noted that "leisure and consumption for pleasure, more than the political arena," provided the opportunity "to produce new forms of identification and understanding of one's own culture."[5] And, to be sure, the intersections of social practice and deliberate meaning-making help reveal how beer transformed from something Germans drank into something with which Germans identified.

Contrary to the claims of brewers, advertisers, and journalists, beer became the drink of West Germany not simply because it was popular, but because it helped create a new old Germany. This was a Germany where structures of inclusion, from broadly conceived advertisements to ordoliberal policy, papered over provincial differences, social inequalities, and the legacies of National Socialism. This chapter explores the rise of the new old Germany through two concurrent shifts: first, the rise of community advertising and brewers' efforts to present a unified German culture, and, second, the ways that patterns of consumption depended on normative forms of public and private sociability. For many brewers, the tensions between national and provincial interests shaped industry approaches to the market in the 1950s and 1960s. During this time, West German and Bavarian brewers developed parallel campaigns of *Gemeinschaftswerbung*. The existence of

[3] Hasso Spode, 'Trinkkulturen in Europa: Strukturen, Transfers, Verflechtung', in *Die kulturelle Integration Europas*, ed. Johannes and Christiane Weinand (Wiesbaden: VS Verlag für Sozialwissenschaften, 2010), p. 380.

[4] Mark E. Spicka, 'Gender, Political Discourse, and the CDU/CSU Vision of the Economic Miracle, 1949–1957', *German Studies Review* 25, no. 2 (May, 2002): pp. 305–32; Erica Carter, *How German is She? Postwar West German Reconstruction and the Consuming Woman* (Ann Arbor: University of Michigan Press, 1998); Alice Weinreb, *Modern Hungers: Food and Power in Twentieth Century Germany* (Oxford: Oxford University Press, 2017); and Frank Trentmann, *Empire of Things: How We Became a World of Consumers, from the Fifteenth Century to the Twenty-First* (New York: Harper Collins, 2016), pp. 308–10.

[5] Julia Sneeringer, '"Assembly Line of Joys": Touring Hamburg's Red Light District, 1949–1966', *Central European History* 42 no. 1 (Mar. 2009): pp. 65–96, here p. 96.

twin regional and national advertising platforms evinces the ongoing tensions between Bavaria and the nation. Such divisions, however, would ultimately become the target of advertising itself. Advertisers ultimately sought to displace long-standing tensions between the industries and cultures of the major beer-producing regions. Advertising content and consumption patterns reveal the ways that beer increasingly bound together West Germans of various stripes as they worked to rebuild the nation. Still, any visions of social unity not only papered over persistent regional differences but were also built on conventional social hierarchies in both advertising and the social practices of consumption.

Uncertain Beginnings and Parallel Paths: Brewers and the World of Goods, 1946–1954

Emerging out of the war, the brewing industry as a whole was disheveled, divided, and disorganized. The western zones of occupation and the early Federal Republic were marked by provincial and provisional dynamics. These included, and go far beyond, the case of agricultural policy and fiscal structures discussed in the previous chapter, permeating all social facets, from competing visions of organizing political and cultural space to the structures and practices of commercial life.[6] In the brewing sector, most trade organizations, such as the Business Groups and Brewers Associations, were outlawed by the occupation authorities after capitulation in 1945. In most parts of Germany, nominal trade organizations ranged from single breweries operating in the name of collective interests to informal associations between select companies. The Bavarian Brewers Association was reconstituted in May 1946, making it the first major brewing trade organization of the postwar era. The nationwide German Brewers Association was not resurrected until 1949. The three-year disparity both testifies to the uncertain and provisional nature of western Germany in the occupation years and reflects the extreme devastation of the economy more generally, and brewing specifically. Only a handful of breweries had been permitted to brew full-strength beer for the Allied occupation forces, and this reality created both economic hardships and resentments. As the Bavarian organization put it, the chaotic economic conditions of 1945–1949 "lead to a certain weariness...The spirit of solidarity suffered severely under the demoralizing influences of the postwar period, and many believed it was better to elbow through economic struggle rather than to close ranks and struggle shoulder-to-shoulder for the common goals of the trade." Such a state of affairs

---

[6] Peter Jakob Kock, *Bayerns Weg in die Bundesrepublik* (Stuttgart: Deutsche Verlags-Anstalt, 1983), pp. 33–7, 116–30; see also Jeremy DeWaal, 'Redemptive Geographies: The Turn to Local Heimat in West Germany, 1945–1965', (PhD diss., Vanderbilt University, 2014), pp. 142–240.

and a perceived lack of industrial "self-awareness" led many brewers to worry that the industry as a whole may not last in the expanding market of the early 1950s.[7]

Concerns about industrial solidarity were thrown into sharp relief by the promise of economic recovery. Lingering agricultural scarcities and an increasing American commercial presence combined to produce a general sense among brewers that they would not be able to compete in the emerging market. While we might assume demand for beer far outweighed supply, brewers themselves mostly worried that demand for everything else far outweighed that for beer. And, indeed, in March 1949, only 11 per cent of West Germans regarded beer as their drink of choice. The high price and low quality made it a less attractive purchase than milk, coffee, tea, wine, and liquor.[8] But, while brewers largely agreed that they should band together to heal the "spirit of solidarity" and navigate the rapidly competitive marketplace, any sentiment of unity was racked by concerns about regionally distinct consumer bases. At the regional and national levels, brewers embraced a collective approach, resurrecting Weimar-era plans for *Gemeinschaftswerbung*, or community advertising, which would promote beer as a type of commodity regardless of brand.[9] For the trade organizations of both Bavaria and West Germany, an approach revolving around beer devoid of brand seemed well suited for embedding beer in the popular consciousness of consumers on the precipice between extreme scarcity and an ostensibly overwhelming world of goods. The war and postwar scarcities may have made quality beer a distant memory, but it was nonetheless a familiar good—and this familiarity could be both an advantage and a disadvantage, as American economic power and European market integration made foreign goods accessible. In the early 1950s, the two trade organizations embarked on twin community advertising operations. These advertising wings provided a cornerstone of economic growth that would come to shape the culture of consumption in subsequent decades. It is both ironic and a testament to ongoing provincial tensions that such efforts at solidarity and communal benefit developed simultaneously in Bavaria and in West Germany more broadly. Focusing on their origins and approaches reveals how they drew on divergent political and cultural repertoires in an effort to speak to different communities.

By 1951, the German Brewers Association founded an Advertising and Publicity Department (*Werbe- und Propagandaabteilung*), which was replaced

[7] Bayerischer Brauerbund e.V. *Geschäftsbericht 1949*, p. 3.

[8] Elisabeth Noelle and Erich Peter Neumann, eds., *Jahrbuch der öffentlichen Meinung, 1947–1955* (Allensbach am Bodensee: Verlag für Demoskopie, 1956), pp. 35–8.

[9] See Chapter 1; Theobald Simon, *Die Werbung der Brauereien* (Nuremberg: Verlag F. Carl, 1931), pp. 123–6; and Dirk Schindelbeck, 'Werbung für Alle? Kleine Geschichte der Gemeinschaftswerbung von Weimarer Republik bis zur Bundesrepublik Deutschland', in Clemens Wischermann, Peter Borscheid, and Karl-Peter Ellerbrock, eds., *Unternehmenskommunikation im 19. und 20. Jahrhundert: neue Wege der Unternehmensgeschichte* (Dortmund: Ges. für Westfälische Wirtschaftsgeschichte, 2000), pp. 63–97.

two years later by a separate legal entity called the *Bierwerbe GmbH*.[10] This nationwide organization fused long-standing German approaches to advertising with international insights and successes. First and foremost, while legally independent, the *Bierwerbe* was effectively in-house; a common German approach that only very gradually lost ground to American-style full-service advertising agencies. Aesthetically too, ads by the *Bierwerbe* resurrected an earlier aesthetic form of German advertising that was simple and bold, with minimal text; a form, it should be noted, that had almost seamlessly blurred into political propaganda.[11] Still, brewers overlooked such continuities—willfully or otherwise—claiming their approach drew inspiration from American advertising titan Coca-Cola, which had produced, "the best advertisement in the beverage industry, namely the well-known, well-designed Coca-Cola cap." They took a cue to adopt bright colors, to keep the design simple, to press metal signs, and to incorporate three-dimensionality in print ads. As they told the trade organization membership, "we are not at all ashamed to admit that American advertising not only inspired us, but has also, to a certain extent, created a route to be followed given the existing competition between beer and non-alcoholic beverages."[12]

What emerged from these combined commitments was the flagship ad of the *Bierwerbe*, the so-called Blue Medallion. The image featured a blue oval with the word "beer" written in yellow and accompanied by a frosty glass of beer. There were variations on the theme that included slogans like "fresh beer" or "cold beer," but often it was just the lone word "beer." From its inception, the West German organization set its sights on a market-saturation approach convinced, as it was, that "only through continuous advertising can something stay in the consciousness of the public."[13] In its first year, the Blue Medallion was plastered across West Germany; upwards of 300,000 signs and posters were produced, paid for with a communal budget of 900,000 DM, generated by collecting 10 Pfennigs per hectoliter from member breweries.[14] Such campaigns expanded as the *Bierwerbe* became a sister organization to the Brewers Association, launching massive and consistent advertising initiatives ranging from posters to ads in magazines and newspapers and, eventually, on radio and television.

---

[10] Jan. 1, 1951, Notes on the 12th meeting of the Advisory Committee of the Bavarian Brewers Association, BayHStA Bayer. Brauerbund 1338.

[11] Pamela Swett, *Selling under the Swastika: Advertising and Commercial Culture in Nazi Germany* (Stanford: Stanford University Press, 2014), pp. 31, 109–10; and Molly Loberg, *The Struggle for the Streets of Berlin: Politics, Consumption, and Urban Space, 1914–1945* (Cambridge: Cambridge University Press, 2018).

[12] 'Die Biergemeinschaftswerbung 1951', memo dated only 1951, BayHStA Bayer. Brauerbund 441; on the embrace of American approaches, see Pamela E. Swett, S. Jonathan Wiesen, and Jonathan R. Zatlin, eds. *Selling Modernity: Advertising in Twentieth-Century Germany* (Durham: Duke University Press, 2007), pp. 11–12.

[13] 'Die Biergemeinschaftswerbung 1951'.   [14] Ibid.

Figure 4.1 Heinz Fehling, "Blue Medallion," reproduced courtesy of the German Brewers Association.

While the *Bierwerbe* and the Blue Medallion emerged at the national level, the Bavarian Brewers Association pursued a path that was both complementary and discordant. Bavarian brewers shared concerns with their West German colleagues regarding the fate of beer in the expanding marketplace. Convinced of regional difference, however, the Bavarian Brewers Association doubted that plastering Blue Medallions everywhere was an adequate strategy for the Bavarian market. Indeed, in 1951 Bavarian brewers nearly torpedoed the fledgling national advertising approach by threatening to pull out altogether. They worried about provincial cultural differences, demanding that "it is imperative to pay more attention to the Bavarian mentality."[15] At the same time, their arguments about the peculiarities of the Bavarian industry—its decentralization and higher rates of production and consumption—resonated with other regional organizations in Baden-Württemberg and North Rhine-Westphalia. The former saw themselves more aligned in culture and industry composition to their southern neighbors than to the northern *Länder*. The latter, representing the second most productive brewing region in West Germany, claimed that they would only join if Bavaria did so on

---

[15] Jan. 1, 1951, Notes on the 12th meeting of the Advisory Committee of the Bavarian Brewers Association, BayHStA Bayer. Brauerbund 1338.

even financial footing and regardless of regional industrial and cultural differences.[16] In an effort to pacify Bavarian concerns, the German Brewers Association offered the position of head of the *Bierwerbe* to Willy Hübsch, a brewer from the city of Augsburg and head of the Swabian district office of the Bavarian Brewers Association. Determined not to be the source of further industry acrimony, the Bavarian organization decided to take part in West German community advertisements while also forming a separate Bavarian counterpart, the *Bayerischer Bierwerbeverein*, which would design ads unique to Bavaria.[17]

Throughout the 1950s, Bavarian brewers paid for and received Blue Medallions and other community advertisements from the *Bierwerbe*, as well as those of the regionally specific *Bayerischer Bierwerbeverein*. The latter took a markedly different approach than the former in both method and content. Rather than consistent market saturation, the approach was more similar to interwar approaches that were periodic and seasonal. In its first year, the *Bayerischer Bierwerbeverein* focused on a series of press events (roughly one per month) that covered issues such as technological developments in the malting and bottling sectors, brewery histories, the history of the *Reinheitsgebot* in Bavaria, and the health benefits of beer. The events were initially proposed to keep public attention on beer during the seasonal sales dip in the winter months between Oktoberfest and Starkbierzeit, which corresponded roughly with Lent in early spring.[18] This was a fully Bavarian approach. Not only was the *Reinheitsgebot* not yet a national touchstone (the subject of the next chapter) but the very chronology of the campaigns was based on two Bavarian, or, more broadly, southern events, rooted in Catholicism and Bavarian politics and culture.

The main thrust of Bavarian collective advertisements from the 1950s to the early 1960s was an explicit effort at regional place-making. The central tagline, "in Bavaria you drink beer" (*In Bayern trinkt man Bier*), appeared in the first print ad by the *Bayerischer Bierwerbeverein*. It was designed by Munich graphic artist Max Bletschacher in September 1952 and reflected not a nationwide embrace of beer but rather cultural and political provincialism. The aesthetics echo not Coca-Cola, but rather political posters of decades past. The fist in the air and the Bavarian flag on the mug may have resonated with the fact that in 1950 the Bavaria Party won 17.9 per cent of the state parliament and by 1954 became part of a ruling coalition in Bavaria with the SPD and the FDP, thereby keeping the once and future dominant CSU out of power for three years. The trade organization produced 60,000 copies of this poster which they sent to Bavarian breweries

---

[16] Apr. 4, 1951, letter from Dr Richard Biergans to the Bavarian Brewers Association, BayHStA Bayer. Brauerbund 1338.

[17] Jan. 1, 1951, Notes on the 12th meeting of the Advisory Committee of the Bavarian Brewers Association.

[18] Oct. 3, 1950, letter from Seeberger to the Presidium and Director Pfülf, BayHStA Bayer. Brauerbund 1338.

Figure 4.2 Max Bletschacher, "In Bavaria you drink beer," Bayerischer Brauerbund e.V., *Geschäftsbericht 1951/52 und 1952/53*, insert. Reproduced courtesy of the Bavarian Brewers Association.

for internal décor and public promotion. Beyond this particular image, the campaign, *In Bayern trinkt man Bier*, is both an imperative to visitors and a conceptual association of a place and the nature of being there. In some cases, this association became quite literal. Beginning in the last days of March 1953, travelers arriving at the Munich Central Train Station were greeted by a banner two meters high and thirty meters long painted in the Bavarian blue and white and reading simply "In Bayern trinkt man Bier."[19] Bookended by the annual

[19] Bayerischer Brauerbund e.V. *Geschäftsbericht 1951/52 und 1952/53*, p. 75.

Starkbierzeit in late March and the closing of the annual Oktoberfest, the banner hung in the train station for six months of high-traffic tourism and travel into the city from the Bavarian countryside and from West Germany more broadly. For all its Bavarian specificity, the simplicity of the statement and its invitation to drink also resonated with the emergence of Bavaria as a jovial tourist destination in "a nation burdened by the recent past and beleaguered by the present."[20]

In spite of the tensions between Bavarian and West German advertising initiatives, both trade organizations agreed that community advertising was particularly useful for navigating the combined difficulties of lingering scarcity and a rapidly expanding marketplace. As an article in the trade journal *Deutsche Brauwirtschaft* counseled, community advertising plans were the best strategy for garnering the attention of the increasingly powerful and overwhelmed modern consumer. The author cited an increase in the standard of living and an expanded supply and diversity of consumer goods that dwarfed the available choices of the previous generation. The truth of the "economic miracle," the author argued, is that "the consumer alone decides. In a free market economy, the consumer is completely free with regard to their purchases... but their decisions are capable of being influenced." Community advertising, he went on, was designed to work with brand advertising but on a deeper level of consumer consciousness. In the apparently (or potentially) overwhelming consumer landscape of the 1950s, community advertising was designed to shape consumer culture: "to get people interested in the good as a whole," to ensure that "people want beer instead of cigarettes."[21] Such a concern was not limited to West Germany; lingering postwar scarcities also led Dutch brewers to adopt community advertising in 1949, to great effect, nearly doubling per capita consumption in less than a decade.[22] Brewers throughout West Germany embraced community advertisements in hopes of ensuring industry success in the rapidly expanding world of goods. Still, the existence of twin Bavarian and West German ad campaigns suggests that brewers were not unanimous in their understanding of the consumers and communities in question. The Bavarian organization developed an approach that resonated with political and cultural provincialism. It was designed to account for such provincialism—the "Bavarian mentality"—and in the process reinforced and reproduced it—*in Bayern trinkt man Bier.*

In the course of the 1950s and early 1960s, economic, political, and social stabilization began to assuage the initial fears of many brewers that they would be left behind. The increasing availability of material goods and the promise of socially inclusive economic growth eased political tensions and sold many West

---

[20] Adam T. Rosenbaum, *Bavarian Tourism and the Modern World, 1800–1950* (Cambridge: Cambridge University Press, 2016), p. 237.

[21] Theobald Simon. 'Werbung für Bier—ein notwendiges Übel oder eine zwingende Notwendigkeit?' *Deutsche Brauwirtschaft* no. 12, June 9 (1953): pp. 169–71.

[22] Theobald Simon, *Werbung für Bier* (Nuremberg: Verlag Hans Carl, 1960), pp. 90–2.

Germans on the structures of the new West German state.[23] Socially and culturally too, the structures and practices of belonging were changing. West Germans increasingly distanced themselves from their immediate pasts, forming new cultures in the opulent but geopolitically polarized world of the 1950s and early 1960s.[24] Within these transitions, producing, buying, and enjoying beer not only helped signal increased stability and plenty; it led the way. Tellingly, between 1945 and 1964 beer sales outpaced increases in real income by a third.[25] This was possible not just because the market restrictions and agricultural scarcities of the 1940s were undone, but also because of the meanings producers and consumers attached to beer. Producers, for their part, explicitly worked to position beer as part of a pleasure-based consumer mentality. Consumers, in turn, were happy to embrace both drinking itself and the broadly emergent culture of consumption. It would be an oversimplification to suggest that advertisements simply established the meanings of beer, but analyzing advertisements in conjunction with consumption patterns does reveal how producers and consumers jointly contributed to a "consumption regime" in which conventional values were projected onto fledging mass consumption.[26]

A Drink of All Germans?

In the course of the 1950s and 1960s, the social and political function of consumption changed dramatically. The hardships of the "Hunger Years" had both encouraged and rewarded saving and frugality. But, beginning in the 1950s, the "mentality of scarcity" was increasingly displaced by a new consumption regime in which West Germans understood consumption to be enjoyable.[27] The history

---

[23] S. Jonathan Wiesen, 'Miracles for Sale: Consumer Displays and Advertising in Postwar West Germany', in David F. Crew, ed., *Consuming Germany in the Cold War* (Oxford and New York: Berg Publishers, 2003), pp. 151–78; Mark Spicka, *Selling the Economic Miracle: Reconstruction and Politics in West Germany, 1949–1957* (New York: Berghahn Books, 2007).

[24] For only a brief list of thematic examples, see, Carter, *How German is She?*; Robert G. Moeller, *War Stories: The Search for a Useable Past in the Federal Republic of Germany* (Berkeley: University of California Press, 2001); Frank Biess, *Republik der Angst: eine andere Geschichte der Bundesrepublik* (Reinbek bei Hamburg: Rowohlt Verlag, 2019); and Monica Black, *A Demon-Haunted Land: Witches, Wonder Doctors, and the Ghosts of the Past in Post-WWII Germany* (New York: Metropolitan Books, 2020).

[25] 'Bier: Sieg der Flasche'.

[26] I use 'consumption regime' in the sense developed in Victoria De Grazia, 'Introduction: Changing Consumption Regimes', in Victoria De Grazia and Ellen Furlough, eds., *The Sex of Things* (Berkeley and Los Angeles: University of California Press, 1996), pp. 11–24.

[27] Michael Wildt, 'Plurality of Taste: Food and Consumption in West Germany during the 1950s', *History Journal Workshop* 39, no. 1 (1995): pp. 24–6; and Arne Andersen, 'Mentalitätenwechsel und ökologische Konsequenzen des Kosumismus: Die Durchsetzung der Konsumgesellschaft in den fünfziger Jahren', in *Europäische Konsumgeschichte: Zur Gesellschafts- und Kulturgeschichte des Konsums (18. bis 20. Jahrhundert)*, ed. Hannes Siegrist, Hartmut Kaelble, and Jürgen Kocka (Frankfurt a.M.: Campus Verlag, 1997), pp. 763–92.

of beer both supports and nuances this interpretation. Community advertisements and consumer patterns in the 1950s suggest that consumption did in fact become more enjoyable, but also that it remained enmeshed in evolving hardships. Rampant food scarcities and the condition of occupation no doubt receded, but the difficulties of rebuilding, often through heavy labor, complicated the transition from scarcity to opulence. While brewers and advertisers sought to make beer the drink of all West Germans—and while West Germans came to drink a remarkable amount of beer by the mid-1960s: over 120 liters per capita—the drink was embraced unevenly across the Federal Republic. Sales and consumption broke along social fault lines including place, profession, and gender. While the next section focuses more centrally on issues of gender, here, community advertisements and demographic data illuminate some of the ways in which the embrace of beer and pleasurable consumption was not a uniform process but, rather, was fundamentally shaped by labor and locale.

Beer became a pillar of postwar consumerism in no small part because of the efforts of the brewing trade organizations to embed it in the public consciousness. And while the direct influence of advertisements is difficult to gauge, in 1953 the Nuremberg-based market research institute, the Society for Consumer Research (*Gesellschaft für Konsumforschung*, or GfK) found that community advertisements had a positive influence on West German consumers and that they were more readily recognizable than brand-specific ads.[28] The brewing industry itself also strongly believed in their success. In the course of the 1950s, nationwide beer production dramatically surpassed pre-war levels and the German Brewers Association largely credited the rise in demand to the successes of the *Bierwerbe* in capturing the minds, and Marks, of West German consumers.[29] The cultural messages "encoded" by advertisers, to borrow the language of Stuart Hall, does not readily translate into linear "decoding" by consumers. And, indeed, the social practices of consumption generate their own meanings, often quite divorced from advertising or other strategic efforts at persuasion.[30] Still, bringing together advertising content and consumption patterns suggests that producers and

---

[28] 'Die Einstellung der Verbraucher zum Bierkonsum', GfK S 1953 013–1, pp. 118–19, 127.

[29] H. Pfülf, 'Wo stehen wir?' Sept. 28, 1957, BayHStA Bayer. Brauerbund 339a. The Bavarian Brewers Association also boasted to their membership that their own community advertising was delivering and well worth the additional money paid. See Bayerischer Brauerbund e.V. *Geschäftsbericht 1953/54*, pp. 65–6.

[30] Stuart Hall, 'Encoding/decoding', Hall, ed., *Culture, Media, Language: Working Papers in Cultural Studies, 1971–1979* (London: Routledge, 1980), pp. 117–27; and Wim van Binsbergen, 'Commodification: Things, Agency, and Identities: Introduction', in Wim van Binsbergen and Peter Geschiere, eds., *Commodification: Things, Agency, and Identities (The Social Life of Things Revisited)* (Münster: Lit Verlag, 2005), pp. 9–53, esp. p. 46; John Brewer and Roy Porter, eds., *Consumption and the World of Goods* (London: Routledge, 1993); Jeremy Prestholdt, *Domesticating the World: African Consumerism and the Genealogies of Globalization* (Berkeley: University of California Press, 2008), p. 8; Michael R. Redclift, 'Chewing Gum: Mass Consumption and the "Shadow-lands" of the Yucatan', in John Brewer and Frank Trentmann, eds., *Consuming Cultures, Global Perspectives: Historical Trajectories, Transnational Exchanges* (Oxford and New York: Berg, 2006), pp. 167–88, esp. p. 179.

consumers alike used beer to construct new forms of sociability. Both producers and consumers associated beer with pleasure and reprieve. Brewers and advertisers moved away from the provincial peculiarities seen in the previous section and even worked to downplay them in the name of a shared national culture. Consumers, for their part, integrated the purchase and consumption of beer into the rhythms of daily life in the miracle years.

In the 1950s, the content of community advertisements shifted to reflect the state of the economy and the concerns of consumers. Focusing in on the very earliest advertisements helps to make the point. At the turn of the 1950s, the *Bayerischer Bierwerbeverein* had initially attempted to attract consumers by locating beer within the scarcity mentality of the immediate postwar world. More than a half a dozen black and white advertisements tied beer to values and concerns that emerged out of the occupation and testified to the scarcity mentality of the early 1950s. According to the main Bavarian trade publication, these ads were quite explicit in their effort to "bring awareness to the meaning of beer and its by-products for human and animal nutrition."[31] They built on discourses first popularized in the occupation period, spanning from the agricultural value of by-products to the nutritional benefits of brewers' yeast. They compared the caloric value of beer, beef, bread, fish, butter, and eggs, and emphasized the increased productivity of milk cows reared on feed enriched with spent brewers' grain. These ads were clearly designed to attract consumer interest in beer for very practical nutritional and agricultural reasons. A legacy of the hunger years in general, and the struggle against Allied regulations on beer in particular, these ads sought to capitalize on the prominent place of scarcity among the concerns of consumers. It is hardly surprising, then, that they were sidelined by 1954. Not only did beer production across West Germany return to pre-war levels that year, but also, compared to 1948, unemployment had decreased by half and output across industries had tripled.[32]

By the mid-1950s, community advertisements reflected consumer concerns not with managing scarcity but with navigating economic recovery and locating pleasurable consumption within the realities of daily life. Advertisements in the mid-1950s departed dramatically from those of earlier years, displaying beer as part of a fun-loving and pleasurable form of consumption to be enjoyed after work, in the home, and in public recreational settings. One ad designed specifically for Carnival featured anthropomorphized glasses of beer, dancing and kissing, smiling and licking their lips. Another promoted the leisure of summer vacation by depicting an iconic beach town at a distance, foregrounded with a frosty beer glass and reading simply, "summer...sun...cool beer." This iconography was,

---

[31] Bayerischer Brauerbund e.V. *Geschäftsbericht 1951/52 und 1952/53*, p. 74.
[32] Unemployment and output statistics from Konrad H. Jarausch, *After Hitler: Recivilizing Germans, 1945–1995* (Oxford: Oxford University Press, 2008), p. 89.

for many West Germans, quite divorced from their lived realties. While the *Bundesländer*, and later the federal government, instituted minimum vacation days in the 1950s, most West Germans did not travel very far, making sunny beach idylls (at least beyond the Baltic and North Seas) more aspirational than realistic.[33] And, indeed, passive leisure more generally was often at odds with labor-driven economic recovery. In spite of generally improving trends nation-wide, income inequality remained rampant in the 1950s and the working class, including skilled workers, was chronically overworked and underpaid. Many workers felt forgotten by their state, with some 40 per cent in 1955 claiming they were more valued by the Nazi regime than the young Bonn Republic. Wages and purchasing power undoubtedly increased across the board, but blue-collar wages remained 20–25 per cent lower than the national earnings average.[34] Labor itself proved extremely demanding, resting at least as much on old-fashioned sweat and elbow grease as it did on modernization and mechanization. Until the 1970s, West German workers maintained a 48-hour work week, and, even as their wallets fattened, one worker recalled that "not much time remained for having fun after work."[35]

Accordingly, brewers and advertisers also actively worked to locate beer and pleasurable consumption within the labor realities of the 1950s. And it was here, more than anywhere else, that the *Bierwerbe* actively sought to use beer to bridge regional differences in the name of national recovery. Bavaria and North Rhine-Westphalia—the two largest beer regions in the Federal Republic—at first appear as different as two *Länder* could be. Most readily, they represent polar opposites of German society, culture, and history: rural, agricultural, majority Catholic, and traditionally Austria-facing on the one hand, and urban, industrialized, majority Protestant, and Prussian on the other. Their divergent historical trajectories likewise informed and manifested in disparate practices of production and consumption. Take, for example, the composition of the regional brewing industries. Between them, Bavaria and North Rhine-Westphalia produced close to 60 per cent of all beer in West Germany in 1957. But where Bavaria was home to nearly 2,000 smaller, decentralized breweries, North Rhine-Westphalia had fewer than 200, producing far more beer per company. Bavaria accounted for only 17 per cent of large-scale breweries nationwide—those producing more than 120,000 hl per year—but was home to 78 per cent of those producing less than 15,000 hl.[36]

Regional differences also factored into different cultures of consumption. While beer loomed large in Bavarian or Rhenish culture—different though they

[33] Sneeringer, '"Assembly line of Joys"', fns. 30 and 32.
[34] Hans-Ulrich Wehler, *Deutsche Gesellschaftsgeschichte: Fünfter Band, Bundesrepublik und DDR, 1949–1990* (Munich: Verlag C.H. Beck, 2008), pp. 153–7.
[35] Quoted in Jarausch, *After Hitler*, p. 89.
[36] Bayerischer Brauerbund e.V. *Geschäftsbericht 1956/57 und 1957/58*, calculated from tables on pp. 154 and 156–7.

were—it was far less important in other parts of Germany, like, for example, Schleswig-Holstein in the far north. Beer was a quotidian mass consumer good with deep, if provincial, historical roots, and those remained palpable in consumption patterns. According to one market research report in 1953, beer consumption was "all but predestined" by where West Germans lived and worked.[37] More than half of all surveyed respondents in Bavaria (52.4 per cent) claimed to drink beer regularly. In North Rhine-Westphalia just over 40 per cent (41.4 per cent) declared the same. Precisely what "regularly" meant was not specified, but it indicates how respondents understood their own consumption habits. Both numbers should be read against a national average of 38.2 per cent and the regional low from Schleswig-Holstein (26.5 per cent).[38] Low beer consumption usually aligned with the existence of alternative drinks and well-established cultures of consumption. Survey correspondents in Ratzeburg and Timmendorfer Strand in Schleswig-Holstein reported that beer bars were simply not visited with the frequency seen elsewhere and that locals preferred to drink spirits. Such habits of local consumption also manifested in Baden-Württemberg where, in spite of beer having a well-defined cultural presence, locals tended to drink more wine and must (*Most*). From Lörrach to Crailsheim, on opposite sides of Baden-Württemberg, respondents may have enjoyed beer, but they had nonetheless relegated it to a drink for special occasions. In their day-to-day lives, they drank cheaper fermented beverages based on available fruits and often produced at home.[39]

If regional traditions and cultures of production and consumption informed where beer was and was not regularly enjoyed, labor most directly informed the ubiquity of consumption. The excessively high consumption rates in both Bavaria and North Rhine-Westphalia reflect not only vibrant brewing sectors, but also the fact that the two *Länder* were West Germany's most important agricultural and industrial states. Here, as elsewhere, beer represented a pleasurable commodity but one that captured just how closely consumption was tied to hard labor. In their down time, farmers and industrial workers were significantly more likely to consume beer than those in other professions. During the work week, farmers and heavy laborers were, respectively, two and three times more likely to drink beer on work breaks than civil servants and white-collar workers.[40] Farmworkers in Swabia included beer as part of their worktime snacks (*Brotzeit*), especially during the hot months and at harvest time. In mining towns around Dortmund and Duisburg too, beer was integrated into the balance of labor and leisure. Consumption spiked on paydays in particular but, as one survey administrator put it, "beer consumption is simply considerable" among miners who seek to

[37] 'Die Einstellung der Verbraucher zum Bierkonsum', p. 40.   [38] Ibid., pp. 41–2.
[39] Ibid., pp. 43–5.   [40] 'Die Einstellung der Verbraucher zum Bierkonsum', pp. 58, 83.

"quench their thirst" after a day of "very hard physical labor." Even during the work day, blue-collar workers were between three and four times more likely to drink beer on the job—often in factory canteens—than their white-collar counterparts.[41] By the late 1950s, the regional brewing industries of Bavaria and North Rhine-Westphalia were fully aware of the connection between beer and physical labor. In response, they collaborated to develop a new campaign for the *Bierwerbe* that emphasized beer as a reward for a hard day's work. The campaign stressed that beer was so refreshing and rewarding that it even made the experience of thirst enjoyable: "*Bier macht den Durst erst schön.*" In a flagship print ad, a smiling glass of beer drips with condensation legible as sweat. In 1958 the slogan went on to be the foundation of a ten-minute film shown to theatergoers across the Federal Republic, and by 1960 it was "on every tongue."[42] In laboring communities, particularly in Bavaria and North Rhine-Westphalia, beer played an important role in making the toil of reconstruction bearable—and even enjoyable.

macht den *Durst* erst *schön*

Figure 4.3 Thomas Abeking, "Beer makes thirst enjoyable," reproduced courtesy of the German Brewers Association.

---

[41] Ibid., pp. 60, 79.
[42] Bayerischer Brauerbund e.V. *Geschäftsbericht 1958/59 und 1959/60*, p. 89.

While the realities of provincial differences in lifestyle and culture undoubtedly remained, by the late 1950s and early 1960s the brewing industry had not only found common ground—as in the case of *Bier macht den Durst erst schön*—but they also began actively working to downplay regional differences. On an institutional level, this is most abundantly clear in the fact that the *Bayerischer Bierwerbeverein* was incorporated into the West German *Bierwerbe* in 1962. The organization that had been created in the name of the peculiar "Bavarian mentality" quietly became a national subsidiary. But such an effort is clear in public relations work too. Since the mid-1950s, the *Bierwerbe* had been accepting submissions for songs they could produce for circulation at festivals and at drinking establishments—songs that provided "a valuable contribution to the design of a sales-favorable atmosphere."[43] Part of that project was explicitly avoiding highlighting cultural difference. In 1964, for example, a composer from a small town in central Bavaria wrote to the Bavarian Brewers Association promoting his hymn "*Sauf Bruder, sauf*" (swig, brother, swig). The lyrics, composed in Bavarian dialect and featuring a yodeling refrain, focused on a distinctly provincial culture with local, agricultural, and Catholic references. In his response, the director of the Bavarian trade organization declined to promote the song to the *Bierwerbe*. The dominant position of beer in the West German beverage market, he claimed, had everything to do with it being "regarded as a national drink." The distinctly Bavarian flair of the song, he went on, "is in no way in harmony with the target approach of our advertisements. Moreover, we do not believe that the diction of the song would be well received throughout Germany."[44] By the mid-1960s, then, concerns about Bavarian peculiarity had given way to minimizing provincial difference in the name of national success.

It was in this moment that the president of the *Bierwerbe*, Theobald Simon touted the successes of advertising in making beer the West German people's drink.[45] From 1950 to 1956 West German beer consumption per capita doubled, and by 1960 it had tripled. By 1964 West Germans had quadrupled their beer consumption, drinking an average 122.4 liters per person per year. This figure amounts to a liter of beer every three days and includes men, women, children, and the abstinent.[46] Such a development is particularly striking in light of the fact that the postwar prohibition had been overturned only 16 years earlier, and beer production had surpassed pre-war levels only 10 years earlier. In some ways, drinking beer had become a collectively West German experience—perhaps

---

[43] Feb. 11, 1963, letter from Werner Schladenhaufen to the membership of the Bavarian Brewers Association, BayHStA Bayer. Brauerbund 1340.

[44] See correspondence between Werner Schladenhaufen and Carl Jung in July and August 1964, BayHStA Bayer. Brauerbund 1340.

[45] 'Zehn Jahre Deutsche Bier-Gemeinschaftswerbung', speech by Theobald Simon delivered at the Internationaler Bierwerbe-Kongress held in Munich, September 4–6, 1963, Bayerisches Hauptstaatsarchiv (henceforth BayHStA) Bayer. Brauerbund 443.

[46] 'Bier: Sieg der Flasche'.

analogous in aspiration to sociologist Helmut Schelsky's "leveled middle-class society" (*Nivillierte Mittelstandgesellschaft*)—and, as in other commercial sectors, the embrace of material stability and pleasure-based consumption was a crucial component of West German stabilization. The political appeal of Ludwig Erhard's promise of "prosperity for all" became a cornerstone of what it meant to be a West German, and drinking beer appeared to be part of that. As Erica Carter has written, "the transition to popular affluence" was less about "the mass accumulation of wealth than the recasting of everyday life."[47]

But what *kind* of Germany was recast in the 1950s? It was not, of course, "leveled" or homogenous. First, in spite of industrial efforts to minimize them, it was a Germany with strong provincial cultures and traditions. In the same year that the head of the Bavarian Brewers Association declined to advocate for "*Sauf Bruder, sauf,*" annual per capita consumption surpassed 200 liters in Bavaria, dwarfing the national average of 122.4. Still, such differences lost much of their political and economic vibrancy; the brewing industry downplayed them and separatist political movements faded into the background.[48] The fist in the air and the imperative that "*In Bayern trinkt man Bier*" quietly receded even if it remained true that in Bavaria, they drank a lot of beer. Second, and related, this was a Germany where economic growth became a key part of stabilizing public life and sociability in the aftermath of dictatorship. That thirst became enjoyable under the promise of beer spoke to both solidarity between industrial and agricultural workers and a respectable conviviality to be found on breaks and after work. Finally, while differences including geography and profession informed variations of West German life, one distinction—gender—remained perhaps the most important.

Gendering Beer in Private and Public Life

The stabilization of West German society in the first postwar decades depended on the re-establishment of conventional values. The core of such values was the paternalistic family which, throughout the immediate postwar decades, was simultaneously propped up and limited by everything from legislative reforms and state welfare programs to economic practices and the modes of consumerism.[49]

---

[47] Carter, *How German Is She?*, p. 59.

[48] The Bavaria Party, for example, experienced its highest electoral successes both in state and federal elections between 1949 and 1954. By the early 1960s it held no seats in the Bundestag and less than 5 percent (and falling) in the Landtag.

[49] Robert G. Moeller, *Protecting Motherhood: Women and the Family in the Politics of Postwar West Germany* (Berkeley: University of California Press, 1993); Elizabeth D. Heineman, *What Difference Does a Husband Make? Women and Marital Status in Nazi and Postwar Germany* (Berkeley: University of California Press, 1999), esp. 137–75; Alexander Badenoch, 'Time Consuming: Women's Radio and the Reconstruction of National Narratives in Western Germany, 1945–1948', *German History* 25, no. 1

This latter sphere was particularly important in and far beyond West Germany, functioning as "the lynchpin of the conservative restoration" across western Europe and the United States.[50] In West Germany, political stabilization relied upon a gendered bifurcation of male producer-citizens and female consumer-citizens.[51] The rapid growth of beer consumption in West Germany both depended on and contributed to emerging forms of public and private sociability from bar talk to family life. Political and social stabilization in West Germany depended on economic growth, and the advertisements, consumption patterns, and social norms of drinking beer aided in recasting gendered norms of sociability. Beer consumption, as a behavior, in turn contributed to shaping a stable West German society.

Up to this point we have seen how beer functioned in the material lives of heavy laborers, most of whom were men, but the conservative restoration in West Germany also hinged on the marginalization of women in public life. Perhaps not surprisingly, men made up the vast majority of waged laborers in the 1950s, precisely because of state regulations that supported a male breadwinner model and restricted full-time employment for married women. On the level of representation, community advertisements for beer, like so many other commercial representations, evince a broader social transformation of women from public laborers to sexualized objects. In one of the earliest community advertisements—from the era of the "scarcity mentality"—a milkmaid foregrounds a comparison of milk yields from dairy cows with and without feed enriched by brewing by-products. The advertisement speaks to consumers' interests in optimizing nutrition and the presence of the milkmaid seems obvious, reflecting the social reality of the labor of women in the immediate postwar period. Just a few years later, in the context of emerging notions of pleasure-based consumption, another woman appears, but here the woman is more objectified, sexualized, and passive. Dressed in a bathing suit, she smiles and waves at the viewer while the text plays, perhaps, on a gendered moniker for beer—kühle Blonde, or cool blonde. The female form marked a radical departure from both the milkmaid and the late 1940s iconic "woman of the rubble."[52] For many, once again, the imagery would have been aspirational, capturing a scene from a beach vacation that only a few would have taken. Still, it targeted men, sexualizing the woman and equating both her and beer with the simple pleasures of growing stability. As Heinrich Tappe wrote of beer advertising more generally, while women occasionally appeared as beer

(Jan. 2007): pp. 46–71; and Alexandra Ruble, *Entangled Emancipation: Women's Rights in Cold War Germany* (forthcoming with University of Toronto Press, 2023).

[50] Trentmann, *Empire of Things*, p. 309.

[51] Erica Carter, *How German is She?*; Spicka, 'Gender, Political Discourse, and the CDU/CSU Vision of the Economic Miracle, 1949–1957'; and Weinreb, *Modern Hungers*, pp. 122–95; and Trentmann, *Empire of Things*, pp. 308–10.

[52] See further, Elizabeth Heineman, "The Hour of the Woman: Memories of Germany's 'Crisis Years' and West German National Identity," *The American Historical Review* 101, no. 2 (Apr. 1996): pp. 354–96.

Figure 4.4 Heinz Fehling, "Cool Beer," reproduced courtesy of the German Brewers Association.

drinkers themselves, more often than not they were framed as "an erotic reward or prize" for male beer drinkers into at least the 1970s.[53]

Beyond representation, the social norms of beer consumption also reveal the gendered dynamics of bourgeois models of the individual and the family. In the early 1950s, West German women tended to drink beer in public only when accompanied by men; according to West German consumers, to imbibe in public without male company would be considered "crude" (*unfein*) and "improper" (*unpassend*).[54] Such convictions mirrored those of the past; as recently as the Nazi period, beer consumption had remained beyond the boundaries of feminine propriety.[55] Advertising personnel in the brewing industry—and far beyond it—no doubt recognized women as an untapped consumer market. In the late 1950s, they developed campaigns to appeal to women as beer drinkers. However, the series, known as "the woman

---

[53] Heinrich Tappe, 'Der Genuß, die Wirkung und ihr Bild. Werte, Konventionen und Motive gesellschaftlichen Alkoholgebrauchs im Spiegel der Werbung', in *Bilderwelt des Alltags: Werbung in der Konsumgesellschaft des 19. und 20. Jahrhunderts. Festschrift für Hans Jürgen Teuteberg*, eds. Peter Borscheid and Clemens Wischermann (Stuttgart: Franz Steiner Verlag, 1995). pp. 222–41, here p. 234.
[54] 'Die Einstellung der Verbraucher zum Bierkonsum', pp. 62, 77.   [55] See Chapter 2.

with the blouse," got almost no ad space in leading women's publications such as *Madame, Nachrichten für die Hausfrau,* and *Frauenwelt.*[56] Such publications remained focused on an emerging culture of domesticity and the role of the housewife in managing domestic affairs. By this point, women had been largely hemmed in by the paternalist and pro-natalist government of Konrad Adenauer, and social norms and cultural representation kept pace. While women's part-time employment was ramping up in the 1950s, marginalization remained palpable, especially for married women, who faced bureaucratic hurdles to being viewed as real workers by the welfare state.[57] In the male-breadwinner model of the 1950s, one telling community advertisement simply proclaimed that beer "fosters sociability." It portrays a markedly normative sexual sociability, featuring male and female glasses of beer kissing; the male glass knowingly eyeing the viewer. Sociability, in this context, meant explicitly heteronormative and ultimately reproductive sexuality.

While women drank far less beer than men, they bought far more of it in their roles as managers of the modern household. Already in 1953, West German women were disposing of 73 per cent of expendable household income, versus 27 per cent by men, a trend that continued into the 1960s.[58] Moreover, women were readily aware of their new responsibilities for domestic stability and growth. As one article in *Nachrichten für die Hausfrau* put it, " 'The economy' is not a process that takes place far away...We are all a part of the economy, because we are all consumers...More than 100 billion [DM] passed through a woman's hand in the year 1959."[59] In their role as consumers, then, West German women increasingly played a crucial role in economic and political recovery in the Federal Republic. In the case of beer, the policies and practices that buttressed the emergence of the consuming housewife went hand-in-glove with changes in technology, from packaging to domestic appliances. As part and parcel of an emerging consumer Cold War between the two Germanys—and the American and Soviet spheres generally—Federal Economics Minister Ludwig Erhard developed programs to improve material life by subsidizing domestic technologies such as refrigerators (in 1953) and washing machines (in 1955).[60] Ordoliberal market regulation fed

---

[56] For the specifics of the ad campaign and the plan to saturate women's magazines, see Bayerischer Brauerbund e.V. *Geschäftsbericht 1956/57 und 1957/58*, pp. 87–8; in the course of research, however, the author found no single instance of the ad being printed in any of these magazines.

[57] Christine von Oertzen, *The Pleasure of a Surplus Income: Part-Time Work, Gender Politics, and Social Change in West Germany, 1955–1969* (New York: Berghahn Books, 2007), p. 72.

[58] 'Die Bedarfsstruktur im Käufermarkt', August 1953 survey by the GfK, p. 21, qtd. in Heinz Pritzl, 'Die absatzwirtschaftliche Bedeutung der Verpackung für Bier' (PhD diss., Hochschule für Wirtschafts- und Sozialwissenschaften Nürnberg, 1956), pp. 33–5; H. Zurnidden, 'Mehr Haushaltsgeld durch Einkaufs-Disziplin', *Nachrichten für die Hausfrau* 6, no. 12 (Dec. 1959): p. 14.

[59] 'Die Milliarden der Hausfrau', *Nachrichten für die Hausfrau* 7, no. 9 (Sept. 1960), pp. 22–3.

[60] In the East German case, see Mark Landsman, *Dictatorship and Demand: The Politics of Consumerism in East Germany* (Cambridge: Harvard University Press, 2005) and Weinreb, *Modern Hungers*, pp. 164–95.

Figure 4.5 Thomas Abeking, "Beer fosters sociability," reproduced courtesy of the German Brewers Association.

the gendered politics of consumption—or, as one 1955 campaign advertisement put it: "Erhard helps the housewife."[61]

The technologization of domestic space, particularly the proliferation of refrigerators, influenced what products were appealing and how they could be consumed privately. Women's magazines encouraged the conviction that refrigerators were "no longer a luxury" and that women could have "more free time with a contemporary kitchen."[62] By the early 1970s, 91 per cent of all West German homes had a refrigerator, making it the single most common household appliance—even more common than a radio.[63] This development directly overlapped with the

---

[61] Jan Logemann, *Trams or Tailfins?: Public and Private Prosperity in Postwar West Germany and the United States* (Chicago: University of Chicago Press, 2012), pp. 41–2.

[62] Ursula Höpfl, 'Auf die Reihenfolge kommt es an!' *Nachrichten für die Hausfrau* 5, no. 11 (Nov. 1958): pp. 10–16, esp. p. 11; Juno advertisement, *Madame* (June 1957), p. 109; see also Heinz Bohnenkamp, 'Physik im Haushalt—Technik im Haushalt', *Madame* (June 1957), pp. 120–4, 128–48.

[63] Elisabeth Noelle and Erich Peter Neumann, eds., *Jahrbuch der öffentlichen Meinung, 1968–1973* (Allensbach am Bodensee: Verlag für Demoskopie, 1974), pp. 399–400.

dramatic increase in sales of bottled beer.[64] Before the First World War, bottled beer accounted for only 8 per cent of all beer sold. Bottled beer first outsold barreled in 1951, and by the early 1960s it accounted for 75 per cent of all West German beer sales.[65] As a result, throughout the "miracle years" beer was increasingly drunk with meals in the home, and in front of radios and televisions. Domestic magazines and beer ads featured advice on how to pair beer with meals, what glassware to use, and other tips for incorporating beer into the West German nuclear family lifestyle. The brewing industry, for its part, worked to incorporate beer in the new domesticity. For example, a 1958 ad campaign by the *Bierwerbe* focused on the many benefits of bottled beer. In practical terms, bottled beer stayed fresh longer and, because it was primarily consumed at home, cut down on drunk driving. But perhaps most importantly, having bottled beer in the house kept the family together. In one image from a brochure distributed at points of sale, a child is shown playing with both parents while they enjoy a bottled beer at home.[66] While men did much of their drinking outside the home, domestic consumption likewise reinforced newly emerging ideals of a gentle father figure that could replace the authoritarian, military father of decades past.[67] And while the woman also appears as a beer drinker, she remains safely framed within the confines of traditional domesticity.

Drinking beer at home had a public component: shopping. From 1953 to 1964, an average middle-class family of four nearly tripled their monthly monetary expenditures on beer.[68] Even in the capital of public beer culture, Munich, 91 per cent of the population reported drinking beer in their home and 71 per cent reported that they made a habit of always keeping a supply of bottled beer on hand.[69] By the end of "the boom," beer was by far the most commonly purchased item at West German grocery stores and corner shops. In 1973, for example, 67 per cent of West Germans recalled buying beer in the last two weeks. By contrast, evaporated milk and margarine came in second, at 50 per cent each, with coffee just behind at 49 per cent; chocolate, yogurt, wine, and tea came in at between

---

[64] See further Nancy Bodden, *Business as Usual? Die Dortmunder Brauindustrie, der Flaschenbierboom und die Nachfragemacht des Handels 1950 bis 1980* (Dortmund and Münster: Gesellschaft für Westfälische Wirtschaftsgeschichte e.V., 2019), pp. 120–1.

[65] 'Flaschenbier: Fassbier—in Prozenten vom Gesamtausstoss', Bayerischer Brauerbund e.V. *Geschäftsbericht 1956/57 und 1957/58*, p. 166; 'Bier: Sieg der Flasche'.

[66] Correspondence between the Bayerischer Bierwerbeverein e.V. and the Bayerischer Brauerbund regarding 'Viele tausend Flaschen'. BayHStA Bayer. Brauerbund 1334.

[67] Till van Rahden, 'Wie Vati Demokratie lernte: Religion, Familie und die Frage der Autorität in der frühen Bundesrepublik', in *Demokratie im Schatten der Gewalt: Geschichte des Privaten im deutschen Nachkrieg*, ed. Daniel Fulda, Dagmar Herzog, Stefan-Ludwig Hoffmann, and Till van Rahden (Göttingen: Wallstein Verlag, 2010), pp. 122–51.

[68] 'Der westdeutsche Getränkemarkt', GfK S 1962 046, tbl 17 in both the original study and in the appendix extending the data to 1964.

[69] 'Trinkgewohnheiten der Münchner Stadtbevölkerung und Markenbilder ausgewählter Brauereien', GfK S 1964 029, tbls 2 and 3; see further, 'Untersuchung über Trinkgewohnheiten für Bier und Image für ausgewählte Brauereien bei der Stadtbevölkerung Würzburgs', GfK S 1964 031, tbls 2, 19, 22, and 33.

40 and 20 per cent.[70] A package of tea certainly lasts longer than a bottle of beer, but the point is precisely the frequency of purchase: beer was on West Germans' minds and shopping lists and constituted the most frequent expenditure of their commercial lives. Buying beer was tied to both local and distant identities. In urban areas such as Düsseldorf, grocery stores promoted thematic bundles like "Altbierfest," selling local Hannen Altbier alongside smoked ham and Emmentaler cheese from the Allgäu Alps in Bavaria—a sale that catered to local tastes while promoting products both local and otherwise.[71] In rural areas, especially in much of Bavaria and Baden-Württemberg, consumers bought their beer by the case from home-delivery services.[72] In Bavaria, home deliveries were accompanied by a domestic magazine, *Bavarian Beer Illustrated*, that included news and opinion pieces on issues of Bavarian culture, homemaking tips for housewives, and humor and puzzle sections for children.[73]

The place of the nuclear family in the stabilization of West Germany is hard to overstate. It was the connective tissue that tied sexualized "sociability" in advertising and cultural norms of feminine propriety to pro-natalism and state subsidies programs for domestic technology. Still, if private consumption had become king by the late 1960s, public consumption had likewise played a crucial role in stabilizing West German society. Men reported enjoying drinking in public settings more than women by a factor of three, and public consumption contributed to recasting masculinity in the aftermath of dictatorship and defeat. Take, for example, another community advertisement. Launched in 1953, "the wanderer in the desert" was the single longest running ad from the *Bierwerbe*, remaining in circulation until 1967. Read against the scarcity-based ads discussed earlier, it would be hard to imagine a starker juxtaposition. The image here is dripping with metaphor and allusion. On one level, for consumers well versed in the struggles of scarcity, the desert as a metaphor smacks of the war and postwar scarcity years, while the beer floating in the sky heralds a reprieve—a vision perhaps not yet entirely realized in 1953. Consuming beer—or, given Allied restrictions, even *producing* beer—offered a return to simple pleasure. But the wanderer also conjures the emasculated men of the Third Reich and occupation returning to a Germany only beginning to climb out of material hardship, seeking the simplicity of work, private life, and material security.[74] This was one of the first

---

[70] Elisabeth Noelle and Erich Peter Neumann, eds., *Jahrbuch der öffentlichen Meinung, 1968–1973* (Allensbach am Bodensee: Verlag für Demoskopie, 1974), p. 395.

[71] 'Bier im Lebensmitteleinzelhandel', GfK S 1973 029, p. 11.

[72] 'Einstellung zum Bierverbrauch', GfK S 1964 058, tbl. 60.

[73] For more on *Bayerische Bier-Illustrierte*, see Chapter 5.

[74] On the material components of reconstructing male subjectivities in the Federal Republic, see Frank Biess, 'Men of Reconstruction—The Reconstruction of Men: Returning POWs in East and West Germany, 1945–1955', in *Home/Front: The Military, War and Gender in Twentieth Century Germany*, ed. Karen Hagemann and Stefanie Schüler-Springorum (Oxford and New York: Berg Publishers, 2002), pp. 348–51.

Figure 4.6 Thomas Abeking, "Wanderer in the desert," reproduced courtesy of the German Brewers Association.

male-presenting figures to appear in the catalog of community advertisements, and it can be understood in the context of war, defeat, and shattered military masculinity. Indeed, the ad echoes imagery surrounding the Afrika Korps in general and German Field Marshal Erwin Rommel in particular—an iconography that had been recently immortalized in the 1951 British film, *The Desert Fox*. The commercially successful film whitewashed Rommel's ideological convictions, and, by extension, those of the entire Wehrmacht.[75] The wanderer thus resonated broadly with hardship—whether returning from war or captivity or climbing out of postwar scarcity. Only a few years later, *"Bier macht den Durst erst schön"* would mark a transition from the shattered men of the Third Reich to the toiling producer-citizens of the Federal Republic.

If the imagery of beer resonated with German men seeking reprieve and honest work, the practices of consumption reflected a daily absolution. Public drinking was a profoundly male activity. Men were nearly twice as likely as women to consume beer in bars and restaurants in the early 1950s, and by 1964 they were three times as likely.[76] By the early 1960s, almost two-thirds of West German men gathered on a biweekly basis to drink and socialize with other men. About half claimed to do so at least once a week. When they met, conversation was innocuous. The most frequent topics of discussion were sports, jokes, politics, cars, and work. Heavier topics, including "the war, imprisonment, [or] how it was back then," rarely came up. Respondents to one survey ranked such conversations as the sixteenth most common topic of discussion.[77] West German men who gathered to drink and socialize seem to have avoided discussing perhaps the single most shared facet of their lives—even the survey avoided naming Nazism in favor of "how it was back then." Monica Black has recently and rightly shown that ostensibly harmless rumors and gossip are not categorically distinct from open and frank conversations about the Third Reich.[78] Still, it seems clear that public drinking offered men an opportunity to recast public sociability, embrace emerging abundance, and drown their recent past.

In public life, the brewing industry was once again active in shaping the culture of consumption. In their search for songs to produce—such as the failed *"Sauf Bruder, sauf"*—the brewing industry actively promoted unity through beer. In the autumn of 1964, for example, the song *"Wir gründen eine Bier-Partei"* (We're founding a Beer Party) was written and recorded by the Bavarian group *Hugo und seine Stammtischbrüder* (loosely, Hugo and his Drinking Buddies). The lyrics went as follows:

---

[75] Patrick Major, '"Our Friend Rommel": The *Wehrmacht* as "Worthy Enemy" in Postwar British Popular Culture', *German History* 26, no. 4 (2008): pp. 520–35.

[76] 'Die Einstellung der Verbraucher zum Bierkonsum', p. 76; 'Einstellung zum Bierverbrauch', tbl. 13g.

[77] Elisabeth Noelle and Erich Peter Neumann, eds., *Jahrbuch der öffentlichen Meinung, 1965–1967* (Allensbach am Bodensee: Verlag für Demoskopie, 1967), p. 21.

[78] Black, *A Demon-Haunted Land*.

Refrain:

Prost! Prost! Prost!

We're founding a Beer Party, Beer Party, Beer Party

We're founding a Beer Party, and count me in.

The SPD votes for Willy [Brandt], yeah, yeah, yeah,

The FPD for Erich [Mende], yeah, yeah, yeah

The CDU votes for Ludwig [Erhard], yeah, yeah, yeah

But when I go to the polls, I choose my local pub.

(Refrain)

With us there is no quarrel and struggle, no, no, no,

We have no time for ceremonial honors, no, no, no,

And nor for state visits, no, no, no,

For those we'll just send a case of German beer,

(Refrain)

Today we're paying the founding dues, yeah, yeah, yeah,

And if we all do it, yeah, yeah, yeah,

And if we're very generous, yeah, yeah, yeah,

Our party will build breweries everywhere.

(Refrain)

The lyrics are fairly explicit that beer consumption was a shared experience of German life. According to the song, beer consumption stands beyond the divisive realms of politics. No matter where one fell politically, beer consumption was a shared pleasure and was perhaps more important than politics, acting as it did, apparently, as a cure-all for international diplomacy. The song also captures the stabilization of West Germany in a nutshell: consume more, vote for your party but more so for increased consumption, and feed the expansion of the consumer economy by buying in in daily practice. The song received institutional backing from the Bavarian Brewers Association, which circulated it to their membership, endorsed it for the annual Oktoberfest celebration, and promoted it at a November press ball. Records of it were given to attending members of the press and, according to the conservative newspaper *Die Welt am Sonntag*, the song was the "hymn of the evening."[79]

The outwardly apolitical message of the song—as with all facets of life in the Adenauer/Erhard years—provided only the thinnest veneer to cover the politics of the conservative restoration. The song borrowed composition from March and Foxtrot music and was adorned with repetitive chanting of "Prost!" or "Cheers!" The aesthetic appealed to older Germans and smacked of the marches and chants of their youth. And, to be sure, *"Wir gründen eine Bier-Partei"* was not designed

---

[79] See correspondence between September and November 1964, BayHStA Bayer. Brauerbund 1340.

for the West German youth, in spite of the Beatles-esque "yeah, yeah, yeah." Beer was certainly part of the emerging youth cultures which, by 1964, were taking the world by storm but *Hugo und seine Stammtischbrüder* offered an alternative. Hard working men and women—but mostly men—who drank in public spaces could now associate beer with a shared national culture that was outwardly apolitical but also deeply communitarian, drawing on an aesthetic which sounded a lot like that of an earlier Party. Like the Beer Party, National Socialism had also built its base in beerhalls and taverns, arguing about what was inherent to all Germans.

At the same time, in the autumn of 1964, the West German weekly *Der Spiegel* published a lengthy article about the production and consumption of beer. The opening epigraph came from none other than the Iron Chancellor, Otto von Bismarck, who allegedly claimed that "we Germans can scarcely kill more time than when drinking beer." More than a mere leisurely pastime, the piece began, beer was a symbol of pride. Readers should celebrate—especially since it was an Olympic year—that they had just broken the world record in beer drinking per capita. Less than 20 years after the collapse of the Third Reich, here was a major West German publication invoking the words of the architect of the German nation-state to encourage consumption in the name of cultural nationalism. But the piece went further still by tapping motivational psychologist Ernest Dichter to bolster the significance of beer consumption in contemporary German society. He assured readers, "You can be proud of beer; with beer, you don't have anything to apologize for."[80] The statement was profound when read in the context of the early 1960s. At this very moment, the high-profile Auschwitz Trial for SS guards was at its midway point in Frankfurt. Even in the pages of *Der Spiegel*, the immediately preceding article detailed an international history conference in Berlin revolving around the work of Fritz Fischer and the question of German culpability in the First World War. Just as Bismarck and Dichter sought to persuade readers that "we Germans" have nothing to apologize for, it was becoming increasingly clear that many Germans may actually have quite a lot to apologize for.

Conclusion

By the end of the 1960s, West German annual beer expenditures for the year surpassed 11 billion Marks. The drink had become the single most popular beverage in the Federal Republic, with one in four West Germans drinking beer every day and per capita consumption displacing milk from its historic top spot.[81] Throughout the so-called "miracle years" the brewing industry worked to increase consumption by participating in the conservative modernization and cultural

---

[80] 'Bier: Sieg der Flasche', p. 54.
[81] 'Der Deutschen liebster Saft', *Der Spiegel* no. 33, (1968), p. 34.

democratization of the Federal Republic. An industry that began the postwar period weary of itself and provincial differences in consumer culture shifted in the boom years toward trying to mitigate the celebration of regional difference in the name of a new nationally German market of beer drinkers. The brewing industry in some ways created an early form of cultural democratization in that it cracked the traditional class hierarchies of high and low culture, *Kultur* and kitsch, in German society.[82] And yet if it was democratic, in the sense of its broad popular reach, it was far from progressive. The apolitical façade of quotidian pleasures was deeply entwined not only with a "conservative restoration" and the stabilization of a conventional gender binary, but also with the conspicuous absence of public assessment of Germans' recent pasts. The brewing industry undoubtedly succeeded in securing its place in what they feared would become a new and crowded West German world of goods. But this depended in no small part on the reformation of conservative paternalism and a mass consumerism that celebrated the departure from scarcity while massaging away deep regional differences and the rough edges of the Nazi dictatorship.

As the Federal Republic found political stability and legitimation in economic growth, beer helped create a unified national culture of consumerism through a conviction that the drink of "we Germans" trumped political or provincial animosity. Differences in regional and local consumer cultures no doubt remained, but *beer*, stripped of brand and local consumer culture, became indicative of a new culture of Germany and Germanness where differences in politics and provincialism played a secondary role to the economic miracle as the defining cultural trope of the new West German nation. There is at least one major part of this story, however, which requires more extensive consideration. The next chapter offers a parallel history to the present one, but transitions toward thinking about how West Germans came to understand beer as a particular type of commodity that helped them define themselves in the broader world.

---

[82] Kaspar Maase, 'Establishing Cultural Democracy: Youth, Americanization, and the Irresistible Rise of Popular Culture', in *The Miracle Years: A Cultural History of West Germany, 1949–1968*, ed. Hanna Schissler (Princeton: Princeton University Press, 2001), pp. 428–50, esp. pp. 430–4.

5

Making a National Icon

A Political Economy of the *Reinheitsgebot*, 1953–1975

At the end of the 1940s, brewers in Bavaria collectively chipped in to produce a poster version of the so-called *Reinheitsgebot*. The image is likely familiar to anyone who has spent time in German, and especially Bavarian, bars and beer halls. Designed by Augsburg graphic designer Hermann Müller, the image, which is shown in Figure 5.2 presented both the original Middle High German and the modern transliteration of a 1516 decree regarding the production of beer. The header embellished the now famous word—*Reinheitsgebot*—and, between the two versions of the text, the clearest written script on the poster claims the decree remains "unchanged in application to this day." By the early 1950s, the posters hung in breweries, restaurants, and inns throughout Bavaria. The initiative, undertaken by the regional trade organization, the Bavarian Brewers Association, was intended to fill an "absence" in popular consciousness. While the decree had long informed what beer was produced, and therefore consumed, it had never, in its more than 400-year history, been promoted among the public.[1] Since the 1950s, the *Reinheitsgebot* has become a touchstone of industry standards and commercial sensibilities across the country. Indeed, by the late 1980s, 95 per cent of West Germans insisted that the *Reinheitsgebot* constituted "the guarantee of quality."[2] This transformation from Bavarian curiosity to national icon has its origins in two concentric conflicts of market integration from the 1950s to the 1970s. In both, the perceived threat of market integration prompted anxious brewers to invoke the *Reinheitsgebot* to win political allies, cudgel industry outliers, and generate popular support by mobilizing consumer protection movements and claims to culture and tradition.

As we have seen in the preceding chapters, the regulations, practices, and cultures around beer in Germany were far from uniform. The *Reinheitsgebot* is a case in point. Anchored in 16th century *Altbayern*, and applied piecemeal in Swabia and Franconia in the 19th century, the regulation did not gain traction outside

---

[1] 'Das bayerische Reinheitsgebot in der Bierherstellung', *Mitteilung des Bayer. Brauerbund* 12 Dec. 23, 1950, Bayerisches Hauptstaatsarchiv (henceforth BayHStA) Bayer. Brauerbund 1352; and Bayerischer Brauerbund e.V., *Geschäftsbericht 1951/52 und 1952/53*, pp. 72–4.
[2] Bayerischer Brauerbund e.V., *Geschäftsbericht 1988/89*, p. 64.

A Nation Fermented: Beer, Bavaria, and the Making of Modern Germany. Robert Shea Terrell, Oxford University Press.
© Robert Shea Terrell 2024. DOI: 10.1093/oso/9780198881834.003.0006

Bavaria until the turn of the 20th century. When it did, it remained hotly contested, particularly outside the south, where it was only ever adopted in a modified form.[3] In fact, in legal terms, the signifier *"Reinheitsgebot"* does not refer to an actual law but to sections of the Beer Tax Law (*Biersteuergesetz*) and the Food Law (*Lebensmittelgesetz*), and depending where in Germany one is, it can mean different things. Still, the term became increasingly powerful as Bavarians and later West Germans framed economic integration as a challenge to their commercial and cultural lives. The most heated conflicts around the *Reinheitsgebot* emerged in the "miracle years" of unprecedented economic growth in the postwar decades. The first of the two conflicts surveyed here—the so-called *Süßbierstreit*, or conflict over sweet beer—was sparked by West German market integration and pitted *Altbayerisch* brewers and regulators against other West German brewers shipping beer into Franconia, the culturally contested areas of northern Bavaria. In the 1950s and 1960s, the Franconian borderlands became the object of battles over cultural, economic, and regulatory supremacy between Munich and Bonn. The second conflict followed a parallel development but was initiated by western European market integration and set West Germans in opposition to imports from other member states of the European Economic Community (EEC). Here, capital and regulatory influence in Munich led the way but, well beyond Bavaria, West German regulators and consumer groups likewise joined the charge to rally behind market protectionism. It was in these two conflicts that the *Reinheitsgebot* emerged as the cultural icon and market regulation we often understand it to be. In both cases, the transformation was a local reaction—relatively speaking—to increased integration; market protectionism that rallied regulators and consumers alike in defense of industrial interests.

The popularization of the *Reinheitsgebot* depended on myriad connections between Munich, *Altbayern*, Bavaria proper, the Federal Republic, and the EEC. As historian Sebastian Conrad demonstrated for the turn of the 20th century, "the invocation of national specificity" was often a response to "the threatened loss of national characteristics" via global integration.[4] Here we see not only that similar phenomena occur at the sub-national level, but also that synchronic responses to integration at the local, regional, national, and international levels fed off and shaped one another. The *Reinheitsgebot* was inflated as a marker of cultural identity—both Bavarian and West German—precisely because of the integration of national and international markets and perceived challenges to established economic and political power. While what follows tells the story of market integrations and market protectionism, it shifts between different scales of analysis in order to capture the historical changes that depended on the

---

[3] See Chapters 1 and 3.
[4] Sebastian Conrad, *Globalisation and the Nation in Imperial Germany*, trans. Sorcha O'Hagan (Cambridge: Cambridge University Press, 2010, orig. 2006), p. 337.

interactions between them.⁵ Tracing the emergence of "pure beer" as a national touchstone, it suggests how, as Nancy Reynolds wrote in another case, "the material specificity of consumer goods structured how objects could help define the boundaries of national community and the behaviors deemed suitable in it."⁶ The *Reinheitsgebot* gained traction as a national icon in spite of its long and embattled history because shifts in the conditions of exchange informed new political economic constellations and individual interactions between Munich, Franconia, Bonn, and Brussels. Just as the regulation became more Bavarian through the birth pangs of the West German market, so too did it become more West German through those of the EEC. Through both processes, capital interests, particularly rooted in Munich, invoked the *Reinheitsgebot* and effectively shaped both market regulations and consumer sensibilities.

Franconian Demand, *Altbayerisch* Capital, and the West German Economy

From 1953 to 1965, brewers and regulators in Munich and *Altbayern* waged war on consumer habits in Franconia, the culturally contested northern part of Bavaria. There, most notably in and around the city of Würzburg, a small market existed for beer brewed with the addition of sugar. Later dubbed *Süßbier* in press coverage, this beer was brewed mostly in Hesse and West Berlin and then crossed state lines to satisfy Franconian demand. Such beer was well within the lines of West German brewing law but did not meet stricter Bavarian regulations on production. There was, therefore, an economic issue here: *Süßbier* was cheaper to make and represented an unfair market advantage over brewers bound to Bavarian standards. And yet, the quantities of beer in question were so miniscule as to be non-existent. Rather than purely economic, the ensuing conflict, which positioned Bavarian brewers and political leaders against the larger federal system, was a proving ground for *Altbayerisch* cultural and regulatory power in the face of the integrating West German economy.

What the media styled as the *Süßbierstreit*, or "sweet beer conflict," began in 1953 as a result of the market protectionist anxieties of Bavarian brewers eyeing the trajectory of the West German market. Bavarian consumption had been growing slower than that of other West German states. At home, Bavarian brewers knew that from 1950 to 1953, they had lost more than 3 per cent of their West

---

⁵ In this I follow conceptions of scale articulated in Michael Werner and Bénédicte Zimmerman, 'Beyond Comparison: *Histoire Croisée* and the Challenge of Reflexivity', *History and Theory* 45 (Feb. 2006): pp. 30–50, esp. 44.

⁶ Nancy Y. Reynolds, 'National Socks and the "Nylon Woman": Materiality, Gender, and Nationalism in Textile Marketing in Semicolonial Egypt, 1930–56', *International Journal of Middle East Studies* 43, no. 1 (Feb. 2011): pp. 49–74, here 51.

German market share, thanks in large part to booming large-scale enterprises elsewhere, most notably in North Rhine-Westphalia.[7] This apparently shocking turn of events even made international news in small-town New York, where hearing that "other West German states are drinking more beer than the Bavarians... is like hearing that the Americans are playing more and better cricket than the English."[8] In May 1953, Dr Bernhard Bergdolt of the Munich Löwenbräu brewery wrote to Ernst Röhm, the head of the Bavarian Brewers Association, in an effort to shore up control of the Bavarian market. Each month, he complained, close to half a million liters of beer brewed with the addition of sugar were entering Bavaria and being consumed in Franconia.[9] As we saw in Chapter 2, Röhm and other Bavarian brewers had fought battles over sugar before. And, indeed, when representatives from the trade organization and the Finance Ministry met to discuss the issue, they poured over a dossier of almost 30 documents from Nazi-era conflicts over brewing with the addition of sugar. Beginning in this meeting and spreading well beyond it, the concerns of the Löwenbräu executive quickly found support, including from the board of the Bavarian Brewers Association, the State Minister of Finance, and leading legal scholars.[10] On the legal front, this moment in the early 1950s proved pivotal in knotting together many of the continuities and tensions that have appeared throughout this book. According to Munich law professor Dr Hans Nawiasky, for example, the early modern precedents of Bavarian market protectionism were preserved in the 1871 Reserve Rights; southern legal peculiarity existed in parallel with national regulation since 1906; and that regulatory duality was implicitly codified as national law with the signing of the 1949 Basic Law, and explicitly so with the 1950 Beer Tax Law. Effectively arguing against full West German market integration, Nawiasky wrote that "neither bottom- nor top-fermenting beer which has been adulterated with sugar may be produced *or sold* in Bavaria."[11] The assessment was amplified by the new president of the Bavarian Brewers Association, Werner Schladenhaufen, and soon what had begun as a single brewery's financial argument about market share became, within a year, the foundation of an informal trade barrier within the Federal Republic. In the summer of 1954, the momentum had reached the highest levels of the Bavarian state, leading Minister of the Interior Wilhelm

---

[7] 'Das Bier-Politikum', *Der Spiegel* 9, no. 2 (1955), pp. 13–14.

[8] 'Champ Beer Drinkers Dry Up', *Adirondack Daily Enterprise* Oct. 6, 1952, p. 1.

[9] May 9, 1953, letter from Bernhard Bergdolt to Ernst Röhm, BayHStA Bayer. Brauerbund 587.

[10] Mar. 19, 1954, letter from Friedrich Zietsch to Fritz Schäffer, BayHStA MInn 108,423; Mar. 22, 1954, letter from Werner Schladenhaufen to the Membership, BayHStA Bayer. Brauerbund 587.

[11] Mar. 3, 1954, Hans Nawiasky, 'Rechtgutachten über die Tragweite des bayerischen Vorbehalts beim Eintritt in die Biersteuergemeinschaft zu erstatten'. See also his follow-up letter to the Bavarian Brewers Association, dated Mar. 14, 1954, BayHStA Bayer. Brauerbund 587. Emphasis added.

Hoegner to issue a complete distribution ban (*Vertriebsverbot*) on beer produced with the addition of sugar.[12]

The prohibition sparked a media frenzy and, as the almost non-existent economic factors became clearer, public discourse in newspapers tended to become more dramatized and played up historic provincial tensions. The *Süßbier* itself—brewed with the addition of sugar and sold in Franconia—amounted to just 0.14 per cent of the beer produced in West Germany, and thus coverage quickly pointed out that the dispute was less economic than cultural. One of the earliest pieces to address the ban was a front-page article in the satire column of the *Süddeutsche Zeitung*, which opened "finally Bavaria has a war to which it is well suited: The Beer War, and it is even against the 'Prussians'!" Satire or not, the piece captured the reality that brewers and regulators, particularly in *Altbayern*, were working to rally tradition and southern culture. Going for broke, the article poked fun at the nearly negligible volume of Franconian demand: "one wants to say it is a non-issue. But what a non-issue! It violates the holiest Bavarian sentiments. We are enraged by those above (*die da oben*) that are trying to break our *Reinheitsgebot*! The battle cry of the native brewers echoes throughout all of Old Bavaria."[13] If the rhetoric was overblown, the sentiment was not. Beyond satire, the distribution ban was discussed in trade publications and national newspapers of all political leanings. On the Bavarian side the conflict looked like a challenge to the "magna carta of the Bavarian brewer," while on the northern German side it looked like Bavarian "separatism by proxy."[14] Many claimed the debate was about more than just beer, noting regional differences and even "honor" in articles dripping with the rhetoric of war and historic north–south tensions.[15] By the time the dispute came up for legal process, the provincial question was already pronounced in public discourse: it was a provincialism of *Altbayern* against the north—and a north often reduced to the non-existent Prussia.[16] More often than not, Franconians were rarely present in the early coverage and appeared to be simply caught in the middle. Most probably would have agreed with one

---

[12] See the various correspondences between MInn, MFin, Bayer. Brauerbund, leading up to Jul. 8, 1954, 'Bekanntmachung des Bayerischen Staatsministeriums des Innern, Überwachung des Verkehrs mit Lebensmitteln; hier Inverkehrbringen von Bieren, die unter Verwendung von Zucker bereitet sind', all in BayHStA MInn 108,423; see also, *Bayer. Staatsanzeiger* Nr. 29, July 17, 1954.

[13] 'Das Streiflicht', *Süddeutsche Zeitung*, Aug. 21/22, 1954, p. 1.

[14] 'Streit um gesüßtes Bier', *Deutsche Brauwirtschaft* 63 no. 18, Aug. 31, 1954, pp. 316-7; 'Malzbierkrieg zwischen Nord und Süd—Blauweiser Separatismus erstrebt bei sich das Biermonopol', *Der Fortschritt*, Oct. 21, 1954.

[15] 'Es geht um unsere Bier-Ehre', *Abendzeitung*, Aug. 17, 1954, p. 2; 'Bierkrieg Berlin-Bayern', *Abendzeitung*, Aug. 20, 1954; 'Im Bierkrieg geht's um mehr als ein Zuckerl', *Münchner Merkur*, Aug. 26, 1954; 'Bierkrieg mit Bayern', *Frankfurter Allgemeine*, Aug. 14, 1954; 'Bierkrieg zwischen Nord und Süd', *Der Tag*, Aug. 20, 1954; 'Bierkrieg mit Bayern', *Der Kurier*, Aug. 20, 1954; 'Bayern führt "heißen" Krieg gegen Bierlimonade', *Die Welt*, Aug. 28, 1954.

[16] For a fuller analysis of the discourse of the *Süßbierstreit*, see Birgit Speckle, *Streit ums Bier in Bayern: Wertvorstellungen um Reinheit, Gemeinschaft und Tradition* (Münster: Waxmann Verlag, 2001).

Würzburg beer retailer, who complained that 15th-century conceptions of trade "seem like a bad joke in the era of the free market economy."[17]

By the end of 1954, the distribution ban had been upheld in state and federal court and for the next four years, Bavarian brewers and state officials policed the sale of beers in violation of Bavarian law. The proceedings were relatively simple and upheld the 1954 distribution ban until 1958–1959, when they began to test the limits of what was meant by "beer."[18] In late 1958, the Hofbräuhaus Nicolay A.G. in Hanau, Hesse, on the border of Lower Franconia, was taken to court for selling a beverage brewed with the addition of sugar, but sold under the name "*Nährtrunk*" and "*Malztrunk*."[19] Such beverages were most often called *Malzbier* and had previously fallen under the purview of the distribution ban, but in January 1959 the Second Criminal Court ruled that the drink could still be sold in Bavaria because the word "*Bier*" (as in *Malzbier*) did not appear on the label.[20] The ruling fundamentally shifted the course of the *Süßbierstreit* because while it found the limits of what could be policed under the distribution ban, it also led brewers to seek yet more stringent market protectionist legislation, now in the language of consumer protection. Soon after the ruling, they began developing a new argument in which, regardless of the word -*bier*, such products were allegedly capitalizing on the imagery and reputation of beer, thereby misleading consumers.

The allegation of consumer manipulation was exceedingly hard to make concrete. In leveling such a critique at Frankfurt-based Karamalz, for instance, Bavarian brewers accused the product of attempting to "to conjure the appearance" of being beer—a phrase from §10 of the 1950 Beer Tax Law which they had invoked several years earlier in the context of international market protectionism.[21] Appealing to the Ministry of the Interior, the Bavarian Brewers Association provided copies of Karamalz advertising, arguing that the use of a foaming pint glass too closely resembled the image everyone associated with beer, thanks to the brewing industry's community advertising program.[22] Going even further, they sent complete schematic diagrams detailing the sizes, shapes, angles, proportions,

[17] 'Der bittere Kampf ums süße Bier', *Süddeutsche Zeitung*, Sept. 15, 1954, p. 6; In northern Franconian newspapers, the issue received very little coverage at first and was treated a bit more neutrally. One might even read a sense of passiveness and even powerlessness. See, for example, 'Kleiner Vorgriff auf mögliche Entscheidung', *Main Post*, Sept. 8, 1954.

[18] 'Berliner Zuckerbier in Bayern verboten', *Abendzeitung*, Mar. 29, 1955, p. 2; May 23, 1956, 'Urteil des Bayerischen Obersten Landesgerichts', Bundesarchiv Koblenz (henceforth BAK), B 126/23409; 'Gesüßtes Bier darf nicht nach Bayern', *Abendzeitung*, May 24, 1956; 'Der Süßbierkrieg geht weiter', *Süddeutsche Zeitung*, June 4, 1956, p. 8.

[19] 'Weitere Runde im Süßbierstreit', *Gastwirt und Hotelier*, June 5, 1958.

[20] W. Zipfel, 'Bier und doch kein Bier, aber "kein Bier" ist doch Bier', *Der Brauer und Mälzer* 13, no. 19 (Oct. 15, 1960): pp. 3–6; and Speckle, *Streit ums Bier in Bayern*, pp. 70–1.

[21] Nov. 20, 1959, letter from Werner Schladenhaufen to Knies, with attachments, BayHStA MInn 108427.

[22] See Chapter 4.

neck lengths, and types of glass typical of bottles used for *Bier, Malzbier*, water, and other beverages, arguing that Karamalz was intentionally using a bottle that too closely resembled a beer bottle.[23] Such evidence and argumentation depended on minute attention to detail and an impractical case-by-case scrutiny. And so, rather than just legislating piecemeal, the trade organization also pushed the Bavarian state to consider an explicit law on the circulation of such beverages. Their lobbying ultimately led Franz Elsen (CSU) to introduce the Beer Transport Law (*Gesetz über den Verkehr mit Bier*) in the early summer of 1960. Section 1, Paragraph 1 forbade the circulation of fermented beverages in Bavaria that did not meet Bavarian production standards, regardless of whether the product was called "beer."[24]

Debates around the law proposal in the early 1960s brought the rhetoric of consumer protection firmly into political discourse while also reframing the *Reinheitsgebot* as a consumer—rather than a producer—oriented tradition. But still, consumers themselves were mostly absent, used as rhetorical objects and ones that, as it turned out, could be used just as well by the opposition. In Franconia, a special interest group called the Action Group of *Nährtrunk* Distributors in Bavaria (*Aktionsgemeinschaft der Nährtrunkverleger in Bayern*) petitioned the Bavarian Parliament and Bavarian representatives to the Bundestag to reject the "superfluous" restriction on consumer freedom. They even went so far as to equate the restriction with authoritarianism and produced pamphlets lamenting how hard such an act would be to explain later. The pamphlet told of a fictional elderly woman, years in the future who explained to her children how one day the state government "proclaimed to its unsuspecting voters: 'we can determine what beverages are allowed to be placed on the table in Bavaria.' The citizens living beyond the white-blue border shook their heads anxiously... But just like that, there was no more freedom of beverage choice in Bavaria."[25] While the parallel was overstated, by the early 1960s it seems likely that the experience of explaining an uncomfortable past would have hit close to home. The group had many supporters, including the regional chairman of the free-market liberal FDP in Middle Franconia, Klaus Dehler. As he put it in 1962, the Law was "patronizing to the consumer" in that it undermined the ability of Franconians, and indeed all Bavarians, to drink what they want, when they want.[26] Still, when the Beer Transport Law went to committee, it was agreed that the beverages in question qualified as "falsified" (*verfälscht*) in accordance with §4 Nr. 2 of the 1927 Food

[23] Nov. 20, 1959, letter from Werner Schladenhaufen to Knies, with attachments, BayHStA MInn 108427.

[24] Details of the proposed law described in Bayerischer Brauerbund e.V. *Geschäftsbericht 1960/61 and 1961/62*, pp. 39–47.

[25] 'Süßbierhändler fordern Getränkefreiheit', *Süddeutsche Zeitung*, Oct. 2, 1962, p. 17.

[26] 'Landtag billigte Süßbierverbot—Verfassungsklage droht', Oct. 24, 1962, cutout marked only *Tagblatt*, Archiv für Christlich-Soziale Politik (henceforth ACSP) NL Elsen, Franz: 6.7.14.

Law (*Lebensmittelgesetz*). The term was ambiguous but brought legal power to industrial and political discourses of consumer protection. It also legitimized the convictions of brewers and legislators alike that even if consumers did not know about the *Reinheitsgebot*, it had informed consumer expectations and habits for more than 450 years. Indeed, *Verbrauchererwartungen*, or consumer expectations, became a catchphrase of political discourse, and ultimately many in the Bavarian state government concluded that consumers needed to be protected whether they knew it or not.[27] This argument had been wielded by brewers across Germany for decades—from north German opposition to the 1906 tax law to Bavarian intransigence in the face of Nazi-era resource management—but only in this moment did it turn so explicitly to a legislative action to leverage capital interests into market regulation.

At the core of the conflict, producers and regulators in Munich and *Altbayern* were attempting to shape market sensibilities—and, indeed, Bavarian culture—in the absence of a shared or cultivated value system among Bavarians. Indeed, most Bavarians confessed ignorance about what "sweet beer" even was.[28] As late as 1962, 34 per cent of the Bavarian population firmly believed that the *Reinheitsgebot* actually *allowed* sugar in beer, some 45 per cent knew without question that it was *not* allowed, and a final 21 per cent had no conviction either way.[29] The *Süßbierstreit* did not reflect any sort of consolidated or homogenous consumer demand. It was instead a site of working out the temporal and spatial authority of tradition. Put differently, the question was whether Franconia, in spite of being part of a federated republic, would be governed in the economic and cultural spheres first and foremost by political and capital interests in Würzburg, Munich, or Bonn. Ultimately, the law narrowly passed in the Bavarian Landtag in October 1962 but was never ratified by Minister President Alphons Goppel, who argued that the trafficking of food and stimulants was the jurisdiction of the federal rather than the state government. Leaders in the brewing industry were devastated. The president of the trade organization, Werner Schladenhaufen, expressed his shock and sense of betrayal by claiming that the Minister President had "stabbed us in the backs" (*ist uns...in den Rücken gefallen*).[30] This linguistic formulation, though not entirely uncommon in German, conjures its most infamous usage—the Nazi-era "Stab in the Back Myth"—suggesting, perhaps, that for

---

[27] 'Bericht des Wirtschaftsausschusses und des Rechts- und Verfassungsausschusses', May 24, 1962, BayHStA Bayer. Brauerbund 1355; see also, Oct. 19, 1962, letter from Peschel and Sedlmayr to the Representatives of the Bavarian Parliament, ACSP NL Elsen, Franz: 6.7.14.

[28] 'Verbraucher kennen sich nicht aus', *Süddeutsche Zeitung* Oct. 19, 1962, p. 12.

[29] 'Zum Reinheitsgebot bei Bier: Die Einstellung der Bevölkerung in Bayern Ergebnisse einer Repräsentativ-Umfrage'. This survey was commissioned by the Bavarian Brewers Association from the Institut für Demoskopie in Allensbach. It was conducted in 1962 but published in 1964. BayHStA Bayer. Brauerbund 1355.

[30] 'Ein "Handvoll Chemie" in den Sudhäusern?', *Süddeutsche Zeitung*, May 15, 1965; 'Ende des Süßbierkrieges?', *Süddeutsche Zeitung* Jan. 28, 1965, p. 6.

Schladenhaufen, Goppel's commitment to federalism constituted first order treason against Bavaria.

If abandoning the law was indeed treason, it was because it appeared to go against the grain of a larger process of constructing Bavarian political and cultural identity in the 1950s and 1960s. In those years, Goppel's party, the CSU, had worked to construct an integral Bavarian political identity—a sort of umbrella for Bavarian subregional peculiarities, which remains the basis of their hegemony in Bavarian politics to this day.[31] In the course of the *Süßbierstreit*, the political economic utility of the *Reinheitsgebot* elevated *Altbayerisch* capital interests but ultimately did not seem to fit in the political program of the CSU—at least according to Goppel. Still, while political federalism won the day, the *Süßbierstreit* was in effect an effort to pressure both cultural and market sensibilities throughout Bavaria, particularly in Franconia. This market protectionist conflict initiated by a single Munich brewery percolated into the state government and sought to legislate a dominant regional culture of beer (down to the very use of the word). But while the law died in 1965, and while less than half of Bavarians knew what the *Reinheitsgebot* even said in the mid-1960s, the rhetoric of adulteration and consumer protection was a genie that would never be put back in the bottle.

Making the *Reinheitsgebot* German

At the height of lobbying for the Beer Transport Law, Alfons Schubert, the head of the Franconian opposition organization, wrote to the delegates of the Bavarian Parliament asking just how far the alignment of capital and political interests would go. Hoping to highlight the futility of support for the proposed law, he pointed to the newly signed Treaty of Rome, which guaranteed the economic integration of the six western European signatory countries. Surely European integration would do away with trade barriers like those at stake in the *Süßbierstreit*. In obvious hyperbole, Schubert quipped "Is the idea of Europe to collapse so soon on account of the beer trade?"[32] In the next decade, the spirit of the inquiry would become far less preposterous than it at first seemed. In the late 1960s and early 1970s, a second conflict of market integration expanded the contours of debate around the *Reinheitsgebot*. Often called the *Europäischer Bierkrieg*, or European Beer War, by contemporaries and historians alike, it ran from 1958 to 1975.[33] The conflict paralleled much of the rhetoric, interest groups, and course

---

[31] Graham Ford, 'Constructing a Regional Identity: The Christian Social Union and Bavaria's Common Heritage, 1949–1962', *Contemporary European History* 16, no. 3 (Aug. 2007): pp. 277–97.
[32] July 3, 1960, letter from Alfons Schubert to members of the Landtag, BayHStA Minn 108,421.
[33] Speckle, *Streit ums Bier in Bayern*, pp. 95–156.

of the *Süßbierstreit*, but, as the name suggests, it operated on a larger scale. Bavaria once again provided the spark of conflict but Franconia got lost as brewers and politicians across West Germany now became major advocates of the *Reinheitsgebot* as particularly German, not just Bavarian or southern German. New as well was the mass mobilization of consumers, not just as political objects, but increasingly as political agents rallying around the *Reinheitsgebot* as a consumer protectionist measure.[34]

A year after the Treaty of Rome, the national brewing associations of the six member states of the European Economic Community (EEC) founded the Working Community of Common Market Brewers (*Communauté de Travail des Brasseurs du Marché Commun*, or CBMC). The organization aimed to consider market harmonization in advance of any explicit directive from Brussels. As Pierre Falcimaigne, the head of the French national brewing trade organization, the *Union Générale Nationale des Syndicats de la Brasserie Française*, put it in April 1960, the brewing industries of the six member states faced "enormous differences," ranging from, "on one extreme, complete freedom in Belgium and on the other the strictest adherence to the *Reinheitsgebot* in Bavaria."[35] His recognition of the difference between West German and Bavarian stringency is noteworthy in foreshadowing the course of events at the national level, but in the early negotiations most sights were set on international differences. For five years, the CBMC held smooth if somewhat unproductive meetings in which representatives took turns suggesting that the member states simply adopt the production standards of one country or another. In his pitch for Europeanizing West German production standards, delegate Richard Biergans argued that the *Reinheitsgebot*—referring to the looser national version rather than its stricter southern counterpart—guaranteed consumers freedom from fear of additives by ensuring that beer was "natural." But such categories were cultural, not universal, and Falcimaigne pushed back, arguing that unmalted grains were also "natural," and that the prohibition of unmalted grain had nothing to do with making beer a "natural product." Consumers had nothing to fear, another French delegate chimed in: "a beer is not unpure because it is produced in part with rice." The comment prompted a gestalt shift that the German delegation was not willing to accept. Going on the offensive, one West German representative asked why the other European brewers were so adamant about the addition of raw grain and

---

[34] It was thus an early iteration of consumer capitalism: a phase of advanced capitalism in which the interests of consumers "set the terms for government policy formation and for company-level product market strategies." See Gunnar Trumbull, *Consumer Capitalism: Politics, Product Markets, and Firm Strategy in France and Germany* (Ithaca: Cornell University Press, 2006), p. 3; see, further, Matthew Hilton, 'Consumers and the State since the Second World War', *Annals of the American Academy of Political and Social Science* 611, no. 1 (May 2007): pp. 66–81.

[35] Falcimaigne's report of April 20, 1960, cited in Nov. 28, 1960, 'Zusammenfassung der ersten Versammlung der Kommission Gesetzgebungen—CBMC'. BayHStA Bayer. Brauerbund 1382.

rice. Members of the other delegations insisted that it was the Germans, not they, who put too much emphasis on their own practices.[36]

Such early attempts at international negotiation were often fruitless, but by 1964 the other member organizations of the CBMC had chipped away at West German intransigence. In 1964 the West German representatives began to make concessions on a harmonization proposal to include unmalted grains as long as other members agreed to limit the sorts of sugars they used to those permitted by the 1950 Beer Tax Law.[37] From a West German perspective, the arrangement was sensible, but when talk of concession reached southern Germany, Bavarian brewers dug in their heels. As noted earlier and elsewhere, Bavarian brewers had long been the most stubborn on production standards and, since 1906, had enjoyed and repeatedly defended parallel legal restrictions. Likely fuming that the 1962 Beer Transport Law had still not been ratified, the Bavarian brewing leader Werner Schladenhaufen wrote to Biergans that he received the compromise proposal "with surprise and consternation." Indeed, his marginalia on the proposal draft were mostly thick red exclamation points. He insisted that the Bavarians held "firmly to the *Reinheitsgebot* without compromise and without restrictions," and therefore renounced confidence in CBMC negotiations, demanding they be halted until West German brewers could come to a consensus.[38]

For the next four years, southern intransigence halted all progress on international negotiations. When the West German brewers had met in Munich in 1965, any hopes at creating a national consensus ran up against a north–south division. The regional trade organizations of Bavaria, Baden-Württemberg, Hessen, and Rhineland Palatinate stood firmly on the side of the unconditional retention of current brewing standards, while those of North Rhine-Westphalia, Lower Saxony, Bremen, Hamburg, West Berlin, Schleswig-Holstein, and the Saarland were all willing to accept negotiations and the loosening of national brewing law.[39] This almost perfect north–south split was a peculiar industrial geography. While Baden-Württemberg had long adhered to stricter Bavarian production standards, Hesse had found itself in opposition to Bavaria in the *Süßbierstreit* only a few years prior. But the split nonetheless effectively dispensed with the guiding hope of the CBMC that European brewing trade organizations could collectively define the terms of their own integration. In the immediate aftermath of the Munich meeting of the German Brewers Association, there was

---

[36] Apr. 12, 1962, 'Zusammenfassung der zweiten Tagung der Kommission Gesetzgebung—CBMC'. BayHStA Bayer. Brauerbund 1382.

[37] Ibid., and, Jan. 10, 1964, 'Kurzbericht über die dritte Sitzung der Kommission Gesetzgebung—CBMC', held in Milan, Nov. 21, 1963; Jun 1, 1964, 'Kurzbericht über die vierte Sitzung des Legislativausschusses der CBMC', held in Rome, May 11, 1964, all in BayHStA Bayer. Brauerbund 1382.

[38] Nov. 16, 1964, letter from Werner Schladenhaufen to the German Brewers Association, BayHStA Bayer. Brauerbund 1382.

[39] May 4, 1965, Circular P 14/B 16/65 on the 'Harmonisierung der Gesetzgebung für Bier in den Mitgliedstaaten der Europäischen Wirtschaftsgemeinschaft', BayHStA Bayer. Brauerbund 1382.

little incentive to deal with the north–south split head on. Indeed, this was nothing new, reflecting instead the decentralized cultures and regulations that dominated German brewing since 1871. Even as recently as the *Süßbierstreit*, the national trade organization had remained conspicuously silent.

The process of European integration, however, represented a qualitatively new condition. In 1969, the European Economic Community turned to harmonizing regulations on foodstuffs—a process that promised to turn to beer before too long. The threat was sufficient to spark a response. When members of the West German trade organization met at the end of July 1969, they finally resolved to hold uniformly to the *Reinheitsgebot* without compromise.[40] In effect, this meant rallying around the somewhat looser national restriction rather than the stricter southern one, but this distinction also receded in subsequent discourse thanks to the shared threat of market competition. The spark came the next summer, in June 1970, when the Council of Ministers of the EEC presented its harmonization proposal. At the core of the proposal was a directive allowing unmalted grain and a number of additives. Conceptually, this proposal should have been a simple choice. West German brewing law was in effect a non-tariff trade barrier and the Federal Republic had signed an international agreement to pursue free trade. Here, now, was a policy proposal that would establish precisely that and needed only to be approved by the federal government. Over the next few years, however, free trade arguments were buried under industrial, political, and ultimately popular pressure on officials in Bonn and Brussels to retain the *Reinheitsgebot*, and, indeed, to rally behind it.

At the level of both political procedure and popular opinion, opposition to the 1970 harmonization proposal emerged from Bavaria more than anywhere else. In the Bundesrat, for example, special committees considered the agricultural, economic, and public health implications of the proposal and, in each, Bavarian voices were the loudest. The switch to unmalted grain and the opening of the market to cheaper foreign beers would wreak havoc on the smaller decentralized malters and brewers, disproportionately in Bavaria, and on West German agriculture, dominated since 1949 by the Bavarian breadbasket.[41] As brewers were keen to point out, the West German, and especially Bavarian, industries were extremely decentralized, making them particularly susceptible to market displacement. The Federal Republic was home to 1,815 breweries, some 1,247 of them in Bavaria, respectively producing an average of 479,000 and 194,000 hectoliters per brewery.

---

[40] N.a., 'Brauertag in Dresden—nur eine Frage der Zeit', *Brauwelt* 23 (1996): pp. 1046–60, esp. p. 1055; and Bayerischer Brauerbund e.V. *Geschäftsbericht 1968/69–1969/70*, pp. 9–12; Bayerischer Brauerbund e.V. *Geschäftsbericht 1970/71*, pp. 7, 39–42.

[41] Simon Bulmer, *The Domestic Structure of European Community Policy-Making in West Germany* (London: Routledge Revivals, 2016, orig. 1986), pp. 299–333; Raphael Gerhardt, *Agrarmodernisierung und europäische Integration: Das bayerische Landwirtschaftsministerium as politischer Akteur, 1945–1975* (Munich: Verlag C.H. Beck, 2019), pp. 267–442; and Chapter 3 of this book.

By comparison, Great Britain, which was in the process of negotiating their entry to the European Community, was home to a mere 177 breweries producing a whopping average of 3,120,000 hectoliters each.[42] This was a production structure with much more centralized capital and lower operating costs that would allow British breweries, and other centralized European breweries, to undersell their West German counterparts. This was all the more true since production costs were cheaper in Britain and current EEC member states that could brew with the addition of cheaper ingredients not allowed in West German law.

While those arguments made political sense, they did not receive the public attention generated by consumer protection and public health arguments. Here, brewers and their allies papered over the regional differences in brewing standards to rally around the *Reinheitsgebot* as a long-standing *German* form of consumer protection. Brewers put on a public exhibition about the *Reinheitsgebot* at the Bavarian *Landesvertretung* in Bonn, frequented by both the public and federal representatives to the Bundesrat and Bundestag. It claimed that the *Reinheitsgebot* had been in effect in Germany since 1906—a partial truth that glossed over decades of provincial fragmentation. Elsewhere, brewers extended that further. Blending regional history into national, they argued to the Bundesrat that the *Reinheitsgebot* had protected German consumers from "health-damaging beer" for 450 years.[43] This exaggeration of four centuries appeared in an extensive report by the German Brewers Association in October 1970 that became the basis of political action for the next half decade. It was distributed to all levels of political engagement: federal and state ministers, federal and state parliamentarians, German representatives in Brussels, special interest groups, and allied industry organizations in agriculture, brewing, malting, packaging, and logistics. It was directly cited and circulated in political and popular discourse from the Bundestag and Bundesrat to publicity campaigns by Federal Ministers.[44]

As regulators considered the EEC proposal and brewers rallied around tradition, the *Reinheitsgebot* developed as a major theme of consumer protectionist politics. Here too, Bavarian advocacy for the *Reinheitsgebot* preceded and ultimately shaped national parallels. In the 1960s, home delivery was perhaps the single most common mode of acquiring beer in Bavaria.[45] Beginning in the late 1960s, many such deliveries came with a complementary domestic magazine, *Bayerische Bier-Illustrierte*, or *Bavarian Beer Illustrated*. The magazine catered to the nuclear

---

[42] Deutscher Brauer-Bund e.V., *13. Statistischer Bericht: 1977* (Bonn: 1977), pp. 38, 166.
[43] 'Zur Angleichung der Rechtsvorschriften für Bier im Gemeinsamen Markt', Oct. 1970 report by the German Brewers Association, BAK B 189/10312.
[44] 'Niederschrift über die 292. Sitzung des Agrarausschusses des Bundesrates am 11. Sept. 1970', BAK B 189/10310; 'Ansprache von Frau Minister Käte Strobel zur Stimmkartenübergabe des Aktionskomitees "Reines Bier" am 23. März 1971 in Bonn', BAK B 189/10312.
[45] One market research report in 1962 found that 41 per cent of Bavarians listed home delivery as their single most common mode of purchase. See, 'Einstellung zum Bierverbrauch', *Gesellschaft für Konsumforschung* (henceforth GfK) S 1964 058, tbl. 16, and, further, pp. 27–9.

family, including homemaking tips, political essays, and puzzles and jokes for children. The threat of foreign, mass-produced "chemical beer" (*Chemiebier*) was a common topic. So too was the *Reinheitsgebot* as a point of Bavarian pride and a traditionalist shield against the dangers of advanced capitalism, from automation to unfettered market globalization.[46] Once the EEC issued its harmonization proposal, *Bavarian Beer Illustrated* featured the *Reinheitsgebot* more explicitly as a consumer protectionist measure. Just as the proposal was first being discussed in the state and federal governments, readers learned that while drinking their Bavarian beer, they could have "absolute certainty of its pure and unadulterated production." The EEC proposal, by contrast, allowed myriad forms of adulteration. And the motivation was simple:

> The advantage is not for the consumers, the brewers, nor the malters, nor the German farmers, and not for the workers in these industries. The only advantage would be for foreign breweries...It cannot be the purpose and goal of the EEC to suppress what is tried and tested, because something new is profitable. It cannot be the purpose of the EEC to replace the variety of beer types...with a unity swill (*Einheitsgesöff*) of undefined origin and composition.[47]

The article featured strong images to round out the argument, putting the onus on consumers themselves to insist that their interests and health mattered. In one image, the hammer of European regulation descends on consumers taking cover behind the *Reinheitsgebot*; in another, rioting consumers storm the barricades with banners demanding "pure beer," pitchforks in hand; in yet another, a responsible consumer vehemently rejects any potential European "unity swill."[48] These would have been the same consumers who, as we saw, admitted confusion about the contents and purpose of the *Reinheitsgebot*. But now they were cast as having a crucial role to play in retaining tradition and, of course, the market share of local brewers.

News of the harmonization proposal also led to other forms of consumer mobilization beyond Bavaria—namely, the founding of a special interest group called the *Aktionskommitee reines Bier* (ArB) rooted in Düsseldorf. The capital of North Rhine-Westphalia, Düsseldorf had been a center of opposition to "Bavarian separatism" in the *Süßbierstreit*. But now, the ArB followed the lead of the

---

[46] Rudolf Oleschko, 'Das Reinheitsgebot: Gedanken eines Egoisten', *Bayerische Bier-Illustrierte* no. 1 (1967), p. 9; 'Robotor-Bock—Computer-Pils und was sonst noch auf Sie zukommen könnte', *Bayerische Bier-Illustrierte* no. 1 (1969), pp. 12–13; and 'Wünschen Sie uniformes Einheitsbier?' *Bayerische Bier-Illustrierte* no. 4 (1969), pp. 11–12. On the place of such fears in the political culture of Federal Republic, see Frank Biess, *German Angst: Fear and Democracy in the Federal Republic* (Oxford: Oxford University Press, 2020), pp. 130–57.

[47] 'Um das Reinheitsgebot', *Bayerische Bier-Illustrierte* no. 4 (1970), p. 10.

[48] Ibid. On the question of the capitalistic "purpose and goal" of European integration, see Chapter 7.

Figure 5.1 "ArB ballot box in Bad Neustadt a.d. Saale." Bayerischer Brauerbund e.V., *Geschäftsbericht 1970/71*, insert. Reproduced courtesy of the Bavarian Brewers Association.

Bavarian and West German brewing industries and rallied around the *Reinheitsgebot*. Its public relations work effectively helped popularize and politicize the very concept of "pure beer," thereby leveraging consumer interests into policy-making. In 1971, their most successful action involved the circulation of ballots allowing consumers to voice their support for "pure beer." Ballots were made available in various locations, including as mail-in cutouts in domestic magazines such as *Bavarian Beer Illustrated* and at ballot boxes in both cities and small towns. They proclaimed that "Our beer must remain pure! Vote for pure beer!" and juxtaposed a "yes" vote for pure beer with a *reductio ad absurdum* "no" vote—a vote for the inclusion of "chemical additives: ascorbic acid, tannins, sulfur dioxide, and proteolytic enzymes." Across the Federal Republic, the ArB circulated 750,000 ballots, half a million fliers, and 26,000 posters, which were hung in breweries and around towns, in order to generate popular resistance toward what they and others called "chemical beer" and advocating instead for "pure beer."

The activities of the ArB and the consumer protectionist rhetoric of Bavarian and West German brewers readily fed into public health policy and discourse. As early as the summer of 1969, Bavarian brewers had been in contact with Federal Minister of Health Käthe Strobel, a self-identified Bavarian from Nuremberg. A long-time advocate of consumer protection, she was drawn to the idea that the *Reinheitsgebot* ensured that consumers knew what was in their beer. Without the law, she claimed, the housewife could unknowingly expose her family to uncertain and even unhealthy substances.[49] Even before the EEC proposal, Strobel appeared in television campaigns alongside the Bavarian Brewers Association promoting the *Reinheitsgebot* as a staple of public health policy.[50] She had similarly been in contact with the ArB since at least late 1970, when they requested that she start consolidating allies in relevant federal ministries, in the federal parliament, and in the European Commission in Brussels.[51] In March of 1971 she held a public spectacle event in Bonn at which representatives of the ArB delivered more than 200,000 ballots endorsing the protection of "pure beer." She noted that it was a wave of popular support she could not easily ignore and joked that her advocacy would be for all Germans, and not just because she was a Nuremberger or a Bavarian.[52]

Minister Strobel came to spearhead the publicity campaigns for the *Reinheitsgebot*, appearing on television and at press events to taste "pure beer" and talk about consumer protectionist virtues. But she was not alone in a wave of mass mediatization. Current and former Federal Ministers of Nutrition and Agriculture, Josef Ertl and Hermann Höcherl, also both Bavarians, launched public campaigns defending "pure beer," railing against additives, and advocating for consumer protection. Höcherl, for example, appeared in a late 1970 television public service announcement in which he spoke to West German consumers about the various chemicals that were included in "unpure" foreign beers. Speaking directly into the camera, a glass of German beer in front of him, he explained that the ten laboratory vials surrounding him contained various dangerous and risky ingredients not permitted under the *Reinheitsgebot*. He concluded that, "for me, beer adulterated with chemicals is an abomination!"[53]

Beyond the advocacy of political notables, perhaps the single broadest media push came from the brewing industry, which launched a nationwide advertising campaign to make the *Reinheitsgebot* a shared German icon. Their 1971 platform "The purity is in the beer" (*Im Bier ist die Reinheit*), claimed that, "Since time immemorial, Germany's brewers brew beer according to the *Reinheitsgebot*. From hops, malt, yeast, and water. And nothing else. So it is, and so it will remain." The print ad appeared in more than 150 newspapers, reaching an estimated two-thirds of West German households. The campaign also involved television ads that reached more than 16.5 million West German homes. By 1972, the West

---

[49] On her approach to public health policy, see, 'Für Beibehaltung des Reinheitsgebotes', *Gesundheitspolitik aus erster Hand* Nr 17 (May 19, 1969); and, further, Christian Sammer, 'Die "Modernisierung" der Gesundheitsaufklärung in beiden deutschen Staaten zwischen 1949 und 1975: Das Beispiel Rauchen', *Medizinhistorisches Journal* 50 no. 3 (2015): pp. 274–6.

[50] Bayerischer Brauerbund e.V. *Geschäftsbericht 1968/69–1969/70*, p. 89.

[51] Nov. 12, 1970, letter from the Aktionskommitee Reines Bier to Federal Minister Käthe Strobel, BAK B 189/10312.

[52] Mar. 23, 1971, speech by Käthe Strobel at the submission of the voting cards by the Aktionskommitee Reines Bier, BAK B 189/10312; and '200,000 Stimmzettel in 10 Bierfässern. Plebiszit über die Reinheit des Bieres: "Akt verantwortungsbewußten Bürgersinns,"' *General Anzeiger* 24.3.71.

[53] *Bayerische Bier-Illustrierte* no. 1 (1971), p. 14.

Figure 5.2 "Federal Minister Käthe Strobel tests pure Bavarian beer at a televised event in Summer 1969." Bayerischer Brauerbund e.V. *Geschäftsbericht 1968/69–1969/70.* Reproduced courtesy of the Bavarian Brewers Association.

German brewing industry estimated that the multi-platform campaign had reached 96 per cent of the West German adult population.[54] "Since time immemorial" was a bold claim indeed. The *Reinheitsgebot* had only gotten outside of Bavaria at the turn of the 20th century, and was contested at that. The final act of

[54] Bayerischer Brauerbund e.V. *Geschäftsbericht 1971/72*, pp. 77–9.

Anzeige
der Deutschen Bierwerbung 1971

Deutschlands reiner* Fluß:

Bier

Seit eh und je brauen
Deutschlands Brauer Bier nach dem Reinheitsgebot.
Aus Hopfen, Malz, Hefe und Wasser.
Und sonst nichts.
Darauf ist und bleibt Verlaß.
Die deutschen Brauer.

* Ohne chemische Zusätze,
ohne Aromastoffe,
ohne künstliche Farbstoffe.

Im Bier ist die Reinheit.

Figure 5.3 "Germany's source of Purity: Beer," reproduced courtesy of the German Brewers Association.

the *Süßbierstreit* had only closed in 1965. Not only had the list of permissible ingredients been a point of political and industrial contention for centuries, contemporary brewing restrictions actually allowed the production of ales with cane, beet, and invert sugar as well as coloring agents derived from sugar and starch sugar.[55] The content of the campaign was simply not true, on basically all counts.

This campaign encapsulated much of the transition of the *Reinheitsgebot* in the postwar decades. To some critical observers, such as *Der Spiegel*, the play was legible as capital interest disguised as consumer protection: "The 'struggle for pure beer,' which the Brewers Association allegedly wants to fight 'for the protection of consumers,' still quite informally serves the interests of beer makers…frightened by the competition from foreign beer producers."[56] But if it was a play, it worked. West German delegates to the European Council repeatedly stalled or vetoed the proposal, spurred on, as they were, by the recommendations of the Bundesrat and Bundestag, the leading charge of Käthe Strobel and the Ministry of Health, and the wave of industrial and apparent popular opposition. From 1971 to 1973, an international working group on the beer question repeatedly met in Brussels, expressing confusion and frustration with the intransigence

[55] *Biersteuergesetz in der Fassung vom 14. März 1952 mit Durchführungsbestimmungen zum Biersteuergesetz (BierStDB) in der Fassung vom 14. März 1952* (Nuremberg: Brauwelt Verlag Hans Carl, 1952), Sect. 9, Para. 1–2.

[56] 'Bier/ Reinheitsgebot—Leer und pappig', *Der Spiegel* 15, 1971, p. 49.

of West German opposition. They were unmoved by both the unmalted grain argument, which amounted to a question of technique rather than raw materials, and by the additive argument, which made monsters out of naturally occurring substances: ascorbic acid (vitamin C), tannins (bittering agents), and proteolytic enzymes (which breakdown protein molecules). Still, by 1973, and a few versions of the proposal later, the process had stalled completely. In May of that year, Strobel's ministry representative to the EEC, Dr Nickels, hit the nail on the head with a rarely present critical tone noting that the brewing industry had succeeded in making the "so-called *Reinheitsgebot*" into a "sacred cow" by "popularizing it amongst the people, the federal parliament, and the federal council."[57] Further amendments were made in the European Council, but by 1975 the plan was officially withdrawn because the West Germans were completely unwilling to compromise on their newfound commitment to beer purity. And so, this effort at market protectionism had lasting cultural effects. The claim to tradition was a claim of timelessness and purity that energized a collective past that never was. It was an appropriation of regional peculiarity into an ahistorical national touchstone that was particularly well-suited to the postwar condition. Indeed, the language of beer purity resonated not only with emerging forms of consumer capitalism but also with discursive continuities of German purity in the shadow of National Socialism. The *Reinheitsgebot* in some ways did become a "sacred cow," but a shared one, and a point of collective pride in an era in which many Germans sought safe modes of collective identification.

Conclusion

The historian Celia Applegate once noted that after 1945, "Germany was rebuilt from the regions outward and upward."[58] That certainly rings true in the case of the *Reinheitsgebot*, as a long embattled provincial industrial standard became a national icon. The impetus for this rebuilding and recasting of tradition and place often emerged from locally rooted interests. Just as the *Reinheitsgebot* became more Bavarian through West German market integration, so too did it become more West German through European integration. Locating the *Reinheitsgebot* in the entangled regional, national, and international political economies of the boom years reveals how capital interests became consumer protectionism, and how a provincial curiosity became a national crusade. When the EEC proposal

---

[57] May 17, 1973 memorandum, BAK B 189/10311. Nickels had been a critical voice for some time. See, for example, his early assessment in: May 12, 1969, Dr Nickels Vermerk, II B6–49 780–6250/69. Betr. Angleichung der Rechtsvorschriften über Bier in Brüssel, Fragestunde am 13/14 Mai 1969, BAK B 189/1481.

[58] Celia Applegate, *A Nation of Provincials: The German Idea of Heimat* (Berkeley: University of California Press, 1990), p. 229.

died in 1975, the *Reinheitsgebot* remained king, becoming the subject of extensive advertising and public relations work. It remained that, as we will see in Chapter 7, even when it was overturned as a trade barrier by the European Court of Justice in the 1980s. There remains one more sphere, however, in which Bavarian cultures, practices, and business interests shaped the German nation. We turn now to a yet broader scale of entanglements, and to the international and global perception of Germany as a jovial, alpine, beer-drinkers' paradise—a postwar transformation in which selling beer often meant rebranding the nation.

6

The Munich Effect

Löwenbräu, Bavarian Beer, and the Global Imaginary

In the summer of 1952, an ad in the London newspaper *The Evening Standard* announced to readers that, after a wartime hiatus, "Löwenbräu is back!" The re-emergence of the beer in London offered a "really potent reminder that the world's best beer since 1383 is still brewed at Munich."[1] Only a decade earlier German bombs had fallen on London, and the United Kingdom was still rationing foodstuffs including sugar, meat, and cheese. Reviving the product by associating it with long-standing German excellence likely conflicted with lingering British animosities toward their erstwhile enemy. Indeed, many in Britain considered the nascent power of Germany an equal threat to that posed by the Soviet Union.[2] And yet, the advertisement reminded consumers that Germany—and even Munich, a city Hitler had called the "capital of the movement"—was more than Nazism: it was the centuries-long home of the "world's best beer." If Londoners were to order the beer, they would have to pronounce it first, so the ad suggested that they "repeat 'Lurvenbrow' ten times."[3] As a whole, the ad presented the beer as an introduction, or a reintroduction, to a different Germany than the one they had recently known—a Germany that was home to a past everyone could enjoy and appreciate. Such a development was not limited to London, or even Great Britain. Beer from Bavaria, and especially from Munich-based Löwenbräu, shaped and informed a whole host of international perceptions of West Germany and obfuscated the Nazi past in an expanding world of goods.

Beer operated as a medium for rebranding Germany thanks to two primary developments: First, the unprecedented economic growth of the postwar decades, and, second, a marketing strategy that revolved around place-based claims to authenticity. On the first count, well beyond beer alone, exports became an important part of how people around the world made sense of the West German nation. This was a function of Economics Minister and later Chancellor Ludwig Erhard's intentional rejection of great power politics in favor of market

---

[1] Löwenbräu ad, *The Evening Standard*, June 12, 1952; the same ad appeared in London several times; see for example, *The Times*, June 26, 1957.
[2] Spencer Mawby, *Containing Germany: Britain and the Arming of the Federal Republic* (London: Palgrave Macmillan, 1999), p. 197.
[3] Löwenbräu ad, *The Evening Standard* and *The Times*.

A Nation Fermented: Beer, Bavaria, and the Making of Modern Germany. Robert Shea Terrell, Oxford University Press.
© Robert Shea Terrell 2024. DOI: 10.1093/oso/9780198881834.003.0007

globalization and a "trade-state paradigm."[4] Across business sectors, West German export strategy targeted the unprecedented economic boom in Western Europe and particularly the United States.[5] But because beer was relatively cheap and quotidian compared to, say, automobiles, it also boasted a more complex trade geography, following German migrants with a taste for home, entering global diplomatic relations from decolonization to Cold War imaginaries, and seeking out development booms in the United States, East Asia, and beyond. Throughout, claims to authenticity underpinned almost all the success of Löwenbräu, which dominated German international sales in profits, markets, and volume. Löwenbräu and their global partners in distribution, marketing, and advertising built their success on linking the product with Munich-based claims to authenticity and quality. Selling an imagery of Munich and a culture of consumption as much as a singular product, Löwenbräu came to inform how people around the world perceived West Germany broadly.

International cultural understandings of Germany as a place were shaped in the course of capitalist expansion. On the one hand, Löwenbräu is a private enterprise that merely followed the standard formula of capital growth: seeking markets, defining markets, shaping product image, expanding product placement, and protecting the exclusivity of the product. On the other, Löwenbräu and their global partners sold more than beer. Demand, to borrow from Arjun Appadurai, "is a socially regulated and generated impulse," and thus to understand the life of a high demand commodity it is crucial to interrogate the production of cultural value—to study the value makers, the so-called "experts," and those with capital interests at stake who informed the landscape of meaning.[6] Löwenbräu was particularly active in this process as a result of their intensive focus on exports, but their beer also shaped an imagery of Germany informed by Bavarian and Munich iconography. Beer drinkers around the world came to understand that when they bought Löwenbräu or attended an Oktoberfest, they were approximating an authentic German experience. The greatness of Munich's beer culture, long a staple of Munich tourism, had been fully turned outward, becoming part of West Germany's global cultural repertoire.[7] As beer traveled the world, so too did information *about* it. In the process of shaping the market scaffolding that would

---

[4] Reinhard Neebe, *Weichenstellung für die Globalisierung: Deutsche Weltmarktpolitik, Europa und Amerika in der Ära Ludwig Erhard* (Cologne: Böhlau Verlag, 2004), p. 18.

[5] See, for example, Werner Abelshauser, *Deutsche Wirtschaftsgeschichte seit 1945* (Munich: C.H. Beck Verlag, 2004), pp. 258–62; and Bernhard Rieger, *The People's Car: A Global History of the Volkswagen Beetle* (Cambridge: Harvard University Press, 2013), pp. 188–232.

[6] Arjun Appadurai, *The Social Life of Things: Commodities in Cultural Perspective* (Cambridge: Cambridge University Press, 1986), p. 32. For a similar discussion of authenticity, see Robert Ji-Song Ku, *Dubious Gastronomy: The Cultural Politics of Eating Asian in the USA* (Honolulu: University of Hawaii Press, 2014), esp. pp. 17–48.

[7] On beer and Munich tourism, see Adam T. Rosenbaum, *Bavarian Tourism and the Modern World, 1800–1950* (Cambridge: Cambridge University Press, 2016), p. 189.

ensure sales, people in diverse fields—from patent law to advertising and from event organizing to international diplomacy—produced meanings about the product and its consumption that took on larger significance for global re-imaginings of Germany.

Going Global: Patterns and Pathways of International Sales

The era of the two world wars and the postwar occupation wrought multilayered havoc on the brewing industry. As in most sectors of the global economy, trade decreased between the wars. In broad strokes, German beer exports in 1913 remained unrivaled in volume until 1959, from which point they consistently expanded.[8] But war itself had also driven the industry into the ground. In addition to those issues facing production for the domestic market in the 1940s—from material shortages to piecemeal conversion of many large breweries toward civil defense—the export market was hampered by an Allied naval blockade. In the final stage of the war, Allied bombing likewise dealt a significant blow to the productive potential of many breweries. The Spaten Brewery, for example, stopped brewing altogether in the last months of the war, in part because it had been converted to war purposes, but also because it was bombed at least nine times from March 1943 to February 1945.[9] A similar fate awaited Löwenbräu, which by April 1945 had been reduced to a "rubble heap."[10] Production got a boost immediately after the war when the American Military Government designated Löwenbräu one of the seven breweries tasked with supplying full-strength beer to American soldiers. Still, the prohibition on sales for civilian consumption, the physical damage to the brewery, and the material scarcities of the late 1940s all kept production levels remarkably low. In the first twelve months of postwar production, Löwenbräu produced less beer than they had in a single month in the pre-war Third Reich and earlier. Almost all of it stayed local, consumed by occupation soldiers, and only about 5 per cent went abroad, sold on dining cars of the *Compagnie Internationale des Wagons-Lits*, a Paris-based international overnight train service.[11] But for Löwenbräu, more so than any other major brewery, exporting was the way of the future. It provided their solution to at least three problems: the Allied prohibition, the lingering scarcities of the 1950s, and the difficult fact

[8] Uwe Paulsen and Franz Meyer, *7. Statistischer Bericht des Deutschen Brauer-Bundes e.V.* (Bad Godesberg, 1966), p. 78.

[9] Wolfgang Behringer, *Die Spaten-Brauerei, 1397–1997: Die Geschichte eines Münchner Unternehmens vom Mittelalter bis zur Gegenwart* (Munich and Zurich: Piper Verlag GmbH, 1997), pp. 326–34.

[10] Wolfgang Behringer, *Löwenbräu: Von den Anfängen des Münchner Brauwesens bis zur Gegenwart* (Munich: Süddeutscher Verlag, 1991), pp. 249–51.

[11] Export statistics June 1, 1945–Sept. 30, 1945; and Oct. 1, 1945–Sept. 30, 1946, Bayerisches Wirtschaftsarchiv (henceforth BWA) F002-495.

that the brand was relatively unpopular among consumers in Munich and Bavaria. While their export efforts were not unique, they began remarkably early and, more importantly, were unmatched in scope. For the next few decades, the success of Löwenbräu depended on a conscious choice by brewery leadership to focus their reconstruction on exports almost immediately after the war.[12]

One of the primary vectors of Löwenbräu's explosive global growth in the postwar decades was the established history of German exports and the consumption patterns of the German diaspora. Löwenbräu's first major international deal, for example, was with a former import partner, Hans Holterbosch Inc. in New York City. Agreed to in the summer of 1947, Löwenbräu beer was among the earliest consumer goods to be produced for export following the shift in Western Allied strategy toward nourishing German economic productivity. The deal of $700,000 for 12 monthly deliveries of 20,000 cases was a radical quantity given the scarcity of the postwar years. Indeed, Holterbosch had to supply the barley for production as a condition of the deal. Such terms won the approval of Lucius Clay who, as we have seen, was deeply concerned about questions of raw materials in the production of beer.[13] Holterbosch was a known quantity for Löwenbräu. Born in Düsseldorf, he had migrated to New York City in the mid-1920s and eventually opened a German restaurant and sports club in Yorkville on the Upper East Side. He rose to distinction in the German community, ultimately working with New York City mayor James Walker to welcome notable German visitors, including athletes and scientists, in the late 1920s and early 1930s. When American prohibition was lifted in 1933, German migrants in the United States wanted German beer and the German breweries wanted a piece of the American market. Bavarian beer had long been held in high regard in the United States, but most imports had shut down and Löwenbräu itself had not been available for almost 20 years.[14] Holterbosch, who had never worked in importing, got the contract through personal connections from his soccer club, and between 1933 and 1939 worked "to make the name and the taste well known."[15] Business grew along the northeastern United States, primarily through sales to German restaurants, and as late as June 1940 Holterbosch boasted that his was the only German beer "still available in this country 10 months after the outbreak of the European War."[16] In 1947, Holterbosch made the deal through negotiations overseen by the Military Government, but for a variety of practical reasons on both sides of the Atlantic,

[12] Löwenbräu A.G., *Geschäftsbericht 1944/45*; 'Technischer Bericht für die Aufsichtsratssitzung vom 22.12.1954', BWA F002-917; Behringer, *Die Spaten-Brauerei*, pp. 345–6.

[13] 'Bavarian Beer Coming. US to Get 20,000 Cases a Month, Gen. Clay Discloses', *New York Times*, Aug. 4, 1947, p. 25.

[14] On the high regard, already in 1849 consumers in and around Hoboken, NJ enjoyed unnamed Bavarian beer, 'justly deemed…vastly preferable to any ale ever made in this country'. See 'The Bavarian Beer Garden, Hoboken', *New York Herald*, May 23, 1849, p. 4.

[15] 'One Way to Get a Big Beer Franchise is to Play Soccer', *The New York Times*, June 1, 1957, p. 21.

[16] Behringer, *Löwenbräu*, p. 247.

imports did not begin in earnest until 1949. Less than ten years later, the New York importer had increased imports from 100,000 gallons a year to 1.3 million, which amounted to more than half of the German beer (and almost a third of all European beer) imported to the United States in the late 1950s.[17]

This trend of reopening older export channels, and, more importantly, of tapping German diasporic demand, explains much of the initial success of Löwenbräu in the export market. In the 1950s, German-Canadians and Germans in Canada placed a high premium on beer as part of their cultural life. During the war, many social clubs had closed their doors, as was the case with Club Edelweiss in Alberta, in operation since 1906 but shuttered from 1939 to 1953. In subsequent years, German communities—often maintaining German-language newspapers—began to organize folk festivals, including Oktoberfest, which Club Edelweiss helped bring to Edmonton in 1958, for example. Beer was imagined as a fundamental part of the experience. As the *Edmonton Nachrichten* put it in anticipation of the event, "those who have been away from Germany for years want very much to simply feel the taste of German beer on the tongue once again."[18] Sadly, it was not to be that year, much to the disappointment of the "flood of visitors" that more than doubled the event capacity and came from as far as British Columbia. This influx of visitors, the paper reported, had come for the Munich beer to heal their homesickness but, at the eleventh hour, the Alberta Liquor Control Board blocked the import of German beers in an effort to stimulate the local brewing sector.[19] In other cases, however, the absence of German beer at such events was short-lived and depended on location. Indeed, in Regina, Saskatchewan, local Oktoberfest celebrations included Löwenbräu already in 1955, when the beer sold out and left the yodeling crowd demanding more. By 1959, the beer could also be had in the home and at numerous German celebrations in Ontario, where it marked a return to a high-quality German life. As the *Torontoer Zeitung* put it on Christmas Eve 1959, "those in Toronto or many other provinces, who had learned to appreciate the quality and excellence of a bottle of Löwenbräu beer in their old homeland no longer has any reason to play the role of the have-nots."[20]

Another important trend in opening the export market to Bavarian and German beer, and especially to Löwenbräu, was a circle of diplomats and international elites as well as American, British, and French military forces around the world. In the mid-1950s the geography of Löwenbräu exports expanded

---

[17] 'One Way to Get a Big Beer Franchise'.

[18] 'Oktoberfest mit deutschem Bier', *Edmonton Nachrichten* n.d., likely from late October 1958, clipping in BWA F002-8916.

[19] 'Überschäumendes Oktoberfest in Edmonton', *Edmonton Nachrichten*, Nov. 6, 1958; and 'Deutsches Bier ist unerwünscht', *Edmonton Nachrichten*, Oct. 16, 1958.

[20] '"Feuchte" Festtags-Perspektiven', *Torontoer Zeitung* Dec. 24, 1959, pp. 4–6; above, 'Oktoberfest in der Praerie', *Der Courier* (Regina) Oct. 27, 1955.

dramatically, in lockstep with geopolitical developments. In 1955, for example, the beer became available in the Belgian Congo, hot on the heels of new colonial reform programs to "emancipate" Congolese elites through proof of "civil merit." The advertisements targeted colonial agents and new Congolese elites, promising to deliver the highest quality beer available the world over.[21] Shortly after, on the eve of the Suez Crisis, the American Embassy in Tel Aviv thanked the Munich brewery in advance for meeting their larger order in preparation for their embassy Christmas party. Importers in Baghdad and Aden—that is, on the other side of Suez—continued to make the beer available to embassies and clubs even after the Suez Crisis, but had to dramatically increase shipping rates to account for the lingering canal closures.[22] Around the globe, importers in Pusan and Seoul that serviced the demand of American GIs stationed in South Korea since the Korean War advocated for a more direct trade relationship with Munich in 1956 to cut out price hikes charged by their middleman in Japan—a long-time importer in Yokohama, Hans Haenschel & Co., who had been bringing the beer into Japan since the early 1930s.[23] The beer was shipped to exclusive circles around the world, and sometimes to places where drinking alcohol was not the norm or not even legal. The beer was sold, for example, in Pakistan, Iran, and most of the Levant and North Africa, but was mostly consumed in embassies, consulates, and elite homes and clubs. In all these markets, importers held power over the flow of the commodity and sometimes sought to leverage that. In 1958, for example, the New Delhi–based Lavena Trading Corporation argued for a higher commission on sales while also wanting to sell beer to diplomats for reduced prices, which they claimed was common practice. All told, Löwenbräu beer traveled with the American military, followed the contours of decolonization, lubricated the banquet halls of embassies around the world, and stayed in the spaces of lingering colonial influence and neocolonial interest. In 1958, the brewery even contacted Wasel Gabriel Bespolka, the General Service Officer of the United Nations Truce Supervision Organization in Jerusalem, to see if peacekeeping in the Middle East might benefit from the highest quality beer in the world, already exported to more than eighty countries worldwide.[24] While shipping quantities to these countries were low, the expansive export geography fed the marketing claims to quality and global status that became staples of Löwenbräu's global image.

Alongside catering to the German diaspora and capitalizing on international developments, a third and final way that Löwenbräu and other Bavarian

---

[21] See, for example, Löwenbräu ads in *Le Courrier d'Afrique*, July 20 and 21, 1955.

[22] Oct. 22, 1956, letter from US Embassy in Tel Aviv to Löwenbräu in Munich; Feb. 27, 1957, letter from Joseph N. Loka (Baghdad) to Löwenbräu Munich; Apr. 16, 1957, letter from S.E. Delbourgo Import & Export (Aden) to Löwenbräu Munich, BWA F 002–364.

[23] See correspondence from Aug. to Sept. 1956 between Tradeship Ltd Pusan & Seoul and Löwenbräu Munich, BWA F 002–364.

[24] Feb. 1958, letter from Lavena Trading Corporation, New Delhi, to Löwenbräu Munich; letter marked only 1958 from Löwenbräu Munich to W.G. Bespolka of UNTSO, BWA F 002–366.

breweries tapped into major markets was by more broadly targeting new consumer opulence in radically booming economies such as those in England and especially the United States. The 1960s proved a pivotal decade. From 1959 to 1969, West German and Bavarian exports increased by 146 per cent and 259 per cent respectively.[25] Löwenbräu and other major exporters, most notably Würzburger and Beck's, actively targeted wealth centers. In the United Kingdom, for example, Löwenbräu wanted a foothold in London of course, but also eyed major industrial and trade centers such as Manchester, Birmingham, Liverpool, and Edinburgh. In the United States, Löwenbräu established three main centers of distribution: one in New York (Holterbosch) that could cater to the Eastern seaboard, one jointly based in Detroit and Chicago, and one based in Los Angeles. In each case, Löwenbräu worked with their international distribution team to target new opulence and gain practical knowledge of the difference between regional markets, especially when it came to import competition such as that from Würzburger (Franconian/northern Bavarian), Beck's (north German), Heineken (Dutch), and Tuborg and Carlsberg (both Danish). Booming economies in western Europe and the United States were not alone, however. Beginning in the 1960s, Löwenbräu and their partners began ramping up sales, distribution, and marketing in the growing economies of East Asia. In particular, Hong Kong and Tokyo became major sales hubs as Löwenbräu rode, and contributed to, both the well-worn and the newly emerging pathways of growth in a shifting terrain of global capital.[26] While German diasporic communities may have had reasons to seek out German products, many others around the world did not. All this expansive market growth thus brought with it numerous challenges, namely convincing consumers that the beer was unique, high quality, and worth the frequently higher price tag. The story of Löwenbräu, then, is a story not just of logistics, but also of meanings: defining, constructing, and protecting the meanings of the thing.

Quality, Authenticity, and the Political Economy of Taste

At the same time that Bavarian breweries such as Löwenbräu were reopening and expanding their export networks, they were also working to ensure that their product would remain unique in the global market. Individual breweries and the Bavarian Brewers Association had the most at stake in the success of their product and fought hard to protect it very early in the period of postwar economic

---

[25] Calculated from 'Außenhandel mit Bier 1950–1969 Bundesrepublik—Bayern', Bayerischer Brauerbund e.V., *Geschäftsbericht, 1968/69–1969/70*, p. 124.

[26] Beyond Löwenbräu, see Jeffrey Pilcher, '"Tastes Like Horse Piss": Asian Encounters with European Beer', *Gastronomica: The Journal of Critical Food Studies* 16 no. 1 (Spring, 2016): p. 34.

growth. Officials at the Löwenbräu brewery and their partners in Bavaria actively policed the image of their product in an effort to hold on to and expand their global market share. The sorts of knowledge, expertise, and claims *about* the commodity that they exercised did much to shape the cultural and economic values attached to it. The claims of commodity "experts," to return to Appadurai, are part of the "political economy of taste." Put differently, meaning and value, and thus demand, are shaped by those who lay claim to specific commodity knowledge.[27] In Munich, this meant actively policing the image and language of the product in an effort to hold on to and expand the global market share. In pursuing capital growth, Löwenbräu and their domestic partners worked to preserve, and indeed construct, cultural values such as "quality" and "authenticity." In the case of Löwenbräu, the political economy of taste that underpinned the exclusivity of claims to Bavarian quality and authenticity was rooted in the legal institutions of capitalism: patents, naming rights, and proprietary claims. Throughout the 1950s, the Bavarian Brewers Association and its industrial allies responded to complaints from Löwenbräu and other export breweries, ultimately engaging in a number of national and international legal battles in the name of preserving the exclusivity of Bavarian beer.

In January 1952, a representative of Löwenbräu complained to a legal counsel of the Bavarian Brewers Association about an export brewery in Hamburg called the *Bavaria-und-St.-Pauli-Brauerei*. The Hamburg brewery had been exporting a beer called, in English, "Bavaria Beer" that the Löwenbräu representative felt was a "conscious attempt to mislead consumers" in the global market. He argued that this fell under Section 16 of the Law Against Unfair Competition, which dealt with product descriptions and labeling.[28] The initial determination was that the Hamburg brewery violated no laws because the spirit of its label meant "in the Bavarian style," a logic which may have reflected the fact that, by this time, "Bavarian style" beerhalls were relatively well established throughout Germany, including in Hamburg. The Löwenbräu brewery remained unsatisfied, however. Indeed, as seen in the previous chapter, this was the exact same moment that Löwenbräu and other Bavarian breweries were insisting on the importance of parallel Bavarian and West German production standards. The case here transferred those efforts at domestic market protection to a larger, international scale. Unless the Hamburg brewery was matching Bavarian standards, which they were not, the original critique about proprietary use of the name "Bavaria" stood. Indeed, just as he would years later in the case of the *Süßbierstreit*, Werner Schladenhaufen of the Bavarian Brewers Association drew on the language of the West German Beer Tax Law, accusing the Hamburg brewery of attempting

[27] Appadurai, *The Social Life of Things*, p. 45.
[28] Jan. 11, 1952, letter to Carlo Proebst, Bayerisches Hauptstaatsarchiv (henceforth BayHStA) Brauerbund 1453.

to develop an appearance or pretense (*Anschein*) of being Bavarian and thus misleading consumers.[29]

The issue slowly simmered until 1956, when Löwenbräu encouraged the Union of Bavarian Export Breweries—an allied organization of the Brewers Association—to enlist the services of patent lawyers in Berlin and Munich. The ensuing legal entanglement lasted for years—and, in some respects, decades. At stake, the lawyers argued to the German Patent Office, was "a delocalizing effect" (*entlokalisierende Wirkung*) on the very word "Bavaria." As precedent for this phenomenon, the team offered the case of Pilsner beer. In the late nineteenth century, the German court ruled that "Pilsner beer" had become a style all its own, devoid of geographical peculiarity, and we have seen how the style took the German nation by storm. It also, of course, rose to prominence around the world.[30] Speaking to this precise issue, the Bavarian legal team claimed that even within West Germany the English word "Bavaria" would immediately conjure the German federal state of Bayern. According to the patent lawyers, "Bavarian beer," as a *type* of beer, could thus not be as transferrable as "Pilsner beer" had been in previous decades. Both terms—Bavarian beer and Pilsner beer—indicated a product from a place but in the case of Bavarian beer, they argued, the product and the place could not be separated because of the stricter provincial adherence to the *Reinheitsgebot*.[31]

There were, in fact, legal concerns about how the law in different regions of West Germany, and other parts of Europe, mattered for the production of beer intended for export. Beyond the domestic distinctions discussed in the previous chapter, brewers in Bavaria were beholden to the law for export beer where other states of the Federal Republic were not. While the economic ramifications were real, the Munich brewery was explicitly *not* arguing for their release from them. Instead, they deployed a legal argument that used their own market constraints to protect their market share. Correspondence between the lawyers, the Munich and Hamburg breweries, the Bavarian Brewers Association, and the Union of Bavarian Export Breweries debated the semantics and symbols at play. Discussions on the delocalizing effect ranged from the use of words—Bayerisch, Bayern, Bavaria, Bavarian, and even the nonsensical Bavariana—to typography and even the size of the spaces on the labels which might, when viewed from just the right angle, mislead the consumer as to product origins.[32] The Hamburg brewery ceded

---

[29] Jun. 10, 1953, letter to Carlo Proebst, BayHStA Brauerbund 1453.

[30] Malcolm F. Purinton, *Globalization in a Glass: The Rise of Pilsner Beer through Technology, Taste and Empire* (London: Bloomsbury Academic, 2023); and Jeffrey M. Pilcher, "Imperial Hops: Beer in the Age of Empire," *Global Food History* (published online Jun. 21, 2023), DOI: 10.1080/20549547.2023.2226526.

[31] Apr. 9, 1956, letter from Walter Meissner and Herbert Tischer to the German Patent Office, BayHStA Brauerbund 1453.

[32] Mar. 8, 1957, letter from Löwenbräu to the Bavarian Brewers Association; and Dec. 15, 1959, letter from Meissner and Tischer to the Union of Bavarian Export Breweries, both in BayHStA Brauerbund 1453.

some ground on the phrase "Bavarian Beer," but they were not the only brewers using the name. As that dispute reached a fever pitch, Löwenbräu moved to protect their market once again, this time setting their sights on the Dutch Brouwerij-Bavaria-Lieshout. Complaining to the patent lawyers, Löwenbräu officials noted that the Dutch brewery had been overcharging for their beer in Tripoli, literally capitalizing on the Bavarian reputation.[33] The Hamburg brewery had likewise been accused of overcharging in Lebanon. Under pressure of these concerns, the lawyers conducted an international study of how these non-Bavarian "Bavaria beers" were being sold in more than twenty countries worldwide, ranging from England to Nigeria, Haiti to Japan.[34]

Ad hoc solutions, some technical, some legal, satisfied the various parties in the late 1950s. Efforts at larger holistic solutions would come only in subsequent decades with the institutionalization of protected geographical indications, a subject discussed later. In the short term, however, some resolutions were quite small. In 1959, for example, the Hamburg brewery made changes to their bottle labels, all of which were worked out in a dizzyingly mundane discussion of spacing and typography. In the global register, naming disputes had to be worked out in the various import locations. Indeed, the disputes were always ultimately about global perception, and nowhere were the stakes as high as in the United States, which was by far the dominant market for Bavarian, German, and all export beers in the 1950s and 1960s. Moving to clamp down on wording, the Union of Bavarian Export Breweries filed a US federal trademark registration for "Genuine Bavarian Beer," which was accepted in 1960 by the Bavarian Brewers Association. Further disputes in the 1960s brought additional trademarks on "Bayrisch Bier" and "Bayerisches Bier" in 1968. Case-by-case litigation and protection remained an important vector of market protectionism by Löwenbräu and other Bavarian breweries; indeed, as recently as 2011 the Bavarian Brewers Association engaged in legal action with the Dutch Bavaria Brewery in the European Court of Justice.

What such solutions have in common—from typography to supranational systems of market legislation—is the interests of provincial capital in the global market. At every stage in the early disputes, Löwenbräu kicked off and exacerbated tensions around proprietary claims to being *from* Bavaria and *being* Bavarian. These Bavarian brewers and trade organizations were actively policing the exclusivity of their product in hopes of avoiding a Pilsner-like "delocalizing effect." In the process they sharply limited who could make truth claims about the nature of the commodity. At the top of the knowledge network were the Bavarian brewers themselves. They were not alone, however. As we expand the political economy of taste, we see how international importers, distributors,

---

[33] Apr. 12, 1957, letter to Bavarian Brewers Association, BayHStA Brauerbund 1453.
[34] See letters from Apr. 4, May 2, and May 13, 1957, BayHStA Brauerbund 1453.

and marketers of Bavarian beers such as Löwenbräu came to have a profound global cultural impact as beer sales soared.

"A Magnificent Advertisement"—From Quality to Authenticity

In the summer of 1958, Dudley Mozely of Fremlins Ltd, the UK-based importer and distributor of Löwenbräu, attended the World's Fair in Brussels. The Munich brewery had set up a beer hall as part of the fair and had been promoting it to their clients around the world, from Fremlins itself to their Indian distributor in New Delhi, Lavena Trading Corporation. The Löwenbräu Beer Hall in Brussels was a massive 3,500-person establishment adorned with traditional décor and even featuring a large roaring lion, a staple of the Löwenbräu tent at the Munich Oktoberfest. Mozely was impressed by both the scale and the potential. Upon his return to England, he wrote to Munich that, "the whole 'set up' is a magnificent advertisement, and although it must certainly have cost a lot of money to finance the Hall, you seemed to be taking a lot of money judging by how crowded it was with visitors." After conveying his impression of the experience, he concluded that, "if a cellar could be procured in London about half the size it might also be a good advertisement."[35] In the next decade, Fremlins associate J.C. McLaughlin collaborated with the Munich brewery to open ten establishments across Britain, increasing UK sales ten-fold and promising, in the case of their Soho tavern, that visitors could "Travel to 'Old Bavaria' without leaving London!"[36] These establishments, much like the beer halls and Oktoberfests that similarly sprouted up around the world, promised an authentic experience by crafting the environment down to the last detail. Such establishments were a lot of fun, certainly, but at their core they were magnificent advertisements that sought to, and did, convince many consumers to buy expensive imported beer. By the time Mozely visited Brussels, claims to quality were standard in crowded markets and the sale of an authentic product and experience provided a new tactic to generate growth. It was developed by the Munich brewery itself in conjunction with decentralized agents in the political economy of taste: international importers and distributors looking to protect their own local market interests.

The standard copy of Löwenbräu's global marketing in the 1950s was essentially the same regardless of language. In the company records, newspaper ads from this period include languages ranging from French to Japanese, English to Arabic, but all revolve around the somewhat unoriginal claims that the drink was of the "highest quality" or "the world's best beer." The claim to quality was

---

[35] July 8, 1958, letter from Dudley Mozley to F. Kugelstatter, BWA F 002–385.
[36] Egon Larsen, 'Münchner Bierkeller in Soho. Lederhosen aus dem Kostümverleih', *Süddeutsche Zeitung* Aug. 19, 1965, p. 3.

generally motivated by the need to overcome the exceptionally high price point, which had been a consistent barrier to growth. In the United Kingdom, where wartime rationing on some goods continued until 1954, margins were thin. J.C. McLaughlin, who held the marketing contract for Löwenbräu beginning in 1952, had worked tirelessly to establish niche demand in luxury hotels and bars, but confessed that sales were dipping in the early 1950s. The problem, as Dudley Mozley explained in 1954, was locating and isolating "circles receptive to a luxury beer."[37] In the booming United States sales were higher, but the marketing approach was a similar refrain of quality and luxury. One newspaper advertisement in Chicago, for example, featured a man stopped at customs, giving up smuggled jewels but begging to keep his Löwenbräu.[38] In the United States, the United Kingdom, and Japan, magazines and newspapers played up the beer as being more like Champagne than conventional beer, drawing attention to the green bottle, the gold foil top, and the high price point.[39] Even closer to home, Löwenbräu placed ads in trade publications for the Austrian hospitality industry informing restaurateurs that "Löwenbräu is expensive. But also good. Beer aficionados in 149 countries know that. Restaurateurs in 149 countries profit on that."[40] Claims to quality would never entirely go away but, as readers likely know from their own lives, claims to the world's best burger or the world's best coffee often come from the most suspect of kitchens and cafes.

In most markets, Löwenbräu sales were slow and depended on consumers remaining convinced that claims to connoisseurship, expense, and exclusivity were true. But around the world, especially in the vibrant American economy, the beer market was flooded with products that boasted luxury and refinement. And, before too long, local Löwenbräu agents worried that such drinks were also encroaching on the authenticity of their product. In the winter of 1955, for example, the head of Löwenbräu's Detroit-based importer Premium Beer Sales, Felix Faber, encountered a Cincinnati beer called Wunderbräu while on vacation in Florida. For Faber, the beer posed a clear and direct challenge. The beer was a "miserable imitation," he explained, incapable of competing even with a good American beer. And yet, in bars and restaurants it was often listed as an import and carried an import price tag. The Cincinnati brewery, he claimed, was quite literally "capitalizing on the merit and esteem which good German imported

---

[37] Oct. 27, 1953, letter from J.C. McLaughlin to Dudley Mozley; and Apr. 27, 1954, letter from Dudley Mozley to Löwenbräu, both in BWA F 002–384.

[38] Löwenbräu ad, *Chicago Tribune*, May 8, 1956, p. A7.

[39] See ads ranging from the mid-1950s to mid-1960s in BWA F 002–8902. This approach eventually even became an emulative marketing strategy for brewing upstarts in later decades. In the 1990s, for example, the Indian brewery Sand Pipers adopted the "champagne of beers" motto, the green bottle, and gold foil, effectively increasing sales ten-fold. See, Pilcher, ' "Tastes like Horse Piss" ', p. 37.

[40] Ad from 1970 presented as an unmarked clipping in BWA F 002–8895. A note in the file claims similar ads were run in trade publications, including *Österreichisches Gastgewerbe Zeitung, Gastwirt, Hotelier, Cafetier*, and *Lebensmittelhändler*.

beer enjoys." As he explained to two of the Munich brewery heads, "The entire promotional advertising used for Wunderbräu is calculated to deceive the public into thinking that it is an authentic German beer." Indeed, the six-pack cartons, which featured lions and a coat of arms reminiscent of Munich iconography, even claimed, in German, that you won't find one better: "*Ein besseres findest du nicht.*" Faber fumed that the beer was advertised with an illegitimate German heritage. The claim on the cans that the beer was "now brewed in Cincinnati...by its original Braumeister" implied the beer was once brewed in Germany, which, according to Faber, it was not.[41]

There was very little the Munich brewery could do about this sort of issue directly. In the case of Wunderbräu, the beer actually never made any claims to being Bavarian, and Faber's concern was that it was pretending to be *German*. When the Bavarians could flex their trademarks, they did. In 1955, for example, American brewing giant Anheuser-Busch launched their "Busch Bavarian," which was branded with a snowy mountain scene complete with buildings in the Bavarian Alpine architectural style. Known today simply as Busch—in part to satisfy Bavarian trademarks—the beer is still branded with snowy mountains in spite of hailing from the prairie and floodplain of St. Louis, Missouri. But the case of Wunderbräu makes clear—as Eva Göbel argued well beyond the case of beer—that conceptions of Germany abroad became intricately tied to Bavarian traditions, imagery, stereotypes, and, of course, capital interest.[42] This conflation of things Bavarian and things German testifies to the provincial inflections of the nation on the global stage and undergirds a Bavarian stereotype of West Germany. Foundational in this case was the emergence of Löwenbräu as an ambassador of Germanness—not just a luxury, but a metonym for West Germany itself. Far from an intentional national rebranding, the process arose out of the desire of Löwenbräu and its global partners to sell more beer. They sought, in short, to overcome the claims of competitors like Busch Bavarian and Wunderbräu by selling the most authentic beer in the most authentic experience. Unlike the versatility of "Pilsner beer," the authenticity of Bavarian beer was inherently tied to the place. It was thus also tied to mythologies and stereotypes *about* the place and, beginning in the 1960s, the commodity and the mode of consumption became intimately related. The conviction that the product and the place were linked in an approximation of an authentic experience was part of expanding the political economy of taste as distributors and marketers sought to increase sales.

In the United States, the three distributors of Löwenbräu became increasingly active in selling not only beer but an experience of drinking it. In 1957, for example, the Los Angeles–based Wisdom Import Sales Co. worked with local

---

[41] Feb. 21, 1955 and Mar. 1, 1955, letters from Felix Faber to Karl Messner and Josef Kuglstatter; and Mar. 14, 1955, letter from Messner and Kuglstatter to Faber, BWA F 002-405.
[42] Eva Göbel, *Bayern in der modernen Konsumgesellschaft: Regionalisierung der Konsumkultur im 20. Jahrhundert* (Berlin: Weißensee Verlag, 2005), pp. 251–70, 333–52.

notables in Monterey, California to develop the Monterey Bay Oktoberfest. The festival was first thrown in 1956 by GIs at the Fort Ord Soldier's Club and was a relatively small gathering, likely serving a San Francisco brew called Wunder Beer.[43] In 1957, however, local businessman and community notable Tinsley C. Fry chaired a committee to expand the event and worked with Wisdom Import Sales to get the Munich Löwenbräu brewery involved. Fry wanted to stage an authentic Oktoberfest celebration complete with draft Löwenbräu beer, décor, Bavarian Trachten outfits, and glassware. He even invited the Mayor of Munich to attend the 1957 Monterey Oktoberfest, but the latter does not seem to have abided.[44] The festival turned a small profit and became a regular event, growing each year for the next few decades. Similarly, in 1961, importer Felix Faber enlisted the help of the Munich brewery in remodeling a German restaurant in Detroit. The owner of Krager's Restaurant, Frank Krager, wanted to remodel to "make a 'true Bräuhaus' of his restaurant." Krager was considering renaming the restaurant after Löwenbräu and requested that the Munich brewery send sample luncheon and dinner menus, postcards, pictures of the interior and exterior of their Munich location, samples of their glassware, and pictures of the uniforms worn by their waiters and waitresses.[45] On the other side of the Atlantic too, the popularity of the 1958 World's Fair exhibition generated local demand in Brussels for the style of consumption, and by the early 1960s restaurateurs and hoteliers in Belgium were working to capture and capitalize on the authentic sensory experience of proper consumption.[46]

By the end of the 1960s, the alleged authenticity of this Bavarian German experience had circled the globe. Bavarian and German quality had long been a staple of international sales, and while themed drinking had emerged in some places decades earlier, the 1960s witnessed an explosion of beer gardens and Oktoberfests from Australia to Japan, Gibraltar to Edmonton, and Hong Kong to California. At each, Löwenbräu beer anchored claims to the authenticity of the experience. In 1966, for example, the Palace Hotel in Kowloon opened to welcome Hong Kong socialites to the annual Oktoberfest celebration. The event had been promoted in the local magazine, *What's Doing in Hong Kong*, as "one of the thumpingest down-to-earth good times of the year," complete with beer directly from Löwenbräu in Munich. Lapsing into broken and nonsensical German, the promotion told of "two weeks of nightly singing, dancing, beer and wine gedrinken, German food zu essen, and alles zusammen good time gehaben [sic]."

---

[43] This had been the standard of German beer drinking in the area for decades. See, Tim Thomas, *The Abalone King of Monterey: 'Pop' Ernest Doelter, Pioneering Japanese Fishermen & the Culinary Classic that Saved an Industry* (Charleston: American Palate/The History Press, 2014).

[44] Aug 2, 1957, letter from Tinsley Fry to Löwenbräu, BWA F 002-651.

[45] Dec. 21, 1961, letter from Faber to Kugelstatter, BWA F 200-411.

[46] 'Munich et son 'Oktoberfest'', *le C.H.R.—Organe officiel de la Confédération Nationale des Unions Professionnelles des Cafetiers, Hôteliers et Restaurateurs de Belgique*, Nov. 3, 1961.

The event promised a welcome disruption from the normal tranquility of everyday life, noting that "the flowing of the beer in Munich sets off a gemutlich [sic] reaction in Hong Kong and the King's Lodge becomes a Munich Hofbrau [sic] Haus with an air of merriment that is rarely, if ever, seen in Hong Kong."[47] *Gemütlich* roughly translates as "cozy," but the word goes beyond physical coziness to include social acceptance and friendliness; it is a coziness of mind, body, and social environment. The piece included advice for how to manage Munich-style communal drinking practices lest readers get caught unaware in the "gemutlich reaction." At the same time, "German" beer bars opened throughout Tokyo, and, in 1967, Yokohama hosted their "Bavaria Festival." At the Tokyo Bazaar, visitors to the "Frankfurter und Bier" tent would be served by young Japanese women in dirndls, signaling the globalization of a stereotyped Bavarian mode of consumption made all the more authentic by the availability of Löwenbräu beer.

This transition toward authenticity as both an advertising pitch and an experience was not only a boon to sales, but also reshaped the experience of Germany around the world. Back in the United Kingdom, ad man J.C. McLaughlin had worked hand in hand with the Munich brewery to open ten establishments across Britain between 1965 and 1967—an investment that increased British consumption of Löwenbräu beer tenfold, from about 10,000 gallons to more than 100,000. According to a piece in London newspaper *The Sun*, these were "authentic German beer 'kellers' [where]...for six shillings a pint for Lowenbrau draught or bottled, keller customers get a real German night out with accordionist, plenty of rousing song and waitresses in traditional German dress."[48] McLaughlin, who had struggled to locate a market for Löwenbräu for a decade and a half, finally created one by selling an authentic experience of drinking to the newfound opulence of the English youth.[49]

In these British bars and restaurants, there was a deeply convoluted understanding of what was Bavarian and what was German. Indeed, such confusions seem to have permeated most international manifestations of the Löwenbräu–Munich–Germany nexus. We get a granular narrative from London's *Daily Express*, which boasted a circulation above 4 million, and in which readers were taken through a night out at an "authentic German beer-cellar in Aldwych." Our narrator is taken out by an old drinking friend who promises "a new and diverting view of the British drinking classes." Inside the "keller," [sic] English, Scots, and Irish were singing the First World War song " 'Waltzing Matilda' at the tops of their voices and thumping beer mugs on the table top." They were greeted with a "Guten Abend" from the accordion player and then given Löwenbräu beer

---

[47] 'Time again for Oktoberfest at the Palace', *What's Doing in Hong Kong*, Oct. 1966, BWA F 002–8901.

[48] 'The Toast is "prosit"', *The Sun*, Dec. 11, 1967.

[49] See, for example, William Osgerby, *Youth in Britain since 1945* (London: Wiley-Blackwell, 1998).

"imported from Bavaria, [and] the dearest in Britain." Stronger than British beer, the Löwenbräu "put you in a great trim for a sing-and-shout session." The waitresses wore dirndls "that squeeze their bosoms up," and at least one song in twenty was in German to keep up the "echt Deutsche stimmung [sic]"—genuine German mood or atmosphere. Other songs included American classics, British war songs, folk songs of Wales and Scotland, and the theme songs of West Ham FC "immediately followed" by that of Tottenham Hotspur. "By 10 o'clock the 'stimmung' [sic] was at its height. Eyes glazed, beer mugs thumped the boards," and our narrator had had enough. He stumbled home, leaving his friend to continue his "sing-and-shout session," and concluded that he could "see the point of the bierkeller [sic]...Singing and shouting appeal to all." The experience apparently departed from other London establishments that encouraged quiet, passive, and even lethargic drinking. This "authentic German Bierkeller" and the approximation of a convoluted stereotype that it encouraged apparently did offer a "new and diverting view of the British drinking classes." It leveled national difference, transcended football rivalries, and cut across social classes—provided one could afford the six-shilling beers. It seemed to fill a niche in London culture where singing and *Stimmung* were all that mattered. It was "German," but also somehow British. Indeed, the author closed by joking that by next year American tourists in Britain would be told "Now the next call on our schedule is a visit to a typical British bierkeller [sic]."[50]

Unbeknownst to the author, and perhaps also to J.C. McLaughlin, many Americans would have already been familiar with this experience if they had ever visited Krager's Restaurant or any of the many other examples from across the United States in the late 1950s and early 1960s. Ranging yet further, the Munich effect echoed around the world in Oktoberfests from Edmonton to Gibraltar, Monterey to Hong Kong. The stakes of this experience, however, went far beyond what many in the business of beer sales could fathom. Not only was this a good way to make money, it also came to shape the conception of West Germany itself at a time of great global instability.

What Was Being Sold? Beer, West Germany, the Present, and the Past

By the mid-1960s, Löwenbräu had established a sizeable market, in large part thanks to the meanings assigned to it by brewers, lawyers, importers, distributors, marketers, and consumers. Because so much of its international presence depended on claims to an authentic experience, the drink also entered into larger

---

[50] Peter Chambers, 'Booming Now in Britain—The German Style 'Pub': Shout as you Drink!' *Daily Express*, Dec. 11, 1967.

reckonings with West Germany: how the world might understand the country, its place in the Cold War–world, and its recent Nazi past. Such confrontations were most visible around the 1964–1965 World's Fair, when Bavarian, West German, and international commentators opined about the extent to which the economic success of the Bavarian brewing industry—chief among it Löwenbräu—could and should represent the West German success story. At stake was the vibrancy of the Cold War–capitalist west and the culture not just of Munich but of all of the Federal Republic. Held only a couple years after the construction of the Berlin Wall, the World's Fair provided an opportunity to showcase the successes of capitalism in the West German "economic miracle." Löwenbräu entered these conversations through their participation in the fair but for many, their flavor of German authenticity was hardly appropriate to the task. Here, then, we expand the political economy of taste as beer, and the imagery of the beer-drinking German entered the highest levels of international relations, national branding, and the politics of memory. In disputes around the fair, the lines between selling beer and selling a nation increasingly blurred.

The 1964–1965 New York World's Fair threw into sharp relief the extent to which beer participated in an international politics of memory and the representation of the West German nation. Two years before the fair began, the West German state pulled out of formal participation. This was primarily in response to the fact that in their preparations, the fair organizers had violated a number of the organizational principles of the Bureau of International Expositions. Still, while the state would not officially take part, it ultimately came to support the participation of a number of West German corporate representatives. The reasons for this were directly tied to the Cold War and the urging of American businessmen and diplomats who sought to showcase the successes of West German capitalist recovery. As the president of the New York World's Fair Corporation Robert Moses put it, the fair was "an unparalleled opportunity for Germany to demonstrate to the American people all that has been achieved since the War."[51] The geopolitical purpose was clear. Almost exactly a year after construction had begun on the Berlin Wall, the former High Commissioner of Germany, John J. McCloy, wrote to West German Chancellor Konrad Adenauer that,

> There has never been a fully adequate representation in the United States of the progress and strength of the growth of West Germany since the war and I believe the times almost demand it now both for economic and, more importantly, political reasons. The constitutional and cultural progress is, to my mind, comparable with the economic progress and too few people here sense the advances which have been made in the former fields...Other countries are

---

[51] June 13, 1962, letter from Robert Moses to John J. McCloy, New York Public Library (henceforth NYPL), New York World's Fair, 1964–1965, Box 271.

making their preparations (notably the Soviet Union) and I would very much like to see the German Exhibit made truly representative of the full achievements of the country.[52]

Adenauer sympathized with the argument but remained determined to honor the West German state's commitment to the Bureau of International Expositions. He reiterated that the state would not formally participate but endorsed an ad hoc committee to support the participation of German industries.[53]

Löwenbräu was one of the West German companies to participate, and was perhaps the most visible. Thanks to a stroke of good luck in the planning stages, the "Löwenbräu Gardens" was situated smack between the Ford, Chrysler, and General Motors exhibitions and less than 300 meters from the iconic Unisphere at the center of the fairgrounds. In now familiar fashion, the Munich brewery and their New York distributor Hans Holterbosch oversaw the contracts for and construction of the half-million-dollar beer garden, complete with all the appropriate Munich flair. In the course of preparations, however, a number of voices of concern emerged. While Moses, McCloy, and Adenauer agreed not to let the opportunity of representing West Germany to the world slip away, others became concerned about what this representation would look like. Edwin Hartrich, who had been a correspondent for the *New York Herald Tribune* and the *Wall Street Journal* in Germany in the late 1940s, felt compelled to intervene. In the spring of 1963 he wrote to West German Minister of Economics Ludwig Erhard, praising him as the architect of the "economic miracle" and the "almost fifteen years of unprecedented economic, social and political recovery, during which time Germany resumed her place and prestige in the Western family of nations." But for Hartrich, all of that now stood in jeopardy. Unless the West German state officially participated, he lamented that "the outward 'face' of Germany" would be "just beer and sauerkraut!" In a "World's Fair that will be visited by 80 million people of all nations, races, and political creeds," surely this would not do.[54] His concern seems to have been shared by many in the American government. Indeed, in late June 1963, American President John F. Kennedy himself proved unsuccessful in swaying Adenauer's reconsideration of formal participation when the two met in Bonn.[55]

[52] McCloy to Konrad Adenauer, qtd in Aug. 27, 1962, letter from Gates Davison to Scholten, NYPL, New York World's Fair, 1964–65, Box 271.

[53] Aug. 30, 1962, letter from Adenauer to McCloy; and Sept. 12, 1962, letter from Edwin Hartrich to Davison, NPYL New York World's Fair, 1964–1965, Box 271; 'Bonn will shun New York's Fair', *The New York Times International Edition*, Dec. 21, 1962.

[54] Mar. 26, 1963, letter from Hartrich to Ludwig Erhard, NYPL, New York World's Fair, 1964–1965, Box 271.

[55] 'Germany Restudies World's Fair Role', *New York Times*, June 27, 1963, p. 12; 'Neue Hoffnungen auf eine Teilnahme Westdeutschlands', *Sonntagsblatt Staats-Zeitung und Herold*, June 30, 1963; and July 12, 1963, letter from Hartrich to Jameson Parker, NYPL, New York World's Fair, 1964–1965, Box 271.

If the "beer and sauerkraut" image of Germany struck some as apolitical, for others such a partial and commercial representation was entirely *too* political in its moral failings. The month after Kennedy had failed to persuade Adenauer, the former governor of New York, Charles Poletti, spoke out against the commercial representation of West Germany at an Overseas Press Club luncheon. Poletti was a World War Two veteran and the Vice President for International Exhibits at the New York World's Fair. In addition to being the former governor of New York, he had been involved with de-fascistization in postwar Italy, even expanding the system that would ultimately be adopted in occupied Germany.[56] Such experiences lent weight to his critique of West German industrialists, whose participation he saw as using the fair to "erase an image here of a Nazi Germany." The claim drew the ire of the German-American Chamber of Commerce (GACC), an institution whose very raison d'être was to protect and advance the capital interests of German companies. Gordon Michler of the GACC was quick to the defense. He did not deny that the effect of industrial participation weakened the memory of the Nazi past, but instead reemphasized the importance of West Germany in ongoing Cold War tensions. "At this particular time," he wrote, "the German government and public are giving [the United States] the staunchest possible support in the defense of Western democracy." Going further, he praised the decision of the West German state to honor its commitments to the Bureau of International Expositions, which he characterized as a healthy respect for international agreements and a testament to how West Germany had abandoned Nazi lawlessness and "thrown off Nazism [and] Nazi methods." He charged Poletti with "a most objectionable and ill-timed resurrection of the Nazi image," emphasizing the recent public embrace of Kennedy in West Germany and the continued promises of now-Chancellor Ludwig Erhard to honor West Germany's NATO commitments.[57]

The New York World's Fair ran from April to October of 1964 and 1965. Instead of being located next to the pavilion of participating countries, as noted, the Löwenbräu Gardens stood at the center of the fair, less than 300 meters from the Unisphere. Not only was it thus part of a high-traffic path, it also drew visitors from across the park with a horse-drawn wagon featuring barrels of beer and a Trachten-clad crew that would circle the fairgrounds at regular intervals. Once inside the gardens, the space was meticulously designed by Munich architect Rupert Augustin to resemble an Alpine village square, complete with wooden benches and material details down to the flags, coasters, and glassware. Much to the enjoyment of visitors, eleven of the waitresses were titled nobility—countesses and baronesses—flown from Munich to serve beer at the "Bavarian hamlet."

---

[56] Thanks to Mikkel Dack for making this connection.
[57] July 22, 1963, letter from Gordon H. Milcher to Charles Poletti, NYPL, New York World's Fair, 1964–1965, Box 271.

For the women it was a chance to experience New York City on the ground. For Holterbosch and Löwenbräu, the women were preferable to professional waitresses because instead of wanting to make money, they would "make good ambassadors for Germany."[58] Beyond heads of state, then, this formulation from the *New York Times* suggests that brewers, importers, distributors, and journalists likewise understood that it was not just beer for sale, but an entire country.

Beer, the women who served it, and the entire experience of the "Bavarian hamlet," complete with horse-drawn wagons, comprised a particular sort of ambassadorship. If Charles Poletti had overstated his case that industrialists at the World's Fair were working to erase the memory of Nazi Germany, it was not by much. Already at the 1958 World's Fair in Brussels, West German architects had consciously suppressed the Nazi past in designing their pavilion.[59] And at the New York Fair, as Michler had noted, the Nazi past certainly proved inconvenient for both the economic interests of West Germany and for the Cold War interests of the capitalist West and the United States. But far beyond the World's Fairs, West German industrialists, politicians, and cultural commentators were explicitly using the commercial successes of companies such as Volkswagen to suppress the Nazi past and rebuild diplomatic relations with the United States.[60] Löwenbräu, like Volkswagen, became an ambassador of West German recovery and capitalist vitality. But unlike an automobile, beer was not a high-tech commodity, and the success of Löwenbräu depended not on its versatility—like the Beetle, which spanned from suburbia to the counterculture—but on deep historical roots and claims to the timelessness of production and consumption. This was even less a rival to American power than the Beetle had been. Indeed, reading through the World's Fair visitor guide, one is struck by how out of place Löwenbräu really was. The "picturesque village square" described in the guide stood next to the GM pavilion which offered "a fascinating look at the future...a foretaste of lunar commuting, Antarctic ports, jungle cities and resorts on the ocean's floor." In the other direction, the Ford Motor Company presented "suggestions of a city of tomorrow" and other exhibitions in the immediate vicinity boasted "undersea adventures" and "space vehicles."[61] The "Bavarian hamlet" was no doubt as far away as an imagined Germany could get from the technical, high-modern efficiency of engineering, tanks, Blitzkrieg, mass executions, endless trains of cattle-cars, and bureaucratic industrialized mass murder. In the Cold War era, World's Fairs were almost always about deploying science and technology to impress visitors and capture the imagination, but the Löwenbräu Gardens seemed to do the exact

[58] Walter Carlson, 'Noble Frauleins tend Bar at Fair', *New York Times* May 21, 1964, p. 45.
[59] Greg Castillo, 'Making a Spectacle of Restraint: The Deutschland Pavilion at the 1958 Brussels Exposition', *Journal of Contemporary History* 47, no. 1 (Jan. 2012): pp. 97–119.
[60] See, for example, Rieger, *The People's Car*, pp. 222–8.
[61] Editors of Time-Life Books, *1965 Official Guide: New York World's Fair, all new for 1965* (New York: Time Inc., 1965), p. 190.

opposite.[62] Taking yet another step back, this was an image of Germany that ran across the grain of a number of other "Holocaust moments" in the mid-1960s.[63] Poletti's criticism had come only months after *The New Yorker* had run Hannah Arendt's serialized account of Adolf Eichmann's high-profile trial in Jerusalem, in which she famously articulated the "banality of evil" in the bureaucratic mass murder of the European Jewry.[64] If those articles had lost some of their public presence by 1964 or 1965, fairgoers may have been equally interested in the ongoing press coverage of the Frankfurt Auschwitz Trials, which overlapped almost completely with the World's Fair, spanning from 1963 to 1965. We may never know just how far fairgoers tried to reconcile the two encounters with Germany, but it seems likely that some tried. In the two opening months of the fair (April and May of 1964), *The New York Times* alone published nineteen articles on the Auschwitz trial, or roughly one every three days.[65]

It would be hard to directly argue that the beer-drinking Bavarian directly crowded out the Nazi as the synecdoche of the German nation. Indeed, in some ways the two were entering popular discourse simultaneously, and commentators like Hartrich clearly would have preferred some other national personification. For him and others, the World's Fair offered the opportunity to recast Germany—to reintroduce the place and the people. The case of the New York World's Fair captures the extent to which the contested meanings of beer spanned not just marketing schemes from Japan to the American Midwest, but also diplomats and heads of state arguing about the Cold War benefits of showcasing western capitalism. If this was a contest of meanings—an engagement in the political economy of taste—it was one in which the lines between commodity and country got particularly muddled.

Conclusion: Business and Tragedy

In the upper echelons of cultural representation and international relations, it can be easy to lose sight of beer, brewers, and the real Munich. For surely, while

[62] Arthur P. Molella and Scott Gabriel Knowles, eds., *World's Fairs in the Cold War: Science, Technology, and the Culture of Progress* (Pittsburgh: University of Pittsburgh Press, 2019).

[63] I borrow the term from historian Atina Grossman, who wrote that the history of the Federal Republic was characterized by a series of "Holocaust moments" from the Nuremberg Trials to the major—and majorly public—debates of the 1980s and 1990s, including the *Historikerstreit* and the Goldhagen debates. In each moment, the legacies of Nazism and the Holocaust were particularly visible and primed for piecemeal social engagement. See Atina Grossman, 'The "Goldhagen Effect": Memory Repetition, and Responsibility in the New Germany', in Geoff Eley, ed., *The 'Goldhagen Effect': History, Memory, Nazism—Facing the German Past* (Ann Arbor: University of Michigan Press, 2000), pp. 89–90.

[64] Hannah Arendt, *Eichmann in Jerusalem: A Report on the Banality of Evil* (New York: Viking Press, 1963); the book is an expansion of a five-part series that ran in *The New Yorker* from February to March 1963.

[65] According to a Proquest Historical Newspapers search.

Munich and Löwenbräu became many things representationally, they undoubtedly remained real, tangible places and products. In the 1950s and 1960s, Löwenbräu and their international partners built their global success on exaggerating and marketing a simplistic Bavarian culture of consumption. It was a product that touted and depended on claims to authenticity. But back home, in Munich, Löwenbräu beer was tremendously unpopular and carried a negative connotation among consumers. The local market had long eluded Löwenbräu, in no small part because they had built their postwar success on exports. Along with kindred tourist favorite Hofbräu, Löwenbräu was among the least-esteemed beers in Munich. According to a 1964 market research report, a whopping 45 per cent of Münchner named Löwenbräu as their least favorite local beer, dwarfing second-place Hackerbräu with only 5 per cent. In contrast to its global image, Münchner knew Löwenbräu primarily as an export beer that "does not meet Munich tastes."[66] Beer remained an important part of how Münchner and Bavarians self-identified, but at this scale, the case of Löwenbräu highlights the spatial disconnect between global and local conceptions of place and culture.

More broadly, the provincial peculiarities of Munich and Bavarian beer cultures were hardly a selling point for most West Germans. They were, quite to the contrary, something to downplay. Just as the World's Fair was ending in 1965, leaders of the Christian Social Union, including Alphons Goppel and Franz Josef Strauss, teamed up with the West German Olympic committee to pitch Munich as a candidate for the 1972 Olympic Games. Their application package aimed to present the city and its rural environs as a romantic alpine wonderland, a kind of timeless German paradise, complete with "generously endowed Fräuleins, and fun-loving atmosphere (Oktoberfest!)."[67] But once the city had won the bid, the planners were often at loggerheads over the issue of whether Munich's beer culture should play a role in the organizing efforts. The 1972 Munich Games were overwhelmingly understood as a foil to the 1936 Berlin Games. In the run-up, the primary aesthetic planners—including graphic designer Otl Aicher, architect Günther Behnisch, and landscape architect Günther Grzimek—opted to downplay Munich's provincial beer culture in an effort to make the games a German national event rather than an explicitly Bavarian or Munich one.[68] The 1972 Olympic Games are of course infamous for the murder of eleven Israeli athletes and coaches by a Palestinian militant group, Black September. But if the games became a cloud over the city, the record-setting Oktoberfest that followed

---

[66] 'Trinkergewohnheiten der Münchner Stadtbevölkerung und Markenbilder ausgewählter Brauereien', Gesellschaft für Konsumforschung (henceforth GfK) S 1964 029, 34 and *Tabellenteil*, tbl. 13.

[67] David Clay Large, *Munich 1972: Tragedy, Terror, and Triumph at the Olympic Games* (Lanham: Rowman & Littlefield Publishers, Inc., 2012), p. 48, more generally, pp. 30–40.

[68] Kay Schiller and Christopher Young, *The 1972 Munich Olympics and the Making of Modern Germany* (Berkeley: University of California Press, 2010): on downplaying provincial beer culture, pp. 113–114; on the legacies of the Berlin Games, pp. 56–86.

brought some financial and cultural sunshine. Prices increased 30 per cent over the previous year, netting the vendors and local economy some 110 million DM. As much as the planners for the games had sought to eschew Munich and Bavarian beer culture, it ultimately aided in boosting the economy and the reputation of the city in the wake of tragedy. Only 11 days after the closing ceremonies of the Olympic Games, the Hamburg-based newspaper *Die Zeit* gestured toward the city's drunken redemption, noting that, "for the reputation of Munich, the Oktoberfest is priceless."[69]

By the 1970s, the Munich brewing industry—Löwenbräu first and foremost—had succeeded in linking the product, the place, and the mode of consumption. In hindsight, the international history of Löwenbräu looks like a precursor to other globalized sites of ostensibly authentic consumption—say, for example, the Guinness-based "Irish pub."[70] Even more than in the Irish case, however, Löwenbräu's success is noteworthy in that it marked a conceptual transition in the global imaginary. Marketers, advertisers, regulators, and consumers participated in displacing the legacies of Nazi militarism with a jovial and unthreatening capitalism—effectively rebranding an entire country. The authenticity of the experience of drinking in Monterey, London, or Hong Kong—of being swept up in the "gemutlich reaction"—in many ways came to stand in for journeying to Munich or Germany. How beer was sold, marketed, coveted, protected, and imbued with meanings helps explain how beer and Bavaria came to inform global conceptions of West Germany, render it distinct from both a militaristic predecessor and a Cold War twin, making it legible as a western capitalist success story. This was provincial capitalism communicating the nation on the global scale. For the Löwenbräu brewery, as for much of the brewing industry and, indeed, the global economy, the recessions of the 1970s and 1980s proved disastrous, as we will see. Ultimately, the legacy of Löwenbräu and authentic beer as a cultural ambassador far outlived the economic realities: the stereotypes of the beer drinking German remained even as the Löwenbräu empire deteriorated. But as we will see, it was not only shifts in global capital that challenged the Germany that Bavaria made. The recession was joined by a number of other formidable challenges in the 1970s and 1980s that stripped away some of the major regulatory and geopolitical scaffolding upon which an entire conception of Germany had been built.

---

[69] Hermann Bößenecker, 'Oktoberfest: Fingerhakeln um Bierpreise', *Die Zeit*, Sept. 22, 1972.

[70] Jan Blommaert and Piia Varis, 'Enough is Enough: The Heuristics of Authenticity in Superdiversity', *Tilburg Papers in Culture Studies* 2 (2011); see also Cliona O'Carroll, '"Cold Beer, Warm Hearts": Community, Belonging and Desire in Irish Pubs in Berlin', in *Drinking Cultures: Alcohol and Identity*, ed. Thomas M. Wilson (Oxford: Berg Publishers, 2005), pp. 43–64; and John Simmons, 'Guinness and the Role of Strategic Storytelling', *Journal of Strategic Marketing* 14 no. 1 (2006), pp. 11–18.

7

Gone Flat?

Reconfigurations from the Recession to the *Wende*

In the first half of the twentieth century, centralizing pressures—from fiscal integration to dictatorship and occupation—catapulted long-standing Bavarian and southern German interests to the forefront of national discourse and practice. Bavarian brewing taxonomies and standards of production became increasingly national. As the new West German nation found its footing, Bavarian brewers and their associates in advertising and policy shaped markets, regulations, and consumer culture from Franconia to Hong Kong. In the decades of explosive postwar economic growth, brewers, regulators, marketers, and consumers in Bavaria and West Germany associated product and place in many different ways. Public relations slogans proclaimed that "in Bavaria you drink beer" or that beer is "Germany's source of purity," while industrial and regulatory insistence on the peculiarities of regional and national production ranged from Würzburg to global market protectionism. In the last decades of the century, however, shifts in three crucial spheres—capital, regulation, and geopolitics—transformed the ways that Bavarian brewers and their associates operated on global, national, and local scales.

In the case of capital, the recessions of the 1970s and 1980s hollowed out the place-based claims to authenticity by which the Munich Löwenbräu brewery had helped shape global conceptions of the German nation. The Bavarian stereotype would remain, but after the 1970s, producers, marketers, and promoters in Bavaria scaled back their promotion of cultural approximation. In addition to deflating the capital and cultural scope of Löwenbräu's global market, the recessions of the 1970s and 1980s initiated a shift in the relative power of regulatory bodies. It was in this moment that the European Court of Justice (ECJ) emerged as the cutting edge of neoliberal European market integration, overturning West German regulations that had limited access to the national market. West Germans retained their cultural insistence on the importance of the *Reinheitsgebot*, but during the 1980s the ECJ defanged it as a market barrier. For West Germans weary of surrogate imports, the *Reinheitsgebot* became a purely cultural standard—an insistence on national culture in a supranational economy.

These stories of capital and regulation centered on the recession and the ECJ resonate with a growing body of scholarship exploring the extent to which the 1970s marked a fundamental rupture. In broad strokes, historians have

A Nation Fermented: Beer, Bavaria, and the Making of Modern Germany. Robert Shea Terrell, Oxford University Press.
© Robert Shea Terrell 2024. DOI: 10.1093/oso/9780198881834.003.0008

highlighted the shift from Keynesian economics to Chicago School monetarism, the birth of the digital age and the neoliberal self, and the erosion of traditional labor markets through "deindustrialization" and the rise of developing economies, particularly in East Asia. But rupture and decline are not entirely sufficient to explain the industrial west "since the boom."[1] The collapse of Löwenbräu and the repeal of the *Reinheitsgebot* are ambiguous as ruptures: Munich remained a—or perhaps *the*—heart of German beer around the world and, in the longer view, the ECJ ruling marked only the most recent transformation of the "Purity Law." And, in fact, thanks to the collapse of the German Democratic Republic, the *Reinheitsgebot* would soon expand its territorial purchase. As West German producers and consumers embraced the regulation as a form of market nationalism in the face of cheaper, surrogate imports, the reunification of the two Germanys brought brewers a new opportunity for capital growth, initiating a wave of market expansion and privatization. Many former East German breweries worked to meet the production standards of the Federal Republic, but most failed to secure sufficient private investment or fell to western conglomerates. Meanwhile, eastern expansion provided a salve but not a cure for the anxieties of Western brewers that their own markets would be overwhelmed by mass-produced beers from international competitors. Thus, while the reunification of Germany likewise marked a kind of rupture, it also provided the conditions under which long-standing southern German concerns about capital consolidation and industry centralization emerged as a part of the national industrial agenda.[2] The consolidation of the German brewing industry reaches back to at least the nineteenth century, but in the decades after the 1970s the conditions of global capital and supranational economic integration sparked a coordinated national response. By the mid-1990s, the reunified brewing industry circled the wagons, rallying around both small- and mid-sized brewers as the lifeblood of the industry and around the *Reinheitsgebot* as a fundamentally *German* tradition. Major structural transitions from the 1970s to the 1990s thus took down the scaffolding of explosive

---

[1] In particular, see the essays in Sebastian Voigt, ed., *Since the Boom: Continuity and Change in the Western Industrialized World after 1970* (Toronto: University of Toronto Press, 2021). The volume provides a synthesis of relatively siloed American and European (namely German) literatures on the effects of the global recession, seeking to intervene in both by arguing for a more nuanced and ambiguous history than that of "deindustrialization," "rupture," or "decline." See further, for example, Niall Ferguson, Charles S. Maier, Erez Manela, and Daniel J. Sargent, eds., *The Shock of the Global: The 1970s in Perspective* (Cambridge: Harvard University Press, 2010); and Anselm Doering-Manteuffel and Lutz Raphael, *Nach dem Boom: Perspektiven auf die Zeitgeschichte seit 1970*, 2nd ed. (Göttingen: Vandenhoeck & Ruprecht GmbH, 2010); alternatively, Frank Bösch has pointed to 1979 as the geopolitical rupture that underpins the contemporary world: see Frank Bösch, *Zeitwende 1979: Als die Welt von heute began* (Munich: C.H. Beck, 2019).

[2] In the three decades before reunification in 1990, the number of breweries in the Federal Republic declined dramatically, from 2,218 to 1,168, with nearly 70 per cent of all closures coming from Bavaria. Bayerischer Brauerbund e.V., *Daten und Fakten der bayerischen Brauwirtschaft 1988/89*, tbl 3 & 4; and 'Struktur der bayerischen Brauwirtschaft', *Brauwelt* 16 (1993), p. 642.

economic growth and political division, but they did not fundamentally undo the Bavarian influence of decades past.

Recession, Consolidation, and Place

The first major structural challenge came in the form of a global recession. Between 1971 and 1974, a series of transformations shook the foundations of postwar western capitalist states. The turn to floating exchange rates and the first oil crisis proved to be inflection points in longer processes of deindustrialization and western dependence on cheaper manufactured goods from emerging East Asian economies.[3] At the level of everyday consumption, the price of food and non-fuel commodities increased and consumption slowed.[4] During this period, West German beer production continued to grow, but at a slower clip than in previous decades, and consumption rates declined for the first time since the end of the Second World War.[5] Beyond consumption patterns, the end of the boom era had profound structural consequences. In Bavaria, long home to the most decentralized brewing sector, the number of breweries fell from 1,556 in 1960 to only 931 in 1980.[6] Smaller breweries either went out of business or were bought out by larger companies—part of a larger consolidation that would inform many facets of the industry for the next three decades. Beyond such domestic mergers, Bavarian and West German brewers also now had to decide how to navigate higher export costs. Some, most notably Löwenbräu, outsourced production around the world. The story of Löwenbräu is noteworthy because the brewery's business choices in the 1970s cleaved apart the cultural and economic value it had once worked so hard to fuse together. Perhaps more importantly, it is indicative of how the culture of Bavarian beer turned inward.

The Munich Löwenbräu brewery had played a large role in globalizing the Bavarian imagery of a traditional, jovial, beer-drinking West Germany. As we have seen, the postwar recovery of Löwenbräu was built on exports increasingly marketed with place-based claims to the authenticity of the product and its mode

---

[3] Konrad H. Jarausch, *Out of Ashes: A New History of Europe in the Twentieth Century* (Princeton: Princeton University Press, 2015), pp. 620–2.

[4] Historians continue to debate the extent to which the recessions represented a fundamental rupture. See, for example, Sina Fabian, 'Crisis? What Crisis? Mass Consumption in Great Britain in the 1970s and Early 1980s', in *Since the Boom: Continuity and Change in the Western Industrialized World after 1970*, ed. Sebastian Voigt (Toronto: University of Toronto Press, 2021), pp. 56–77; and, more broadly, Frank Trentmann, 'Unstoppable: The Resilience and Renewal of Consumption after the Boom', *Vorgeschichte der Gegenwart: Dimensionen des Strukturbruchs nach dem Boom*, ed. Anselm Doering-Manteuffel, Lutz Raphael, and Thomas Schlemmer (Göttingen: Vandenhoeck & Ruprecht GmbH, 2016), pp. 293–308.

[5] Bayerischer Brauerbund e.V., *Geschäftsbericht, 1972/73*, pp. 32–8; Behringer, *Die Spaten-Brauerei*, pp. 360–1.

[6] Lothar Ebbertz, 'Die Entwicklung der bayerischen Brauwirtschaft', *Brauwelt* 4 (1996), pp. 146–51.

of consumption. Such marketing suggested that drinking imported Löwenbräu in manufactured beer halls and Oktoberfests allowed consumers to approximate a real German experience. By the end of the 1960s, beer halls, beer cellars, and Oktoberfest celebrations—made all the more authentic by the presence of Löwenbräu—spanned California to Japan, Toronto to Australia, Gibraltar to Hong Kong, and Detroit to Tokyo. Yet a few years later, beginning in the early 1970s, the profitability and reputation of Löwenbräu began to collapse on the global stage. The brand had never been a domestic success and the costs associated with sustaining a global export market quickly became insurmountable. In an effort to navigate the recession, the brewery chose to outsource production, most importantly, in its largest markets: England and the United States. This decision—along with emerging connoisseur markets and consumer experimentation—sealed Löwenbräu's fate by rendering its dependence on place of origin virtually irrelevant. As before, beer would undoubtedly remain part of the global imaginary of Germany and, also as before, keen observers would note that the association more often than not massaged away the rough edges of the Nazi past. But the beer in question and the rhetoric of representation was no longer markedly Bavarian. As Beck's and other competitors capitalized on Löwenbräu's fateful response to the recession, the culture of Bavarian beer turned inward—something to experience firsthand, not by proxy.

In 1974 Löwenbräu made licensing agreements in the United States and England for local companies to brew their beer. In the United Kingdom the agreement was with the Ind Coope & Sons brewery of Burton-on-Trent, part of the Allied Breweries conglomerate in London. In the United States the contract went to Miller Brewing of Milwaukee, part of the Philip Morris Corporation since 1969. This transition marked a watershed. In New York City, Hans Holterbosch, Löwenbräu's long-time importer for the Eastern United States, had been their single greatest global partner for the past four decades. When Löwenbräu made its licensing agreement with Miller, Holterbosch and Universal Brands, their distributor in Florida, brought an anti-trust suit for breach of contract against the Munich brewery, Miller, and Philip Morris in the New York Supreme Court. While the court ruled against them, judge Gerald Bard Tjoflat also warned against the "marked and steady trend toward economic concentration" in the beer industry. The fact that "Miller is the fifth largest brewer in the United States" and that "Löwenbräu is the largest importer of beer into the United States," he argued, may be an "unhealthy concentration of the beer market as a whole."[7] But the court had spoken, Holterbosch was out of the Löwenbräu story, and by 1977 the import of

---

[7] United States v. Pabst Brewing Co. 384 U.S. 546 (1966), cited in Tjoflat's dissent. See Universal Brands, Inc., etc., Plaintiff-appellant-cross Appellee, v. Philip Morris Inc., Etc, Defendant-appellee, Löwenbräu-München Aktiengesellschaft, Etc., defendant-appellee-cross Appellant, 546 F.2d 30 (5th Cir. 1977) *Justia US Law,* accessed Sept. 4, 2016, http://law.justia.com/cases/federal/appellate-courts/F2/546/30/204878/.

Löwenbräu beer from Munich to the United States had stopped completely as all American demand was met by Miller-produced Löwenbräu from Milwaukee. By 1983, the Munich brewery made similar deals in Nicaragua, Australia, Yugoslavia, Sweden, Ecuador, Panama, Hong Kong, Greece, Japan, Canada, and Portugal, with the cumulative effect that, from 1973 to 1986, more Löwenbräu beer was produced outside Munich than in it.[8] The repercussions of this transition for a brand that depended on placed-based claims to quality and authenticity would be catastrophic.

The knowledge economy that Löwenbräu depended on collapsed like a house of cards. Hans Holterbosch and his son and business partner Dieter openly pointed to the absence of German quality in light of the Miller cut-corners approach. Even Löwenbräu officials in Munich were skeptical; export manager Johann Daniel Gerstein told West German reporters, "There is no need to be ashamed" of the financial decision, but "whether we actually like [the beer] or not, that's another question."[9] The Löwenbräu deal signaled the end of the beer's global stature, and the void was filled almost immediately by competitors from beyond Bavaria and beyond West Germany. Foremost among them was the Dutch Heineken brewery, which by 1978 singlehandedly outpaced the entire West German export sector.[10] This was in no small part thanks to the precipitous decline in Bavarian exports. Bavarian exports in the 1960s and early 1970s had increased by an average of 8.6 per cent per year, outpacing the 5 per cent annual growth in the rest of West Germany. But in 1974, Bavarian exports increased by only 1 per cent, and the rest of West Germany by more than 7 per cent—a general trend that continued for decades.[11] Qualitatively too, Bavaria no longer held the market on German authenticity. In 1979 the north German Beck's brewery ran an ad in the United States asking, "Are you drinking a well-known German beer that isn't really German?...Read the label...Beck's: the only leading German beer that's really made in Germany."[12]

As the Beck's campaign suggests, the collapse of Löwebräu was not just the downfall of a brand. Löwenbräu was one of the first brewing giants to be swept into what Judge Tjoflat called a "marked and steady trend toward economic concentration" since the 1960s.[13] Their decisions to outsource may have made some sense to the company board, but it was not the only way. Indeed, when Alfred Heineken was asked about Löwenbräu's licensing agreements in the early 1970s,

[8]   Behringer, *Löwenbräu*, pp. 280–82.
[9]   Barbara Smit, *The Heineken Story: The Remarkably Refreshing Tale of the Beer that Conquered the World* (London: Profile Books Ltd, 2014), p. 297.
[10]   'German Brewers Looking to US Market', *The New York Times*, Dec. 29, 1979, p. 29.
[11]   Export statistics 1950–1974 in Bayerischer Brauerbund e.V., *Geschäftsbericht, 1973/74–1974/75*, p. 175.
[12]   'The Titans of Beer Head to Head: A Battle full of Foam and Fury', *The New York Times* Apr. 29, 1979, p. E20.
[13]   Universal Brands, Inc., v. Philip Morris Inc.

he sneered "I mean, can you believe anybody could be so damn stupid?"[14] Heineken, unlike so many national flagship breweries around the world, managed to survive the capital consolidation of the brewing industry, in part by driving it. At the time of writing, it owns more than 100 breweries in almost 70 countries, making it the third largest brewing company in the world. But in the decades since the 1970s, almost every other major international beer—Stella Artois, Beck's, Hoegaarden, Labatt; Pilsner Urquell, Peroni, Amstel, Carlsberg, Boddingtons, Sapporo, Singha, Guinness, and the Budweiser, Busch, Miller, and Coors families, to name only a few—has been bought out and "delocalized" by a conglomerate or holding company producing in a multitude of cost-cutting breweries around the world. Claims to authenticity in such a market remained high stakes. In 1978, for example, Anheuser-Busch protested to the US Federal Trade Commission that Miller was trying to "mislead or deceive consumers into thinking [Löwenbräu] is still an imported beer, or that it is brewed according to the original German formula."[15] From the beginning, Miller's goal with acquiring Löwenbräu was to combat Anheuser-Busch's Michelob brand, which was often mistaken as an import.[16] The actors were bigger, the brands stronger, and the financial stakes higher, but the fault lines of the debate echo the complaints of Löwenbräu agents decades earlier: market protectionism under the banner of authenticity and consumer protection.

Beyond being a casualty of capital consolidation, the story of Löwenbräu also points to other shifts in the material and spatial experience in late-20th-century capitalism. The Munich brewery, perhaps more than any other beer in the world until the 1970s, had created for itself a global aura of authenticity linking product, place, and mode of consumption. When the Löwenbräu brewery severed the only connection between the actual place and their global consumer base, they not only isolated themselves from potential growth but also relegated their product to a delocalized cut-corners beer abroad. Claims to authenticity in the case of Löwenbräu consumption had fundamentally been claims to similitude of place. After the outsourcing deals in the 1970s, the Beer Kellers in London closed their doors, and Canadian, American, and Australian Oktoberfests transitioned to serving domestic beers. In smaller markets such as Malta, Löwenbräu worked to reconstruct its shattered global quality by changing licensing contracts to adhere to the *Reinheitsgebot*, but such efforts never reestablished the global reputation of the brand.[17] Around the world, but particularly in the large export market of the United States, a "new social environment of television and suburbia—totally privatized, fully home-oriented, and daily saturated with entertainment," challenged

---

[14] Smit, *The Heineken Story*, pp. 192–3.
[15] 'F.T.C. Opens an Inquiry on Löwenbräu Formula', *The New York Times* Jul. 23, 1978, p. 21.
[16] 'Löwenbräu of US in Test', *Chicago Tribune*, May 20, 1976, p. C11; see also, 'Miller's Löwenbräu Is Target of Complaint by Anheuser-Busch', *The Wall Street Journal* Nov. 11, 1977, p. 22.
[17] 'Löwenbräu mit neuem Auslandskonzept', *Brauwelt* 25 (1990), p. 975.

the social context of "authentic" experiences in large social settings.[18] Transitions in both capital and consumption in the decades after 1970 thus not only brought "social developments of revolutionary proportions," they also had the power to hollow out place-based concepts of authenticity in the global imaginary.[19]

Still, as Löwenbräu's global market fell apart, their work in the cultural sphere remained. The Munich brewery had contributed so much to making an association between beer and conceptions of Munich, Bavaria, and Germany that it had—as we saw in the previous chapter—begun to rival other, less savory conceptions of the nation. Even after the implosion of Löwenbräu, keen observers were quick to point out the importance of beer culture as a means to understand Germany as a place. In 1976, Regina Krummel, a Jewish-American professor of English at Queens College (CUNY), published her poem responding to an ad in a liberal intellectual Jewish journal promoting tourism to Israel. Her poem, "Stop off in Germany for a Beer," reflects on promises of safe travel to Germany and Israel: kosher food on a German airline, and, implicitly, the certainty of making it out of Germany "still clothed in my Jewish flesh." German tourist commodities— clocks, sweaters, music, and beer—testified to the new Germany, purged of its Nazi past. Above all, "It's the beer that's special about Germany / And the Jew can have it now with kosher food minus / The incinerated flesh of the inept six million / Who came without invitation."[20] The poem oozes hostility to both the new Germany and the zeal of Israeli nationalism, pointing to the ghosts of the past and the relatively rapid process by which beer and other consumer goods managed to supersede the popular memory of German atrocities.[21] Published in the midst of a broader transition in international Holocaust memory, the poem attests to the silencing power of material goods and the role of economic stability in rebranding the German nation.

The tourist promotion that sparked Krummel's reflection and its title also points to the larger process by which international approximations of German authenticity turned inward. To experience the full effect, Krummel and other travelers needed to "stop off in Germany for a Beer" rather than visit an international beerhall. As Löwenbräu collapsed, the authenticity of consumption became increasingly exclusive to Munich and Bavaria. In a 1985 *New York Times* article, for instance, Erfurt-born journalist John Dornberg touted the lore of Munich drinking culture, the wide diversity of beer styles and "distinctive" brewery differences known only to "local connoisseurs." The formulation proves

---

[18] Luca Massidda, 'The Cold War, a Cool Medium, and the Postmodern Death of World Expos', in *World's Fairs in the Cold War: Science, Technology, and the Culture of Progress*, ed., Arthur P. Molella and Scott Gabriel Knowles (Pittsburgh: University of Pittsburgh Press, 2019), p. 189.

[19] Doering-Manteuffel and Raphael, *Nach dem Boom*, pp. 12–18.

[20] Regina P. Krummel, 'Stop off in Germany for a Beer', *The English Journal* 65, no. 5 (May, 1976), p. 51.

[21] See also Rieger, *The People's Car*.

instructive when read against earlier claims by other commodity experts: lawyers, distributors, marketers, and festival-goers. Munich was a unique place, one to visit and experience rather than to approximate, where the people not only "consider beer their national beverage" but also "do not view it as a drink, rather a liquid bread—a food." Matching this anthropological curiosity, Dornberg ended with a simple statement of apparent fact: "To think of Bavaria without beer or Munich without its enormous beer halls and cellars is almost to not think of Bavaria and Munich at all."[22] The claim seems to suggest there was no other past to associate with the "capital of the movement." But the heyday of the "gemutlich reaction" which had spread from Munich around the world was apparently over. Media coverage about how British consumers could "travel to 'Old Bavaria' without leaving London" receded and the conditions by which the King's Lodge in Hong Kong, among many places, "*becomes* a Munich Hofbrau Haus" through the mere presence of Bavarian beer imploded.[23] In this resurgence of the local, what remained was the city itself, a place you had to visit; a city experienced through beer and gaiety and increasingly stripped of its radical past—beer halls more than the Beer Hall Putsch.

The Fate of the *Reinheitsgebot* and the Cultural Regime of Beer

While the recessions of the mid-1970s challenged the business scaffolding and cultural work of a company like Löwenbräu at the global level, it also triggered a wave of regulatory changes that similarly undermined the market structures for which Bavarian and West German brewers had fought. In the 1960s and early 1970s many Bavarians, and, ultimately, West Germans, rallied around the market protectionism of the *Reinheitsgebot*. They allied with law makers, public health officials, and special interest groups to enshrine the regulation as a timeless German tradition. As we have seen, legal, regulatory, and marketing campaigns to protect the cultural value and market exclusivity of "pure beer" spanned from targeting nearly negligible consumer preferences in Franconia to global jockeying with northern German, Dutch, and American rivals. But the recessions of the 1970s and 1980s, and the subsequent triumph of neoliberal economic thought, presented an important challenge in the history of regulating the politics, economics, and culture of beer. This challenge was most explicit at the level of European integration, where, in the mid-1980s, the European Court of Justice (ECJ) worked toward the repeal of the *Reinheitsgebot* as an informal trade barrier.

---

[22] John Dornberg, 'In Bavaria, Beer is Both Food and Drink', *The New York Times* Mar. 3, 1985, p. XX6.
[23] Both quotes discussed further in previous chapter. Egon Larsen, 'Münchner Bierkeller in Soho. Lederhosen aus dem Kostümverleih', *Süddeutsche Zeitung* Aug. 19, 1965, p. 3; 'Time again for Oktoberfest at the Palace', *What's Doing in Hong Kong* Oct. 1966, BWA F 002-8901.

The market protectionist dynamics which brewers and regulators had worked so hard to establish now faced renewed criticism in the name of European integration and the language of consumer sovereignty. But while the ECJ had the power to undo the legal platform of market protectionism, they could not undo the cultural regime that advocates for "pure beer" had made.

The recessions of the 1970s and 1980s accelerated the process of European market integration through changes in both economic thought and market regulation. Until the 1970s, the harmonization of market standards on goods and services was usually carried out on a case-by-case basis. We saw in Chapter 5 how the West German rejection of the EEC harmonization proposal in the early 1970s held integration at bay, embracing regional qua national production standards and emboldening the federal state to protect consumers. By the early 1980s, however, advocates for further European market integration had abandoned harmonization, or at least added to it the principle of mutual recognition. This held that in the event that there was no specific Community-wide regulation, each member state was obliged to accept goods from other member states as long as they were produced and marketed according to the legal standards of their country of origin. It was a markedly post-boom approach, in effect challenging state regulations in the name of unfettered markets. In theory it allowed the consumer, rather than the state, to shape the market by generating (or not generating) demand for a product.[24] In this new wave of market integration, the institutional importance of the ECJ can hardly be overstated. Rooted in the 1957 Treaty of Rome, the precise role of the Court began to take shape only in the 1960s and 1970s. Its goal, to borrow the words of ordoliberal lawyer Ernst-Joachim Mestmäcker, was to "exclude control of interstate trade as an instrument of national economic policy."[25] Put differently, the aim of the ECJ was to undermine precisely the sort of market trade barriers represented by the *Reinheitsgebot*.

The ECJ case against the *Reinheitsgebot* opened in 1983 and triggered a familiar and predictable response. West German brewers, politicians, lawyers, brewing scientists, and others responded by repeating the *German* history of the Purity Law and its public health benefits. Bavarians were once again the most vocal, with legal and nutritional assessments coming out of Weihenstephan, and the old fighters dating to the *Süßbierstreit*, such as Hermann Höcherl and Joseph Ertl, taking up roles in both discourse and policy meetings. Brewers, for their part, not only developed public relations and advertising material, but also directly rallied consumers. Even before the case began, the German Brewers Association coordinated a massive public relations campaign seeking to mobilize the West German

---

[24]   Christoph Hermann, 'Neoliberalism in the European Union', *Studies in Political Economy* 79 no. 1 (2007): pp. 61–90, esp. 69–73.

[25]   Qtd in Quinn Slobodian, *Globalists: The End of Empire and the Birth of Neoliberalism* (Cambridge and London: Harvard University Press, 2018), p. 209, more broadly on the ECJ, pp. 202–17.

populace. They placed ads in more than 4,000 newspapers, with an estimated total circulation of 105 million; launched television and radio campaigns; helped develop a traveling public relations program that visited each of the federal states; and distributed a petition to 25,000 hotels, restaurants, and grocery stores. In September 1983, they delivered this petition—complete with the signatures of 2.5 million West German citizens—to the Federal Ministers of Health and Agriculture.[26] Support for the *Reinheitsgebot* went so deep that West German Chancellor Helmut Kohl, a strong advocate of European integration, entered the fray. In May 1983, Kohl wrote to the President of the European Commission, Gaston Thorn, that "the Federal Government, in agreement with the German Parliament, the Federal Council, and the German public attaches the utmost importance to the maintenance of the Purity Law." He criticized the ECJ case and asked that Thorn "work to ensure that the infringing process is immediately ter-minated."[27] Thorn was unmoved. He acknowledged the concern but noted that "the Commission must ensure that the beer of other member states receives the same opportunities as German beer."[28] Without the intervention of the Commission, the final decision came down the ECJ. Already in late 1983, legal experts noted the increasingly active role of the Court in the service of unre-stricted capital and predicted that the ECJ would likely rule to open the West German market under the banner of mutual recognition and market integration.[29]

By the end of 1984, most West German politicians had resigned themselves to the repeal, but it took more than two years for the ax to fall. When, in March 1987, the court lifted the *Reinheitsgebot* as an informal trade barrier to the free movement of goods in the European Community, West Germans—particularly Bavarians—were shocked. Since at least 1982 the German and Bavarian Brewers Associations had rallied around the law in press conferences and public relations work. In Bavaria, beer-related media such as the magazine *Bier und Wir* had assured readers that their politicians were on the job.[30] The shockwaves of the decision went deep. In Neumarkt in der Oberpfalz, about 40km southeast of Nuremberg, for instance, one Andreas Z. felt so moved by the ECJ ruling that he wrote a letter of complaint to the Federal President, Richard von Weizsäcker. "Much has been written about the *Reinheitsgebot* lately," he began, referencing recent food scandals, chemical additive concerns, and cases of food poisoning

---

[26] Bayerischer Brauerbund e.V., *Geschäftsbericht 1981/82*, p. 50; and n.a., 'Über ein Vierteljahrhundert erfolgreich für den Erhalt des Reinheitsgebots', *Brauwelt* 23 (1996), pp. 1064–71. The circulation estimate of 105 million, found in the first source, nearly doubled the West German population at the time.

[27] May 20, 1983, letter from Helmut Kohl to Gaston E. Thorn, Bundesarchiv Koblenz (henceforth BAK) B 189/30450.

[28] July 8, 1983, letter from Gaston E. Thorn to Helmut Kohl, BAK B 189/30450.

[29] 'Mitteilung der Regierung der Bundesrepublik Deutschland, re: Vertragsverletzungsverfahren wegen des Reinheitsgebotes für Bier', no date, but makes reference to an EC Commission circular dated Aug. 25, 1983, BAK B 189/30450; see also a memo on the Nov. 25, 1984 press conference by EC Commissioner Karl-Heinz Narjes, BAK B 189/36039.

[30] 'Ist das Reinheitsgebot in Gefahr?' *Bier und Wir* 29 (1982), p. 5.

tied to "unpure" beer in the United States and Canada. The age-old regulation, he claimed, protected consumers from such adulteration, and the ECJ decision now exposed them to it. "Would it not be better," he asked in the language of market nationalism, "if the people in the countries that do not observe the *Reinheitsgebot* drank their own beer and were not allowed to send it to us?"[31]

What is most remarkable about this letter is that in the summer of 1987, Andreas Z. was an eleven-year-old, fifth-grade student at the Willibald-Gluck-Gymnasium. His letter is written on stationary whimsically decorated with cartoon kittens and today lives sandwiched between official government correspondence in the Federal Archive in Koblenz. Andreas may well have been the coolest kid in school when he received a response a week later from Dr Pieper in the office of President Weizsäcker. Pieper dodged the eleven-year old's demands, explaining that, according to the ECJ, West Germany was now obligated to unconditionally open its market to members of the European Community (EC). But while EC member states could now send beer to West Germany that was not brewed in accordance with the *Reinheitsgebot*, "the consumer still has the choice which beers with which additives he chooses to drink."[32] This was a curious exchange. Eleven-year-old Andreas was likely not a frequent beer drinker. Moreover, it proves hard to imagine a rural fifth-grade student spending his free time staying current on food poisoning, chemical additives, and the goings-on of the European Court of Justice. His interest in the issue, he admitted, stemmed from the fact that his father worked at a local brewery.[33] And so while Dr Pieper took the opportunity to reminded Andreas that children his age should not be drinking beer anyway, his response was less directed to Andreas personally than it was a repetition of faith in individual consumer choice as a foil to the potentially exploitative unregulated market.

While West German brewers had feared that the ECJ ruling would leave the national market "flooded" with adjunct competition, such was not the case. Already in May 1989, the Federal Cartel Office, a market competition watchdog, announced to the Bundestag that brewers' fears had not materialized, in large part because consumers did not generate demand for foreign adjunct beers.[34] By the end of the 1980s, "pure beer" had become so embedded in consumer culture that regulators deployed it as a discursive object for economic moralizing across the political spectrum. In a February 1990 Bunderstag debate, Ulrich Irmer of the free market liberal FDP invoked the regulation and the ECJ decision as proof

---

[31] July 15, 1987, letter from Andreas Z. to Weizäcker, BAK B 122/36039.
[32] July 22, 1987, letter from Dr Pieper to Andreas Z, BAK B 122/36039.
[33] July 15, 1987, Andreas Z. to Weizäcker.
[34] 'Bericht des Bundeskartellamtes über seine Tätigkeit in den Jahren 1987/1988 sowie über die Lage und Entwicklung auf seinem Aufgabengebiet (§ 50 GWB)', Deutscher Bundestag 11. Wahlperiode, Drucksache 11/4611 (May 30, 1989), p. 81.

positive that in spite of market protectionist anxieties, the free market works. "One realizes," he jested, "that today there are still more types of beer in Germany than there are different types of cheeses in France or soldiers in Luxemburg."[35] Whether the spirit or the letter of the joke was true, the workings of the free market were hardly the reason. Consumer choices had been hemmed in by decades of market protectionism, public relations work, and industrial lobbying. For others on the political spectrum, the successes of wedding regulatory and business interests to consumer tastes became a model for navigating integrated Europe. In the summer of 1991, CSU parliamentarian Dr Martin Mayer offered beer as an example of how to approach the branding of meat, milk, and other agricultural products. Advocating for closer cooperation with trade, he noted that "when it comes to beer, every child knows: only beer brewed in accordance with the German *Reinheitsgebot* is good enough." Heckled about the drinking age by the SPD, he responded, "yeah, but children already know that anyway." Andreas Z. would have agreed. And, returning to his point, he noted that "corn and millet beer produced according to the regulations of the European Community can also be sold here...We just don't drink it."[36] Consumer sentiments and convictions around beer, shaped by decades of regulation and PR work, now offered a model for market nationalism in the European market.

The destruction of the legal basis of Bavarian and West German market protectionism by the ECJ testifies to crosscurrents in the institutions of integrating Europe. The case is a textbook example of ascendant neoliberal market regulation. Neoliberalism is not simply a constellation of market values—liberalization, deregulation, and privatization—but rather the advocacy for, and construction of, a series of institutions that construct and "encase" rather than "free" markets.[37] As Quinn Slobodian put it, neoliberalism is a drive toward the "complete protection of private capital rights, and the ability of supranational judiciary bodies like the European Court of Justice...to override national legislation that might disrupt the global rights of capital."[38] The fate of the *Reinheitsgebot* as a market protectionist measure certainly aligns with such a drive. But the case also testifies to another important role of supranational institutions such as the European Union: the creation of structures intended to preserve bounded cultural economies. Beginning in the late 1980s and continuing into the early 1990s, brewers leaned into an emerging system of protected indications to identify regional origin and quality for the consumer. Almost immediately after the ECJ decision, for instance, brewers in Baden-Württemberg sought a protected indication, insisting that beer

---

[35] Deutscher Bundestag Plenarprotokoll 11/194 (Feb. 8, 1990), p. 14893.
[36] Deutscher Bundestag Plenarprotokoll 12/30 (June 12, 1991), pp. 2332–3.
[37] Slobodian, *Globalists*. Philipp Ther, *Europe since 1989: A History*, trans. Charlotte Hughes-Kreutzmüller (Princeton and Oxford: Princeton University Press, 2016).
[38] Slobodian, *Globalists*, pp. 12–13.

produced from local barley malt captured the tradition and taste of place; it embodied the *terroir*. Such claims not only in Germany but throughout integrating Europe fed into the 1992 emergence of the EU system of geographical indications. Throughout the 1990s, more and more producers worked to protect their products through this sort of market signaling. Bavarian brewers likewise lobbied the federal government to petition for a Protected Geographical Indication (PGI) on "Bavarian Beer," and in 1995 "German Beer" was one of only nine products— out of more than 300 applicants—to be recognized by the EU Commission. To be labeled and sold as "German Beer," the beverage had to be brewed according to German regulations—namely, the national version of the *Reinheitsgebot* as set out in the Beer Tax Law.[39] Such an international system protects the name, enshrines the product, and communicates authenticity to consumers now allegedly awash in a flooded "free market." From a business perspective, the more restrictive the geographical indication, the greater the financial benefit to the controlled good.[40] And, thus, the PGI system—though it operates in the logic of the neoliberal sovereign consumer—tends to work as a counterbalance to the opening of markets to unfettered capital by protecting localized capital in the name of tradition. Since the 1950s, cultural meaning-making around the *Reinheitsgebot* had centered on discourses of tradition and an alleged timelessness which, by the early 1990s, meshed with the value structures of the evolving marketplace.

The ECJ ruling on the *Reinheitsgebot* flung open the West German market. Breweries in the member states of the European Community could henceforth send beer to West Germany that was not brewed in accordance with German standards, but, as Dr Pieper noted in his response to Andreas Z., German producers and consumers did not have to like it. And they didn't. By the time it was overturned, the *Reinheitsgebot* had become so embedded in the fabric of West German culture that it remained the norm of production and consumption. Even after the ECJ ruling, the *Reinheitsgebot* remained an indication of quality well beyond market protectionist measures such as the PGI system. According to one survey, 95 per cent of West Germans insisted that the regulation continued to be "the guarantee of quality and taste for our beer," while 91 per cent demanded that beer should be brewed according to the law in spite of the ruling. A more conservative survey found that two-thirds of beer drinkers identified the *Reinheitsgebot* as

[39] N.a., 'Deutsches Bier ist traditionelles Produkt', *Brauwelt* 19/20 (1995), p. 930.

[40] See, for example, Brian Ilbery and Moya Kneafsey, 'Registering Regional Specialty Food and Drink Products in the United Kingdom: The Case of PDOs and PGIs', *Area* 32 no. 3 (Sept. 2000): pp. 317–25; Michaela DeSoucey, 'Gastronationalism: Food Traditions and Authenticity Politics in the European Union', *American Sociological Review* 75 no. 3 (June 2010): pp. 432–55; Oana C. Deselnicu, Marco Costanigro, Diogo M. Souza-Monteiro, and Dawn Thilmany McFadden, 'A Meta-Analysis of Geographical Indication Food Valuation Studies: What Drives the Premium for Origin-Based Labels?' *Journal of Agricultural and Resource Economics* 38 no. 2 (Aug. 2013): pp. 204–19; and Fabio Parasecoli, *Knowing Where It Comes From: Labeling Traditional Foods to Compete in a Global Market* (Iowa City: University of Iowa Press, 2017).

the pre-eminent feature of good, German beer.[41] Such convictions evince the broad, nationwide internalization of a provincial peculiarity that was, until just a few decades earlier, almost completely unknown. By the late 1980s, then, the concept of "pure beer" had evolved from regional to national icon in West Germany and the ECJ ruling served to entrench the cultural value of the tradition. But while pure beer became an icon of the nation, the nation itself was dramatically transforming.

Brewing the New Nation—Beyond the Bonn Republic

The fall of the Berlin Wall and the hasty reunification of the two Germanies provided a twofold opportunity. First, many West German brewers who worried about competition from breweries in other EEC member states recognized a fertile market for continued growth. As many breweries of the former East were bought out, providing temporary relief for larger market anxieties among western brewers, voices of dissent quickly emerged. Some were from the former East, as we might expect, but others were from the former West, particularly from small- and mid-sized enterprises, disproportionally located in the south, who saw potential for national kinship in the language of industry decentralization. Second, reunification forced the issue of industrial structure into national relevance, with advocates for industry decentralization emerging most forcefully from the south. Just as historians have debated continuity and rupture in the 1970s, so too have they sought to integrate and renarrate German histories in view of the political transformations of 1989/90.[42] In the case of beer, the reunification of Germany featured both ruptures, particularly for East German producers and consumers, and transformations of longer industrial processes and values, most notably two initially southern convictions: a deep opposition to industry consolidation paired with a broad deference to the *Reinheitsgebot*.

In West Germany, *German* beer had been promoted, sold, legislated, and internalized as essentially and fundamentally "pure beer," thanks in no small part to the efforts of Bavarian brewers and regulators. Even before the emergence of the two German states, the areas that became East Germany had already abandoned the *Reinheitsgebot*. As we saw in earlier chapters, many had opposed the Bavarian infatuation with purity as early as 1906, while others readily adopted Herbert Backe's sugar adulteration proposal in 1938. In the aftermath of the Second World War, the Soviet Zone and later the East German state formally

---

[41] Bayerischer Brauerbund e.V., *Geschäftsbericht 1988/89*, 64; and results from the Centrale Marketinggesellschaft der deutschen Agrarwirtschaft, in 'Aktuell' *Brauwelt* 20 (1990).
[42] For example, Christoph Kleßmann, ed., *The Divided Past: Rewriting Post-War German History* (Oxford: Berg, 2001); and the essays in the special issue 'New Narratives for the History of the Federal Republic', *Central European History* 52 no. 1 (March 2019).

rejected the *Reinheitsgebot* in all its forms.[43] All mention of it disappeared from GDR government documents as economic planners worked to optimize resources and make beer compatible with the rationalized economy and socialist consumption through massive adulteration efforts. Beer production increased steadily, particularly after about 1960, and economic planners devoted significant attention to rationalizing production and industrial organization. Following a shift in state policy toward prioritizing consumer goods, the brewing industry was restructured and expanded in the early 1970s. At the start of that decade, state planners consolidated the production of beer and other beverages into fifteen regional beverage combines (*Getränkekombinaten*) managing 457 firms, some 270 of which produced beer. The beer of the consolidated industry was overwhelmingly lager, and, more specifically, Pilsner. Indeed, Helles declined in market share from 60 per cent in 1970 to only 13 per cent in 1990. But East German beer was also the product of scarcity. The portion of sugar and unmalted grain fluctuated throughout the four decades of the regime, sometimes ranging as high as 65 per cent. Eastern brewers were allowed to brew with rice, corn, and unhusked barley, as well as additional enzymes required to break down these ingredients.[44] Culturally, beer played a similar role as we saw in Chapter 4 in that it "fostered a sense of cultural unity," but the East German state also used it to more explicit political ends, pointing to beer as evidence for the people of the workers' state "that the planned economy had their best interests in mind."[45] Eastern beverage combines, like so much of the East German state, seemed to be functional and highly stable. Indeed, per capita beer consumption in the GDR had risen steadily, peaking in 1988 at 143 liters per annum.

The deterioration of the East German dictatorship came as a shock, but one welcomed by many brewers, particularly those in the West. For them, the opening of the eastern market offered an opportunity to line their coffers as they braced for the influx of cheaper foreign beers coming on the heels of the ECJ ruling. In early 1990, *Der Spiegel* reported that western brewers were looking "at the map of the GDR with covetous eyes," sizing up market weaknesses and "undreamt-of possibilities."[46] Inroads were almost immediate. In December 1989, the Hamburg Holsten brewery shipped some 700,000 liters of beer to the eastern city of Dresden. In the winter and spring, western German brewers regularly

---

[43] See Chapters 1 and 2; John Gillespie, 'The People's Drink: The Politics of Beer in East Germany (1945–1971)' (MA thesis, Middle Tennessee State University, 2017), pp. 80–1; and Hans-J. Manger and Peter Lietz, *Die Brau- und Malzindustrie in Deutschland-Ost zwischen 1945 und 1989: Ein Beitrag zur Geschichte der deutschen Brau- und Malzindustrie im 20. Jahrhundert* (Berlin: VLB Berlin, 2016), p. 446.

[44] N.a., 'Brauwirtschaft in der DDR', *Brauwelt* 12 (1990), p. 404; N.a., 'Zusatzstoffe und Rohfrucht bleiben in der DDR erlaubt', *Brauwelt* 13 (1990), p. 466; N.a., 'Senkung der Stammwürze bei der DDR-Bieren', *Brauwelt* 19 (1990), p. 719.

[45] Gillespie, 'The People's Drink', pp. 30–1.

[46] 'Galle statt Hopfen', *Der Spiegel* Mar. 19, 1990, pp. 148–9.

toured the East, carrying with them free samples and paraphernalia in hopes of building their reputations among consumers. When they returned, they brought with them "true horror stories" of adulteration. According to rumor, some Eastern brewers were reportedly adding cow bile to provide bitterness absent sufficient hops. Such claims likely reflected cultural bias more than commercial reality. Indeed, even more objectionable than cow bile, western brewers reported "shuddering" that sugar cane was also regularly used.[47] This sensibility can only be fully understood in the wake of decades of fighting over the inclusion of sugar, from the 1930s to the 1970s. It also glosses over some of the lingering disparities between law and popular understanding. By federal law, brewers in West Germany were still allowed to use sugar cane in top-fermenting beer—though Bavarians were not—but that fact had got lost in the popular exaltation of the four-ingredient *Reinheitsgebot* for bottom-fermenting beer. Here, the use of sugar cane thus points less to a technical difference—though it remains true that most beer in the West was sugar-free lager—than to an effort to demarcate the cultures of the two Germanys.

The Western gaze—both covetous and alienating—sparked opposition from brewers in the East. In the spring of 1990, many Eastern brewers voiced their willingness to brew according to West German standards, claiming that they just needed time to adjust. In March, for example, Dr M. Siebert, the director of the *VEB Wissenschaftlich-Technisch-Ökonomisches Zentrum der Brau- und Malzindustrie* (WTÖZ), spoke to Western industry leaders, explaining that their Eastern counterparts were already moving to reduce the inclusion of sugar and unmalted grain in good-faith deference to the *Reinheitsgebot*.[48] Other Eastern brewers organized among themselves. In the early summer of 1990, many breweries in East Germany founded new trade organizations. By June, the brewers of Berlin-Brandenburg and Saxony had resurrected the pre-war Brewers Associations, hoping to align themselves with the industrial organizations legible in the West. While almost all member breweries were state owned, the remaining eight private breweries in the GDR organized themselves into the "Brau Ring," citing both the "unrestrained market offenses" of Western brewers and the uncertainties of the looming introduction of the Deutsche Mark. Their effort at solidarity was admirable, but many Western brewers were skeptical, dubbing the strategy the "Allianz syndrome," in an apparent reference to the recent and unsuccessful political alliance of East German non-communist parties in the March elections.[49] The assumption in the West seemed to be that even in the context of coalitions among themselves, East Germans would not fare well in the course of privatization and market competition. And most did not.

---

[47] Ibid.   [48] N.a., 'Brauwirtschaft in der DDR', *Brauwelt* 12 (1990), p. 404.
[49] N.a., 'Brau Ring in der DDR', *Brauwelt* 18 (1990), p. 680.

In the early 1990s, former East German breweries followed the course of other industries that were rapidly privatized, often to the detriment of East German workers and certainly to that of former East German goods.[50] Almost immediately in 1990, more than 300 employees of the Schultheiss "Kulturbrauerei" in Prenzlauer Berg, East Berlin, were laid off in successive waves as the company was "swallowed" by private capital from West Berlin.[51] The competitive capacities of GDR breweries were limited by a lack of technological modernization. Most breweries had been built before 1930 and little updated since, meaning that the primary need in 1990 was private investment, which was slow in coming, and breweries tended to either collapse or be bought out by Western competitors.[52] Such was the case for the Berliner Bürgerbräu in Friedrichshagen, which initially stayed afloat thanks in large part to an investment by the Kindl Brauerei in Neukölln, on the opposite side of the formerly divided city. Bürgerbräu had opened in the 1860s, boomed in the transformative Pilsner years of the turn of the century, and operated as a publicly owned enterprise (*Volkseigene Betriebe*, or VEB) throughout the Cold War. By 1992, however, the development costs required to maintain and update the brewery moved the interim trust agency (*Treuhand*) to sell. It was bought by Hofmark Brauerei KG in Loifling, in the Upper Palatinate region of Bavaria, for 35 million DM, with an estimated 20 million DM needed in investments to bring the facilities up to the standards of the new Bavarian owners.[53] On a larger scale, three of the largest and best-known Eastern breweries—Radeberger Exportbrauerei, Köstrizer Schwarzbierbrauerei, and Mecklenburgische Brauerei Lübz—were simply bought out in 1990 and 1991 by West German breweries Binding, Bitburger, and Holsten.

As western capital and standards rapidly penetrated the former East, a number of critical voices emerged. According to the new WTÖZ director Achim Beubler, most Western brewers were interested not in investment, but rather in expanding their monopolies on production and distribution. Prior to reunification, Eastern brewers had appealed to the GDR government for a battery of protectionist measures: credits, tax breaks, bans on publicly owned bars and restaurants converting

[50] Patricia J. Smith, 'The Illusory Economic Miracle: Assessing Eastern Germany's Economic Transition', in *After the Wall: Eastern Germany since 1989*, ed. Smith (Boulder: Westview Press, 1998), pp. 109–42, esp. 111–12; more recently, see Rainer Land, 'East Germany 1989–2010: A Fragmented Development', in *United Germany: Debating Processes and Prospects*, ed. Konrad H. Jarausch (New York: Berghahn Books, 2013), pp. 104–18, esp. 109–13; and Holger Wolf, 'German Economic Unification Twenty Years Later', in *From the Bonn to the Berlin Republic: Germany at the Twentieth Anniversary of Unification*, ed. Jeffrey J. Anderson and Eric Langenbacher (New York: Berghahn Books, 2010), pp. 321–30, esp. 322–4.

[51] Gabriele Oertel, 'Ein schaler Geschmack', *Neues Deutschland* Nov. 20, 1990.

[52] N.a., 'DDR-Brauereien fordern Schutzmaßnahmen', *Brauwelt* 27 (1990), pp.1102–3.

[53] 'Alte Berliner Bier-Traditionen sollen bewahrt werden', *Neues Deutschland* Apr. 27, 1992; on the Neukölln investment, see Friedrich-Karl Helmholz, 'Schwacher Gerstensaft für die Damen', *Neues Deutschland*, Feb. 22, 1991.

to western products, and tariffs on imports for 2–3 years.[54] Such appeals were short-lived, not least because, soon afterward, the East German state ceased to exist. But they suggest that critics lamented not only the economic, but also the cultural stakes of privatization. In the summer of 1991, for example, the Sächsischen Brau-Union in Dresden (formerly the VE Getränkekombinat) was acquired by the Hamburg-based Holsten multinational. In his reporting on the issue, Alfred Michaelis of the former East German communist party newspaper *Neues Deutschland* lamented both the emerging "monopoly" of western breweries and the ways in which it displaced local tastes and cultures. While the new Hamburg owners claimed an interest in continuing to produce Dresden favorite Feldschlößchen, the first beers produced there were Holsten, not Feldschlößchen. Michaelis noted that the displacement "speaks volumes" about the plans of western capital. For the foreseeable future, he wrote, the prevailing wisdom in Dresden appeared to be "people buy Saxon beer—first and foremost from Holsten." Across the newly reunified country, beer increasingly flowed from West to East. Since 1976, Bavarian and West German beer production had virtually stagnated, with annual production often decreasing, and never gaining more than 1.5 per cent. But in 1990, their total outputs increased 14 per cent and 12 per cent respectively, a growth rate not seen since the 1950s, with almost all increases heading to the East.[55] By 1991, western beer production had increased by some 11 million hectoliters, eight million of which had gone to the former East, while the sales of former East German breweries declined by up to 40 per cent.[56]

Privatization and the displacement of Eastern products is not the entirety of the story, however. Brewers on both sides of the political divide united in their support of a decentralized brewing structure and the industrial retention of the *Reinheitsgebot*. Industrial composition had changed dramatically since the 1970s, as the long-touted mid-sized structure of the West German brewing industry consolidated in response to economic recessions.[57] While consolidation meant increased tax revenues and greater profits, many in the industry, particularly in southern Germany, bemoaned the process as one of homogenization and the destructive capacities of unrestricted capital. For these advocates of a decentralized industry, the embattled East appeared to be a kindred spirit. In the summer of 1990, Wilhelm Kumpf, the head of the Association of Midsized Private Breweries in Baden-Württemberg, openly criticized larger Western brewers for

---

[54] N.a., 'DDR-Brauereien fordern Schutzmaßnahmen'.

[55] 'Bierausstoß Bayerns und Deutschlands nach Kalenderjahren seit 1950', Bayerischer Brauerbund e.V., *Geschäftsbericht 1993/95*, p. 97.

[56] Alfred Michaelis, 'Der Poker um das Dresdner Traditionsbier geht weiter', *Neues Deutschland* July 31, 1991. https://www.neues-deutschland.de/artikel/317863.der-poker-um-das-dresdner-traditionsbier-geht-weiter.html. See also N.a., 'Gesamtdeutscher Biermarkt wächst zusammen', *Brauwelt* 27 (1990), pp. 1100–1.

[57] Bayerischer Brauerbund e.V., *Daten und Fakten der bayerischen Brauwirtschaft 1988/89*, tbl 3 & 4; and 'Struktur der bayerischen Brauwirtschaft', *Brauwelt* 16 (1993), p. 642.

their assault on the mid-sized structure of the East German industry. He called for regulators in both Bonn and Berlin "to hinder private capitalistic monopoly structures in the GDR."[58] Thus, even as Western brewers insulated themselves from the European market opened by the 1987 ECJ ruling, some hoped to reunify the national beer market. Small-scale industry and the *Reinheitsgebot* were often at the core of their convictions. Such a position made its way into the upper reaches of the trade industry as well. The president of the German Brewers Association, Dieter Soltmann was himself a Munich brewer, and by the summer of 1990 he had begun to urge caution in the privatization of the East. Rather than imagine the "undreamt-of possibilities" of the East, he now advocated protecting East German breweries, especially small- and mid-sized enterprises. Eventually, he maintained, they would take on the standards of "pure beer" as the reincorporated *Länder* adopted the West German Beer Tax Law (*Biersteuergesetz*). These breweries' continued existence would ensure that more brewers adhered to the so-called "Purity Law." For those concerned about industrial structure, such an interest quickly became a parallel goal to mere capital growth.[59] Cultural–industrial convictions about industry decentralization, long a staple of southern brewing, gained new purchase as a sort of market nationalism thanks to the twin pressures of market integrations and reunification.

As more and more Eastern breweries fell, advocates from East and West rallied around the *Reinheitsgebot*. The impetus was partly international. In the summer of 1990, the European Community considered a series of rulings on foodstuffs that would further undermine German production standards. In response, the DBB appealed directly to Chancellor Helmut Kohl, arguing that Western qua national standards were essential for the future of the industry in a reunified Germany. The retention and application of the "*Reinheitsgebot* is essential for the future of the GDR brewing industry, [which] can only survive in market-based competition if a high-quality standard is consistently applied."[60] These regulations came to naught in the case of the brewing sector, but the support for the *Reinheitsgebot* that they sparked maintained at the national level. In October 1990, hot on the heels of reunification, the Ministry of Finance announced that brewers in the former East had until the end of 1992 to convert their production to conform to the Beer Tax Law. In the interim, beers produced outside of it could only be sold in the former GDR.[61] Like the rest of German reunification, the process of reuniting the brewing industry unfolded faster than expected. While the industry was largely consolidated under the German Brewers Association through 1991, the process was distinctly regional. Brewers in East Berlin and

---

[58] N.a., 'Mittelständische Struktur der DDR-Braubranche soll erhalten bleiben', *Brauwelt* 18 (1990), p. 680.
[59] N.a., 'Gesamtdeutscher Biermarkt wächst zusammen'.
[60] 'Appel zum Reinheitsgebot', *Brauwelt* 30/31 (1990), p. 1240.
[61] 'Aktuell', *Brauwelt* 41 (1990).

Brandenburg joined the *Wirtschaftsverband Berliner Brauereien*; Mecklenburg-Vorpommern joined the *Landesverband Nord*; and the newly reformed trade organizations in Saxony, Saxony-Anhalt, and Thuringia joined the German umbrella organization. The brewing industries of the three latter regions were also proud to announce that by February 1991, only four months after reunification, they were brewing according to the *Reinheitsgebot*.[62]

In the years after 1991, the adoption of Western standards, the eastward flow of private capital, and a focused marketing push toward things local aided growth in the former GDR. While reunification drastically challenged eastern brewers, with nearly 80 per cent of businesses bought out and combined sales dropping from 24.5 to 7.8 million hectoliters between 1989 to 1991, by the end of 1992 the industry of the former East had begun to grow.[63] From 1993 to 1994, the sale of beer in the *Bundesländer* of the former GDR often outpaced that of the old Federal Republic.[64] A shift in individual behavior was partly responsible, as many consumers abandoned the euphoria of western goods, and acknowledged their own role in business failures and widespread unemployment when they did not buy local.[65] This behavioral change went hand-in-hand with industry advocacy for small and mid-sized production. Beer drinkers on both sides of the former divide testified to the importance of localism in the production and consumption of beer.[66] But these convictions were not independent of the industry itself. Beginning in 1991, the German Brewers Association sponsored a massive public relations campaign spanning print, radio, and television, and revolving around the slogan "Beer needs *Heimat*." Notoriously difficult to translate, the word *Heimat* is most often rendered as home or homeland, but with a deeper and more localized sense of belonging. Beer, the slogan maintained, needs a spatial orientation, a rooted sense of belonging. While the campaign benefitted brewers throughout Germany—and perhaps especially in the former East—it was a national and local response to European and global market integration. Both producers and consumers seemed to agree that beer can't be from just anywhere—it is constitutive of identity and place.

At the core of what made German beer German in the reunified country was the legal peculiarity that had been little known outside the south only a generation earlier: the *Reinheitsgebot*. Both nationally and internationally, it emerged as the linchpin of popular and industrial convictions that beer was a near timeless

---

[62] 'Deutscher Brauer-Bund wieder vereinigt', *Brauwelt* 1/2 (1991), p. 4; 'Bier nach dem Reinheitsgebot in Thüringen, Sachsen und Sachsen-Anhalt', *Brauwelt* 10 (1991), p. 325.

[63] 'Bericht des Bundeskartellamtes über seine Tätigkeit in den Jahren 1991/92 sowie über die Lage und Entwicklung auf seinem Aufgabengebiet', Deutscher Bundestag 12. Wahlperiode, Drucksache 12/5200 (June 24, 1993), pp. 112–13.

[64] 'Gesamtbierabsatz nach Bundesländern im Dezember 1994', *Brauwelt* 135, no. 9 (1995), p. 419.

[65] 'Bier nach dem Reinheitsgebot in Thüringen, Sachsen und Sachsen-Anhalt', *Brauwelt* 10 (1991), p. 325.

[66] "Bier braucht Heimat,' *Brauwelt* 5 (1993), 187; and 'Aktuell', *Brauwelt* 35 (1990).

tradition, belonging to and defining people and place. Although the ECJ had stripped the regulation of any international standing in 1987, in 1995 the Commission of the EU granted "German Beer" recognition as a traditional product; 1 of just 9 commodities out of more than 300 applicants to win this supranational recognition.[67] To count as "German," beer had to be produced according to the four-ingredient list commonly called the *Reinheitsgebot*. We might note that this distinction, which only applied to bottom-fermented lager, meant that all top-fermented ale which was legally brewed with other sugar sources might be German beer, but it was not "German Beer." On the national level, German brewers—again led by Bavarians—launched a new holiday to celebrate the *Reinheitsgebot* as a marker of German tradition. The so-called Day of German Beer was inaugurated in 1995—more precisely, on April 23: the date of the 1516 Bavarian decree. The German Brewers Association hoped that the event would have a loud "media echo" across the nation as brewers reaffirmed their oath (*Eid*) to the *Reinheitsgebot*.[68] Economic nationalism and supranational market regulation buttressed consumer behaviors enshrining "pure beer" in the pantheon of the new, reunified Germany.

By the 1990s, the concept of "pure beer" had become so commonplace—the invented tradition so normalized—that even critics of the industry operated within its logic. On the occasion of the Day of German Beer, for instance, Hans-Dieter Schütt, the features editor of *Neues Deutschland*, reflected on the holiday, the *Reinheitsgebot*, the changing market, and the German love of beer. The piece both perpetuates and critiques the notion that drinking beer is a marker of the sentiment of belonging to the German nation. On the one hand, he lamented the rapid market takeover of the former East by western breweries and standards. On the other, he perpetuated the alleged timelessness of "German beer," noting that the *German* Purity Law had existed for 479 years. Flipping the slogan "beer needs *Heimat*" on its head, he noted that "the reverse is also true: *Heimat* needs beer. The more beer in the blood, the more *Heimat* in the heart. And on the tongue... [The] *Reinheitsgebot* finally clarifies the question, wherein the German nation exists: mainly in the existence of beer."[69] In the soul-searching, post–Cold War moment, as the readership of *Neues Deutschland* rapidly deteriorated, Schütt was manifestly critical of the reduction of the idea of Germany to a mere commodity. Yet for all his cynicism, he simultaneously confirms an important transition that has been at the heart of this book: how the production and consumption of beer evolved from a mere industry and cultural behavior to an identity expressed both inwardly, "in the heart," and outwardly, "on the tongue." And, tellingly, he does so by writing over the entangled dynamics by which a provincial

---

[67] 'Deutsches Bier ist traditionelles Produkt', *Brauwelt* 19/20 (1995), p. 930.

[68] 'Bier—ein emotionales Lebensmittel', *Brauwelt* 15/16 (1995), p. 717.

[69] Hans-Dieter Schütt, 'Wege vom Ich zum Bier—Gedanken zum Tag des deutschen Bieres am 23. April', *Neues Deutschland* April 22, 1995, https://www.neues-deutschland.de/artikel/544928.wege-vom-ich-zum-bier.html.

standard became a national cultural touchstone. To be sure, the conquest of the former East by western capital and standards was just the most recent reconfiguration of space. Only a hundred years earlier, the Old Bavarian dynastic proclamation in question had yet to even be called the *Reinheitsgebot* and was still decades away from informing regulations and production standards beyond Bavaria.

The emergence of the *Reinheitsgebot* as a reunified national icon depended on a series of immediate conditions, including accelerating industrial centralization and reunification, but it also stands as a triumph of Bavarian influence on the German nation. The "German *Reinheitsgebot*" emerged as a market sentiment in spite of decades of attack. In the 1920s, northern brewers railed against the Bavarian obsession with "purism." In the 1930s, northern brewers readily adopted Herbert Backe's sugar proposal. And as recently as the 1960s, northern brewers had been ready to compromise on production standards in the process of European integration. The recession and the ECJ ruling likewise posed a threat, but cultures of market protectionism emerging from the 1970s and industrial responses to reunification in the 1990s ultimately came to prop up long-contested southern convictions. The founding of the Day of German Beer in 1995 was an industry effort to fortify market sensibilities in the wake of the ECJ decisions against the *Reinheitsgebot* as a trade barrier. If the new, reunified Germany was a nation of "pure beer," it was in no small part thanks to provincial dynamics that shaped the economic and cultural structures across different iterations of the German nation-state. In the 1990s, the combined political and economic pressures of reunification and neoliberal globalization forced the long-standing issue of industry structure to the fore, and decentralized production came to stand alongside the veneration of the *Reinheitsgebot* as a defining feature of the national industry.

Conclusion

From the global collapse of Löwenbräu to sweeping industrial and cultural responses to market and political integrations, the decades "after the boom" witnessed structural shifts in capital, regulation, and geopolitics. Some of these were direct consequences of changing global markets, such as the turning inward of Munich beerhall culture as the similitude of place constructed by Löwenbräu and their global partners came crashing down. Other transitions were less disruptive as decades-long processes assumed urgency in new contexts. Bavarian insistence on the *Reinheitsgebot* as a *cultural*—and not just industrial—marker became nationally hegemonic just as the market and the nation expanded thanks to neoliberal integration and German reunification. By the turn of the 21st century, southern regulations and production standards that had remained broadly unknown and had been industrially contested 80 years earlier became the fully national standard—a mark of industrial practice and cultural identity. As brewers of the former East adhered to the new standards and regulations, they found allies in the former West who viewed their plight as akin to the delocalizing threats of late modern globalization and neoliberal market integration. Countervailing impulses led many regulators and small and mid-sized brewers to work toward incorporating and investing in the stability of Eastern enterprises as long as they adhered to the standards of the Federal Republic—namely, the *Reinheitsgebot*. Bavaria continued to follow stricter production standards than the rest of Germany, but the multiplicity of meanings and applications became less immediately important as long everyone adopted the language of "beer purity." By the turn of the 21st century then, the standards that Bavarians had fought to make West German had become fully national as the reunified Germany sought to position itself in the shifting global economy.

Conclusion

At the end of May 2017, then Chancellor Angela Merkel stood in a Munich beer tent addressing members and supporters of the Bavarian Christian Social Union (CSU), the sister party to her own Christian Democratic Union (CDU). While cooperation between the CSU and CDU had been remarkably durable for more than half a century, disputes over the so-called refugee crisis had recently strained the relationship. Addressing the Bavarian party, Merkel sought to ensure the stability of the alliance for what was sure to be a rough road ahead. The event took place the day after the 2017 G7 summit—Merkel's first sustained diplomatic engagement with a number of new international leaders, among them Theresa May and Donald Trump. In the context of these newly complicated diplomatic relationships, she worked to bring the increasingly anti-refugee CSU in line with her pro-European position. Reflecting on ascendant nativist politics in the United States and the United Kingdom, she proclaimed that "we Europeans truly have to take our fate into our own hands." Some international commentators found this image laughable and dismissed the speech, noting that "were Merkel to signal a German pivot away from the United States, she would hardly choose a Bavarian beer party as the venue."[1]

The critique may have been fair at the level of international relations, but a "Bavarian beer party" was precisely the place to appeal to the CSU on questions of national solidarity and European unity. The CSU has long been perhaps the most conservative of postwar German political parties—a conception immortalized in the 1987 claim by the iconic Franz Josef Strauss that "to the right of us is only the wall." Animated by that spirit of ultimate conservatism, the CSU had been slipping away from Merkel since at least 2015 in an effort to outdo the far-right Alternative for Germany (AfD). Beyond her speech, Merkel mingled with the more than 2,000 attendees and raised her *Maß* with Lederhosen-wearing Bavarians. She clinked glasses with CSU-head Horst Seehofer as they worked to bury the hatchet over refugee policy and "close the election flank" of the CSU—that is, its increasing right-wing sympathies with ascendant xenophobic populism around the world, in Britain, the United States, and Germany itself.[2] In this

---

[1] Matthew Karnitschnig, 'What Angela Merkel meant at the Munich beer hall', *Politico* May 28, 2017, https://www.politico.eu/article/what-angela-merkel-meant-at-the-munich-beer-hall/.

[2] Daniel Brössler and Robert Roßmann, 'In aller Freundschaft', *Süddeutsche Zeitung* May 29, 2017, https://www.sueddeutsche.de/politik/usa-in-aller-freundschaft-1.3526198.

A Nation Fermented: Beer, Bavaria, and the Making of Modern Germany. Robert Shea Terrell, Oxford University Press.
© Robert Shea Terrell 2024. DOI: 10.1093/oso/9780198881834.003.0009

Munich beer tent, national politics catered to regional peculiarity for the sake of supranational commitments and in light of transnational migrations and a globally ascendant radical right.

Far more than an obscure "Bavarian beer party," the episode captures the ways that Germany constructs and represents itself between provincial cultures, national economies, and international relations. An image from the late–Cold War era is particularly illuminating in this regard, revealing how Bavaria fits in the representations and real trajectories of the German nation. It appeared in July 1987, in *EG-Magazin*, which aimed to keep West Germans up to date with the goings-on of the European Community. In it, two journalists question which image of Germany they want to use that day. Taken clockwise from the top left, they are the German Michael (*Deutscher Michel*), a Prussian imperialist, a modern financier, a Nazi (perhaps Hitler himself), and a beer-wielding Bavarian. The journalistic decision-makers in the image are more ambiguous. If they are Germans, they are apparently not a representative option, and they are not

„Welches Deutschlandbild nehmen wir heute?"   Zeichnung: Peter Leger

Figure 8.1 Peter Leger, "Which image of Germany should we use today?" *EG-Magazin: Politik-Wirtschaft-Kultur* no. 7/8 (July, 1987), p. 7. Reproduced courtesy of the Haus der Geschichte der Bundesrepublik Deutschland.

particularly thrilled about their choices. Portrayed here with uncharacteristic angel wings, the gullible German Michael is perhaps no longer viable in a world that Germany twice plunged into war and catastrophic violence. The other options are more readily legible: the military might of the imperialist, the formalized practices of finance, and the space-claiming salute of the Nazi militarist. The mere presence of the Bavarian among these other characters is initially confusing. For many Germans, Bavaria is the national backwater—"our Texas," as a German once told me. But this Bavarian and his beer embody the ways that provincial capital interests, political economy, and discourses of tradition shaped the multiplicities of the German nation in ways this book has tried to take seriously.

The preceding chapters have revealed some of the ways that Bavaria shaped the German nation, from the ubiquity of lager and the decentralized structure of the beer tax to the national cultural embrace of the *Reinheitsgebot*. In many cases, conflicts between centralization and provincialism dating to German unification smoldered and transformed national structures. Taxation is an especially notable case. The reversal of the 1871 Reserve Rights through federal fiscal policy in the Weimar Republic sparked Bavarian opposition that directly informed the West German legislation that remains in force to this day. In the immediate postwar period, Bavarians who had resented federal centralization in the 1920s invoked the legacies of the Nazi past and the well-being of the German people to advocate for a decentralized beer tax. Meanwhile, in both law and culture, the *Reinheitsgebot* transformed from a relatively unknown Bavarian peculiarity into a popular staple of the nation in the last third of the century. Partially adopted in 1906, it remained a point of contestation into the postwar decades. Market protectionism in the 1960s and 1970s, initially by Bavarians and later by West Germans, elevated the Purity Law in the name of protecting consumers. While few had even heard of the law as late as the 1950s, as recently as 2016 some 85 per cent of Germans held firmly to the ostensibly timeless production standard. Finally, a similar Bavarian influence is manifest in the stereotype of the beer-drinking German. Far from an accident of global history, it was a product of postwar economic and political conditions. The accessibility and apparently irrelevant provincialism of the Bavarian imagery ultimately worked to resuscitate both the Bavarian cradle of National Socialism and the nation more broadly. By 1987, as the image clearly shows, the Bavarian and his beer literally stand beside the Nazi as an alternative image of the nation.

In both discourse and structure, southern producers, regulators, lobbyists, advertisers, and consumer interest groups consistently exerted transformative pressure on the national whole. In southern Germany, particularly Bavaria, capitalists with a provincial face pushed to uphold their traditions and standards. In the early 20th century, such convictions manifested across the nation, particularly as northern brewers critiqued the homogenization of the lager market, but southern brewers were unmatched in their intransigence and in their effect on national processes. This was in large part thanks to a rotating cast of political allies throughout the century. In both the Weimar Republic and the postwar occupation, Bavarian legislators from the Depression-era BVP to the Parliamentary Council and early Bundestag acted in the service of provincial beer and brewing. The relationships between brewers and legislators became most explicit in the 1960s and 1970s when lobbying for economic interests successfully stemmed the tide of European integration, at least temporarily. In that moment, the embrace of the *Reinheitsgebot* as a staple of West German commercial sensibilities showed just how far regional identities and practices inflected national cultural discourses. From the embrace of "beer purity" as a hallmark of German commercial sentiments to the consolidation of an international stereotype of the beer-drinking German, southern brewers and their partners in government and trade transformed the nation.

Provincial Nation

Decades of debate on the importance of Prussia in German history provide an enduring historiographical reminder that Germany is not simply the sum of equal parts. In its repeal of a Prussian-centered history, however, a great deal of historical scholarship has embraced plurality and the plethora of localized German experiences and senses of belonging, at times at the expense of acknowledging the transformative power of particular centers of gravity. Focusing on beer and Bavaria, I have attempted to show how provincialism and its global entanglements transformed the national whole throughout the 20th century. Going one step further, we might fruitfully understand Germany as a *provincial nation*: a place defined by relatively decentralized politics, industry, and culture but where centers of gravity—Bavaria, in the case of beer—shape the nation writ large. The provincial nation is not the same thing as a nation unified by its multiplicity.[3] In the history of beer in Germany, there certainly *is* multiplicity and there *are* many local histories worth telling that can bring texture to specific places and animate questions of place and belonging. For instance, the cultural rivalry between Cologne and Düsseldorf and their respective beers, Kölsch and Altbier, is desperately in need of a finely grained microhistory. But such localized histories would likely not speak to the kinds of national and international transformations that this book has revealed through the focus on Bavaria and Munich. Indeed, in 1998, Thuringians were happy to promote the recent discovery of the 1434 *Statuta thaberna*, a Thuringian code restricting beer to only water, malt, and hops that pre-dated the Bavarian restrictions that became the *Reinheitsgebot*. But the fact of

---

[3] Celia Applegate, *A Nation of Provincials: The German Idea of Heimat* (Berkeley: University of California Press, 1990).

predating does not undo the process by which restrictions on ingredients traveled the nation, and the world, by way of Bavarian interests and advocacy. That story, I have tried to show, depended on a constellation of global and local conditions and opportunities.

Reorienting the geography of Germany in this way has implications for the temporalities of the German nation. A Nation Fermented has built on a sizeable body of scholarship concerned with continuity and rupture. A whole generation of historians has identified some of the many continuities that stretch across political regimes, either in the form of postwar legacies of conflict and genocide, or in terms of long-standing thematic developments (e.g. capitalism, socialism, or political Catholicism) which are bent by the weight of the mid-century.[4] To take one particularly relevant example, Alice Weinreb's study of hunger demonstrated how modern governmentality evolved as ostensibly divergent regimes adopted and deployed markedly similar biopolitical methods of regulating and managing the body. While the present book takes issue with her claim that "the country's identity has…not been shaped by the production or consumption of a specific or charismatic foodstuff," it has taken inspiration from her insistence that historicizing modes of governance—rather than types of states—opens new avenues for thinking holistically about German history.[5] A Nation Fermented reveals how German (and particularly southern German) producers, regulators, advertisers, and consumers of beer proved remarkably malleable and adaptable across, in response to, and often regardless of dramatic and fundamental social and political challenges. But the narrative arc and provincial vantage point of this book hopefully does more than simply provide a regional angle on conventional German history. Looking from the south, this book has not only added to the trajectory of national history, but has also revealed new moments in which the German nation took shape both locally and globally thanks to provincial interests and cultures.

---

[4] For an overview of the analytic challenges and some of the many solutions, see Konrad H. Jarausch and Michael Geyer, Shattered Past: Reconstructing German Histories (Princeton: Princeton University Press, 2003). In terms of the two approaches identified here, see, for example, Robert G. Moeller, War Stories: The Search for a Useable Past in the Federal Republic of Germany (Berkeley: University of California Press, 2001); S. Jonathan Wiesen, West German Industry and the Challenge of the Nazi Past, 1945–1955 (Chapel Hill: University of North Carolina Press, 2001); Elizabeth Heineman, What Difference does a Husband Make: Women and Marital Status in Nazi and Postwar Germany (Berkeley: University of California Press, 2003); Frank Biess, Homecomings: Returning POWs and the Legacies of Defeat in Postwar Germany (Princeton: Princeton University Press, 2006); and Frank Biess and Robert G. Moeller, eds. Histories of the Aftermath: The Legacies of the Second World War in Europe (New York: Berghahn Books, 2010); Wolfgang Abendroth, ed. Faschismus und Kapitalismus: Theorien über die sozialen Ursprünge und die Funktion des Faschismus (Frankfurt a.M.: Europäische Verlagsanstalt, 1967); Catherine Epstein, The Last Revolutionaries: German Communists and Their Century (Cambridge: Harvard University Press, 2003); Wolfram Kaiser, Christian Democracy and the Origins of the European Union (Cambridge: Cambridge University Press, 2007); and James Chappel, Catholic Modern: The Challenge of Totalitarianism and the Remaking of the Church (Cambridge: Harvard University Press, 2018).

[5] Alice Weinreb, Modern Hungers: Food and Power in Twentieth-Century Germany (Oxford: Oxford University Press, 2017), p. 8.

The provincial moments discussed here—including disputes over tax law in 1906, 1919, and 1950, or the market protectionist campaigns of the early 1970s and early 1990s—suggest an unconventional emplotment of German history. The arc of this book and the concept of the provincial nation complicate "linear state-centric periodization," as Shelly Chan wrote in a different context, revealing some of the ways that "the nation is multispatial, polyrhythmic and always incomplete."[6]

There are, potentially, many more iterations of the provincial nation than this book has been able to delineate. A parallel commodity history of coal, for example, would predictably focus on the Rhineland, North Rhine-Westphalia, and, most explicitly, the Ruhr Valley, and it would range from industrialization and heavy labor to foreign occupation, the social question, European integration, and beyond. Coal exists outside these areas, and coal miners or energy consumers do not become Rheinlanders or Duisburgers any more than beer drinkers become Bavarians or Münchner. And yet, the standards of production, the practices of consumption, and the emergence of regulations are nonetheless disproportionately shaped by the respective power centers. While a history of coal might reflect many of the well-known histories of the German nation and German capitalism, one can hope that the regional frame can do more than confirm or question the teleologies of modernization theory.[7] Indeed, one of the points here is that Bavaria—an unassuming and long-agrarian region, the butt of German jokes—has shaped German history and practice in ways obfuscated by conventional histories of the nation. Here, provincial industrial and regulatory interests have shaped the nation both from within (e.g. production standards, tax law, and commercial sentiments) and from without (e.g. limiting international market access and shaping stereotypes).

Well beyond the German case, the present history resonates in many other contexts. In the case of Spain, for example, a number of historians have revealed how flamenco—a form of song and dance often derided for its association with "Gypsies" and the allegedly backward region of Andalusia—came to stand among the icons of the nation. There, as in Germany, a combination of local tradition, cultural promotion, state sponsorship, and international cultural recognition transformed regional practices into national discourses and structures.[8] In histories of wine too, a significant amount of research has emphasized the ways that

---

[6] Shelly Chan, *Diaspora's Homeland: Modern China in the Age of Global Migration* (Durham: Duke University Press, 2018), pp. 194–195.

[7] Celia Applegate, 'A Europe of Regions: Reflections on the Historiography of Sub-National Places in Modern Times', *The American Historical Review* 104, no. 4 (Oct., 1999): pp. 1157–1182.

[8] Yuko Aoyama, 'Artists, Tourists, and the State: Cultural Tourism and the Flamenco Industry in Andalusia, Spain', *International Journal of Urban and Regional Research* 31, no. 1 (Mar. 2009): pp. 80–104; Sandie Holguín, *Flamenco Nation: The Construction of Spanish National Identity* (Madison: University of Wisconsin Press, 2019); and Timothy Dewaal Malefyt, ' "Inside" and "Outside" Spanish Flamenco: Gender Constructions in Andalusian Concepts of Flamenco Tradition', *Anthropological Quarterly* 71, no. 2 (Apr. 1998): pp. 63–73.

questions of scale and place have shaped broader structures and practices. Claims to *terroir* from Hungary to Israel, for example, provide "a cultural narrative that positions a commodity in a regional political economy," politicizing space and laying claim to belonging.[9] But as histories of wine go, the present story perhaps most closely parallels that of France. As Kolleen Guy has shown, capital interests in rural Champagne promoted their regional product as a national good and, in the process, transformed the structures and culture of the French nation.[10] But, more recently, French historians have also pointed out how wine structured senses of place and identity, from the "folklorization" of the vineyard in interwar Burgundy, to the massive shift in the postwar decades away from the mass production and consumption of Algerian wine, to the refined consumption of artisanal appellation wines. These works have collectively demonstrated that cultural discourses, geopolitical transitions, and state promotion played a crucial role in transforming the relationships between particular places, consumer goods, and conceptions of national culture.[11] These cases might also be understood as provincial nations—defined by relatively decentralized politics, industry, and culture, but nonetheless featuring centers of gravity that shape national politics and culture even, and perhaps especially, in the context of 20th century globalization and connectivity.

In each of those cases, similar entanglements, rooted in specific regions and cities, embedded in states and nations, exert cultural, economic, and regulatory influence on national and global processes, imaginaries, and power differentials. As we saw in Chapter 7, the discourses and structures developed in previous decades remained as the boom of the miracle years went bust, as the ECJ repealed the *Reinheitsgebot*, and as the two Germanys reunified. There is "no transhistorical concept of the German nation," and change is slow, overlapping, and piecemeal.[12] Even within Bavaria the residues of this history remain as the faces of Bavaria and the nation have changed. Perhaps no single politician is more representative of this transformation than Edmund Stoiber, who was Bavarian Prime Minister from 1993 to 2007 and is often credited with catapulting it into being one of the wealthiest states in Germany, a center of high tech, media, engineering, and finance. This is the new Bavaria, leading German capitalism in new

[9] Daniel Monterescu, 'Border Wines: Terroir across Contested Territory', *Gastronomica: The Journal of Critical Food Studies* 17, no. 4 (2017): pp. 127–140, here p. 128.

[10] Kolleen M. Guy, *When Champagne became French: Wine and the Making of a National Identity* (Baltimore: The Johns Hopkins University Press, 2003), pp. 5–7.

[11] Gilles Laferté, 'The Folklorization of French Farming: Marketing Luxury Wine in the Interwar Years', *French Historical Studies* 34, no. 4 (2011): pp. 679–712; Joseph Bohling, *The Sober Revolution: Appellation Wine and the Transformation of France* (Ithaca: Cornell University Press, 2018); Owen White, *Blood of the Colony: Wine and the Rise and Fall of French Algeria* (Cambridge: Harvard University Press, 2021).

[12] Helmut Walser Smith, *Germany: A Nation in its Time: Before, During, and After Nationalism, 1500–2000* (London and New York: W.W. Norton, 2020), p. xi.

directions. After traveling through South America and Japan, Stoiber returned home to note that "Bavaria can be proud of its good reputation in the world. I was occasionally confronted with the cliché that Bavaria might just be equated with roast pork, beer, and Lederhosen. But that is now increasingly taking a backseat. More and more, Bavaria is becoming known as a high-tech center."[13] But a year and a half later, as Stoiber addressed Bavarian brewers, he reversed these sentiments, noting that "economic success is only part of what distinguishes Bavaria." The other part is cultural. Indeed, he assured them that "beer as a Bavarian national drink (*Nationalgetränk*) is indispensable. And our beer is not only a national drink; it has long since become, so to say, an international drink, and one with an unmistakable primordial Bavarian (*urbayerischem*) character!"[14] The speeches testify to both the residues of the preceding history and the reconfiguration of the provincial nation in a global integration moment. As much as Germany will continue to transform at the nexus of shifting local and global conditions, Merkel's presence at the "Bavarian beer party" and Stoiber's balance of tradition, collective culture, and thriving industry reveal the ongoing resonance of the Germany that Bavaria made.

---

[13] Jan. 9, 1998, speech by Dr Edmund Stoiber, Archiv für Christlich-Soziale Politik (henceforth ACSP) PS I Stoiber RS 1998: 0109.

[14] Sept. 14, 2000, speech by Dr Edmund Stoiber, ACSP PS I Stoiber RS 2000: 0914.

Bibliography

Archives

Akten der Reichskanzlei, Weimarer Republik (online)
Archiv der sozialen Demokratie der Friedrich-Ebert-Stiftung-Bonn
Archiv für Christlich-Soziale Politik (ACSP)
Bayerisches Hauptstaatsarchiv (BayHStA)
Bayerisches Wirtschaftsarchiv (BWA)
Bundesarchiv Berlin-Lichterfelde (BAB)
Bundesarchiv Koblenz (BAK)
Gesellschaft für Konsum Forschung, Nürnberg (GfK)
Historical Archives of the European Union (HAEU)
Institut für Zeitgeschichte-Munich (IfZ)
National Archives and Records Administration in College Park, MD (NARA)
New York Public Library (NYPL)
Staatsarchiv München (StAM)
University of Wisconsin Digital Collections

Cited Periodicals and Trade Journals

Abendzeitung (Munich)
Auf der Wacht
Bayerischer Staatsanzeiger
Bayerische Bier-Illustrierte
Berliner Tageblatt
Bier und Wir
Chicago Tribune
Daily Express
Daily News
Der Angriff
Der Bayerische Bierbrauer
Der Brauer und Mälzer
Der Courier (Regina)
Der Fortschritt (Düsseldorf)
Der klein- und mittelbrauer
Der Kurier (Berlin)
Der Spiegel
Der Spiegel—Online
Deutsche Brauwirtschaft
Deutsche medizinischen Wochenschrift
Deutsches Reichsgesetzblatt
Die Brauwelt

Die junge Gefolgschaft. Monatsschrift der fränkischen Hitlerjugend
Die Welt (Hamburg)
Die Zeit
Edmonton Nachrichten
EG-Magazin
Frankenpost
Frankfurter Allgemeine
Gastwirt und Hotelier (Munich)
General Anzeiger
Geschäftsbericht (Bayerischer Brauerbund e.V.)
Geschäftsbericht (Löwenbräu A.G.)
Le CHR—Organe officiel de la Confédération Nationale des Unions Professionnelles des Cafetiers, Hôteliers et Restaurateurs de Belgique
Le Courrier d'Afrique (Leopoldville)
Madame
Mitteilung der Wirtschaftsgruppe Brauerei und Mälzerei
Mitteilung des Bayer. Brauerbund
Münchner Merkur
Nachrichten für die Hausfrau
Neue Ruhr-Zeitung
Neues Deutschland
Politico
Simplicissimus
Sonntagsblatt Staats-Zeitung und Herold
Soziale Praxis. Zentralblatt für Sozialpolitik und Wohlfahrtspflege
Süddeutsche Zeitung
Tätigkeitsbericht (Bayerischer Brauerbund e.V.)
Tätigkeitsbericht (Der Deutsche Brauerbund e.V.)
The Evening Standard
The New York Times
The New York Times International Edition
The Sun
The Times (London)
The Wall Street Journal
The Washington Post
Torontoer Zeitung
Wir und Bier

Selected Published Primary Materials

Bayersichen Statistischen Landesamt. *Statistisches Jahrbuch für Bayern, 1947*. Munich: Carl Gerber, 1948.

Biersteuergesetz in der Fassung vom 14. März 1952 mit Durchführungsbestimmungen zum Biersteuergesetz (BierStDB) in der Fassung vom 14. März 1952. Nuremberg: Brauwelt Verlag Hans Carl, 1952.

Boberach, Heinz, ed. *Meldungen aus dem Reich: Die geheimen Lageberichte des Sicherheitsdienstes der SS, 1938–1945*, vol. 1. Herrsching: Pawlak Verlag, 1984.

Borkenhagen, Erich. *100 Jahre Deutscher Brauer-Bund e.V., 1871–1971: Zur Geschichte des Bieres im 19. und 20. Jahrhundert.* Berlin: Westkreuz-Druckerei, 1971.

Busemann, Melchior. *Der Deutsche Brauer-Bund 1871–1921.* Berlin: G. Asher, 1921.

Deutscher Brauer-Bund e.V. *12. Statistischer Bericht des Deutschen Brauer-Bundes e.V.* Bonn-Bad Godesberg: Leopold, 1975.

Deutscher Brauer-Bund e.V. *13. statistischer Bericht: 1977.* Bonn: Deutscher Brauer-Bund, 1977.

Deutscher Bra uer-Bund e.V. *500 Jahre Reinheitsgebot—Das Buch zum Jubiläum.* Frankfurt: Deutscher Fachverlag GmbH, 2016.

Deutscher Brauerbund e.V. *Das Bier: vom Halm bis zum Glase.* Duisberg: Carl Lange Verlag, 1953.

Deutscher Brauerbund, e.V. *Schlußwort zum Deutschen Brauertag 1934. Von. Dr Ernst Röhm, Stellvertr. Führer des deutschen Braugewerbes.* Berlin: Buchdruckerei Gebrüder Unger, 1934.

Deutscher Brauerbund e.V. *Vom Trank der alten Germanen.* Duisberg: Carl Lange Verlag, 1953.

Die Tagebücher von Joseph Goebbels. Edited by Elke Fröhlich. Teil 2, Diktate 1941–1945, Band 2, Oktober–Dezember 1941. Munich: K.G. Saur, 2001.

Editors of Time-Life Books. *1965 Official Guide: New York World's Fair, all new for 1965.* New York: Time Inc., 1965.

Elster, Alexander. *Das Konto des Alkohols in der deutschen Volkswirtschaft.* Berlin: Neuland Verlag, 1935.

Feldkamp, Michael F. and Inez Müller, eds. *Der Parlamentarische Rat, 1948–1949: Akten und Protokolle.* Vol. 12 Ausschuß für Finanzfragen. Munich: Harald Boldt Verlag, 1999.

Feuerstein, Gerhart. *Rauschgiftbekämpfung—ein wichtiges Interessengebiet der Gemeindeverwaltung.* Berlin: Auf der Wacht Verlag, 1936.

Gaeßner, Heinz. *Bier und bierartige Getränke im germanischen Kulturkreis.* Berlin: Gesellschaft für die Geschichte und Bibliographie des Brauwesens e.V., Institut für Gärungsgewerbe, 1941.

Goebel, Ferdinand. *30 Experimente zur Alkohol- und Tabakfrage.* Berlin-Dahlem: Reichsgesundheitsverlag, 1940.

Goebel, Ferdinand. *Schulungsheft der Reichsbahn-Zentralstelle gegen den Alkoholmißbrauch.* Berlin-Dahlem: Reichsgesundheitsverlag, 1940.

Gräße, J. G. T. *Bierstudien: Ernst und Scherz. Geschichte des Bieres und seiner Verbreitung über den Erdball. Bierstatistik. Bieraberglauben. Bierfeste. Bierorden. Bierspiele. Bierlieder aller Zeiten und Völker. Biersprichwörter. Brauergeheimmnisse.* Dresden: R. v. Zahn Verlag, 1872.

Hitler, Adolf. *Die Reden Hitlers am Parteitag der Freiheit 1935.* Munich: Zentralverlag der NSDAP, 1935.

Hollmann, Michael, ed. *Der Parlamentarische Rat, 1948–1949: Akten und Protokolle.* Vol. 7 Entwürfe zum Grundgesetz. Boppard am Rhein: Harald Boldt Verlag, 1995.

Kaetzel, Gertrud. *Volksgift und Frauenpflichten: Schulungshefte der NS-Frauenschaft.* Leipzig: G. Fischer, 1935.

Krummel, Regina P. 'Stop off in Germany for a Beer.' *The English Journal* 65, no. 5 (May 1976), p. 51.

Lammert, Norbert. 'Von der besonderen Qualität deutscher Braukunst.' In *500 Jahre Reinheitsgebot—Das Buch zum Jubiläum,* release of Der Deutscher Brauer-Bund e.V., 10–12. Frankfurt: Deutscher Fachverlag GmbH, 2016.

Liebig, Justus. *Organic Chemistry in its Applications to Agriculture and Physiology*. Translated by Lyon Playfair. London: Taylor and Walton, 1840.

Michel, Carl. *Geschichte des Bieres von der ältesten Zeit bis zum Jahre 1900*. Augsburg: Verlagsbuchhandlung von Gebrüder Reichel, 1901.

Noelle, Elisabeth and Erich Peter Neumann, eds. *Jahrbuch der öffentlichen Meinung, 1947–1955*. Allensbach am Bodensee: Verlag für Demoskopie, 1956.

Noelle, Elisabeth, and Erich Peter Neumann, eds. *Jahrbuch der öffentlichen Meinung, 1965–1967*. Allensbach am Bodensee: Verlag für Demoskopie, 1967.

Noelle, Elisabeth, and Erich Peter Neumann, eds. *Jahrbuch der öffentlichen Meinung, 1968–1973*. Allensbach am Bodensee: Verlag für Demoskopie, 1974.

Paulsen, Uwe, and Franz Meyer. *7. Statistischer Bericht des Deutschen Brauer-Bundes e.V.* Bad Godesberg: Deutscher Brauer-Bund e.V., 1966.

Pritzl, Heinz. 'Die absatzwirtschaftliche Bedeutung der Verpackung für Bier.' PhD diss., Hochschule für Wirtschafts- und Sozialwissenschaften Nürnberg, 1956.

Propaganda Amt der Deutschen Arbeitsfront u. Hauptamt für Volksgesundheit der NSDAP. *Tatsachen zur Alkoholfrage. Wissenschaftlich-praktische Unterlagen Schulungs- und Vortragsmaterial*. Berlin-Dahlem: Reichsgesundheitsverlag, 1940.

Rätsch, Erich. *Gefährliche Freiheit? Der Rausch als Regulierendes Prinzip*. Berlin: Kurt Elsner Verlag, 1934.

Reichsamt des Innern. *Verzeichnis der im Deutschen Reiche bestehenden Vereine gewerblicher Unternehmer zur Wahrung ihrer wirtschaftlichen Interessen*. Berlin: Ernst Siedfried Mittler u. Sohn, 1903.

Schlögl, Alois. *Bayerische Agrargeschichte: die Entwicklung der Land- und Forstwirtschaft seit Beginn des 19. Jahrhunderts*. Munich: Bayerischer Landwirtschaftsverlag, 1954.

Schlögl, Alois. 'Bayerns Landwirtschaft im Aufbau.' In *Bayern: Wirtschaft in Wort und Bild*, edited by Josef Oesterle, 9–16. München: Graphische Betriebe GmbH, 1954.

Schmucker, Gottlieb. *Die wirtschaftliche Bedeutung des deutschen Braugewerbes*. Nuremberg: Verlag Hans Carl, 1951.

Schranka, Eduard Maria. *Ein Buch vom Bier. Cerevisiologische Studien und Skizzen* 2 volumes. Frankfurt a.O.: B. Waldmann Verlag, 1886.

Simon, Theobald. *Die Werbung der Brauereien*. Nuremberg: Verlag F. Carl, 1931.

Simon, Theobald. *Werbung für Bier*. Nuremberg: Verlag Hans Carl, 1960.

Smith, Jean Edward, ed. *The Papers of General Lucius D. Clay: Germany, 1945–1949* Vol. 1. Bloomington: Indiana University Press, 1974.

Stepp, Wilhelm. *Bier, wie es der Arzt sieht. Altes und Neues vom Bier*. München: Verlag Carl Gerber, 1954.

Stresemann, Gustav. 'Die Entwicklung des Berliner Flaschenbiergeschäfts.' PhD diss. University of Leipzig, 1901.

United States Department of State. *Germany 1947–1949: The Story in Documents*. Washington DC: U.S. Government Printing Office, 1950.

von Krafft-Ebing, Richard. *Psychopathia Sexualis: The Classic Study of Deviant Sex*. Translated by Franklin S. Klaf. New York: Arcade Publishing, 2011.

von Pistorius, Theodor. 'Die Entwicklung der Reichsfinanzen und das deutsche Wirtschafts- und Finanzelend.' *FinanzArchiv/Public Finance Analysis* 48, no. 1 (1931): pp. 1–99.

von Viebahn, Georg Wilhelm. *Statistik des zollvereinten und nördlichen Deutschlands* Vol. 3. Berlin: Verlag Georg Reimer, 1868.

Wirtschaftliche Abteilung der Versuchs- und Lehranstalt für Brauerei in Berlin. *Das Bier in Zahlen*. Berlin: Institut für Gärungsgewerbe, 1937.

Selected Secondary Sources

Abelshauser, Werner. *Deutsche Wirtschaftsgeschichte seit 1945*. Munich: C.H. Beck Verlag, 2004.

Abendroth, Wolfgang, ed. *Faschismus und Kapitalismus: Theorien über die sozialen Ursprünge und die Funktion des Faschismus*. Frankfurt a.M.: Europäische Verlagsanstalt, 1967.

Alexander, Jeffrey. *Brewed in Japan: The Evolution of the Japanese Brewing Industry*. Vancouver: University of British Columbia Press, 2013.

Alff, Kristen. 'Levantine Joint-Stock Companies, Trans-Mediterranean Partnerships and Nineteenth-Century Capitalist Development.' *Comparative Studies in Society and History* 60 no. 1 (Jan. 2018): pp. 150–77.

Allen, Fal. *Gose: Brewing a Classic German Beer for the Modern Era*. Boulder, CO: Brewers Publications, 2018.

Andersen, Arne. 'Mentalitätenwechsel und ökologische Konsequenzen des Konsumismus: Die Durchsetzung der Konsumgesellschaft in den fünfziger Jahren.' In *Europäische Konsumgeschichte: Zur Gesellschafts- und Kulturgeschichte des Konsums (18. bis 20. Jahrhundert)*, edited by Hannes Siegrist, Hartmut Kaelble, and Jürgen Kocka, 763–92. Frankfurt a.M.: Campus Verlag, 1997.

Andersen, Knud, Ursula Bitzegeio, and Jürgen Mittag, eds. *'Nach dem Structurbruch?' Kontinuität und Wandel von Arbeitbeziehungen und Arbeitswelt(en) sein den 1970er-Jahre*. Bonn: Dietz Verlag, 2011.

Aoyama, Yuko. 'Artists, Tourists, and the State: Cultural Tourism and the Flamenco Industry in Andalusia, Spain.' *International Journal of Urban and Regional Research* 31 no. 1 (Mar. 2009): pp. 80–104.

Appadurai, Arjun, ed. *The Social Life of Things: Commodities in Cultural Perspective*. Cambridge: Cambridge University Press, 1986.

Applegate, Celia. 'A Europe of Regions: Reflections on the Historiography of Sub-National Places in Modern Times.' *The American Historical Review* 104 no. 4 (Oct., 1999): pp. 1157–82.

Applegate, Celia. *A Nation of Provincials: The German Idea of Heimat*. Berkeley: University of California Press, 1990.

Badenoch, Alexander. 'Time Consuming: Women's Radio and the Reconstruction of National Narratives in Western Germany, 1945—1948.' *German History* 25 no. 1 (Jan. 2007), pp. 46–71.

Barthes, Roland. *Mythologies* Revised Edition. London: Vintage Books, 2009.

Batchelor, Robert. 'On the Movement of Porcelains: Rethinking the Birth of Consumer Society as Interactions of Exchange Networks, 1600-1750.' In *Consuming Cultures, Global Perspectives: Historical Trajectories, Transnational Exchanges*, edited by John Brewer and Frant Trentmann, 95–122. Oxford and New York: Berg, 2006.

Bauer, Franz. 'Aufnahme und Eingliederung der Flüchtlinge und Vertriebenen: Das Beispiel Bayern, 1945-1950.' In *Die Vertreibung der Deutschen aus dem Osten*, edited by Wolfgang Benz, 158–72. Frankfurt am Main: Fischer Verlag, 1995.

Beckert, Sven. *Empire of Cotton: A Global History*. New York: Vintage Books, 2014.

Behringer, Wolfgang. *Die Spaten-Brauerei, 1397-1997: Die Geschichte eines Münchner Unternehmens vom Mittelalter bis zur Gegenwart*. Munich and Zurich: Piper Verlag GmbH, 1997.

Behringer, Wolfgang. *Löwenbräu: Von den Anfängen des Münchner Brauwesens bis zur Gegenwart*. Munich: Süddeutscher Verlag, 1991.

Bennett, Judith M. *Ale, Beer, and Brewsters in England: Women's Work in a Changing World, 1300-1600*. Oxford: Oxford University Press, 1996.

Bera, Matt. *Lobbying Hitler: Industrial Associations between Democracy and Dictatorship*. New York: Berghahn Books, 2016.

Berghahn, Volker R. 'Recasting Bourgeois Germany.' In *The Miracle Years: A Cultural History of West Germany, 1949-1968*, edited by Hanna Schissler, 326-40. Princeton: Princeton University Press, 2002.

Berghahn, Volker R., and Sigurt Vitols, eds. *Gibt es einen deutschen Kapitalismus? Tradition und globale Perpektiven der sozialen Marktwirtschaft*. Frankfurt: Campus Verlag, 2006.

Berghoff, Hartmut, Jan Logemann, and Felix Römer, eds. *The Consumer on the Home Front: Second World War Civilian Consumption in Comparative Perspective*. Oxford: Oxford University Press, 2017.

Berghoff, Hartmut, Philip Scranton, and Uwe Spiekermann, eds. *The Rise of Marketing and Market Research*. New York: Palgrave Macmillan, 2012.

Biess, Frank. *Homecomings: Returning POWs and the Legacies of Defeat in Postwar Germany*. Princeton: Princeton University Press, 2006.

Biess, Frank. 'Men of Reconstruction – The Reconstruction of Men: Returning POWS in East and West Germany, 1945-1955.' In *Home/Front: The Military, War and Gender in Twentieth Century Germany*, edited by Karen Hagemann and Stefanie Schüler-Springorum, 335–58. Oxford and New York: Berg Publishers, 2002.

Biess, Frank. *Republik der Angst: eine andere Geschichte der Bundesrepublik*. Reinbek bei Hamburg: Rowohlt Verlag, 2019.

Biess, Frank and Robert G. Moeller, eds. *Histories of the Aftermath: The Legacies of the Second World War in Europe*. New York and Oxford: Berghahn Books, 2010.

Black, Monica. *A Demon-Haunted Land: Witches, Wonder Doctors, and the Ghosts of the Past in Post-WWII Germany*. New York: Metropolitan Books, 2020.

Blommaert, Jan and Piia Varis. 'Enough is Enough: The Heuristics of Authenticity in Superdiversity.' *Tilburg Papers in Culture Studies* 2 (2011).

Bodden, Nancy. *Business as Usual? Die Dortmunder Brauindustrie, der Flaschenbierboom und die Nachfragemacht des Handels 1950 bis 1980*. Dortmund and Münster: Gesellschaft für Westfälische Wirtschaftsgeschichte e.V., 2019.

Bodden, Nancy. 'Kraftwagen und Flaschenbier—Neue Herausforderungen für die Dortmunder Brauwirtschaft.' In *Die 1920er Jahre. Dortmund zwischen Moderne und Krise*, edited by Karl-Peter and Günther Högl. Dortmund: Historischen Verein für Dortmund und die Grafschaft Mark, 2012.

Bohling, Joseph. *The Sober Revolution: Appellation Wine and the Transformation of France*. Ithaca: Cornell University Press, 2018.

Bönker, Dirk. *Militarism in a Global Age: Naval Ambitions in Germany and the United States before World War I*. Ithaca: Cornell University Press, 2012.

Bösch, Frank. *Zeitwende 1979: Als die Welt von heute began*. Munich: C.H. Beck, 2019.

Brewer, John, and Roy Porter, eds. *Consumption and the World of Goods*. London: Routledge, 1993.

Brewer, John, and Frank Trentmann, eds. *Consuming Cultures, Global Perspectives: Historical Trajectories, Transnational Exchanges*. Oxford and New York: Berg, 2006.

Brückweh Kerstin, ed. *The Voice of the Citizen Consumer: A History of Market Research, Consumer Movements, and the Political Public Sphere*. Oxford: Oxford University Press, 2011.

Bulmer, Simon. *The Domestic Structure of European Community Policy-Making in West Germany*. London: Routledge Revivals, 2016, orig. 1986.

Carter, Erica. *How German is She? Postwar West German Reconstruction and the Consuming Woman.* Ann Arbor: University of Michigan Press, 1998.

Castillo, Greg. 'Making a Spectacle of Restraint: The Deutschland Pavilion at the 1958 Brussels Exposition.' *Journal of Contemporary History* 47, no. 1 (January 2012): 97–119.

Chan, Shelly. *Diaspora's Homeland: Modern China in the Age of Global Migration.* Durham and London: Duke University Press, 2018.

Chappel, James. *Catholic Modern: The Challenge of Totalitarianism and the Remaking of the Church.* Cambridge: Harvard University Press, 2018.

Cheta, Omar Youssef. 'The Economy by Other Means: The Historiography of Capitalism in the Modern Middle East.' *History Compass* 16 no. 4 (2018): e12444.

Cohen, Benjamin R. *Pure Adulteration: Cheating on Nature in the Age of Manufactured Food.* Chicago and London: Chicago University Press, 2019.

Confino, Alon. *The Nation as a Local Metaphor: Württemberg, Imperial Germany, and National Memory, 1871–1918.* Chapel Hill: University of North Carolina Press, 1997.

Conrad, Sebastian. *Globalisation and the Nation in Imperial Germany.* Translated by Sorcha O'Hagan. Cambridge: Cambridge University Press, 2010.

Conrad, Sebastian. *What is Global History?* Princeton: Princeton University Press, 2016.

Crawford, Robert. '"Drink Beer Regularly–It's Good for You [and Us]": Selling Tooth's Beer in a Depressed Market.' *Social History of Alcohol & Drugs* 21 no. 2 (Mar. 2007): 160–82.

Cullather, Nick. 'The Foreign Policy of the Calorie.' *The American Historical Review* 112 no. 2 (Apr., 2007): 337–64.

De Grazia, Victoria, and Ellen Furlough, eds. *The Sex of Things: Gender and Consumption in Historical Perspective.* Berkeley and Los Angeles: University of California Press, 1996.

DeWaal, Jeremy. 'The Reinvention of Tradition: Form, Meaning, and Local Identity in Modern Cologne Carnival', *Central European History* 46 no. 3 (Sept. 2013): 495–532.

Dering, Florian, and Ursula Eymold. *Das Oktoberfest, 1810–2010.* Munich: Süddeutsche Zeitung Edition Verlag, 2010.

Deselnicu, Oana C., Marco Costanigro, Diogo M. Souza-Montiero, and Dawn Thilmany McFadden. 'A Meta-Analysis of Geographical Indication Food Valuation Studies: What Drives the Premium for Origin-Based Labels?' *Journal of Agricultural and Resource Economics* 38, no. 2 (August 2013): 204–19.

DeSoucey, Michaela. 'Gastronationalism: Food Traditions and Authenticity Politics in the European Union.' *American Sociological Review* 75, no. 3 (June 2010): 432–55.

DeWaal, Jeremy. 'Redemptive Geographies: The Turn to Local Heimat in West Germany, 1945–1965.' PhD diss., Vanderbilt University, 2014.

Dietrich, Richard. 'Foederalismus, Unitarismus oder Hegemonialstaat?' In *Zur Problematik 'Preussen und das Reich'*, edited by Oswald Hauser, 49–81. Cologne: Böhlau, 1984.

Długoborski, Wacław. *Zweiter Weltkrieg und sozialer Wandel: Achsenmächte und besetzte Länder.* Göttingen: Vandenhoeck & Ruprecht, 1981.

Doering-Manteuffel, Anselm, and Lutz Raphael. *Nach dem Boom: Perspektiven auf die Zeitgeschichte seit 1970* 3rd Edition. Göttingen: Vandenhoeck & Ruprecht GmbH, 2012.

Doering-Manteuffel, Anselm, Lutz Raphael, and Thomas Schlemmer, eds. *Vorgeschichte der Gegenwart: Dimensionen des Strukturbruchs nach dem Boom.* Göttingen: Vandenhoeck & Ruprecht GmbH, 2016.

Dornbusch, Horst. *Prost! The Story of German Beer.* Boulder: Brewers Publications, 1997.

Dornbusch, Horst, and Karl-Ullrich Heyse. 'Reinheitsgebot.' In *The Oxford Companion to Beer.* Edited by Garrett Oliver, 692–3. Oxford: Oxford University Press, 2012.

Eckert, Astrid M. *West Germany and the Iron Curtain: Environment, Economy, and Culture in the Borderlands.* Oxford: Oxford University Press, 2021.

Eley, Geoff, ed. *The 'Goldhagen Effect': History, Memory, Nazism—Facing the German Past.* Ann Arbor: University of Michigan Press, 2000.

Eley, Geoff. 'Historicizing the Global, Politicizing Capital: Giving the Present a Name.' *History Workshop Journal* 63, no. 1 (Spring 2007): 154–88.

Ellerbrock, Karl-Peter, ed. *Zur Geschichte der westfälischen Brauwirtschaft im 19. und 20. Jahrhundert.* Dortmund: Gesellschaft für Westfälische Wirtschaftsgeschichte e.V., 2012.

Epstein, Catherine. *The Last Revolutionaries: German Communists and Their Century.* Cambridge: Harvard University Press, 2003.

Erdmann, Manfred. *Die vefassungspolitische Funktion der Wirtschaftsverbände in Deutschland, 1815–1871.* Berlin: Duncker & Humblot, 1968.

Erker, Paul. *Ernährungskrise und Nachkriegsgesellschaft: Bauern und Arbeiterschaft in Bayern, 1943–1953.* Stuttgart: Klett-Cotta Verlag, 1990.

Ernst, Waltraud, ed. *Alcohol Flows Across Cultures: Drinking in Transnational and Comparative Perspective.* New York: Routledge, 2020.

Fabian, Sina. 'Between Criticism and Innovation: Beer and Public Relations in the Weimar Republic.' In *Reshaping Capitalism in Weimar and Nazi Germany*, edited by Moritz Föllmer and Pamela Swett, 183–207. Cambridge: Cambridge University Press, 2022.

Fahrenkrug, Hermann. 'Alcohol and the State in Nazi Germany, 1933–1945.' In *Drinking: Behavior and Belief in Modern History*, edited by Susanna Barrows and Robin Room, 315–34. Berkeley: University of California Press, 1991.

Ferguson, Niall, Charles S. Maier, Erez Manela, and Daniel J. Sargent, eds. *The Shock of the Global: The 1970s in Perspective.* Cambridge: Harvard University Press, 2010.

Foda, Omar D. *Egypt's Beer: Stella, Identity, and the Modern State.* Austin: University of Texas Press, 2019.

Föllmer, Moritz, and Pamela E. Swett, eds. *Reshaping Capitalism in Weimar and Nazi Germany.* Cambridge: Cambridge University Press, 2022.

Ford, Graham. 'Constructing a Regional Identity: The Christian Social Union and Bavaria's Common Heritage, 1949–1962.' *Contemporary European History* 16, no. 3 (August 2007): 277–97.

Fritzsche, Peter. *Germans into Nazis.* Cambridge, MA: Harvard University Press, 1998.

Fritzsche, Peter. *Life and Death in the Third Reich.* Cambridge, MA: Harvard University Press, 2008.

Fuchs, Walter Peter. 'Bundesstaaten und Reich: Der Bundesrat.' In *Zur Problematik 'Preussen und das Reich'*, edited by Oswald Hauser. Cologne: Böhlau, 1984.

Gattinger, Karl. *Bier und Landesherrschaft: Das Weißbiermonopol der Wittelsbacher unter Maximillian I. von Bayern.* Munich: Karl M. Lipp Verlag, 2007.

Gerhard, Gesine. 'Food and Genocide: Nazi Agrarian Politics in the Occupied Territories of the Soviet Union.' *Contemporary European History* 18 no. 1 (Feb., 2009): 45–65.

Gerhard, Gesine. *Nazi Hunger Politics: A History of Food in the Third Reich.* London: Rowman & Littlefield, 2015.

Gerhardt, Raphael. *Agrarmodernisierung und europäische Integration: das bayerische Landwirtschaftsministerium als politischer Akteur, 1945–1975.* Munich: Verlag C.H. Beck, 2019.

Giles, Geoffrey. 'Student Drinking in the Third Reich: Academic Tradition and the Nazi Revolution.' In *Drinking: Behavior and Belief in Modern History*, edited by Susanna Barrows and Robin Room, 132–43. Berkeley: University of California Press, 1991.

Gillespie, John. 'The People's Drink: The Politics of Beer in East Germany (1945–1971).' MA thesis, Middle Tennessee State University, 2017.

Göbel, Eva. *Bayern in der modernen Konsumgesellschaft: Regionalisierung der Konsumkultur im 20. Jahrhundert.* Berlin: Weißensee Verlag, 2005.

Gockerell, Nina. *Das Bayerbild in der literarischen und 'wissenschaftlichen' Wertung durch fünf Jahrhunderte: Volkskundliche Überlegungen über die Konstanten und Varianten des Auto- und Heterostereotyps eines deutschen Stammes.* Munich: Kommissionsbuchhandlung R. Wölfle, 1974.

Götschmann, Dirk. *Wirtschaftsgeschichte Bayerns. 19. und 20. Jahrhundert.* Regensburg: Verlag Friedrich Pustet, 2010.

Green, Abigail. 'The Federal Alternative? A New History of Modern German History.' *The Historical Journal* 46 no. 1 (Mar., 2003): 187–202.

Gries, Rainer. 'Cultures of Products and Political Cultures: Looking for Transfer Performances.' In *The Voice of the Citizen Consumer: A History of Market Research, Consumer Movements, and the Political Public Sphere,* edited by Kerstin Brückweh, 243–72. Oxford: Oxford University Press, 2011.

Gries, Rainer. *Die Rationen-Gesellschaft: Versorgungskampf und Vergleichsmentalität: Leipzig, München und Köln nach dem Kriege.* Münster: Westfälisches Dampfboot, 1991.

Gries, Rainer. *Produktkommunikation: Geschichte und Theorie.* Vienna: UTB Verlag, 2008.

Gries, Rainer. *Produkte als Medien: Kulturgeschichte der Produktkommuniktion in der Bundesrepublik und der DDR.* Leipzig: Leipziger Universitätsverlag, 2003.

Grimm, Dieter. 'Was the German Empire a Sovereign State?' In *Imperial Germany Revisited: Continuing Debates and New Perspectives,* edited by Sven Oliver Müller and Cornelius Torp. New York: Berghahn Books, 2011.

Groeneveld, Sabina. 'Far away at home in Qingdao, 1897–1914.' *German Studies Review* 39, no. 1 (2016): 65–80.

Gütermann, Eugen. 'Die Karlsruher Brauindustrie.' PhD diss. Ruprecht-Karls-Universität zu Heidelberg, 1908.

Guy, Kolleen M. *When Champagne became French: Wine and the Making of a National Identity.* Baltimore: The Johns Hopkins University Press, 2003.

Hackel-Stehr, Karin. 'Das Brauwesen in Bayern vom 14. bis 16. Jahrhundert, insbesondere die Entstehung und Entwicklung des Reinheitsgebotes (1516).' PhD diss., Technische Universität Berlin, 1988.

Hall, Peter A., and David Soskice, eds. *Varieties of Capitalism: The Institutional Foundations of Comparative Advantage.* Oxford: Oxford University Press, 2001.

Hall, Stuart, ed. *Culture, Media, Language: Working Papers in Cultural Studies, 1971–1979.* London: Routledge, 1980.

Hau, Michael. 'The Dialectic of Medical Enlightenment: War, Alcohol Consumption and Public Hygiene in Germany, 1910–1925.' *History: The Journal of the Historical Association* 104 no. 359 (Jan. 2019): 149–68.

Haupt, Heinz-Gerhard, Michael G. Mulle, and Stuart Woolf, eds. *Regional and National Identities in Europe in the XIXth and XXth Centuries.* The Hague: Kluwer Law International, 1998.

Hayes, Peter. 'Corporate Freedom of Action in Nazi Germany.' *Bulletin of the German Historical Institute* 45 (Fall 2009): 29–42.

Heindl, Wolfgang. *Die Haushalte von Reich, Ländern und Gemeinden in Deutschland von 1925 bis 1933.* Frankfurt a.M.: Peter Lang, 1984.

Heineman, Elizabeth. 'The Hour of the Woman: Memories of Germany's 'Crisis Years' and West German National Identity.' *The American Historical Review* 101, no. 2 (Apr. 1996): 354–96.

Heineman, Elizabeth. *What Difference does a Husband Make: Women and Marital Status in Nazi and Postwar Germany.* Berkeley: University of California Press, 2003.

Hermann, Christoph. 'Neoliberalism in the European Union.' *Studies in Political Economy* 79, no. 1 (2007): 61–90.

Hilton, Matthew. 'Consumers and the State since the Second World War.' *Annals of the American Academy of Political and Social Science* 611, no. 1 (May 2007): 66–81.

Hobsbawm, Eric, and Terence Ranger, eds. *The Invention of Tradition.* Cambridge: Cambridge University Press, 1983.

Hockerts, Hans Günter, and Günther Schulz, eds. *Der Rheinische Kapitalismus in der Ära Adenauer.* Paderborn: Schöningh, 2016.

Holguín, Sandie. *Flamenco Nation: The Construction of Spanish National Identity.* Madison: University of Wisconsin Press, 2019.

Hughes, Michael L. *Shouldering the Burdens of Defeat: West Germany and the Reconstruction of Social Justice.* Chapel Hill: University of North Carolina Press, 1999.

Huntemann, Hans. 'Bierproduktion und Bierverbrauch in Deutschland vom 15. bis zum Beginn des 19. Jahrhunderts.' PhD diss., University of Göttingen, 1970.

Ilbery, Brian, and Moya Kneafsey. 'Registering Regional Specialty Food and Drink Products in the United Kingdom: The Case of PDOs and PGIs.' *Area* 32, no. 3 (Sept. 2000): 317–25.

Jacobson, Lisa. 'Beer goes to War: The Politics of Beer Promotion and Production in the Second World War.' *Food, Culture & Society* 12, no. 3 (2009): 275–312.

James, Madeline. 'Domesticating the German East: Nazi Propaganda and Women's Roles in the "Germanization" of the Warthegau during World War II.' MA thesis, University of North Carolina—Chapel Hill, 2020.

Jarausch, Konrad H. *After Hitler: Recivilizing Germans, 1945–1995.* Oxford: Oxford University Press, 2008.

Jarausch, Konrad H. *Out of Ashes: A New History of Europe in the Twentieth Century.* Princeton: Princeton University Press, 2015.

Jarausch, Konrad H., and Michael Geyer. *Shattered Past: Reconstructing German Histories.* Princeton: Princeton University Press, 2003.

Judt, Tony. *Postwar: A History of Europe since 1945.* New York: Penguin Books, 2005.

Kaiser, Wolfram. *Christian Democracy and the Origins of the European Union.* Cambridge: Cambridge University Press, 2007.

Klaus, Helmut. *Der Dualismus Preußen versus Reich in der Weimarer Republik in Politik und Verwaltung.* Mönchengladbach: Forum Verlag Godesberg GmbH, 2006.

Kleßmann, Christoph, ed. *The Divided Past: Rewriting Post-War German History.* Oxford: Berg, 2001.

Kloiber, Andrew. *Brewing Socialism: Coffee, East Germans, and Twentieth-Century Globalization.* New York: Berghahn Books, 2022.

Kluge, Ulrich. *Vierzig Jahre Agrarpolitik in der Bundesrepublik Deutschland* Vol. 1. Hamburg and Berlin: Verlag Paul Parey, 1989.

Kock, Peter Jakob. *Bayerns Weg in die Bundesrepublik.* Stuttgart: Deutsche Verlags-Anstalt, 1983.

Kocka, Jürgen. *Capitalism: A Short History.* Translated by Jeremiah Riemer. Princeton: Princeton University Press, 2016.

Koonz, Claudia. *The Nazi Conscience.* Cambridge: Harvard University Press, 2003.

Ku, Robert Ji-Song. *Dubious Gastronomy: The Cultural Politics of Eating Asian in the USA.* Honolulu: University of Hawaii Press, 2014.

Laferté, Gilles. 'The Folklorization of French Farming: Marketing Luxury Wine in the Interwar Years.' *French Historical Studies* 34 no. 4 (2011): 679–712.

Land, Rainer. 'East Germany 1989–2010: A Fragmented Development.' In *United Germany: Debating Processes and Prospects,* edited by Konrad H. Jarausch, 104–18. New York: Berghahn Books, 2013.

Landsman, Mark. *Dictatorship and Demand: The Politics of Consumerism in East Germany.* Cambridge: Harvard University Press, 2005.

Large, David Clay. *Munich 1972: Tragedy, Terror, and Triumph at the Olympic Games.* London: Rowman & Littlefield Publishers, Inc., 2012.

Levsen, Sonja, and Cornelius Torp, eds. *Wo liegt die Bundesrepublik: Vergleichende Perspektiven auf die westdeutsche Geschichte.* Göttingen: Vandenhoeck & Ruprecht, 2016.

Lewy, Jonathan. 'A Sober Reich? Alcohol and Tobacco Use in Nazi Germany.' *Substance Use & Misuse* 41, no. 8 (2006): 1179–95.

Lipartito, Kenneth. 'Reassembling the Economic: New Departures in Historical Materialism.' *The American Historical Review* 121 no. 1 (Feb. 2016): 101–39.

Liu, Andrew B. *Tea War: A History of Capitalism in China and India.* New Haven: Yale University Press, 2020.

Loberg, Molly. *The Struggle for the Streets of Berlin: Politics, Consumption, and Urban Space, 1914–1945.* Cambridge: Cambridge University Press, 2018.

Logemann, Jan L. *Trams or Tailfins?: Public and Private Prosperity in Postwar West Germany and the United States.* Chicago: University of Chicago Press, 2012.

Maase, Kaspar. 'Establishing Cultural Democracy: Youth, Americanization, and the Irresistible Rise of Popular Culture.' In *The Miracle Years: A Cultural History of West Germany, 1949–1968*, edited by Hanna Schissler, 428–50. Princeton: Princeton University Press, 2001.

Maga, Christian. 'Prälat Johann Leicht (1868–1940): Konservativer Demokrat in der Krise der Zwischenkriegszeit.' PhD diss. Julius Maximilian University of Würzburg, 1990.

Major, Patrick. '"Our Friend Rommel": The *Wehrmacht* as "Worthy Enemy" in Postwar British Popular Culture.' *German History* 26, no. 4 (2008): 520–35.

Malefyt, Timothy Dewaal. '"Inside" and "Outside" Spanish Flamenco: Gender Constructions in Andalusian Concepts of Flamenco Tradition.' *Anthropological Quarterly* 71 no. 2 (Apr. 1998): 63–73.

Mallmann, Nadine. *Kölsch—mehr als ein Getränk: Eine Biersorte als Medium regionaler Identitätskonstruktionen.* Munich: GRIN Verlag, 2011.

Manger Hans-J., and Peter Lietz. *Die Brau- und Malzindustrie in Deutschland-Ost zwischen 1945 und 1989: Ein Beitrag zur Geschichte der deutschen Brau- und Malzindustrie im 20. Jahrhundert.* Berlin: VLB Berlin, 2016.

Marchand, Suzanne. *Porcelain: A History from the Heart of Europe.* Princeton: Princeton University Press, 2020.

Massey, Doreen. 'A Global Sense of Place.' *Marxism Today* (June, 1991): 24–9.

Massey, Doreen. 'Places and their Pasts.' *History Workshop Journal* 39 (Spring, 1995): 182–92.

Mawby, Spencer. *Containing Germany: Britain and the Arming of the Federal Republic.* London: Palgrave Macmillan, 1999.

Milov, Sarah. *The Cigarette: A Political History.* Cambridge: Harvard University Press, 2019.

Mintz, Sidney. *Sweetness and Power: The Place of Sugar in Modern History.* New York: Viking, 1985.

Mitchell, Allan. '"A Real Foreign Country": Bavarian Particularism in Imperial Germany, 1870-1918.' *Francia* 7 (1979): 587–96.

Moeller, Robert G. *Protecting Motherhood: Women and the Family in the Politics of Postwar West Germany.* Berkeley: University of California Press, 1993.

Moeller, Robert G. *War Stories: The Search for a Useable Past in the Federal Republic of Germany.* Berkeley: University of California Press, 2001.

Moeller, Robert G., ed., *West Germany Under Construction: Politics, Society, and Culture in the Adenauer Era.* Ann Arbor: University of Michigan Press, 1997.

Molella, Arthur P. and Scott Gabriel Knowles, eds. *World's Fairs in the Cold War: Science, Technology, and the Culture of Progress*. Pittsburgh: University of Pittsburgh Press, 2019.

Monterescu, Daniel. 'Border Wines: Terroir across Contested Territory.' *Gastronomica: The Journal of Critical Food Studies* 17 no. 4 (2017): 127–40.

Moreton, Bethany. *To Serve God and Wal-Mart: The Making of Christian Free Enterprise*. Cambridge: Harvard University Press, 2010.

Neebe, Reinhard. *Weichenstellung für die Globalisierung: Deutsche Weltmarktpolitik, Europa und Amerika in der Ära Ludwig Erhard*. Cologne: Böhlau Verlag, 2004.

Norton, Marcy. *Sacred Gifts, Profane Pleasures: A History of Tobacco and Chocolate in the Atlantic World*. Ithaca, NY: Cornell University Press, 2008.

O'Carroll, Cliona. '"Cold Beer, Warm Hearts": Community, Belonging and Desire in Irish Pubs in Berlin.' In *Drinking Cultures: Alcohol and Identity*, edited by Thomas M. Wilson, 43–64. Oxford: Berg Publishers, 2005.

Osgerby, William. *Youth in Britain since 1945*. London: Wiley-Blackwell, 1998.

Parasecoli, Fabio. *Knowing Where It Comes From: Labeling Traditional Foods to Compete in a Global Market*. Iowa City: University of Iowa Press, 2017.

Penny, H. Glenn. *German History Unbound: From 1750 to the Present*. Cambridge: Cambridge University Press, 2022.

Perkins, John. 'Sugar Production, Consumption and Propaganda in Germany, 1850–1914.' *German History* 15 no. 1 (1997): 22–33.

Perry, Heather R., and Heather M. Benbow, eds. *Food, Culture and Identity in Germany's Century of War*. Cham: Palgrave Macmillan, 2019.

Petri, Rolf. 'The Resurgence of the Region in the Context of European Integration: Recent Developments and Historical Perspective.' In *Gesellschaft in der europäischen Integration seit den 1950er Jahren: Migration—Konsum—Sozialpolitik—Repräsentationen*, edited by Arnd Bauerkämper and Hartmut Kaelble, 159–71. Stuttgart: Franz Steiner Verlag, 2012.

Petrick-Felber, Nicole. *Kriegswichtiger Genuss: Tabak und Kaffee im 'Dritten Reich'*. Göttingen: Wallstein Verlag, 2015.

Pilcher, Jeffrey M. Imperial Hops: Beer in the Age of Empire.' *Global Food History*. Published online Jun. 21, 2023. DOI: 10.1080/20549547.2023.2226526.

Pilcher, Jeffrey M. 'National Beer in a Global Age: Technology, Taste, and Mobility, 1880–1914.' *Quaderni Storici* 51, no. 1 (April 2016): 51–70.

Pilcher, Jeffrey M. '"Tastes Like Horse Piss": Asian Encounters with European Beer.' *Gastronomica* 16, no. 1 (Spring, 2016): 28–40.

Planert, Ute. 'From Collaboration to Resistance: Politics, Experience, and Memory of the Revolutionary and Napoleonic Wars in Southern Germany.' *Central European History* 39 no. 4 (Dec. 2006): 676–705.

Press, Steven. *Blood and Diamonds: Germany's Imperial Ambitions in Africa*. Cambridge: Harvard University Press, 2021.

Prestholdt, Jeremy. *Domesticating the World: African Consumerism and the Genealogies of Globalization*. Berkeley: University of California Press, 2008.

Proctor, Robert N. *The Nazi War on Cancer*. Princeton: Princeton University Press, 2000.

Proctor, Robert N., and Londa Schiebinger, eds. *Agnotology: The Making and Unmaking of Ignorance*. Palo Alto: Stanford University Press, 2008.

Purinton, Malcolm F. *Globalization in a Glass: The Rise of Pilsner Beer through Technology, Taste and Empire*. London: Bloomsbury Academic, 2023.

Rappaport, Erika. *A Thirst for Empire: How Tea Shaped the Modern World*. Princeton: Princeton University Press, 2017.

Reynolds, Nancy Y. 'National Socks and the "Nylon Woman": Materiality, Gender, and Nationalism in Textile Marketing in Semicolonial Egypt, 1930–56.' *International Journal of Middle East Studies* 43, no. 1 (Feb. 2011): 49–74.

Rieger, Bernhard. *The People's Car: A Global History of the Volkswagen Beetle.* Cambridge: Harvard University Press, 2013.

Roberts, James S. *Drink, Temperance and the Working Class in Nineteenth-Century Germany.* Boston: George Allen & Unwin, 1984.

Rosenbaum, Adam T. *Bavarian Tourism and the Modern World.* Cambridge: Cambridge University Press, 2016.

Ruble, Alexandria. *Entangled Emancipation: Women's Rights in Cold War Germany* (forthcoming with University of Toronto Press).

Sammer, Christian. 'Die "Modernisierung" der Gesundheitsaufklärung in beiden deutschen Staaten zwischen 1949 und 1975: Das Beispiel Rauchen.' *Medizinhistorisches Journal* 50, no. 3 (2015): 249–94.

Satia, Priya. *Empire of Guns: The Violent Making of the Industrial Revolution.* New York: Penguin Press, 2018.

Schäder, Christian. *Münchner Brauindustrie, 1871–1945: Die wirtschaftsgeschichtliche Entwicklung eines Industriezweiges.* Marburg: Tectum Verlag, 1999.

Schieffenhövel, Wulf, and Helen Macbeth, eds. *Liquid Bread: Beer and Brewing in Cross-Cultural Perspective.* New York: Berghahn Books, 2011.

Schiller, Kay and Christopher Young. *The 1972 Munich Olympics and the Making of Modern Germany.* Berkeley: University of California Press, 2010.

Schindelbeck, Dirk. ' "Ansbach Uralt" und "Soziale Marktwirtschaft": Zur Kulturgeschichte der Werbeagentur in Deutschland am Beispiel von Hanns W. Brose (1899–1971).' *Zeitschrift für Unternehmensgeschichte/Journal of Business History* 40, no. 4 (1995): 235–52.

Schindelbeck, Dirk. 'Werbung für Alle? Kleine Geschichte der Gemeinschaftswerbung von Weimarer Republik bis zur Bundesrepublik Deutschland.' In *Unternehmenskommunikation im 19. und 20. Jahrhundert: neue Wege der Unternehmensgeschichte,* edited by Clemens Wischermann, Peter Borscheid, and Karl-Peter Ellerbrock, 63–97. Dortmund: Ges. für Westfälische Wirtschaftsgeschichte, 2000.

Schissler, Hanna, ed. *The Miracle Years: A Cultural History of West Germany, 1949–1968.* Princeton: Princeton University Press, 2001.

Schmidt, Dorothea. *'Die Kraft der deutschen Erde': Das Bier im Nationalsozialismus und die Hauptvereinigung der Deutschen Brauwirtschaft in Berlin-Schöneberg.* Baden-Baden: Nomos, 2019.

Schramm, Manuel. *Konsum und regionale Identität in Sachsen, 1880–2000: Die Regionalisierung von Konsumgütern im Spannungsfeld von Nationalisierung und Globalisierung.* Stuttgart: Franz Steiner Verlag, 2002.

Selig, Wolfram. *Chronik der Stadt München, 1945–1948.* Munich: Stadtarchiv, 1980.

Siegrist, Hannes, and Manuel Schramm, eds. *Regionalisierung europäischer Konsumkulturen im 20. Jahrhundert.* Leipzig: Leipziger Universitätsverlag, 2003.

Siemens, Daniel. *Stormtroopers: A New History of Hitler's Brownshirts.* New Haven: Yale University Press, 2017.

Sigmund, Monika. *Genuss als Politikum: Kaffeekonsum in beiden deutschen Staaten.* Berlin: de Gruyter Oldenbourg, 2015.

Simmons, John. 'Guinness and the Role of Strategic Storytelling.' *Journal of Strategic Marketing* 14 no. 1 (2006), 11–18.

Slobodian, Quinn. *Globalists: The End of Empire and the Birth of Neoliberalism.* Cambridge and London: Harvard University Press, 2018.

Smit, Barbara. *The Heineken Story: The Remarkably Refreshing Tale of the Beer that Conquered the World.* London: Profile Books Ltd., 2014.

Smith, Helmut Walser. *Germany: A Nation in its Time: Before, During, and After Nationalism, 1500–2000.* London and New York: W.W. Norton, 2020.

Smith, Patricia J. 'The Illusory Economic Miracle: Assessing Eastern Germany's Economic Transition.' In *After the Wall: Eastern Germany since 1989,* edited by Patricia J. Smith, 109–42. Boulder: Westview Press, 1998.

Sneeringer, Julia. '"Assembly Line of Joys": Touring Hamburg's Red Light District, 1949–1966.' *Central European History* 42 no. 1 (Mar. 2009), 65–96.

Snyder, Timothy. *Black Earth: The Holocaust as History and Warning.* New York: Tim Duggan Books, 2015.

Snyder, Timothy. *Bloodlands: Europe between Hitler and Stalin.* New York: Basic Books, 2010.

Specht, Joshua. *Red Meat Republic: A Hoof-to-Table History of How Beef Changed America.* Princeton and Oxford: Princeton University Press, 2019.

Speckle, Birgit. *Streit ums Bier in Bayern: Wertvorstellungen um Reinheit, Gemeinschaft und Tradition.* Münster: Waxmann Verlag, 2001.

Spengler, Jörg. 'Wer von Bier spricht, muss von Geschichte reden.' *Jahrbuch der Gesellschaft für Geschichte des Brauwesens e. V.* (2007): 221–48.

Spicka, Mark E. 'Gender, Political Discourse, and the CDU/CSU Vision of the Economic Miracle, 1949–1957.' *German Studies Review* 25, no. 2 (May 2002): 305–32.

Spicka, Mark E. *Selling the Economic Miracle: Reconstruction and Politics in West Germany, 1949–1957.* New York: Berghahn Books, 2007.

Spiekermann, Uwe. 'Redefining Food: The Standardization of Products and Production in Europe and the United States, 1880–1914.' *History and Technology* 27, no. 1 (Mar. 2011): 11–36.

Spiekermann, Uwe. 'Vollkorn für die Führer: zur Geschichte der Vollkornbrotpolitik im "Dritten Reich".' *Zeitschrift für Sozialgeschichte des 20. und 21. Jahrhunderts* 16 (2001): 91–128.

Spode, Hasso. *Die Macht der Trunkenheit: Kultur- und Sozialgeschichte des Alkohols in Deutschland.* Opladen: Leske and Budrich, 1993.

Spode, Hasso. 'Trinkkulturen in Europa.' In *Die kulturelle Integration Europas,* edited by Johannes Weinand and Christiane Weinand, 361–91. Wiesbaden: Springer VS, 2010.

Steege, Paul. *Black Market, Cold War: Everyday Life in Berlin 1946–1949.* Cambridge: Cambridge University Press, 2007.

Stephens, Robert. *Germans on Drugs: The Complications of Modernization in Hamburg.* Ann Arbor: University of Michigan Press, 2007.

Streb, Jochen. 'Das Nationalsozialistische Wirtschaftssystem: Indirekter Sozialismus, gelenkte Marktwirtschaft oder vorgezogene Kriegswirtschaft?' In *Der Staat und die Ordnung der Wirtschaft: Vom Kaiserreich bis zur Berliner Republik,* edited by Werner Plumpe and Joachim Scholtyseck, 61–84. Stuttgart: Franz Steiner Verlag, 2012.

Swett, Pamela E. *Selling under the Swastika: Advertising and Commercial Culture in Nazi Germany.* Palo Alto: Stanford University Press, 2013.

Swett, Pamela E., S. Jonathan Wiesen, and Jonathan R. Zatlin, eds. *Selling Modernity: Advertising in Twentieth-Century Germany.* Durham: Duke University Press, 2007.

Szejnmann, Claus-Christian W. 'Nazi Economic Thought and Rhetoric During the Weimar Republic: Capitalism and its Discontents.' *Politics, Religion & Ideology* 14 no. 3 (2013): 355–76.

Szejnmann, Claus-Christian W., and Maiken Umbach, eds. *Heimat, Region, and Empire: Spatial Identities under National Socialism.* New York: Palgrave Macmillan, 2012.

Tappe, Heinrich. *Auf dem Weg zur modernen Alkoholkultur: Alkoholproduktion, Trinkverhalten und Temperenzbewegung in Deutschland vom frühen 19. Jahrhundert bis zum Ersten Weltkrieg.* Stuttgart: Franz Steiner Verlag, 1994.

Tappe, Heinrich. 'Der Genuß, die Wirkung und ihr Bild. Werte, Konventionen und Motive gesellschaftlichen Alkoholgebrauchs im Spiegel der Werbung.' In *Bilderwelt des Alltags: Werbung in der Konsumgesellschaft des 19. und 20. Jahrhunderts. Festschrift für Hans Jürgen Teuteberg,* edited by Peter Borscheid and Clemens Wischermann, 222–41. Stuttgart: Franz Steiner Verlag, 1995.

Teich, Mikuláš. *Bier, Wissenschaft und Wirtschaft in Deutschland 1800–1914: Ein Beitrag zur deutschen Industrialisierungsgeschichte.* Vienna: Böhlau, 2000.

Terrell, Robert Shea. 'Entanglements of Scale: The Beer Purity Law from Bavarian Oddity to German Icon, 1906–1975.' *Contemporary European History.* Published online Jan. 18, 2023. DOI: 10.1017/S096077732200087X.

Terrell, Robert Shea. '"Lurvenbrow": Bavarian Beer Culture and Barstool Diplomacy in the Global Market, 1945–1964.' In *Alcohol Flows Across Cultures: Drinking Cultures in Transnational and Comparative Perspective,* edited by Waltraud Ernst, 204–20. London: Routledge, 2020.

Ther, Philipp. *Europe since 1989: A History.* Translated by Charlotte Hughes-Kreutzmüller. Princeton and Oxford: Princeton University Press, 2016.

Ther, Philipp and Holm Sundhaussen, eds. *Regionale Bewegungen und Regionalismen in europäischen Zwischenräumen seit der Mitte des 19. Jahrhunderts.* Marburg: Verlag Herder-Institut, 2003.

Thomas, Tim. *The Abalone King of Monterey: 'Pop' Ernest Doelter, Pioneering Japanese Fishermen & the Culinary Classic that Saved an Industry.* Charleston: American Palate/ The History Press, 2014.

Tlusty, Ann B. *Bacchus and the Civic Order: The Culture of Drink in Early Modern Germany.* Charlottesville: University of Virginia Press, 2001.

Tooze, Adam. *The Wages of Destruction: The Making and Breaking of the Nazi Economy.* New York: Penguin Books, 2006.

Treitel, Corinna. *Eating Nature in Modern Germany: Food, Agriculture and Environment, c. 1870 to 2000.* Cambridge: Cambridge University Press, 2017.

Trentmann, Frank. *Empire of Things: How We Became a World of Consumers, from the Fifteenth Century to the Twenty-First.* New York: Harper Collins, 2016.

Trentmann, Frank. 'Unstoppable: The Resilience and Renewal of Consumption after the Boom.' In *Vorgeschichte der Gegenwart: Dimensionen des Strukturbruchs nach dem Boom,* edited by Anselm Doering-Manteuffel, Lutz Raphael, and Thomas Schlemmer, 293–308. Göttingen: Vandenhoeck & Ruprecht, 2016.

Trumbull, Gunnar. *Consumer Capitalism: Politics, Product Markets, and Firm Strategy in France and Germany.* Ithaca: Cornell University Press, 2006.

Unger, Richard. *Beer in the Middle Ages and the Renaissance.* Philadelphia: University of Pennsylvania Press, 2004.

van Binsbergen, Wim M.J., and Peter L. Geschiere, eds. *Commodification: Things, Agency, and Identities (The Social Life of Things Revisited).* Münster: LIT Verlag, 2005.

van der Hoog, Tycho. *Breweries, Politics and Identity: The History Behind Namibia's Beer.* Basel: Basler Afrika Bibliographien, 2019.

van Rahden, Till. 'Wie Vati Demokratie lernte: Religion, Familie und die Frage der Autorität in der frühen Bundesrepublik.' In *Demokratie im Schatten der Gewalt: Geschichte des Privaten im deutschen Nachkrieg,* edited by Daniel Fulda, Dagmar Herzog, Stefan-Ludwig Hoffmann, and Till van Rahden, 122–51. Göttingen: Wallstein Verlag, 2010.

Voigt, Sebastian, ed. *Since the Boom: Continuity and Change in the Western Industrial World after 1970*. Toronto: University of Toronto Press, 2021.

von Oertzen, Christine. *The Pleasure of a Surplus Income: Part-Time Work, Gender Politics, and Social Change in West Germany, 1955–1969*. New York: Berghahn Books, 2007.

Wehler, Hans-Ulrich. *Deutsche Gesellschaftsgeschichte: Bundesrepublik und DDR, 1949–1990*. Munich: Verlag C.H. Beck, 2008.

Weinreb, Alice. *Modern Hungers: Food and Power in Twentieth-Century Germany*. Oxford: Oxford University Press, 2017.

Weinreb, Alice. 'The Tastes of Home: Cooking the Lost Heimat in West Germany in the 1950s and 1960s.' *German Studies Review* 34, no. 2 (May 2011): 345–64.

Werner, Michael, and Bénédicte Zimmerman. 'Beyond Comparison: *Histoire Croisée* and the Challenge of Reflexivity.' *History and Theory* 45 (Feb. 2006), 30–50.

Westermann, Edward B. *Drunk on Genocide: Alcohol and Mass Murder in Nazi Germany*. Ithaca: Cornell University Press, 2021.

White, Owen. *Blood of the Colony: Wine and the Rise and Fall of French Algeria*. Cambridge, MA: Harvard University Press, 2021.

Wiesen, S. Jonathan. *Creating the Nazi Marketplace: Commerce and Consumption in the Third Reich*. Cambridge: Cambridge University Press, 2011.

Wiesen, S. Jonathan. 'Miracles for Sale: Consumer Displays and Advertising in Postwar West Germany.' In *Consuming Germany in the Cold War*, edited by David F. Crew, 151–78. Oxford and New York: Berg Publishers, 2003.

Wiesen, S. Jonathan. *West German Industry and the Challenge of the Nazi Past, 1945–1955*. Chapel Hill: University of North Carolina Press, 2001.

Wildt, Michael. *Am Beginn der Konsumgesellschaft: Mangelerfahrung, Lebenshaltung, Wohlstandshoffnung in Westdeutschland in den fünfziger Jahren*. Hamburg: Ergebnisse Verlag, 1994.

Wildt, Michael. 'Plurality of Taste: Food and Consumption in West Germany during the 1950s.' *History Journal Workshop* 39, no. 1 (1995): 23–41.

Wilk, Richard. 'Learning to be Local in Belize: Global Systems of Common Difference.' In *Worlds Apart: Modernity through the Prism of the Local*, edited by Daniel Miller, 110–33. London and New York: Routledge, 1995.

Windell, George G. 'The Bismarckian Empire as a Federal State, 1866–1880: A Chronicle of Failure.' *Central European History* 2, no. 4 (December 1969): 291–311.

Wischermann, Clemens. 'Zur Industrialisierung des deutschen Braugewerbs im 19. Jahrhundert: Das Beispiel der Reichsgräflich zu Stolbergschen Brauerei Westheim in Westfalen, 1860–1913.' *Zeitschrift für Unternehmensgeschichte/Journal of Business History* 30 no. 3 (1985): 143–80.

Wolf, Holger. 'German Economic Unification Twenty Years Later.' In *From the Bonn to the Berlin Republic: Germany at the Twentieth Anniversary of Unification*, edited by Jeffrey J. Anderson and Eric Langenbacher, 321–30. New York: Berghahn Books, 2010.

Woller, Hans. *Gesellschaft und Politik in der amerikanischen Besatzungszone: Die Region Ansbach und Fürth*. Munich: Oldenbourg Verlag, 1986.

Zierenberg, Malte. *Berlin's Black Market, 1939–1950*. Basingstoke: Palgrave Macmillan, 2015.

Zimmerman, Andrew. *Anthropology and Antihumanism in Imperial Germany*. Chicago: University of Chicago Press, 2001.

Index

For the benefit of digital users, indexed terms that span two pages (e.g., 52–53) may, on occasion, appear on only one of those pages.